The Problem of Free Will
and Naturalism

Also available from Bloomsbury:

Freedom After Kant, edited by Joe Saunders
Free Will and Epistemology, by Robert Lockie
Locke on Knowledge, Politics and Religion, edited by Kiyoshi Shimokawa and Peter R. Anstey
The Philosophy of Friedrich Heinrich Jacobi, by Birgit Sandkaulen and translated by Matt Erlin

The Problem of Free Will and Naturalism

Paradoxes and Kantian Solutions

Christian Onof

BLOOMSBURY ACADEMIC
LONDON • NEW YORK • OXFORD • NEW DELHI • SYDNEY

BLOOMSBURY ACADEMIC
Bloomsbury Publishing Plc, 50 Bedford Square, London, WC1B 3DP, UK
Bloomsbury Publishing Inc, 1385 Broadway, New York, NY 10018, USA
Bloomsbury Publishing Ireland, 29 Earlsfort Terrace, Dublin 2, D02 AY28, Ireland

BLOOMSBURY, BLOOMSBURY ACADEMIC and the Diana logo
are trademarks of Bloomsbury Publishing Plc

First published in Great Britain 2024
This paperback edition published 2025

Copyright © Christian Onof, 2024

Christian Onof has asserted his right under the Copyright, Designs and
Patents Act, 1988, to be identified as Author of this work.

For legal purposes the Acknowledgements on p. vii constitute
an extension of this copyright page.

Cover image: Wanderer for his Painting, Artist: Gerard Boersma, 2008

All rights reserved. No part of this publication may be: i) reproduced or transmitted in any form, electronic or mechanical, including photocopying, recording or by means of any information storage or retrieval system without prior permission in writing from the publishers; or ii) used or reproduced in any way for the training, development or operation of artificial intelligence (AI) technologies, including generative AI technologies. The rights holders expressly reserve this publication from the text and data mining exception as per Article 4(3) of the Digital Single Market Directive (EU) 2019/790.

Bloomsbury Publishing Inc does not have any control over, or responsibility for, any third-party websites referred to or in this book. All internet addresses given in this book were correct at the time of going to press. The author and publisher regret any inconvenience caused if addresses have changed or sites have ceased to exist, but can accept no responsibility for any such changes.

A catalogue record for this book is available from the British Library.

ISBN: HB: 978-1-3504-2536-1
PB: 978-1-3504-2540-8
ePDF: 978-1-3504-2537-8
eBook: 978-1-3504-2538-5

Typeset by Deanta Global Publishing Services, Chennai, India

For product safety related questions contact productsafety@bloomsbury.com.

To find out more about our authors and books visit www.bloomsbury.com
and sign up for our newsletters.

To Sabine, Alice, Alexander and Mummy

I was just about to declare boldly that the devil only knows what choice depends on, and perhaps thank God for that, but then I remembered science . . . and stopped dead in my tracks.[1]

Fyodor Dostoevsky

Not all necessity excludes free will[2]

Erasmus

Insofar as man chooses what he wills, he is free; (. . .) Willing is (. . .) not something random, but self-determination that necessarily arises from our ego.[3]

Robert Musil

Contents

List of figures		viii
Preface		ix
Introduction		1
1	Free will and compatibilism	11
2	Kant's idealism and compatibilism	31
3	Libertarian theories of free will	55
4	Kant's Resolution of the Third Antinomy	81
5	Freedom in Kant's practical philosophy	111
6	The temporal dimension of free agency	143
7	The Kantian solution and its requirements	167
Notes		197
References		227
Index		241

Figures

3.1	The Paradox of Self-Determination in the Infinite Regress Argument (R_i stands for a reason or reason-pair, i.e. B_i or D_i or $\{B_i, D_i\}$). 'My agency' stands for 'how I am mentally speaking'	73
3.2	Volitional and psychological accounts of intention to φ	78
3.3	Metaphysical account (full line arrow) in which the agent's willing grounds the causal link of the psychological account (dashed-dotted arrow), thereby bringing about the effect (intention) as required by the volitional account (double arrow). $\{B, D\}$ are both causes (full line arrow) and reasons (dashed-dotted arrow)	78
5.1	The volitional account for the primary incentive (the thin arrows represent the enabling causes; the thick ones the driving causes; the oval shapes are the incorporated primary incentives and the large rectangles the agent's will; the dashed line represents conditioning)	133
6.1	The infinite (Zeno) series from decision to action	161
7.1	Paradox of Observed Totalities arising from the infinite regress in steps (2), (3) (O_i stands for observer number i). 'World' stands for W_s/W_t observed by O_1 in the 'finite' case; in the 'non-finite' case, it is some part of the total world and more gets included at each step. The schematic covers the spatial and temporal cases. © Christian Onof	178
7.2	The causal origin of my sensations. Empirical affection (dashed arrow) results from an empirical causality grounded in reality in-itself (thick arrow). This leads to the latter defining the transcendental cause of sensations, i.e. transcendental affection (dashed-dotted arrow)	183

Preface

As most universities today are streamlined into economically efficient businesses, subjects like philosophy are under pressure to justify their existence. Insofar as a philosopher could be characterised as raising further questions about issues others take as settled, the utility of philosophy might be hard to justify. Socrates's deflating of his confident interlocutors' knowledge claims by exhibiting the precariousness of their assumptions led him to be viewed by the authorities as an undesirable troublemaker.

This tradition of asking further questions is taken a step beyond Plato's Socrates's maieutic method and systematised by Kant's critical questions about the conditions of possibility of various norms such as those governing theoretical objectivity, agency and teleological judgements. The importance, and dare I say, the utility, of this type of critical question is heightened in cases where these normative constraints appear to conflict. The problem of the free agency required for moral responsibility in a causally determined natural world is a case in point. Here, the norms governing our self-conception as controlling our agency and thereby praise/blameworthiness and moral responsibility, clash with the normativity of the natural world.

The interplay of distinct normative constraints in the problem of free will gives rise to questions that it is worth distinguishing to address this problem. In this book, I also argue for the need to examine conditions of possibility of both types of normativity, thereby breaking with the skewed contemporary approach which typically takes the objectivity of nature as unproblematic, hence the book's title. Examining how contemporary philosophy addresses the problem of free will lead me to conclude that certain covert naturalist assumptions must be discarded and that a Kantian solution is required. I therefore claim that on his tercentenary, Kant's place is at the heart of the contemporary debate.

Kant's writings, particularly on the problem of free will, are not reputed to be paragons of clarity. For the exegetical work in this book, I am therefore indebted to the Kant scholarship I refer to in the book, as well as to the impulse given to me years ago by Henry Allison's seminal interpretations and Sebastian Gardner's absorbing lectures. I have also benefitted over the years from exchanges with, in alphabetical order, Lucy Allais, Karl Ameriks, Richard Aquila, Sorin Baiasu, Gary Banham†, Manfred Baum, Talbot Brewer, John Callanan, Kyoshi Chiba, Andrew Cooper, Corey Dyck, Wolfgang Ertl, Sebastian Gardner, Ido Geiger, Dietmar Heidemann, Chris Janaway, Paulo Jesus, Patricia Kitcher, Christine Korsgaard, Leslie Marsh, Meade McLaughlin, Giuseppe Motta, Stephen Palmquist, Derek Parkinson, Adrian Piper, Gerold Prauss, Marcel Quarfood, Valerio Rohden†, Tobias Rosefeldt, Joe Saunders, Dennis Schulting, Lucas Thorpe, Jens Timmermann, Jacco Verburgt, Eric Watkins, David Wiggins, Markus

Willaschek and many more. Special thanks go to my friends Dennis and Wolfgang for their comments on the manuscript.

Last but not least, finding the time to develop the ideas presented here and put the manuscript together came with its own conditions of possibility. I am therefore grateful for the constant support of my mother, wife and two children.

Introduction

Background

Free will, understood as that which makes agents morally responsible for their acts, is one of the central concepts of philosophy. Its importance stems not only from its being a necessary condition for imputability, but also from its key role in relation to human flourishing. It is insofar as agents are free to determine themselves that they have the potential to live good lives. Systems of rights are primarily designed to ensure the obtaining of conditions under which such freedom can be manifested outwardly, i.e. in physical actions.

It is therefore of particular concern, and not just to philosophers, that the common understanding of freedom is prima facie incompatible with the claim that we are determined by natural causes. This common understanding has two essential features: that I am the author of my actions and that I could have acted otherwise. Both are threatened by a determinism that seems to imply that the *source* of my action lies in natural causes which are beyond my control and that there is no *leeway* in my agency because these causes fully determine it. The philosophical discussion around this perceived threat is an old one, but it has gained in intensity, particularly in the English-speaking world, over the past few decades. This is no doubt partially a consequence of the progress in our understanding of the brain and the emergence of artificial intelligence which strengthen the opinion that causal determinism is a threat to free will.

In this book, I take the problem of free will (hereafter 'the Problem') to be that of the possibility of having free will while our actions are determined by natural causality. This is (a) *thought to be a problem*, insofar as such determination is typically (b) *thought to be a complete* determination by a causality that (c) *lies beyond the agent's control*. The two main responses to the problem have involved questioning either (a) or (b). Compatibilists argue that there is in fact no real problem here, as long as freedom is understood properly. Libertarians argue that it is not necessary for the determination by natural causality to be complete, thus leaving room for free will.

That the debate continues is proof that neither approach has met with anything close to unanimity among philosophers. Interestingly, the various positions are rather entrenched, particularly as far as the compatibilist/libertarian divide is concerned. There has been movement on the compatibilist side with the emergence of the semi-compatibilist claim that, while free will as defined above might indeed not be compatible with determinism, it is not needed for moral responsibility. In the incompatibilist camp, some have given up on libertarianism to migrate towards hard incompatibilism which claims that free will is impossible.

Others, like Ted Honderich, have opined that both compatibilist and incompatibilist approaches are fundamentally flawed. Interestingly, in his survey of various historical and contemporary positions, Honderich writes the following thoughtful remark about Immanuel Kant's response to the Problem:

> So he is a determinist of a kind, opposed to the tradition of Compatibilism, not really in the Incompatibilist tradition, but tries to make his determinism and freedom-as-origination consistent by his own private means. You may well wonder if he can succeed in all this – and suspect too, at the beginning of the 21st Century, that something so radical as his view is actually needed. (Honderich n.d.)

There are two lessons to be learnt from this remark. First, in Honderich's opinion, something as radical as Kant's view is needed to make progress in the discussion around the Problem. While Honderich is not endorsing Kant's solution to the Problem, he is at least indicating its relevance to the contemporary debate.

The other lesson is that the use of the tentative 'tries' and 'if he can succeed in all this' indicates, of course first, that there is scepticism as to whether Kant's solution works, but also, second, that this solution is not so well understood that one can be certain about how to judge it. That is, interpretative work is needed. And, as the first lesson teaches us, this interpretative work is of relevance not only to Kant scholars but also to the wider debate around the Problem.

This book takes up the challenge of showing that Kant's approach to the Problem is what is needed to address the issues arising from the contemporary debate and of providing a comprehensive interpretation of his solution. I thereby address the concern that 'Kant scholarship might become a bit too insular, (. . .) through lack of engagement with (. . .) contemporary philosophy' (Saunders 2021: 1187). On the basis of a critical survey of the various main compatibilist and libertarian options, I argue for a fundamental shift: at its core, the Problem defines a paradox sharing its structure with a problem facing naturalism, as I show in the final chapter. By recognising that the Problem is essentially a problem for naturalism, it can be solved by questioning assumption (c), i.e. the claim that all natural causality lies beyond the agent's control. This is the nub of *Kant's solution* which I examine through careful exegesis of his writings. I conclude the book by indicating which aspects of this specific proposal need to be retained as essential to a '*Kantian*' solution to the Problem and where amendments are possible or necessary.

The Chapters

Chapter 1 starts by clarifying the nature of the Problem and the two types of account of freedom, the volitional and psychological accounts, that are essential to any proposed solution. Van Inwagen's Consequence Argument is set out as challenge to any attempt to tackle the Problem. After briefly considering the problems of mysterianism, the chapter provides a review of compatibilist proposals. While traditional compatibilism, stretching from Hobbes to Ayer, sought to redefine freedom in terms of the ability to do what one chooses so as to preserve a conditional notion of leeway, contemporary compatibilism typically focusses upon providing a causal account of action that locates its source in the agent. These proposals are generally centred around sometimes very sophisticated proposals for a psychological account, i.e. explanations of how an action related to prior reasons might be deemed to be free.

Such source compatibilism, however, comes up against the Argument from Manipulation, which shows that this account does not ensure that the action's source lies in the agent. This amounts to saying that the problem is its failure to explain how an account of reasons causing my action leaves any room for understanding these reasons as *my* reasons *qua* agent: starting from a deterministic causal process, the source compatibilist fails to identify a proper place for my agency. I call this the Homeless Agent problem. As a result, contemporary source compatibilism provides no satisfactory volitional account of how the agent's will controls action. Kant's pre-critical views on freedom are a form of compatibilism that encounters similar problems.

Kant understood that the only way of avoiding them was to locate the agent's willings outside the temporal domain of nature. He thus introduced the need for a metaphysical account of the locus of freedom: this played a key role in critical philosophy's adoption of transcendental idealism. I briefly address some initial worries about engaging with such idealist metaphysics to solve the Problem.

Chapter 2 is devoted to providing the reader with a summary presentation of a metaphysical interpretation of Kant's transcendental idealism. This is contrasted with a methodological reading which, I argue, exhibits important shortcomings.

I then present Kant's conceptions of substance and causality and briefly discuss interpretations of Kant's principle of causality, the Second Analogy. With this background in place, I set the scene for the centrepiece of Kant's metaphysical account of free will as it is presented in the Resolution of the Third Antinomy. To do so, I first present the antinomial conflict in its original cosmological setting of which the Problem is a derivative issue. As to whether Kant is a compatibilist or not, I argue that his comments in the preamble to the Resolution clearly place him in the compatibilist camp and, further, that he is a source compatibilist, although this is only a partial characterisation of his position.

I argue, contrary to much of the literature, that Kant is not, however, content with establishing the mere logical possibility of freedom together with determinism. Ignoring this issue could lead to overlooking the importance of two well-known concerns for Kant's solution: the Historical Agency and Timeless Agency problems. According to the first, the free agent must be responsible for the whole of the past leading to his action. I argue that this altered-past interpretation of Kant is inadequate and that Kant endorses the alternative altered-law proposal which has the agent's freedom grounding a natural law, her empirical character. According to the second problem, her freedom is unrelated to any temporal location. Such worries, together with the metaphysical cost of transcendental idealism, provide the cue for considering the alternative of addressing the Homeless Agent problem by questioning the assumption of determinism.

Chapter 3 shows how libertarianism thus takes up the challenge of finding a role for the agent as source of her action that is adequate for a volitional account. The libertarian denies causal determinism because of the requirement of leeway, whether as such or as condition for sourcehood. I argue that Frankfurt-style examples in which the agent allegedly acts freely although no alternative course of action is available do not succeed in making a case against this need for leeway. While noting the problem of endorsing indeterministic causality, I then examine event-causal, agent-causal and non-causal contemporary libertarian theories and discuss how they fare in the light of various forms of the Luck Argument which questions to what extent the libertarian theorist is able to distinguish free agency from mere chance, in which case, his theory would have failed to address the Homeless Agency problem.

There is an important argument that is too easily dismissed by many in the contemporary debate but which I view as a major challenge to any libertarian theory of free will, namely Galen Strawson's Infinite Regress Argument. I examine this challenge in the form of a Paradox of Self-Determination and argue that a way forward which also meets the requirements of the Luck Arguments can be discerned by considering the explanatory self-sufficiency of willings, as pointed out by Thomas Pink. While not endorsing his own further proposal to solve the Problem, I argue that this insight shows the necessity of the same move as in Chapter 1, i.e. placing the agent's will outside time, with the specification that the will grounds her psychological causality. This move is only plausible in the context of Kant's transcendental idealism.

Chapter 4 presents Kant's Resolution of the Third Antinomy as filling in the outline of Kant's metaphysical account presented in Chapter 2 and interprets it as developing the solution derived in Chapter 3. It also defines the materials for the volitional and psychological accounts.

Contrary to a widespread opinion about this text, I show that Kant's argument is well-structured around key objectives. His solution is here confirmed as showing more than the mere logical possibility of freedom and as an altered-law solution. Further, it is libertarian in that it requires the availability of leeway to attribute sourcehood to the agent.

Kant's practical interests are manifested from the outset in this text which distinguishes a notion of practical freedom from the theoretical one, transcendental freedom. By paying due attention to the structure of the Resolution, I argue that an alternative solution to the much-discussed issue of the relation between these two conceptions makes sense of Kant's apparently conflicting statements. Kant's outline of the psychological account involves claims of predictability of actions that, I argue, are fully compatible with the agent's freedom. These materials the Resolution provides for the volitional and psychological accounts leave us with two important questions. First, insofar as the causality of freedom is defined in terms of the causality of reason whose law is the moral law for Kant, how is free immoral action possible? Aside from this Moral Leeway problem, the Temporal Leeway problem looms: How is it possible to act otherwise in time since the empirical character, *qua* law of nature, is unchanging? These are addressed in the next two chapters. This chapter concludes by showing how Kant understood the teleological nature of the causality of freedom.

Chapter 5 draws upon Kant's ethical writings and the *Religion within the Bounds of Pure Reason* (*REL*) to piece together Kant's full volitional account of free agency. I first examine what the *Groundwork to the Metaphysics of Morals* (*GMM*) brings to our understanding of freedom. The first contribution it makes is to show how a specific theoretical activity of reason provides us with grounds for adopting a standpoint from which we have to view ourselves as endowed with transcendental freedom. This does not allow for a sufficient 'proof' of transcendental freedom, however. The *GMM* also presents the so-called Reciprocity Thesis connecting freedom and morality. While I find it wanting, it introduces the all-important prescriptive notion of autonomy which provides a key piece of evidence to address the Moral Leeway problem, namely that causality of freedom cannot simply be equated with causality of reason. Rather, our freedom is our *capacity to use* the causality of reason. The issue of asymmetry in our leeway is thereby also addressed.

I adduce further evidence for this interpretation of freedom in relation to the causality of reason, in particular drawing upon the *Critique of Practical Reason* (*CPrR*), where Kant claims he can dispatch the other problem of free will, i.e. that of how we can be free if God, as our creator, is the ultimate cause of our existence.

REL is the text that provides most of the material for filling in the volitional account and for answering a question which arises from the above if Kant is to avoid objections from Luck Arguments, namely that of the nature of the law of the agent's causality of freedom. In the *REL*, Kant provides a full-blown Theory of Choice in the form of an account of how the agent adopts maxims together with the agent's overall adoption of a *Gesinnung*, i.e. an attitude to the moral law. I endorse Allison's famous Incorporation Thesis which provides us with an account of how the agent acts on different incentives but interpret it causally. This, together with Kant's important distinction *Wille/Willkür*, shows how we should understand the law the agent *actually* acts upon. I also provide an explanation of what is involved in acting immorally to complete my answer to the Moral Leeway question.

Kant's account, I shall argue, does not fully deliver in providing a notion of *Gesinnung* as subjective basis for maxim-adoption. This leads me to outline a broader conception of *Gesinnung* for the volitional account needed to address the Problem.

Chapter 6 focusses upon the psychological account and how it meshes with the volitional account by addressing the issue of how the general maxims the agent adopts determine specific intentions to act. This sheds light upon the nature of the agent's psychological causality and the empirical character which can be interpreted in terms of a Davidsonian belief-desire model at the level of appearances.

The main issue to examine here is Temporal Leeway. Addressing it involves examining Kant's notion of (empirical) consciousness/awareness, inner sense. By drawing upon the *Metaphysical Foundations of Natural Science* and a *Reflexion*, I piece together an account of what is involved in the formation of intentions. This exhibits the role of freedom in identifying given circumstances as circumstances of application of an adopted maxim. Temporal Leeway is available because the future always brings up new circumstances requiring further specifications of the agent's empirical character. This leads to understanding the latter as manifested progressively over time.

That the further issue of how an intention to act leads to a physical action, i.e. the *physical account*, is not a particular problem for Kant stems from the fact that mind-body interaction poses no particular philosophical difficulty within the framework of transcendental idealism. The normative dimension of Kant's theory of freedom does, however, require addressing the 'ought implies can' question where the latter is a physical ability.

Although a physical account of the implementation of intentions is not required, I indicate what it might involve on the basis of some of Kant's unpublished texts and exhibit an interesting parallel with a contemporary account of mind-body causation.

Chapter 7 starts by summarising the coherent picture that emerges from the three accounts of free agency discussed in the three previous chapters and emphasising its intuitive appeal. I then consider what we do and do not need to retain from Kant's theory of free will to fulfil the purpose of this book, i.e. defining *a contemporary Kantian solution to the Problem*.

Since the biggest stumbling block to adopting this solution will doubtless be transcendental idealism, I first argue that the alternative of hard incompatibilism threatens our self-conception as agents. I next argue that naturalist metaphysics exhibits a problem with a similar structure to the Paradox of Self-Determination but on grounds independent of the Problem. I argue that the issues this Paradox of Observed Totalities raises show the truth of transcendental idealism.

I briefly consider worries about how certain features of Kant's transcendental idealism stand in relation to contemporary physics. Further, I indicate that worries about the inaccessibility of fundamental properties of reality arise within naturalism.

In the final part of the chapter, I briefly consider how to ground practical norms appropriate for the broader conception of *Gesinnung* I propose in Chapter 5.

Summary

Overall, the Kantian solution I propose is a *normative-compatibilist-libertarian* one characterised by three central claims. The first is that the connection between freedom and morality which underpins the debate (the issue at stake is the possibility of moral responsibility in a deterministic world) follows from the nature of free will as the capacity to act autonomously. This is central to understanding our *volitions* as manifesting the choice of an attitude to the moral constraints defined by autonomy. But it has an equally important *metaphysical* dimension: this choice determines the agent's use of a causality she is endowed with *qua* moral being, thus defining what a *contemporary libertarian* would call agent-causality. The second claim is that this calls for the metaphysical framework of transcendental idealism: in line with the *contemporary compatibilist*'s focus upon the causal history of an action, together with the implications of the Consequence and Infinite Regress Argument, I show that the only place for free will is outside the temporal domain and that the adoption of this idealism is required to make this plausible. The third claim is that our free choice is that of a law of nature, the law of our *psychological causality*. In the transcendentally idealistic framework, the purely temporal nature of mental acts of intention-formation and the implications of the nature of our consciousness for psychological causality dispel any concerns about the predetermination of action.

Methodological issues

A couple of methodological choices I make are worth spelling out. In this book, I address a number of problems that are familiar in the contemporary free will debate and the Kant literature. Insofar as I seek to propose a coherent theory of free will, I do not take these various debates as my starting point. Rather, I have sought to organise the various issues around a distinction between different accounts of free will that are required to address the Problem. First, I introduce the volitional and psychological accounts as addressing first- and third-person perspectives in Chapter 1, and the need for a metaphysical account arises when it becomes clear that finding a place for the agent's free will raises metaphysical issues. The further issue of an intention's physical realisation calls for a physical account. This distinction between these types of accounts is particularly useful to examine Kant's texts and will prove useful in showing their coherence.

Second, insofar as the book's aim is to argue for a Kantian solution to the Problem, it involves addressing both the contemporary philosophical debate and Kantian exegesis. These are linked in the following way. Chapters 1 and 3 examine contemporary compatibilism and libertarianism, and each lead to introducing key aspects of a solution to the Problem that is characteristically Kantian. This motivates an overview of Kant's theory of free will in Chapter 2 and a detailed examination of its content in Chapters 4 to 6.[1] The elements of Kant's theory that are required to fill in the Kantian solution outlined in Chapters 1 and 3 are then identified and further discussed in Chapter 7. This interaction between strict textual exegesis and questioning from a contemporary philosophical perspective is fruitful, I think, both in enriching our understanding of Kant and in showing the contemporary relevance of his writings.

My aim is thus to present my interpretation of Kant's solution to the Problem, not exclusively to an audience of Kant scholars but to an audience interested in the Problem tout court, as enabling the formulation of a Kantian alternative addressing the problems identified in contemporary positions, where 'Kantian' here means faithful to the core and spirit of Kant's own solution if not to the detail and letter of it. To that end, I argue that the shortcomings of compatibilism and libertarianism are hardly due to a lack of subtlety in developing theories of free will to address various objections found in the literature. Rather, they result from a fundamental problem about the very concept of self-determination in its temporal setting which will require giving up the core naturalist claim that nature is the sum total of reality. I am aware that this is a big ask for most contemporary philosophers, but independently of the Problem, naturalism exhibits an analogous problem, so that the adoption of idealism is no ad hoc fix.

Contributions to the literature

In systematic terms, in this book, I:

- Propose a framework for addressing the Problem which distinguishes between metaphysical, volitional, psychological and physical accounts of free will.
- Examine the merits of the Argument from Manipulation against compatibilism and the use of Frankfurt-style counter-examples.
- Differentiate between two strands of Luck Arguments against libertarianism.
- Defend the central role of the Consequence and Infinite Regress Argument.
- Argue for the metaphysics of transcendental idealism as required in the light of certain limitations of naturalism.
- Relate the Problem to the nature of space/time.
- Show how Kant's metaphysical, volitional and psychological accounts of free will enable a Kantian solution to the Problem to be formulated.

In terms of Kantian scholarship, I:

- Argue for a metaphysical interpretation of transcendental idealism.
- Argue that Kant's theory of free will is a coherent whole across his critical works.
- Argue that Kant's response to the Consequence Argument is source compatibilist.
- Show that his is a form of 'altered-law' compatibilism.
- Identify precisely what Kant achieves in the Resolution of the Third Antinomy.
- Show that Kant's theory of freedom is libertarian.
- Propose an alternative interpretation of the concept of practical freedom.
- Propose a new account of the relation between transcendental freedom and the causality of reason.
- Argue that Kant develops a comprehensive Theory of Choice.
- Contribute to the discussion around the meaning of *Gesinnung*.
- Show how the adoption of maxims of action relates to intention-formation.
- Dispel concerns about predetermination of action by examining the nature of inner sense and its laws.
- Show how Kant's strategy involves separating the free will and mind-body problems.
- Address the question of the meaning and validity of the 'ought implies can' principle.

In this book, I am thereby reacting against a tendency prevalent in large parts of anglophone Kant scholarship of the past half-century, which purports to present a Kant who fits in with contemporary philosophical fashion. This tendency, in its most extreme form (Peter Strawson), involves taking out the idealism from Kant's critical philosophy. This approach has a legacy in the contemporary tendency to seek to 'naturalise Kant'.

This tendency does not necessarily detract from shedding crucial light upon specific topics in Kant's critical philosophy (see Paul Guyer, Patricia Kitcher). Nevertheless, the underlying assumption that certain implications of Kant's transcendental idealism are more of an embarrassment than anything else does not, in my view, do justice to the radical nature of his philosophical project.

A concern for philosophical fashion is also detectable in a more productive response to transcendental idealism that emerged in the latter part of the twentieth century in the work of Gerold Prauss, Henry Allison and Graham Bird. This approach understands transcendental idealism as central to Kant's critical turn while seeking to avoid complaints about the 'extravagance and inconsistency of [Kant's] appeal to noumena' (Bird 2006: 707). It achieves this by reading his metaphysical claims methodologically, i.e. as claims about how cognitive subjects/agents are to conceive of themselves.

More recently, Lucy Allais, like Tobias Rosefeldt, reinstated the importance of understanding the metaphysical dimension of Kant's transcendental idealism. She, however, takes empirical realism as starting point, with the aim of showing that Kant is first and foremost a realist, thereby explaining away the essential noumenal dimension of transcendental idealism.

Noting that, in seeking to make Kant more accessible, the 'strength of some traditional positions' has been overlooked. Karl Ameriks (2003: 99) has spearheaded a revival of metaphysical interpretations of Kant's philosophy that pay due attention to its noumenal dimension (see Eric Watkins, Desmond Hogan, Benjamin Vilhauer, Nicholas Stang and Anja Jauernig, among others) to which this book's exegetical chapters are a contribution. More specifically, I suggest leaving behind reactions ranging from apparent embarrassment about a 'mysterious noumenal power' (Allison 2020: 280), via attempts to appeal to a science-savvy contemporary readership (Dieter Sturma 2018: 138–9), to outrage that the mere possibility of certain metaphysical commitments should be entertained (see Allen Wood 2008: 138, 296). The worry is that these betray what Kant's tribunal of reason was aimed at debunking, namely dogmatism or its tacit endorsement. Today's dogmatism is, of course, of a very different ilk from that of Kant's time. And it is rather diffuse, relying upon an unclear belief about what is acceptable given the constraints that scientific theories supposedly place upon rational thought. This belief should be open to challenge: otherwise, we have not learnt the main message of Kant's critical turn.

With the Problem, I argue that it becomes evident why naturalising/de-idealising, 'de-noumenalising' and methodological strategies are wrongheaded: it is essential to an understanding of Kant's theory that some more fundamental level of reality than that of nature play a grounding role. I shall argue that this metaphysical picture is required in the light of the shortcomings of the contemporary positions on free will and by a problem exhibited by naturalism. Such metaphysical claims need not, however, in any way impact the content of our scientific theories about the natural world, or so I shall argue.[2] But if a radical revision of our self-understanding resulting from the denial of free will is to be avoided, I shall claim that the Problem calls for transcendental idealism. I thereby concur with Allison (1983: 13) that the latter is 'a powerful philosophical position rather than (. . .) a curious anachronism or a mass of confusions'.

1

Free will and compatibilism

In this chapter, I present the problem of free will (hereafter 'Problem'), taking care to differentiate different aspects of it. I shall claim that this entails the need for at least two types of accounts of free will in addressing the Problem. I then use the Consequence Argument as starting point for a review of the main types of response to the Problem. After a brief examination of mysterianism, this chapter focuses upon compatibilist responses. The review of compatibilism is necessarily succinct and concentrates upon the main features of these proposals as well as various issues that have been identified in the literature. I next examine whether these proposals are able to provide the two types of account of free will I introduced at the outset and thereby identify what I call the problem of the Homeless Agent. This will be the cue to introducing the critical Kant's shift away from his pre-critical compatibilist approach. I thereby propose a reconstruction of the logic of that move in terms of the problem of the Homeless Agent.

A. The problem of free will

Setting out the Problem

The first encounter with the Problem is, for most people, a clash between first- and third-person perspectives. I find out that psychology claims that my action is caused by a range of factors that I understand as broadly subsumed under the headings of nature and nurture. These would arguably seem to completely determine what I do: if I did something differently today from yesterday in response to apparently identical circumstances, a psychologist who endorses belief-desire reasoning will seek a cause of this change in some belief (e.g. about those circumstances) or desire (e.g. with respect to these circumstances), which was not operative yesterday. Today I might not rush to the door when the bell rings because I now believe that it is likely to be a salesman or because these interruptions during my working day are beginning to feel disruptive.

A neurobiologist might echo this psychologist's assessment of these events by sketching a causal story connecting my brain's perceptual inputs to behavioural outputs. More broadly, and setting aside quantum indeterminacy which is arguably confined to the micro-scale, I may be convinced that physicists endorse Laplacean determinism according to which 'We ought () to regard the present state of the universe as the effect of its anterior state' through which this present state is fully determined (Laplace 1902: 4).

Either way, these are claims that antecedent causes of my intentions completely determine the nature of my action. Because of the central importance of psychological explanation, in what follows I shall, for simplicity, refer to this as psychological causal determination. The extent to which psychological causes require or are reducible to other sub-personal causal determinants (e.g. neural causes) need not concern us here since the Problem only requires that the causes be deterministic. Such deterministic claims about my intentions' causal history clash with my intuition that what I do is up to me, i.e. I am in control of my action. These 'libertarian intuitions'[1] (Keil 2018: 19–20) are arguably constitutive of what we take to characterise a free action (Aristotle 2006: 1113 b6; von Wright 1980; Kane 2011: 4–5). This clash is the locus of the Problem.

This notion of control of our action has two components: its source and its effectiveness. First, to say that I control my action it must be the case that I, i.e. my will, is the source of this action. Second, effectiveness would seem to require that my control be effective in actualising one among many possible courses of action. Compare, for instance, a car driver and a passenger in an automated vehicle without controls and pre-programmed by someone else. The car driver's free will is manifested in his control of it, whose two features essentially differentiate his situation from that of the passenger in the automated vehicle: (i) the movement of the car has its source in the driver's decisions and (ii) the driver's control is apparently essential to ensure that the car avoids obstacles and moves at an optimal speed, both of which refer to possible alternatives; in Chapter 3, we shall see that this second condition is disputed. These two conditions are usually termed *sourcehood* and *leeway* requirements.

The Problem is not, however, confined to such a disconnect between first- and third-person perspectives. If it were, it could be argued that therapy is what is needed here, in the same way that one living under the delusion their behaviour is controlled by extraterrestrial beings might benefit from therapy. Clashes with the third-person perspective arise for the second- and third-person points of view, from the importance of agents being deemed to be in control (to some degree at least) of their actions if they are to be labelled as *responsible*.[2] Many second-person attitudes, e.g. praising and blaming, as well as third-person institutions, e.g. judiciary and penal, rely upon its being true that a human agent's control of her agency makes her actions *imputable*. So I might praise a car driver for winning a Grand Prix, but he might later be prosecuted for driving as though he were still in the Grand Prix although he is on his way home from the celebratory party. In both cases, what is at stake are certain *norms* which the agent complies with or not.[3]

As in the first-person case, the clash between determinism and responsibility in the light of these norms has two components. The car driver is responsible insofar as the action originates in him so that he receives the praise or the sentence. But this blame or sentence only make sense, it would seem, if he could have done otherwise, i.e. worse or better in terms of the respective second-person and third-person norms. So, again, we have *sourcehood* and *leeway* requirements.

Finally, we should note the relations between the first- and second-/third-person aspects of the Problem. The appropriateness of praise or sentencing is grounded in the assumption that the agent is in control of her actions. This reference to the agent is something the agent herself must be able to endorse because this control means the action was voluntary, which implies a certain first-person authority. Any praise or sentencing must make sense to the driver and this will only be the case if she knowingly acted in the way that attracted these responses, i.e. if the control was *hers*. There is also a converse relation in that the driver derives satisfaction or guilt from her behaviour insofar as she has internalised the second- or third-person aspects of the Problem. This internalisation accounts for the genesis of these subjective features that accompany the sense of control. While the focus of the Problem is often its third-person form,[4] it is important that any purported solution also be satisfactory from the first-person perspective.

In the light of these reflections, the Problem can be defined as that of the possibility of free will together with the natural causal determinism of our actions (hereafter 'determinism'). And the third- and first-person perspectives call for two distinct accounts:

- The *psychological account* must address the issue of how actions which are causally explained psychologically can allow for attributions of responsibility.
- The *volitional account* must show how I can understand these causally determined actions as being under the control of my will.

While these are mostly not differentiated in the debate around free will, this distinction will be useful, specifically in spelling out the implications of certain arguments, as well as in steering our way through Kant's writings about free will.

Further, since the Problem concerns the possibility of free will together with determinism, the requirements on the nature of the possibility at stake need to be specified. The psychological account requires that it be possible to find a place for free will that is compatible with the causal determination of an action: prima facie, this is a matter of logical possibility of a free intention causing an action while it is also accounted for deterministically.[5] In the case of the volitional account, there is a requirement that the agent be able to make sense of her will controlling her action. While this does not require any scientific understanding since the issue is about the first-person perspective, it calls for a specification of the possible place of my free will in an account of the genesis of an action. So this requires more than simply showing the logical possibility of such a place. This characterisation will suffice for now: an exact specification of the modality at stake will be important for an understanding of Kant's proposed solution (see Chapters 2 and 4).

Finally, the psychological and volitional accounts will have to be compatible in the sense that my understanding of my control is compatible not just with the causal determination of my actions but also with their rationality (i.e. their being explained in terms of prior reasons). What this means will become clearer when this issue becomes relevant in Chapter 3. For now, what this entails is that the psychological account will also require more than logical possibility.

The Consequence Argument

It is useful to take as starting point for an examination of the responses to the Problem, van Inwagen's Consequence Argument. This crystallises it in terms of an incompatibility between our actions *qua* free, being up to us, and *qua* determined, not up to us:

> If determinism is true, then our acts are the consequences of the laws of nature and events in the remote past. But it is not up to us what went on before we were born; and neither is it up to us what the laws of nature are. Therefore the consequences of these things (including our own acts) are not up to us. (van Inwagen 1983: 16)

Insofar as van Inwagen is working with the implicit premise that the laws of nature are deterministic, this formulation spells out the crux of the Problem in its original first-person form. The main approaches to the Problem can be presented as responses to this argument.

Most participants in the debate accept the argument's two explicit premises. Indeed, it is widely believed according to current physical knowledge that we are unable to alter the past.[6] Further, the claim that we cannot alter the laws of nature is for many, e.g. naturalists,[7] built into the very notion of what a law of nature is, so this claim has typically not been challenged in the mainstream contemporary debate.

The main strategies in response to the argument are defined in terms of its validity as proof that free will is impossible. *Incompatibilists* accept that, together with the determinism premise, the argument is a valid proof of the impossibility of free will, while *compatibilists* do not. Among the former, we can distinguish *hard incompatibilists* who accept the determinism premise and therefore conclude that free will is impossible. Van Inwagen (1983) himself also accepts this conclusion but argues for *mysterianism*: although impossible, free will nevertheless exists.

The other incompatibilists are *libertarians* who argue for the existence of free will by rejecting the determinism premise.[8] Insofar as they reject that premise, they are not, strictly speaking, addressing the Problem as defined earlier. However, they typically do not reject the existence of causes of agents' behaviour, so they still have to address a looser version of the Problem in which causal determination is replaced by causal explanation.

Only a few compatibilists argue that the argument is not valid tout court.[9] Most compatibilists' disagreement is only with the validity of the argument as proof of the impossibility of free will: they argue that the sense of 'up to us' in the conclusion, which would make the argument valid tout court, is not that which characterises free will when properly understood, so that *free will is possible*. The following compatibilist options will be discussed further:

- Peter Strawson (1974) argues that free will is a feature of our reactive attitudes to ourselves and others that is not affected by objective considerations such as determinism.

- Classical compatibilism is deflationary in arguing for a conditional understanding of the sourcehood and leeway requirements of free will that makes it possible for it to coexist with determinism.
- Contemporary source compatibilism addresses the shortcomings of the latter option by shoring up the sourcehood requirement for the possibility of free will.[10]

As with any attempt to classify philosophical positions, some approaches do not neatly fit in to one class. In particular, locating the critical Kant[11] within this grid is a controversial issue. This classification serves mainly to organise the content of the next chapters. In this chapter, I briefly examine mysterianism before reviewing compatibilist positions. The next Chapter introduces Kant's proposal as a form of compatibilism. Chapter 3 turns to an examination of libertarian proposals. It is followed by an investigation of Kant's libertarianism in Chapter 4. Hard incompatibilism is briefly addressed in Chapter 7.

B. Mysterianism

Van Inwagen claims that free will exists although we cannot understand this, given the truth of determinism and the soundness of the Consequence Argument: 'we are faced with a mystery for free will undeniably exists' (van Inwagen 2000: 1).

While I agree that mysterianism is inherently philosophically unsatisfactory (Ekstrom 2003: 153–4), it is very plausible to claim that there is something beyond our understanding in the existence of free will. However, the incomprehensibility in mysterianism is particularly problematic: the condition for our being morally responsible in a deterministic world conflicts with rationality in the strongest possible way. Indeed, the Consequence Argument exhibits a straightforward logical contradiction in assuming free will and endorsing determinism and the assumptions of the impossibility of altering the past or the laws of nature. So mysterianism involves accepting that the nature of (some aspect of) reality in fact conflicts with something as basic to rationality as propositional logic.

An additional problem is as follows. Mysterianism creates a tension with the rational norms that govern free agency. How is it that my practical judgements should be constrained by the normativity of rationality (e.g. I ought not act in ways which do not further any of my purposes, etc.), while the very possibility of acting according to such norms may be logically incompatible with the facts I know to be true about my agency? This would amount to a conflict between practical and theoretical rationality. I conclude that mysterianism cannot therefore define a philosophically acceptable solution to the Problem.

C. Compatibilist strategies

For the sake of clarity, for each of the compatibilist proposals, I focus upon standard problems typically flagged in the literature, leaving for later any comments upon their psychological and volitional accounts.

Peter Strawson's compatibilism

Strawson (1974) claims that the Consequence Argument's identification of an incompatibility is irrelevant because it concerns two different standpoints. The determinism which makes it impossible for me to change the past or laws of nature which, together, determine my actions belongs to the 'objective' standpoint. Freedom, on the contrary, belongs to the 'participant' standpoint. This is the standpoint of our reactive attitudes towards other agents and ourselves. Strawson's claim is then that these standpoints do not interact. Our reactive attitudes are too well embedded in us to be impacted by any objective claims.

In terms of the distinction I proposed at the outset, this amounts to rejecting the Problem at the first- and second-person levels. Because he has a Humean view of morality in terms of 'moral sentiments' (1974: 24) which define reactive attitudes, moral norms are essentially second person for Strawson and judicial/penal norms are based upon them so that the third-person level does not define a separate problem for him. In thus rejecting the Problem, Strawson is therefore denying that either psychological or volitional accounts are required.

There are two interrelated worries about Strawson's assumption of an independence between the participant and objective standpoints. First, the boundary between the objective and reactive standpoints changes with the widening of the spectrum of what one describes as mental disabilities, for instance: while certain cognitive shortcomings used to attract blame, they are now recognised as objective disabilities such as dyslexia. Second, knowledge-acquisition is something the agent participates in by learning from others and/or doing research. It would be irrational within a judge's participant standpoint, for instance, to continue with strong punitive practices if she were simultaneously learning that agents are not responsible for their acts. Similarly, the resentment Strawson focusses upon would be impacted and probably disappear (see Pereboom 2014b: 119–20). So it seems that the participant standpoint is not insulated from the objective standpoint and determinism remains a threat for our self-conception as free agents. Further, Strawson's proposal is also threatened by the Argument from Manipulation I shall examine in the next section.

Classical compatibilism

Next, I turn to the two most prominent types of compatibilism. What has come to be known as *classical compatibilism* has involved redefining free will as the ability to do what one wills (Hobbes 1651/1997: 108, 1654/1999, 1656/1999, Locke 1690/1975; Hume 1748/1975; Schlick 1939; Ayer 1954).[12] This defines a notion of control that is more restricted than what we have assumed so far, in terms of both sourcehood and leeway. First, I am the source of my action insofar as I do what I will (if it is possible).[13] Second, it allows for a *conditional* notion of the ability to do otherwise: I would have done otherwise had I willed otherwise.

This *conditional analysis* has it that the source of my action is mine insofar as I am identified with what I will. But such an identification is questionable: what I desire or prefer, and thereby will, may be completely out of my control in cases of addiction, phobia or compulsion (Lehrer 1968, 2004). This conditional analysis could arguably be refined 'to rule out the factors that (...) render an agent unable to choose' (Fischer 2014: 51). But there is disagreement as to what these factors are since, unlike the compatibilist, the incompatibilist would include any causal determining factor.

In fact, the incompatibilist critique of compatibilism questions the compatibilist's grounds for claiming that 'there is simply no good reason to suppose that causal determinism in itself (...) vitiates our moral responsibility' (Fischer 1994: 159). This critique is most aptly presented in the Argument from Manipulation, whose aim is to show that it would be arbitrary to distinguish between a type of causal determination that absolves the agent from responsibility and one that does not.

Derk Pereboom (2014b: 94ff) constructs a four-case argument in a way that addresses various forms of compatibilism as we shall see further. He considers the case of Professor Plum who decides to kill White and carries out his plan. This action fulfils egoistic desires, and it is assumed that Plum mostly acts on such desires. Additionally, Plum is, however, sensitive to moral reasons and acts on them when the egoistic reasons are relatively weak. Pereboom considers four ways in which Plum's action might be considered causally determined by factors he has no control over. In the first scenario, Plum is created by neuroscientists and is manipulated so as to go through the process of deliberation that will lead him to kill White. This manipulation begins when he starts reflecting on his situation to ensure that his reasoning will be egoistic. This is however in line with his character as he is often thus manipulated. Pereboom argues that all the compatibilist's conditions are fulfilled although, intuitively, he is not responsible.

The second scenario presents the case of an ordinary human being, and as such, can directly be used to undermine the compatibilist's theory by exhibiting a case of a human agent where the relevant conditions are fulfilled, but there is no moral responsibility. Here, Plum has been programmed at the beginning of his life by a team of neuroscientists in such a way that he often, but not always, gives greater weight to egoistic reasons for action and that in his current situation, he is causally determined 'to undertake the (...) process of deliberation and to possess the set of (...) desires that result in his killing White' (2014b: 95). Pereboom argues, correctly I think, that, just as in the first case, Plum should not be considered responsible for his action here: the greater time lag between the manipulation and the action should not affect the verdict about moral responsibility. Consequently, the compatibilist's proposed conditions for free agency in terms of sourcehood are not sufficient.

Pereboom's next two examples present us, first, with scenario three where, instead of the manipulation in scenario two, we have Plum's rigorous training when he was 'too young to have had the ability to prevent or alter the practices that determined his character' (Pereboom 2014b: 96). With scenario four, the assumption is now physical determinism, i.e. what Pereboom takes to be a scenario corresponding to what actually happens. What is common to all four cases is that the agent 'is causally determined by factors beyond his control to decide as he does' (Pereboom 2014a: 79). That is, a manipulated agent would be indistinguishable from a non-manipulated one in terms of the proposed notion of freedom, i.e. in the case of classical compatibilism, Plum's ability to do what he wants. Our understanding of what sourcehood involves, however, implies that Plum is responsible for his actions only if his situation can be distinguished from that of a manipulated agent. This Argument from Manipulation therefore suggests that compatibilist conditional analyses of free will are unable to capture what makes an agent the source of her actions.[14] Below, I consider objections to this argument in its broader use against any form of compatibilism.

There are other problems with the conditional analysis: it has little to say about the ability to will otherwise. This analysis, when applied to the freedom to choose, leads to the following account of conditional leeway: 'S is able to choose otherwise if and only if, were S to prefer to choose otherwise, S would choose otherwise.' If 'prefer' is understood as 'having the strongest desire', then this is problematic as we do not always act on our strongest desires (Reid 1788/1969; Holton 2009) or indeed on what we desire (see Hobbes 1654/1999, 1656/1999). Lehrer (2004) opts for a broader notion of preference as identifying 'what is preferable, desirable, good for ourselves, and, ideally, good for others. Preference amalgamates these evaluations in a choice disposing state.' He moreover indicates that this analysis can be repeated to explain the freedom to prefer to choose, leading to notions of preferring to prefer to choose, and so on. He argues that this regress is not vicious, however, insofar as S does not have to do anything for all these conditionals to be true. While this is correct, if these conditionals are to be true, the higher-order preferences they refer to must be real features characterising the agent. But, even assuming we could make sense of the meaning of such higher-order preferences, a conception of finite agency characterised by such an infinity of chosen preferences is implausible. If, on the contrary, we stop the regress anywhere, attributions of responsibility become questionable since some set of preferences will ultimately not have been chosen by the agent.

These types of worries prompted a set of moves in contemporary analytic philosophy to go beyond the conditioning upon given willings or desires to identify a plausible notion of the agent as source of her causally determined action. Hume's version of the conditional analysis already prefigures these moves insofar as his account apportions more responsibility to the agent when her actions emanate from what is 'durable and constant' in the agent and when they are 'designed and premeditated' (Hume 1978: 411). This points to two broad approaches depending upon whether it is a particular agent (e.g. characterised by what is 'durable and constant' in her agency) or essential characteristics of rational agency in general (which define the action as 'designed and premeditated') that are at stake.

Source compatibilism: Real-self views

In 'real-self views' (Pereboom 2022: 17f) or 'mesh' theories (McKenna 2011: 175ff), certain features of her psychological make-up are taken as definitive of who the particular agent is. This approach finds its source in the observation that if, as we saw above, it is not satisfactory to simply identify the agent with her willings, it is possible to improve upon that by distinguishing among the psychological causal factors which determine action, those which could rightly be said to characterise who the agent really is. The approach to dealing with this problem is to characterise agency in terms of a mesh between what represents the agent's true volitions and what are the immediate desires that prompt particular actions. With such an understanding of the self, freedom of the will is characterised in terms of actions having their source in a harmonious mesh.

Harry Frankfurt (1971) introduced the first mesh theory in terms of a differentiation between first- and second-order desires. On Frankfurt's *hierarchical theory*, the will is free when our first-order desires are in conformity with our second-order volitions. Alternatively, in the *planning theory* (Bratman 2003), it is general intentions, i.e. policies of practical reasoning, which are viewed as characterising what makes an action the agent's own, so that free actions are those caused by desires that are in line with these general intentions. In the theory proposed by Gary Watson (1975), the agent is characterised by a *valuation system* which encapsulates the agent's practical rationality, i.e. his beliefs about what is good or right. Freedom of the will is characterised by the conformity of the agent's *motivational system* (desires and other motives) to his valuation system.

There are, in the literature, three main types of objections to mesh theories,[15] which question the adequacy of the proposed account of an agent's self as source of agency. It has been objected that

i. it is not successful in dealing with the *Argument from Manipulation*.
ii. the theory does not provide conditions for the *identification* of the agent's self as the action's source.
iii. it does not include cases of free agency where the mesh does not *operate harmoniously*.

The Argument from Manipulation (e.g. Pereboom 2014b: 93–101) has it that, in terms of whatever volitional structure the self is characterised, there is a logically possible scenario in which this structure (i.e. the beliefs and desires characterising it[16]) is brought about through manipulation by a neuroscientist. So, in the case of Frankfurt's proposal, desires of first and second order could be implanted in the agent.[17] Michael Bratman's theory arguably has a further historicist dimension since policies of practical reasoning link the agent's decisions/actions over time. That is, the role of such practical policies would seem to imply that my action at any point in time cannot simply be considered to be the result of manipulation, so that McKenna (2011: 196) concludes that Bratman's proposal is immune to the manipulation objection. Pereboom (2014b: 93–101) responds that his 'four-case argument' of manipulation covers *all* compatibilist theories. In the case of Bratman's theory, the issue is that policies of practical reasoning themselves are sets of beliefs and could therefore be implanted. If Bratman were to respond that the agent would then no longer be free, this means that the origin of these beliefs is relevant to the notion of selfhood at stake, and the theory needs to be revised.

The Identification objection to Frankfurt's theory was part of the motivation for Watson's alternative proposal; Watson (1975) pertinently asks why the higher-order desires have a special relation to the agent's self. This does not appear to be justifiable without appealing to an infinite regress over all higher orders of desires. In fact, Watson's proposal itself seems to suffer from the same problem, as Velleman (1992: 472) points out, since one can certainly ask the same question about an agent's valuational system. As for Bratman's proposal, why describe an agent who acts contrary to his policies of practical reasoning as suffering an 'identity-destroying change' (McKenna 2011: 187) rather than merely altering his identity? On the latter understanding, the source of agency cannot be equated with a set of policies.

The third objection is that mesh theories do not have a satisfactory answer to the question of what happens when the mesh is not operating harmoniously. So, on Frankfurt's hierarchical theory, what if I act on a first-order desire that is not endorsed by a second-order one? The claim that this is not *my* action, i.e. that it is unfree, does not seem an acceptable answer (McKenna 2011: 181–2) as it would absolve the agent of responsibility in cases which are likely to include those actions which are most blameworthy. Bratman also does not appear to have an answer to the question of how we are to make sense of an agent not acting according to her general practical policies (McKenna 2011: 186). Watson (1977) argues that cases of weakness of the will do not arise on his understanding of an agent's volitions: agents do not act in contravention of the evaluations defined by their valuational system. This is, however, problematic insofar as it would exclude from the scope of praise- or blameworthiness all actions that may be prompted by motives which are not fully checked by the agent's valuation system.[18]

Source compatibilism: Rationality accounts

In 'rationality accounts' (Pereboom 2022: 17f) or 'reasons-responsive' theories (McKenna 2017: 27ff), the responsiveness to reasons of the causal mechanism producing the action is definitive of agency. That is, free agency can be distinguished from compulsive-phobic behaviour by the fact that the determination of actions has certain rational features.

The spirit of this second approach has a distant forerunner in Leibniz's understanding of free will: Leibniz has it that the control that characterises our conscious evaluation of reasons for action (Jorati 2017: 297) is definitive of our free will. And the early, pre-critical Kant (i.e. before the late 1770s) espouses such a view as it was adapted by Christian Wolff and Alexander Baumgarten: freedom is a characteristic of actions that are determined by using one's intellect (see Allison 2020: 27).

Insofar as it avoids the thorny issue of explicitly locating a notion of self as source of the individual agent's free actions, the reasons-responsive approach seemingly presents an attractive alternative. On the other hand, by focussing on the mechanism through which the action is brought about, it is prima facie not clear how this approach can accommodate a notion of action ownership in a world where the operation of this mechanism is completely determined by what precedes it.

In a seminal paper, Fischer and Ravizza (1998) argue that by properly understanding the mechanism as responsive to reasons, this can be achieved. In so doing, they however recognise that determinism may be incompatible with the ability to do otherwise (leeway) therefore with a certain understanding of the ability to control one's action. However, in line with Frankfurt (1969; see Chapter 3), they reject the claim that moral responsibility requires an ability of *regulative control*.[19] Rather, they claim that what is needed is *guidance control*, which concerns the sequence of events that leads to the action.[20] That is, they want to preserve the intuition that underpins the sense that an ability to do otherwise is essential for free agency but without commitment to any *actual* such ability. Hence, they introduce a *weak reactivity* to reasons. Guidance control requires only that there should be at least one possible world that is inaccessible to the agent because of the deterministic framework, in which the mechanism leading to the action will respond differently (Fischer and Ravizza 1998: 73).

On this picture, Alice (Carroll 2015) exerts guidance control in voting for Tweedledee rather than Tweedledum in the election to the council of Wonderland,[21] insofar as the mechanism causing this would lead her to vote for Tweedledum had good reasons for so doing been identified *and* were it possible for her to do so. In the current circumstances, it is, however, not possible for her to act otherwise because of determinism. It is in this sense that she is reactive to reasons, but only weakly so since she cannot, as a matter of fact, act differently in identical circumstances, i.e. has no regulative control.

Aside from this condition of weak reactivity, reasons-responsiveness requires *receptivity* to reasons for action, which means that the agent is able to recognise and evaluate them. Additionally, it must be the case that a third-party inquirer could make sense of the pattern of reasons the agent takes as sufficient for action, and some of them should be moral reasons. Finally, Fischer and Ravizza include *ownership conditions* for the mechanism. These are beliefs that the agent can bring about alterations in the world through her action and that she is a target of moral demands and expectations, beliefs which must be based upon the agent's evidence.

Does Fischer and Ravizza's theory capture a notion of sourcehood that can characterise free agency? Of the three types of objection that were made to mesh theories, only the manipulation objection is relevant here, which emphasises the apparent advantage of this approach noted earlier. Thus, first, there are no worries about non-harmonious meshes, and second, there is no attempt to *locate* the agent's self in her psychological make-up (in terms of higher-order desires, etc.). Before turning to the Argument from Manipulation, it is worth reflecting on whether this means that, unlike mesh theories, the reasons-responsive theorist is able to propose a satisfactory notion of sourcehood. On Fischer and Ravizza's theory, I act in a different way in the light of different reasons. This is, however, a mechanistic account which has reasons r_1 ('Tweedledum is the better candidate') leading to action φ_1 ('Alice votes for Tweedledum') and reasons r_2 ('Tweedledee is the better candidate') leading to action φ_2 ('Alice votes for Tweedledee'). This account on its own does not accommodate an explicit conception of self as source of agency: while r_1 are the reasons for φ_1 and r_2 the reasons for φ_2, there is apparently no unified self who can take responsibility for doing either φ_1 or φ_2 (whichever one is causally determined). Rather, this notion of self enters the picture with the *subjective* ownership requirements spelt out earlier, which amount to the condition that the agent take ownership of this mechanism, thereby making him morally responsible. Fischer and Ravizza (1998: 225–8) recognise that if this condition is not fulfilled, the agent is not morally responsible. Some (Mele, McKenna), found this claim controversial, which led Fischer (2006) to make some concessions on this point, but the subjective condition of ownership remains essential to moral responsibility in this reasons-responsive theory.

While this condition is useful to make sense of diminished responsibility, there is a problem with describing it as subjective. If it is *merely* subjective, it is not something that could play any role in legal matters or moral matters (assuming the objectivity of moral norms) for which it would have to find some objective expression. In other words, if this is to play the role of making the agent responsible, there must be an objective dimension to the agent's taking ownership of her mechanism.[22]

Of course, the issue of ownership is one that is subjective, but there is an *equivocation* upon the meaning of this word: it is here subjective in that it pertains to the subject, i.e. the agent, but not subjective in the sense that it has no objective characteristics. Fischer and Ravizza want to use the word in the second meaning to do the work of the word in the first meaning (with objective characteristics). And there is a good reason for this: the reasons-responsive approach has no place for anything objective aside from the mechanism. As a result, this approach fails to deliver a satisfactory notion of sourcehood, for reasons that are analogous to mesh theories, namely that it does not provide a satisfactory notion of the self as source of the action.[23] So a type of Identification Problem does, after all, also affect the reasons-responsive approach (more on this further).

That is also why, just as mesh theories, the reasons-responsive approach falls prey to the Argument from Manipulation. Indeed,

> Plum's [actions] are modified by, and some of them arise from, his rational consideration of the reasons at issue, he is receptive to the relevant pattern of reasons, and if he knew that the bad consequences for himself that would result from killing White would be much more severe than they are actually likely to be, he would have refrained from killing her for this reason. (Pereboom 2014b: 94)

Insofar as this characterisation applies to all four scenarios of the argument, just as with the other forms of compatibilism reviewed earlier, on the reasons-responsive approach, Plum can no more be made responsible in the fourth scenario (i.e. the actual situation for the human agent Plum, assuming physicalism) than he is in the first or second scenarios (i.e. Plum, respectively, as a creation of neuroscientists who control him through a manipulating machine or as manipulated in his youth by a machine).

We can now briefly examine two objections to this argument, applying to its use against any form of compatibilism. Fischer (2006: 231–6) argues that while Plum is not blameworthy in scenarios one and two because of 'the circumstances of the creation of his values, character, desires, and so forth', he is nevertheless morally responsible, hence also morally responsible in the other two scenarios. In effect, while Fischer retains the agent as the recipient of blameworthiness, his notion of responsibility lies rather with the agent's mechanism that produces the action. Pereboom (2014b: 99), rightly in my view, resists this attempt to dissociate responsibility from blameworthiness in these cases. He argues that an agent is responsible for an action if 'he would deserve blame if he understood that it was morally wrong' (2014: 99) and that this 'basic desert' sense of blameworthiness is what is at stake here.

McKenna (2005) questions the way the Argument from Manipulation steers our intuitions by moving from scenario one to scenario four and focussing upon causal determinants. He proposes that the order of the cases should be reversed and that the focus should be not upon causes but upon 'the sort of agential properties that typically serve as a basis for ascribing responsibility' (2005). That is, we would start with the actual professor Plum and, noting that he possesses these properties (i.e. those characterising free agency according to mesh theories and reasons-responsive theories), would deem him responsible. The identification of causal determinants in cases three to one would not alter our verdict of responsibility because they are 'not relevant to [this] psychic structure' (2005).

As Pereboom (2014b: 100–1) points out, the reversal of the sequence of cases would amount to a refusal to engage with the incompatibilist's presentation of the problem and how it steers our intuitions. Further, that there should be a focus upon the psychic structure is not excluded by the incompatibilist: it's just that the incompatibilist does not consider it sufficient for assigning responsibility since she also claims that the existence of causal determinants is relevant. So McKenna's objection largely begs the question against the incompatibilist, and the challenge posed by the Argument from Manipulation remains the major objection to all compatibilist proposals.[24]

D. Further perspectives on the problems of compatibilism

The Problem in its first- and third-person forms

There is a common thread running through the compatibilist theories I have examined: they dismiss (more or less explicitly) the Problem in the first-person form I identified at the outset, i.e. a clash between our intuitions (first-person perspective) and causal determinism (third-person perspective). It is not that these intuitions are not recognised (e.g. Hume 1978: 408; Taylor and Dennett 2011: 222). It is rather that the compatibilist does not see a clash between first- and third-order perspectives. This is either because these perspectives are said to be able to live happily within their respective domains, namely Strawson's participant and objective standpoints respectively; or it is because the first-person perspective is allegedly confused and once it has been properly characterised, the impression that there is a clash will disappear (e.g. Taylor and Dennett 2011: 236).

This confusion, according to classical compatibilists, leads us to think that we need more than a conditional notion of freedom, i.e. the agent's freedom to do what he wills (sourcehood) and therefore to do otherwise if he so wills (leeway). The threat posed by the Argument from Manipulation clearly shows that locating the source of an action in what the agent happens to will is not sufficient, however. This spawned an array of source compatibilist proposals, which in effect amount to arguing that the first-person perspective is not, as was prima facie assumed, in conflict with the third-person deterministic perspective but on the contrary fully integrated with it. This is because the first-person perspective is in fact either that of an agent defined by higher-order desires, a valuation system or policies of practical reasoning it (mesh theories), or that of a rational agent endorsing a reasons-responsive mechanism as her own (reasons-responsive approach) and thereby fully integrated with this deterministic perspective.

Insofar as they thus cast doubt upon the first-person problem as it is formulated, the source compatibilists have essentially focussed upon the third-person problem, i.e. securing an account of agency that enables responsibility to coexist with determinism.[25] In terms of the distinction I introduced earlier, they have therefore proposed psychological accounts of free will but not volitional accounts of how I can understand my control of my action.

Psychological and volitional accounts

It may be objected that all that is needed is for the notion of responsibility from the psychological account to be translated into one of control, thereby defining a volitional account. But, I shall argue that there is no way of effecting such a translation and that this problem summarises the various concerns encountered earlier with these compatibilist proposals.

Starting with mesh theories, the question is essentially one of locating *me* (i.e. my will) in the compatibilist account. The Identification Problem showed that there is necessarily something arbitrary in choosing certain higher-order desires, or a valuation system or policies of practical reasoning as defining my will. If Alice's valuation system leads her to vote for Tweedledee, why should she take that as essentially characterising what she wills, so that if she had voted for Tweedledum, that would not have been a free action?

The problem can be put schematically as follows. There is a causal account, and the compatibilist's problem is to locate me in it, but how can that be achieved? The arbitrariness of any attempt to locate me in it (Identification Problem), i.e. the problem of identifying the 'self' involved in free agency *qua* self-determination, is then reflected upstream and downstream of whatever location my will has been assigned. Upstream, there is room for manipulation of my will (Argument from Manipulation), in which case, is it really *my* will? Downstream, there will be actions that do not conform with this will (problem of non-harmonious mesh) as it has been identified, but does that really mean that such actions are not free?

The reasons-responsive theorist can avoid at least one of these problems by not committing himself to locating my will in the causal flux that produces the action. However, in identifying a reasons-responsive mechanism as essential to free agency, he leaves it open to arguing that the agent can be manipulated. As to the question of where my will is located in relation to this mechanism, the reasons-responsive theorist proposes an answer, namely that it accompanies this mechanism through guidance control and that the agent takes ownership of this mechanism.

Does this provide what is needed for a volitional account? Guidance control is arguably the control exerted when I sit in the driving seat of an automated vehicle constrained to follow a path which has been predetermined but reflects all my reasons for action which can be acted upon given the deterministic constraints. The reasons-responsive theorist would argue that this should satisfy the volitional account since our intuitions about control must be deflated to allow for the constraints of a deterministic setting.

But am I able to view this reasons-responsive mechanism as carrying out what I will? Suppose another identical such causal mechanism were to be operative elsewhere, why am I attached to this one rather than that one? This is obviously a *metaphysical* question, but without addressing it, I am not able to claim that the reasons-responsive theory provides me with a picture of my will controlling my action. To pursue the metaphor, were it possible, I could change to another vehicle following the same path, i.e. switch my ownership claim without this having any impact upon the purpose I pursue: this vehicle has thus not been shown to be mine in the required sense. This problem of the volitional account defines a version of the Identification Problem (as noted earlier) for the reasons-responsive theorist. But unlike this problem in the mesh-theoretic case, it leads to a metaphysical question that needs to be addressed. Doing so satisfactorily must also involve eliminating the possibility of manipulation by leaving no room for any other controlling instance apart from my will. On a naturalistic account, it is not possible to do this, and this metaphysical problem will play a key role in Kant's critical turn as we shall see further.[26]

Of course, a broadly Humean response might involve rejecting the claim that some self must be identified as what wills the action. But that would not only involve a brute rejection of the claim that there is a first- (or indeed second-)person version of the Problem but also beg the question with respect to the Argument from Manipulation.

Importantly, what is clearly at the heart of the Identification Problem here is the lack of alternatives available to the agent.[27] At least in this case, the failure to meet the *leeway condition* makes it impossible to provide a satisfactory notion of *sourcehood* so that the two conditions flagged at the outset are connected. The metaphysical question about how some causal mechanism can really be mine in the sense required by the volitional account can only be answered if such leeway is available. That in general the leeway condition must be met is a much-discussed question following Frankfurt's (1969) seminal paper. I examine this issue in Chapter 3.

These reflections show that the objections to source compatibilism examined above map onto shortcomings with respect to the derivability of a volitional account from a psychological one. That is, in both source compatibilist approaches, the agent finds herself *homeless*: no proper home can be assigned to her in the mesh-theoretic case, and the home assigned to her in the reasons-responsive case is one that she cannot make her own in the required sense. I have also, however, indicated that unlike the mesh theorist, the reasons-responsive theorist does provide materials for a volitional account by addressing, if unsatisfactorily, the issues of control and ownership: what is missing is an answer to a metaphysical question about ownership, one which, I argued, requires the availability of leeway. Below, I shall explain in what way Kant can be understood as precisely addressing this question. Before moving to Kant, it is useful to consider a formalisation of this problem of the Homeless Agent.

The formal problem of the Homeless Agent

Formalising the compatibilist's problem of deriving a volitional from a psychological account sheds further light upon the issues just discussed. What is really needed for a volitional account? Since my action is arguably an intentional relation to a purpose (e.g. Aristotle 1986: iii, 9–10), this account would typically be an explanation of how this action amounts to my pursuit of my purpose (first-person perspective) and would exhibit what makes me morally praise/blameworthy (second-person perspective). Such a reference to the 'I' would ensure that there is no issue of a lack of unity of the self in the account.

A volitional account of an action φ can typically be expressed in the following form:

(1) 'I decide to φ with purpose Φ'

where, to fix ideas, we could take φ = 'vote for Tweedledum' and Φ = 'to get Tweedledum elected to council (of the land beyond the looking glass[28])'.

The teleological nature of a volitional account does not exclude a formulation that refers to reasons, since purpose Φ could be the satisfaction of my desire D:

(2) 'I decide to φ to satisfy desire D'

where D = 'to see Tweedledum sit on the council'.

Now the compatibilist's account is a psychological account of action, involving something like:

(3) 'Because of belief B and desire D, φ occurs'

where B = 'by voting for Tweedledum, I increase his chances of being elected to the council'.

The critique of classical compatibilism points out that the reasons in question are not necessarily endorsed by the agent, which motivates the moves of contemporary compatibilism to introduce the agent into this account. The contemporary compatibilist can thus gesture towards what is required by a volitional account by attempting to refer to the agent as source. Thus, for mesh theories we have:

(3') 'Because of desire D endorsed by 'my' higher-order desire, φ occurs'

or

(3") 'Because of belief B endorsed by 'my' valuational system V or 'my' policies of practical reasoning P, φ occurs.'

In the reasons-responsive theory, a case can be made for introducing a reference to what is mine because of the agent fulfilling certain ownership conditions (see above):

(3''') 'Because of belief B and desire D, and through 'my' reasons-responsive mechanism, φ occurs.'

In these formulations, my will would be represented by the higher-order desire D or valuational system V or policies of practical reasoning P in mesh theories, or introduced as a subjective endorsement of a mechanism as mine, an endorsement that sits next to the psychological account in the reasons-responsive approach. But, as discussed earlier, this cannot yield a proper volitional account of the type (1) or (2). The problem is the arbitrariness of what is defined as mine in mesh theories, i.e. as that which enables free agency to be understood as self-determination, hence the use of 'my' in speech quotes in (3') and (3''). And the merely subjective nature of my role in guidance control in the reasons-responsive approach does not define a proper notion of control for the agent's will hence 'my' in speech quotes in (3'''). As a consequence, we have, in all formulations (3'), (3'') and (3'''), 'φ occurs' rather than 'I (decide to) φ', which is what a volitional account requires.

E. Kant and the Need for a metaphysical account

As indicated earlier, the homelessness of the agent's will in the case of the reasons-responsive theory is less critical than in that of mesh theories: a home is identified and the problem is rather that of the agent making this home her own. This problem of linking the self's will to a particular reasons-responsive causal mechanism in such a way that the latter is not open to external manipulation is a metaphysical one: a *metaphysical account* of how free will and determinism can coexist is therefore required. The critical Kant proposes just such an account.

To understand how Kant's critical proposal makes sense as a response to the shortcomings of the compatibilist theories I examined, let us start with the pre-critical Kant. As noted earlier, Kant was initially a compatibilist espousing something broadly consistent with a reasons-responsive approach. That is, Kant endorsed the Leibnizian conception of freedom in the form it took for Wolff and Baumgarten: 'freedom is attributed to actions determined by the use of the intellect' (Allison 2020: 27). The intellect fulfils the role of the reasons-responsive mechanism bringing about the action.

But there is, in Leibniz-Wolffian compatibilism, no real clash between causal determinism and free will because of the doctrine of pre-established harmony. That is, while my actions are determined, this is not an event-causal determinism (Jorati 2017: 299). Indeed, the inclinations determining my actions are not themselves further determined by antecedent causes. Rather, for Leibniz and Wolff, I am created by God at the beginning of the universe as a monad that would only start developing into a full human being when my parents conceived me (Jorati 2017: 300).[29]

Kant did not endorse pre-established harmony, but rather real causal interaction of substances.[30] Consequently, much as he otherwise subscribed to Leibnizian compatibilism, he was faced with the problem of our actions depending upon causes that are external to the will (MH AA28: 100). Allison (2020: 82) notes that the fact that Kant recognises this problem without offering any solution is probably what led him to make the move away from Leibniz's conception of freedom.[31]

In the 1770s, during his so-called silent decade (2020: 183), Kant developed a radically novel metaphysical stance issuing in the formulation of transcendental idealism as a result of his adoption of a different position on the problem of objectivity, which defines his Copernican Revolution (Buroker 2006: 17–21).[32] While Kant did not publish anything on this metaphysical shift during this decade, we do know that the Problem was at the heart of his thinking (Allison 2020: 183–233) and arguably one of the main motivations for the shift, as Kant himself indicated (Br AA12: 257–8).

Having considered the problems faced by his pre-critical reasons-responsive approach, it is fairly straightforward to reconstruct the logic of such a shift in response to the Problem. These problems, as explained earlier, are (i) that of finding a home for the agent's self, i.e. enabling the causal mechanism that produces the action to be that which implements *what I will* and (ii) ensuring that this home is manipulation-proof, i.e. that nothing else but my will has the ultimate control of my action.

This concern (ii) with manipulation will not disappear as long as what defines my action is located within (mesh theories) or carried by (reasons-responsive) the causal flux: it will always be possible to make room for a manipulator upstream of the relevant part of this causal nexus. So the home that must be found for the will should be located outside the causal nexus. This, however, means placing the will outside nature. If the agent is not to become a supernatural creator, such a move is most plausibly made within the framework of an idealism for which nature is no longer reality in-itself, but rather the appearance of it for beings with our type of cognition. This is transcendental idealism.[33]

Nevertheless, as a metaphysical move, this is prima facie rather unsatisfactory, as it would appear to amount to dodging the Problem by splitting free will away from determinism in some arbitrary metaphysical jiggery-pokery, which, to boot, would arguably leave us with an empty notion of free will outside nature (e.g. Wilkerson 137–8).[34] The concern about arbitrariness can, however, be mitigated with respect to the Problem at least, by noting that requirement (i) also needs to be satisfied. This means that what is in nature as a causal mechanism implementing my will must also be within my ability to exert control over. So my self *qua* agent must straddle the boundary of the natural domain in such a way that what is mine in nature is controlled by what is mine outside nature. It follows that it must be possible for something belonging to the natural domain to be subordinated to what is outside it.

The broader worry about the move to transcendental idealism is, however, thereby compounded by a concern with this apparent demotion of the natural domain. To respond to this concern, consider, first, that Kant's metaphysical shift is not arbitrarily designed simply to make the Problem disappear. This is confirmed by the fact that Kant identified it as required to address the very possibility of objectivity. So it is not only not arbitrary but in fact required, so Kant argues, for the possibility of nature (without which the Problem would vanish). A world of causally connected spatio-temporal objects is only possible, Kant argues, insofar as it is not real in-itself, but rather is the appearance for a possible subject of cognition, of such a reality in-itself (Prol. AA04: 318).

Second, this worry about the apparent demotion of nature can now be crystallised in the concern that nature is mere appearance (A341/A285) where the appearances of my willings would be located. This is a controversial topic in Kant scholarship (Gardner 1999: 269ff; Allison 2004: 50ff; Allais 2015: 3ff; Onof 2019: 198–9) that I shall return to in Chapter 7. For now, I just want to indicate there is a consensus around the view that Kant's intent is not to weaken the standing of the natural sciences as revealing objective truths by giving nature the metaphysical status of appearance. For this just means that nature is not the most fundamental reality, while the status of appearance is, for Kant, precisely what is needed to ensure that our knowledge claims about the empirical world are properly grounded (Gardner 1999: 88–90).

Having, for now, briefly addressed these immediate worries about transcendental idealism, in the next chapter, I turn to how Kant's adoption of transcendental idealism enabled him to propose a source compatibilist solution to the Problem, which avoids the pitfalls of the reasons-responsive approach through the outline of a metaphysical account made possible by the adoption of transcendental idealism.

2

Kant's idealism and compatibilism

In Chapter 1, I introduced Kant's adoption of transcendental idealism as closely connected to his awareness of the shortcomings of his initial compatibilism in the light of problems comparable to those encountered by contemporary source compatibilism, in particular in its reasons-responsive (or 'rationality account') form. I proposed a reconstruction of Kant's thinking in so doing, which showed why this adoption seems required to address such problems.

This chapter shows that this adoption provides the metaphysical framework for Kant's compatibilist proposal to solve the problem of free will (hereafter 'Problem'). Before presenting Kant's version of the Problem in the *Critique of Pure Reason* (hereafter *CPR*), some background is necessary. I present a synopsis of Kant's transcendental idealism and defend my interpretation against methodological alternatives. Kant's understanding of causality and his claims about determinism are then presented. There is a vast literature devoted to these issues to which I cannot do justice to here: I extract only what is essential for my purpose.

I then present the Third Antinomy, which is the form the Problem takes for Kant. In this Chapter, I confine myself to Kant's general approach to solving such so-called *dynamical* antinomies. I shall argue, within the context of the ongoing debate on this issue, that this is sufficient to characterise Kant's solution to the Problem as compatibilist. I shall also argue that this bare solution to the Problem is not sufficient, as it only deals with the logical possibility of a free will and leaves us with two much-discussed problems characterising the psychological and volitional accounts. I consider approaches to these two problems and show that they both lead to the same conclusion as to how to interpret Kant's compatibilism and what more is needed.

A. Transcendental idealism

The metaphysics of transcendental idealism

In Chapter 1, I briefly introduced Kant's idealism as understanding nature, i.e. the spatio-temporal domain of causally connected empirical objects as a domain of appearances for a possible subject of cognition, of some reality in-itself. Kant himself argues that it is fundamentally the spatio-temporality of these objects that calls for a transcendental idealist metaphysics. That is, as Karl Ameriks (2003: 99–100) has pointed out, it is not just the fact that these objects are determined under a certain conceptual scheme (e.g. involving causality and other fundamental concepts that Kant calls 'categories') that transcendental idealism is required. In other words, one could not argue from the mere fact that any objective determination necessarily belongs to some conceptual scheme, that the objects we are dealing are not real in-themselves.

I cannot do justice to the extensive literature on the meaning of Kant's idealism. I just want to draw the reader's attention to the central problem of understanding the relation between appearances and reality in-itself, or things in-themselves as Kant prefers to say, and present the interpretation I shall use in this book. I endorse a widespread but controversial view (see Ameriks 2000; Hogan 2009; Schulting 2017)[1] that when Kant says at the very beginning of the *CPR* that the object 'affects the mind in a certain way' (A20/B34),[2] he is arguing that something independent of my cognition is causing my sensations, i.e. that things in-themselves *affect* me. This is generally referred to as a claim of *transcendental affection* and represents a starting point for our cognition. This amounts to interpreting the relation between appearances and things in-themselves metaphysically, and later, I shall consider an important alternative to this view.

It is, however, also the case that Kant subscribes to a causal theory of perception (e.g. A213/B260; see Aquila 1981: 13) according to which there is an objective causal link between the perceived object and the sensations it produces. Here, the perceived object is the empirical object (appearance) which science can investigate, so that the causal link is describable as *empirical affection*.

The question now is: How are we to make sense of the duality between the empirical object that (empirically) causes my sensation and the thing in-itself grounding it, i.e. causing it in a sense that does not refer to natural causality? There are, prima facie, two problems here: that of the duality between appearance and thing in-itself, and that of the 'double affection' (e.g. Stang 2015) of the empirical object/appearance and the thing in-itself both causing my sensation.

To address these issues, it is important to understand the *object-duality* that lies at the heart of Kant's theory of objectivity. In cognising an object, the subject has to posit some thing beyond her cognition 'this object must be thought as something in general = X, since outside our cognition we have nothing we could set over against this cognition as corresponding to it' (A104). This, Kant calls the transcendental object. Of it, Kant says that appearances are grounded in it (A252; A538/B566). This leads to the claim (e.g. Herring 1953) that 'transcendental object' refers to the thing in-itself grounding appearances.[3]

This transcendental object has a key function in the determination of the empirical object: 'Appearances are the only objects that can be given to us immediately' (A108); these are the empirical objects of our experience. But 'these appearances are not things-in-themselves, but themselves only representations, which in turn have their object, which therefore cannot be further intuited by us, and that may therefore be called the non-empirical, i.e., transcendental' (A109) object. The function of the transcendental object is therefore that in positing it, I posit something existing outside my cognition. My objective determinations can thereby refer to an empirical object as its appearance: while its determinations are nothing but representations, it *exists* outside me.[4]

But the *existence* of the empirical object means nothing more than the existence of the posited transcendental object beyond my cognition. So, *from my cognitive perspective*, these objects define a single existing thing: appearance and reality in-itself are *two aspects* of a single existing thing, whereby the latter grounds the former. Object-duality does not therefore imply a two-world (sometimes called 'two-object') theory of the relation appearance/things in-themselves (e.g. Guyer 1987: 334–5; Stang 2014; Jauernig 2021: ch. 5). Rather, it is a metaphysical *dual-aspect theory* of reality in-itself grounding appearances (see Allais 2015; Rosefeldt 2007) with a *perspectival* dimension (Onof 2019b).[5]

There is nothing more I can know about this thing in-itself than the objective determinations of the empirical object it appears as, because my cognition is constrained by its spatio-temporal nature. There is therefore no concern that objective reality, although it is of so-called appearances, is illusory in any sense. Rather, it is the way some reality in-itself appears to the type of cognition I possess.

While Kant does not discuss the so-called problem of double affection, i.e. of the apparent causal overdetermination of my sensation by empirical object and thing in-itself, this is well-known in the literature since Adickes (1924). Most commentators claim that it defines a serious problem for the Kantian critical system (Vaihinger 1881–92: vol. 2, 53), while others have proposed ways of addressing it (e.g. Stang 2015). I cannot discuss these solutions' merits here other than to indicate that they share an endorsement of the claim that there is indeed a problem of double affection to be addressed. I have argued (Onof 2019b) that the appearance of a problem disappears on a proper understanding of the relation appearance/thing in-itself. That is, the claim of transcendental affection, i.e. the fact that my sensation is grounded in the thing in-itself, does not define any causal overdetermination, as long as the relation appearance/thing in-itself is interpreted as a grounding of empirical causality in things in-themselves.[6] Indeed, the latter thus ground the causality through which the empirical object causes the sensation (empirical affection), thereby defining a causal ground of this sensation (transcendental affection), so that there is only one cause of sensations.[7] That Kant subscribes to such a claim is, for instance, suggested by the reference to causal laws in his stating that, since appearances are not things in-themselves but 'mere representations connected *in accordance with empirical laws*, then they themselves must have grounds that are not appearances' (A536-7/B564-5 my emphasis; see also GMM AA04: 453). Unlike the dual-aspect perspectival claim which is *constitutive* for experience, i.e. necessary for the constitution of objectivity according to my earlier argument, this claim that the grounding of appearances is a grounding of empirical causality should be viewed as what Kant calls *regulative*, i.e. required by the rationality of our cognition, here, the avoidance of the problem of double affection (see Onof 2021a).

The alternative non-metaphysical interpretation of transcendental idealism

Several prominent interpreters have insisted that there is in fact no metaphysical content to Kant's idealism. Typically, they have espoused a *methodological dual-aspect theory* without any claim of existence of things in-themselves. Prauss (1974: 20) thus famously argued that the thing in-itself should be understood adverbially. It is just the thing we experience (empirical object) considered independently of the way it is cognised, i.e. 'as it is in-itself'. Importantly, this merely defines a way of thinking and does not involve any existence claim for things in-themselves.

Allison (1983) developed this into a methodological account of transcendental idealism as 'formal idealism', as Kant (Proleg. AA04: 375) himself calls it to differentiate it from Berkeley's idealism (Berkeley 1848-1957). Correspondingly, Allison's methodological interpretation was developed in response to the dominant English-speaking interpretations of the time. Its targets included Peter Strawson's (1966) influential work, in which he separates Kant's useful 'analytical argument' (1966: 16) from his idealism. Strawson's interpretation of Kant's idealism as that of 'an inconsistent Berkeley', i.e. a mix of phenomenalism with a dogmatic claim of existence of an unknowable supersensible reality, had its roots in Prichard's (1909: 71–100) failure to distinguish between empirical and transcendental forms of the appearance/thing as it is in itself distinction, as Allison (1983: 4–8) puts it.

To wit, on this 'standard interpretation', appearances relate to things in-themselves as the perception of a broken stick (appearance in the empirical sense) held under water to the unbroken stick it really is (the stick as it is itself in the empirical sense).[8] This led to the view that transcendental idealism involves a distinction between an unknowable 'real' reality in-itself and a domain of 'mere' appearances, a view that is generally held to be an untenable metaphysical doctrine, in particular when it involves distinguishing between two worlds (e.g. Guyer 1987).

Allison (1983) introduces the notion of *epistemic condition* with which we make sense of a specifically transcendental sense of appearance that is distinct from that which results from the *psychological conditions* under which we perceive objects, thus avoiding the confusion at the heart of Prichard's interpretation (1983: 11).[9] This notion also captures a central feature of Kant's critical turn against Leibnizian metaphysics, namely the introduction of conditions of objective knowledge that are not *logical conditions* (1983: 10). In this way, Kant introduces the key modal concept of *real* (as opposed to logical) *possibility*: something is really possible if it 'agrees with the formal conditions of experience (in accordance with intuition and concepts)' (B265/A218), conditions which are spelt out by Kant in the Analytic of the *CPR*. Allison then interprets Kant's claim that transcendental idealism is a formal idealism as meaning that 'what is necessary for the representation of something as an object (. . .) must reflect the cognitive structure of the mind' (1983: 27). In particular, this serves to distinguish Kant's idealism from Berkeley's phenomenalism because while 'objects (. . .) are nothing but (. . .) mere representations', it is only 'as they are represented' that they are not an 'existence grounded in itself' (B519).

Problems with the methodological interpretation

While Allison correctly concludes that Kant's idealism does not, therefore, concern the existence of objects, what he infers from this, as regards the issue of affection, is questionable. My interpretation of transcendental affection concurs with Allison's

(2004: 67–73) to the extent that he claims that 'it is a necessary (material) condition of human experience that something affect the mind' and it is a transcendental condition that this 'be viewed (. . .) as the transcendental object' (Allison 1983: 250). But this does not entail that Kant's account of the transcendental object makes 'no reference to entities other than those which are describable in spatio-temporal terms' (Allison 1983: 250).[10] When Kant says of it that it is 'a mere something, about which we would not understand what it is even if someone could tell us' (A277/B333), he is referring to something we thereby conceive as existing.[11] Indeed, when Kant 'posits the ground of the matter of sensory representations (. . .) in something supersensible, which *grounds* these representations and of which we can have no cognition' (UE AA08 215; 306–7), this positing involves an existence claim (see Onof 2019b: 205) which Allison (2004: 71) overlooks.

Further, the methodological interpreter would have it that things in-themselves are just a way in which we can think of the things we cognise as appearances, namely independently of the possibility of cognition.[12] But there is no warrant for such a thought if something existing in-itself has not been posited (Schulting 2017: 391): Why should it be more meaningful than considering the number 2 without the property of evenness (Gardner 1999: 293)? Allison (2004: 53) acknowledges this problem but apparently only offers as warrant the need to avoid Kant's idealism collapsing into Berkeleyan phenomenalism.[13]

That this metaphysical interpretation is also a more natural reading of Kant's formal idealism can be seen from his own explanations of his idealism: 'I leave to things as we obtain them by the senses their actuality and only limit our sensuous intuition of these things' (Proleg. AA04: 292–3). So things of which our intuition is limited to their appearance in space and time exist. This is existence tout court, not that of these things as we intuit them through the senses as opposed to their reality in-itself. It is the reality in-itself of these existing things that causes sensations (transcendental affection) and grounds the empirical affection by which we 'obtain them by the senses' (Proleg. AA04: 292–3). We shall see in subsequent chapters that the deflationist nature of Allison's methodological interpretation of Kant's theory of freedom is problematic (see also Chiba 2012).

The epistemology of transcendental idealism

The epistemology of transcendental idealism is part of the background required for what follows here and in the next chapters. I present its most basic claims in their Kantian context, i.e. in the context of a representational epistemology, while motivating them from a systematic point of view focussing upon perceptual knowledge. At its heart is the distinction between two types of representations: these are representations of an object as a particular token or of it as belonging to a type. The former are *intuitions* and the latter *concepts*.

Intuitions are immediate because they refer directly to the particular in question, the object-token. Analogously to Fregean semantics, a 'sense' needs to be specified to achieve this reference. Depending upon whether the object is thereby determined in any way, this is either a representation that plays the same role in cognition as a demonstrative indexical in language, i.e. of relating the subject to something indeterminate given to her senses, or it involves a conceptual determination. Kant generally refers to the latter intuitions as 'intuitions' tout court or with a unity (B143) and to the former as 'empirical intuitions' (B162).

Concepts are the representation through which an object-token is (further) determined as belonging to a type. Such a determination refers to other possible determinations of object-tokens under this type and is therefore a mediated (by an intuition) representation of this object-token. The categories identify the different ways in which this is achieved, each with its own principle of application.[14]

If we are to have knowledge of a particular determination of an object or state-of-affairs, both types of representation are required. Indeed, a *bare intuition* would correspond to pure ostension, i.e. 'that', but *mere concepts* do not yield knowledge either, because they do not relate to any particular reality (see B75/A51).

Perceptual knowledge requires intuitive representations of an object-token that, through synthesis (B151), are taken by the subject in apperception (self-consciousness) as belonging together. This act of spontaneity has a unity that identifies the token as belonging to a certain type, i.e. as having certain conceptual determinations through which the object-token is comparable to others (possible or actual) included in this unity. This epistemological claim is also definitive of objectivity: such a relation to possible (self-conscious) consciousness is definitive of what it is to be an object in transcendental idealism, since an object is defined in terms of possible experience by a cognising subject.

As we saw earlier, the benchmark of the objectivity of such determinations lies in the subject's positing of an object outside her cognition in unifying the manifold representations in one thought (A108-110), i.e. in self-consciousness. This positing defines something completely independent of cognition (transcendental object, i.e. reality in-itself) as ground for a judgement determining an empirical object as its appearance. Equivalently, objectivity resides in *the* universal validity of this self-consciousness of the manifold representations as mine, i.e. in its defining an impersonal perspective (B131-2).

A natural object[15] is therefore defined as that which, through possible perception, directly or not, can be represented in intuition and recognised conceptually under the synthetic unity of self-consciousness ('apperception' B136-8): objectivity is thus *constituted* by the subject, i.e. by the epistemic spontaneity of her self-consciousness. Further, since we cannot intuit it, reality in-itself is unknowable; it is 'merely intelligible' (B522/A494).

While the principles of the understanding governing the application of the categories are *constitutive*, Kant also identifies a role for ideas of reason (God, the soul, freedom) as defining *regulative* principles that enable our objective knowledge to acquire further unity and systematicity.

These are the basic tenets of Kant's idealist epistemology that are relevant here. I take them to follow from the aforementioned specification of transcendental idealism together with minimal assumptions, although it is beyond the scope of this study to provide detailed arguments for this claim.[16]

B. Substance and causality

Substance

Substance is that which persists 'in all change of appearances' (B224). In the *Metaphysical Foundations of Natural Science* (hereafter 'MFNS'), Kant will identify this as matter (MFNS AA04: 476), but today, in the light of the theory of special relativity, we should extend that to what is manifested either as energy or mass according to Einstein's equation $E = mc^2$. While this notion, which I shall capitalise as 'Substance', seems remote from the common use of 'substance', Kant mostly refers to 'substances' in the plural by which he indicates that we individuate them. This is an empirical issue about which Kant mentions that the Second Analogy, I examine later, will enable us 'to note what is necessary' (B232/A189).

As we shall see, that means that when we observe a change, we thereby assume an unchanging substrate thereof which can be determined as substance. I will thus individuate a sandstone rock as substance as I see it change in position and water content, although I know that it was a scattered collection of grains of sand millions of years ago. The plural 'substances' therefore indicates a way of carving up that which is 'substance (...) the substratum of all change' (B225) that is guided by the determination of change.

Causality

Kant's conception of causality is, as Watkins (2005) has conclusively established, not the default Humean conception of a relation between determinate events. There are historical reasons for this, as Watkins (2005) shows: Kant forms his conception of causality against the background of Wolff and Baumgarten's Leibnizian conceptions of causes as grounds, i.e. possibilities that are essential features of things (2005: 118–21). However, partly in connection with his reading of Hume's *Enquiry*, Kant distances himself from this Leibnizian conception of causes as *logical* grounds in the 1760s (2005: 118–21). A logical ground brings about consequences with logical necessity, i.e. in accordance with the principle of contradiction; real grounds are essential features of a thing through which 'because something is, something else is' (2005: 166). The 'most distinctive feature' of Kant's critical conception of causality in terms of grounds or causal powers is its 'asymmetry': 'a ground that determines the state of another substance does not do so by virtue of a determinate state of its own or by means of its mere existence, but rather through an indeterminate activity that is incapable of ever becoming determinate itself' (2005: 231). Kant refers to this activity as 'the causality of a cause' (2005: 231).

This indeterminacy may seem puzzling. If I put some iron filings close to a magnet, they will organise themselves in a pattern which reveals the shape of the magnetic field. It may therefore seem that the magnet's causal power is determinate in that it has certain spatial properties and that the law governing this causal power can be expressed in mathematical form, in terms of one of Maxwell's equations.

However, appearances are spatio-temporal, so the determinacy of a substance's properties is essentially spatio-temporal. But the magnet's causality is not temporally determinate: the magnet's causal power, expressed by Maxwell's equation, is timeless.[17] So the indeterminacy of causality *qua* causal power is temporal: it defines unchanging grounds (2005: 232; 263–5). And there is a very good reason for this indeterminacy in Kant's idealism. As we shall see further, causality accounts for temporal determinacy.[18] If causality, the source of temporal determinacy, were itself determinate, this determinacy would, in turn, have to be accounted for, thus leading to a regress.

This is the conception of causality I assumed in claiming that empirical causality is grounded in reality in-itself. This helps clarify in what sense this is a double-aspect theory of how appearances relate to things in-themselves: empirical causality is a power characterising a substance whose existence is that of some reality in-itself grounding this power.

To this interpretation of causality that I adopt from Watkins's analysis, I, however, want to add that insofar as the determination that is the effect of some causality is a determination of an alteration, i.e. an event E2, a particular manifestation of the causality of the causing substance is at stake, which defines an event E1. The magnet's causality's manifestation in bringing about the movement of the iron filings defines an event E1 that causally accounts for the start of event E2 even if causality is not *defined* as connecting events.[19]

The Second Analogy

This is one of the a priori principles of the constitution of objectivity in Kant's idealism. It exhibits the function of the category of causality as enabling the determination of an objective order of succession of states S1-S2, which defines an event. The principle states that this determination is made possible by the succession's being governed by a rule according to the 'law of connection of cause and effect' (B232-4).[20]

There are three issues I need to address briefly about how I understand Kant's Second Analogy. First, there is the question of what events must be causally related to account for the order S1-S2. It is clear from Kant's example of the ship (B237/A192) that the rule does not have to be a causing of the occurrence S2 (ship downstream) by the manifestation of the causality of a first substance, i.e. S1 (ship upstream). Since it has to determine that when S1 has occurred, S2 will follow, it is generally the manifestation of the causality C of another substance (e.g. flowing river) which first causes S1, followed by S2 in that order because the occurrence of S1 is among the causally relevant conditions under which this causality will bring about S2.

Second, and more controversial, is the issue of whether the rule in question is an instance of a covering empirical law. The issue at stake is whether the rule which connects cause and effect in this principle is a mere 'local' one which only licences the conclusion that, for every event, there is some cause (e.g. Allison 1983: 229–34; Buchdahl 1992: 195–221; Bayne 2004: 103–36). Others, notably Peter Strawson (1966: 134–8), Arthur Melnick (1973: 82–6), Paul Guyer (1987: 247–52) and Michael Friedman (1992b), argue that Kant's claim in the Second Analogy is that the determination of a temporal order of appearances requires that the same causes occurring at any time have the same effects, i.e. that there be *causal laws* relating them.²¹ Aside from these weak and strong interpretations, one can discern a third position in Watkins's (2005: 286–91) claim that while the argument of the analogy itself does not allow for a 'same cause, same effect' conclusion, the nature of causality as temporally indeterminate property of a substance does justify this strong reading.

I would argue that the strong reading is correct insofar as the concept of *rule* is empty if it does not feature what makes occurrences *regular*, i.e. the same effect's following upon the same cause. That is, even without appealing to the way causality has been interpreted here, the concept of rule refers to something that holds *independently of time* else it could not function as required by the Second Analogy as condition of possibility of time-determinations. This implies that *at any time* the rule would define the same effect to follow from its cause.

A commitment to the strong reading might be shunned on the grounds that it seems too much to require that there be an empirical law (see Guyer 1987: 252ff; Allison 2004: 256ff). However, this worry assumes a narrow reading of 'empirical law', as a law that is discoverable from the multiple instances of repeated occurrences of a certain succession. As Allison (1996: 86) himself observes, laws might be 'instantaneous laws', i.e. only instantiated once or what Benjamin Vilhauer (2010: 59) calls 'limited-instantiation-scope laws'. That is, it may be that the circumstances will in fact never again arise under which causality C is active, once it has caused S2 at time *t*. So, to pursue Kant's example of the ship, such circumstances would obtain if, after the passage of a single ship, the river water were diverted into a canal for ships to bypass Königsberg/Kaliningrad towards the harbour. Such circumstances are *really possible* and therefore sufficient for a law to be defined. Although not 'scientifically interesting', and therefore not the empirical laws that reason requires us to find (A662-3/B690-1) and which are systematised in the *Critique of Judgement* (hereafter CJ; AA06: 185–6), they are laws nevertheless. This is the sense in which Kant uses the term 'law' in explaining how a judgement of experience about a cause is produced: what was merely a 'subjective connection of perceptions' defines an 'empirical rule' which is 'regarded as a law' (Prol AA04: 312).²²

Third, in claiming that S2 follows S1 according to a law, I do not claim to know this law. I merely claim its existence. *Pace* Guyer (1987: 247–52), the Second Analogy is not therefore making the claim that I need to know physical laws to be able to make objective temporal determinations. I agree with Allison (2004: 258) to the extent that the requirement of empirical law defines a *task* of identifying the law in question. But his interpretation is too weak: he claims that there is no guarantee this law is identifiable, even in principle.²³ As I have argued, a rule is nothing if not a law of sorts, which nothing, in principle, should prevent me from identifying.

C. The Third Antinomy

The third antinomial conflict of the Antinomy chapter of the *CPR* is where Kant addresses the Problem. It is one of the four dialectical conflicts that, Kant claims, arise in relation to the idea of the world. This idea, like all so-called transcendental ideas

(B377ff), is a necessary by-product of reason for Kant, i.e. of the fact that we seek the totality of conditions for a given conditioned (B364/A307). What this means in the case of the world is, for instance (First Antinomy), that reason seeks to identify a complete whole of the world of which any spatial region or temporal duration is a part, so that the whole acts as condition for it.

This requirement of reason clashes, however, with the requirement of the understanding, which, in a nutshell, is that there be a further condition for any given conditioned. The antinomial conflict is thus between two claims which are incompatible if transcendental realism, i.e. the thesis that empirical objects are things in-themselves (e.g. as in naturalism), is assumed; for each claim, valid arguments can be formulated.

In the case of the Third Antinomy, *causal* conditioning is at stake. The issue is whether or not there is a causality other than natural causality 'from which all the appearances of the world can be derived' (A444/B472). This other causality is described as a causality 'through freedom' (A444/B472), and this would meet the requirement of reason of providing a *first cause* that brings causal *completeness* to causal series. The understanding, however,[24] asks about what caused this putative first cause to be activated.

We thus see that the demands of reason and the understanding correspond to two aspects of rationality that we are familiar with, and which vie with one another when we consider cosmological matters such as the existence of a world-beginning (First Antinomy) or the existence of a first cause of all the events in the world (Third Antinomy). The Third Antinomy's Thesis claims that there is such a first cause while the Antithesis denies that there could be an uncaused event such as the activity of a first cause.

It is important to stress the cosmological setting of this conflict: freedom is introduced as 'absolute self-activity' (A418/B446), 'unconditioned causality' (A419/B447) or 'the faculty of beginning a state from itself' (A533/B560), whereby 'faculty' is not necessarily connected to a subject: it is a 'power' (Pluhar translation of the *CPR*). This is freedom 'in the cosmological sense', i.e. 'transcendental' freedom (A533/B560). Transcendental freedom is therefore introduced as first cause for *all appearances* in the world. The idea that freedom is a causality is one of Kant's fundamental insights (Gerhardt 2018: 247–9) to which the libertarian idea of agent-causality we shall examine in Chapter 3 can be traced back.

The next obvious question must be, Why is the Third Antinomy the place where Kant addresses the Problem? This follows from a remark Kant makes about the Thesis, namely that if true, then 'we are permitted also to allow' ascribing to substances in the causal series 'in the course of the world (. . .) the faculty of acting from freedom' (A450/B478). To this, the proponent of the Antithesis responds that 'it can never be permitted to ascribe such a faculty to substances in the world' because of the 'connection of appearances necessarily determining one another in accordance with universal laws' (A451/B479). This amounts to the question of the possibility of free will in a deterministic world: it is Kant's formulation of the Problem. So solving the Third Antinomy should also provide a solution to the Problem.

The arguments for the Thesis and Antithesis

Let us briefly examine the arguments. As with the other antinomial conflicts, both arguments are *reductios*. The Thesis thus makes the assumption that there are no first causes of appearances. That is, for any empirical event, once a cause has been identified, a further cause of the 'causality of the cause' would have to be identified (A444/B472). This would lead to a series of causes and therefore insufficient determining grounds because there would be 'no completeness of the series on the side of the causes' (A446/B474). As Allison (2004: 379–81) and Watkins (2005: 307) observe, this incompleteness is only problematic if the principle of sufficient reason is assumed. In the realist setting of the argument, events are completely determinate occurrences: according to this principle, reason requires that all the conditions for this determination be given. So the totality of the causes accounting for the determination of this event must be given. Since this is not the case, the assumption is rejected.[25]

The proponent of the Antithesis will point out that giving in to the demands of reason comes at the cost of not meeting the requirements of the understanding. That is, she argues that transcendental freedom is 'contrary to the causal law' (A445/B473) because such a first cause defines a state which is not causally connected to previous states. Kant describes the problem as the impossibility of a 'unity of experience' (A447/B475). This has prompted commentators to claim that this appeals to the doctrine of transcendental idealism (Allison 1983: 312; Guyer 1987: 411–12). Watkins (2005: 309–10) makes a good case for reading Kant's claim about the unity of experience as following from, rather than being used to justify, the conclusion. The claim is indeed rather that a first cause is incompatible with the 'law of nature', which always requires a further cause. A natural cause defines two states s_1 and s_2: s_1 is any state of the 'not yet acting cause', and s_2 is a state of the beginning of the 'action' brought about by the cause (A445/B473). A further cause is required to account for the transition $s_1 \to s_2$, but none is available in the case of a first cause.

This amounts to infringing the conditions of the unity of experience because of the temporal break at time t when s_2 is manifested, which defines a fragmentation of the possibility of experience into two distinct possible experiences. First, the causal series before t defines what is possible experience after t according to natural causality. But second, the first cause activated at t also defines, together with natural causality, a possible experience after t. These two possibilities are distinct, so there is no *unity* to possible experience, as claimed in the Antithesis.

D. The preamble to, and nature of, Kant's solution

The preamble to the Resolution of the Third Antinomy

Kant prefaces the resolution of the third and fourth (dealing with contingency) antinomial conflicts by explaining how they differ from the first two mathematical ones. The latter are resolved by showing that they illegitimately assume an object, the world, of which contradictory properties can be predicated. Consequently, both Thesis and Antithesis are false for those Antinomies. For the third and fourth conflicts, Kant points out that 'the dynamical ideas allow a condition of appearances outside the series of appearances' so that 'the rational propositions [of Thesis and Antithesis] (...) may both be true' (A531-2/B559-60).

This is because the series constructed from these dynamical ideas are not homogeneous: there is no homogeneity between cause and effect. This contrasts with the homogeneity of series constructed from mathematical ideas, such as in the First Antimony: spatial regions or times are homogeneous as parts of the one space or time. Heterogeneity allows one to seek to terminate a regress in a series of conditions by 'a further condition different in kind' (A520/B558). Kant is here appealing to the fact that the intelligible realm of reality in-itself is not empirically conditioned. As such it defines the conceptual space for an unconditioned condition. For the third antinomial conflict, this will be a 'noumenal' first cause,[26] transcendental freedom, which would not prevent the existence of an empirical causal series of appearances: rather, it would provide its completion.[27]

Kant's argument is therefore simple and thereby convincing: if nature is not the whole of reality, there is room for a completion of causal series of appearances in freedom as a causality outside nature,[28] i.e. in reality in-itself. This logical possibility in the case of appearances that are actions *defines the outline of a solution to the Problem*. Further, I shall examine whether this 'basic solution' is sufficient. But first, I note that Kant's claim that if transcendental idealism is adopted, the coexistence of free will and determinism is a (logical) possibility implies that his solution to the Problem is *compatibilist*.[29]

Kant: A compatibilist?

The debate about how Kant is to be labelled in terms of the contemporary distinctions introduced in Chapter 1 is ongoing in the literature. As with many such debates, much confusion arises from different ways of using labels. But here, this issue becomes particularly acute since authors point out that under different understandings of the labels, Kant can be classified as both a compatibilist and an incompatibilist.[30] Allen Wood's famous comment that Kant's solution to the Problem was designed to show the 'compatibility of compatibilism and incompatibilism' (Wood 1984: 74) is a case in point. Of course, as Matthé Scholten (2022: 84) points out, this is 'strictly speaking a misnomer', but it could nevertheless be informative about Kant's solution to the Problem if it genuinely indicates a way in which Kant could be understood as an incompatibilist (see Ertl 2024). Wood is not alone in making statements that will attract the ire of the logical police: Xie (2009: 53) takes this to another level by adding that aside from being both a compatibilist and an incompatibilist, Kant is also neither. Finally, some authors straightforwardly declare Kant to be an incompatibilist, which is *prima facie* surprising (Pereboom 2006: 542).

In fact, Pereboom (2006: 537) and McKenna and Pereboom (2016: 243) further describe Kant as a libertarian, which helps explain the label of 'incompatibilist' since (Chapter 1) libertarianism is standardly understood as a species of incompatibilism. This classification may, however, have to be revised in the framework of transcendental idealism, In this Chapter, I confine my discussion to the compatibilism/incompatibilism dichotomy. Two questions must be addressed to make sense of these authors' claims: Why is there a reticence in calling Kant a compatibilist? Why is there, *independently* of any such reticence (and of any claims about libertarianism), an inclination to calling him an incompatibilist?

On the first issue, I have already indicated that Kant's solution to the Problem underwent a radical change concomitant with his adoption of transcendental idealism. Given his earlier form of Leibnizian compatibilism (Chapter 1), this move away from Leibniz to transcendental idealism could be adduced as grounds for not calling Kant a compatibilist; this historical dimension probably explains some commentators' (e.g. Allison 2020) views on the matter. The most prevalent reason, however, is Kant's own assessment of the failure of a certain form of compatibilism which he famously describes as 'a wretched subterfuge' (CPrR AA05: 96). What Kant is primarily criticising there is a compatibilism that allows for the freedom to do what one wants if one wants to, which he colourfully describes as the 'freedom of the turnspit' (CPrR AA05: 96). That is none other than the freedom available on the conditional analysis characterising classical compatibilism (Chapter 1).

On this issue, Scholten makes the point that an author who does not endorse classical compatibilism is not therefore an incompatibilist (2022: 83–4).[31] And indeed, as I explained in Chapter 1, contemporary compatibilism replaces the classical compatibilist's focus upon allowing for some notion of leeway freedom with sourcehood requirements. The reticence to call Kant a compatibilist should therefore be overcome.

On the second issue, I agree with Scholten's (2022) claim that the fact that Kant's compatibilism relies upon strong metaphysical assumptions such as transcendental idealism provides no reason 'to withhold the label 'compatibilist'' (2022: 85).[32] I disagree, however, that not withholding the label 'compatibilist' entails having *no* grounds for assigning the label 'incompatibilist' if there are different senses of these words in play.

To see why one might be inclined to use the latter label, consider how Kant's antinomial conflict and his basic solution can be related to van Inwagen's (1983: 16) Consequence Argument (Chapter 1). The reference to 'universal' laws (A451/B479) in presenting the Antithesis reminds us that in a realist setting, agents cannot alter them. And these laws are deterministic: Kant assumes the strong reading of the Second Analogy with the unambiguous claim that 'every occurrence [is] determined in time by another in accord with necessary laws' (A534/B562). Further, insofar as freedom represents an absolute beginning (A445/B473) in time if the setting is realist, its effects can thereby not impact the past prior to this beginning. This agrees with both of van Inwagen's assumptions, as Scholten (2021b) also observes. Importantly, Kant also agrees with van Inwagen's inference that the antinomial conflict therefore defines an *incompatibility* between free will and determinism (A535-6/B563) given the realist setting.[33] So, *conditionally upon the truth of an implicit assumption* of van Inwagen's Consequence Argument, namely that of transcendental realism, an assumption widely endorsed as default today, Kant would be an incompatibilist. Further, in that sense, he would even be a hard incompatibilist since he accepts the truth of determinism. I take these considerations to explain the strong *inclination* to call Kant an incompatibilist.[34]

This does not, however, make Kant a (hard) incompatibilist, for he rejects this implicit realist assumption of the Consequence Argument. Indeed, Kant argues that transcendental idealism, and only transcendental idealism (A535-6/B563-4), can provide the conceptual space for free will together with determinism. Kant is thereby clearly stating that, with the additional assumption of transcendental idealism, the Consequence Argument should lead to the conclusion that free will is logically possible. Insofar as he therefore endorses van Inwagen's explicit assumptions but disagrees with the conclusion of the Consequence Argument, one is again unavoidably led to the conclusion that Kant is a compatibilist.[35]

Importantly, referring to the Consequence Argument shows that Kant's compatibilism will have the option between arguing that introducing transcendental idealism invalidates our inability to alter the past, which defines an 'altered-past' solution, and our inability to alter the laws of nature, i.e. an 'altered-law' solution. The mere logical possibility of transcendental freedom that, as the preamble explains, is available because of transcendental idealism is the denial of the conclusion of the Consequence Argument. This in itself, however, does not enable us to decide between which of van Inwagen's premises are no longer valid under transcendental idealism.

This metaphysical choice requires a *metaphysical account* to adjudicate between the options of altered-past and altered-law. That is, while the move to transcendental idealism has created the conceptual space for a 'home' for the Homeless Agent of naturalist compatibilist proposals, the metaphysical account is tasked with 'locating' this home with respect to the deterministic causal sequence of events leading to an intention/action. Kant presents this in the Resolution of the Third Antinomy (hereafter 'Resolution'), which I examine in Chapter 4, but some initial conclusions about it can be reached as I show in section C.

What kind of solution?

Before that, I want to make three comments about the nature of Kant's compatibilist solution. First, if transcendental idealism creates the conceptual space for a noumenal first cause bringing completion to the causal series in appearance, while this can only mean seeking a termination in the merely intelligible (i.e. thinkable but not knowable) domain of reality in-itself, this does not mean that *any* appeal to this intelligible reality, like a *deus ex machina*, will do. The Third Antinomy deals with the problem of the completeness of causal determination. The inhomogeneity of the causal series therefore allows one to seek a *causality* that is outside appearances. But it does not license the positing of a *distinct substance* outside appearances:[36] this will be the preserve of the Fourth Antinomy, which deals with the existence of substance. In the Third Antinomy, 'the thing itself [which completes the causal regress] as cause (*substantia phaenomenon*) would nevertheless belong to the series of conditions, and only its causality would be thought as intelligible' (A561/B589).

So it is not through any claim about a distinct substance that the Third Antinomy can address the Problem. Rather, what is at stake is the possibility of a thing that both appears and is endowed with an intelligible first cause (transcendental freedom) of its appearance and the natural causal series which ensues from it. For simplicity, I refer to this as a *solution-thing*. For the Problem, this will be the agent who must therefore be understood as belonging to both the intelligible domain of reality in-itself and that of appearances (see Watkins 2005: 360).

Second, the causality of such a solution-thing, which Kant will later characterise by its law, the *intelligible character* (A539/B567), provides completion to the causal series leading to the intention/action:[37] this is described by Kant as a 'complement of sufficiency' (*Zulänglichkeit*) (Ref. 5611, AA18: 252 – see also Ref. 5612, AA18: 253 and Allison 1990: 39). Insofar as a lack of sufficiency is interpreted as a lack of determinacy, this has led certain interpreters to infer that Kant's solution appeals to indeterminism (e.g. Bojanowski 2006: 16).

By clarifying the locus of this insufficiency, this claim can be refuted. What is at stake is the lack of completeness of causal explanations of intentions/actions, *insofar as*, for any cause, it refers to a further cause that conditions it: the complement of sufficiency is what will provide completeness to this series of causal conditions. So, Alice has the intention to vote for Tweedledee because she has a certain belief (that Tweedledee is the better candidate) and desire (to vote for the better candidate); she has these reasons because of other reasons (e.g. the better candidate is the one who seeks to bring about a fairer social order) and events (e.g. her experiencing Tweedledee's speech about the Red Queen's intolerable abuses of power), and these will in turn refer to further causal determinants, and so on. Here, the task of identifying further causal determinants is endless, and it follows that the principle of sufficient reason does not apply to appearances.[38]

This is to be distinguished from the way the causal determinacy of an event (e.g. an intention/action such as that of Alice's voting for Tweedledee) is to be understood in transcendental idealism. I have argued that the causal determination of the event of a succession S1-S2 (e.g. not having and then having the intention to vote for Tweedledee) in transcendental idealism defines a task, according to the Second Analogy, that of identifying the causality (and its law) responsible for it. There is no regress here: it is in principle possible for me to identify any *immediate* causal determinant. Kant, as an advocate of Newton's Universal Theory of Gravitation (Friedman 1992a: 136), would not deny that it is possible in principle to identify causal determinants for any determination of tomorrow's position of Mercury: this means that its position could be determined with any required degree of precision. In Alice's case, Kant would subscribe to the possibility of predicting her intention to vote for Tweedledee in the current circumstances, assuming a complete knowledge of all the relevant immediate causal factors (A549-50/B577-8).[39] There is thus no gap in the deterministic causal flux, hence no indeterminism, even though there is a lack of completeness *of the causal series of causes* for any immediate causal factors responsible for Mercury's position and for Alice's intention/action.

Finally, it is useful to connect this to contemporary source compatibilism. As noted at the end of Chapter 1, Kant's pre-critical compatibilism has affinities with the rationale underpinning Fischer and Ravizza's reasons-responsive proposal. A key problem with the latter was the lack of proper ownership by the agent of the reasons-responsive mechanism that leads to her intentions/actions. We also saw that this problem of ownership concerns the volitional account but is also reflected in the psychological account in terms of the possibility of manipulation. Kant developed his critical theory of freedom in the light of the awareness of the impact of external causal factors upon agency, which is precisely where the threat of manipulation lies. The move to transcendental idealism directly addresses this issue by placing the agent's freedom, as noumenal cause of the causal series that issues in my intention/action, outside time. And the ownership of the reasons-responsive mechanism[40] is, here, the agent's providing the causal completeness to such a causal series (which is here the mechanism in question), thereby underpinning its whole efficacy. This enables us to conclude that Kant's critical theory of freedom is not only compatibilist but primarily *source compatibilist*. Insofar as I also argued that the ownership of the mechanism could only be achieved through the availability of leeway,[41] it is also, secondarily, leeway-compatibilist. In Kant's proposal, it is indeed possible for the agent to do otherwise and thereby bring about a different causal series issuing in a different intention/action. So leeway features in Kant's theory as a *requirement of sourcehood*. In Chapter 3, I shall argue that this is a feature characterising libertarian solutions.

E. The puzzling task of the Resolution of the Third Antinomy

What kind of possibility of freedom?

Since Kant has already, in the preamble, shown that both Thesis and Antithesis may be true, is the Third Antinomy *qua* cosmological problem already resolved before the Resolution officially begins (A532/B560)? After all, Kant has shown that the merely intelligible realm of empirically unconditioned reality in-itself creates the conceptual space for transcendental freedom without disturbing the determinism of the causal series in appearance. That is, he has shown the *logical possibility* of transcendental freedom together with determinism.

Now the majority of commentators take Kant's achievement in the Resolution to be precisely showing this logical possibility of Thesis and Antithesis being simultaneously true (e.g. Gardner 1999: 26; Timmermann 2003: 83; Alison 2004: 388; Guyer 2006: 218; Blöser 2021: 292; Strohmeyer 2013).[42] However, the fact that this is already proven before the Resolution has gone rather unnoticed.[43] It does not seem hermeneutically tenable to claim that the Third and Fourth antinomies are already resolved prior to the thirty-six pages in which Kant officially presents their solutions and while the section I have been considering is a mere 'preamble to the resolution of the dynamic-transcendental ideas' (A528/B556).

Further, such a logical possibility seems unlikely to suffice for Kant. As noted, one of the key differences between Kant's and his Leibnizian predecessors' metaphysics is the introduction of the notion of real possibility: for something to be possible, it must 'agree (. . .) with the formal conditions of experience (in accordance with intuition and concepts)' (B265/A218). The consequence is that 'if one wanted to make entirely new concepts of substances, of forces [i.e. causal powers], and of interactions (...) one would end up with nothing but figments of the brain' (B269/A222). If the existence of a logically possible scenario in which both Thesis and Antithesis are true while we do not know if it is *really* possible, were sufficient to resolve the antinomial conflict, that would mean accepting the concept of a solution-thing that is a mere 'figment of the brain' as solution to the Problem.

While this is not conclusive against it, other considerations weigh against the logical possibility interpretation. As Ludwig (2015) indicates, we must consider the needs of Kant's ethics. When, in the *Critique of Practical Reason* (*CPrR*), Kant claims that 'speculative reason had to assume [transcendental freedom] as at least possible' (*CPrR*, AA05: 47), it is reasonable to assume that Kant is using 'possible' as defined earlier. And, as I shall show in Chapter 4, the Resolution explicitly considers the assumption of the (real) possibility of transcendental freedom in the second and third sections. Further, insofar as Kant contends that the action which an 'ought' defines 'must be possible under natural conditions' (A548/B576),[44] morality requires more than such logical possibility.

The interpretation of Kant's goal in the Resolution is, however, complicated by the fact that in the concluding section, he explicitly states that the Resolution has *not* shown the real possibility of transcendental freedom (and therefore of a solution-thing), a statement that is the main argument for the standard logical possibility interpretation:

> we have not been trying to establish the reality of freedom (...). we have not even tried to prove the possibility of freedom; for this would not have succeeded either. (A557-8/B585-6)

So, if more than logical possibility is at stake, but the Resolution does not show the real possibility of transcendental freedom,[45] and therefore of a solution-thing, what does it show? Looking again at the practical needs of the *CPrR*, as we saw earlier, Kant argues that reason finds it necessary to assume this possibility (Thesis) by which Kant is indicating that this assumption is indeed tenable, i.e. can be reconciled with the Antithesis. So what is at stake in the Resolution must be *to show that the real possibility of a solution-thing with transcendental freedom (Thesis) is compatible with the ubiquity of the determinism claimed by the Antithesis.*[46] This would explain why Kant thought it useful to introduce a concept of 'permissibility' when presenting the results of the Resolution in the *CPrR*. When Kant claims that the 'permissibility [of transcendental freedom] is established in the theoretical Critique' (*CPrR* AA05: 46), this *permissibility* is precisely this compatibility between the real possibility of transcendental freedom and determinism.[47]

What exactly is the difference between the permissibility and the logical possibility interpretations? It lies in the fact that the concept of the real possibility of a noumenal first cause belonging to the intelligible aspect of a solution-thing which appears and impacts appearances is richer than the mere concept of a noumenal first cause. Its additional content is a location for the free agent's freedom in relation to the causally determined appearances, i.e. precisely what is required for a metaphysical account that addresses the Homeless Agent problem. Consequently, showing the former's compatibility with determinism (permissibility interpretation) will entail going beyond showing the compatibility of the latter with determinism (logical possibility interpretation): this defines the task of the Resolution.

Further textual evidence for the correctness of this interpretation can be gleaned from the *CPrR*. In providing a summary of the Problem, Kant prefaces this with a comment about what would be desirable in terms of theoretical philosophy with respect to freedom: 'we are indeed fortunate if we can be sufficiently assured that no proof of its impossibility can be given' (CPrR AA05: 94). Now on my proposed permissibility interpretation, the Resolution addresses the most obvious threat to the possibility of transcendental freedom in the form of natural causal determinism by showing the compatibility of this possibility with this determinism. It follows that no proof of the impossibility of transcendental freedom because of this determinism can be given. While we cannot exclude *other possible grounds* for the impossibility of transcendental freedom in reality in-itself,[48] these are necessarily unknown to us, so 'we can be sufficiently assured' that no proof of this impossibility can be given.

Finally, there are systematic reasons supporting this permissibility interpretation in the light of what I argued is required to solve the Problem in Chapter 1, i.e. the need for psychological and volitional accounts. The logical possibility of a complement of sufficiency provided by a free will is all that is, strictly speaking, required in reply to the Consequence Argument (see Wood 2008: 136–8; Scholten 2021b: 145), but it is not in fact sufficient for the needs of compatible psychological and volitional accounts as I argued in Chapter 1.

Problems for the metaphysical, psychological and volitional accounts

Insofar as a metaphysical account is required as underpinning for the other two accounts of free will, it is therefore not surprising to see that the mere logical possibility of transcendental freedom is insufficient for it. As explained earlier, the question of how to locate the agent with respect to determining psychological causes of an intention/action leaves us with two alternatives according to the Consequence Argument, i.e. two logically possible options ('altered-past' and 'altered-law') for the metaphysical account.

Since transcendental freedom for Kant defines a first cause of the empirical causal series of appearances leading to an intention/action, the Antinomy's thesis might seem to require that it *precede* all the terms of this series, i.e. ground the whole of the causal history of the agent's present intention/action. This 'altered-past' alternative is how Ralph Walker (1978: 148–9) interprets it: the agent 'must have freely chosen the entire causal series that makes up the phenomenal world'. While this is a logical possibility, it would seem to be, as Pereboom (2006: 556) puts it, 'at best insignificantly more credible than an overt contradiction'.

Aside from the need to fill in Kant's account to eliminate such incredible logically possible replies to the Consequence Argument, further infilling is needed in terms of the psychological and volitional accounts to address the problem of the notion of Timeless Agency. Allen Wood (1984: 90) claims that '[t]he temporality of our agency is the necessary ransom that must be paid to the free will problem' if we are to have the kind of control Kant requires (for morality). This conception seems inadequate to represent my agency in a plausible volitional account, because I take it that I pursue various purposes at different points in time. Further, to be responsible for temporally determinate actions requires that the psychological account make room for the possibility of my not performing these actions and for not being determined to repeat them in the future, but it is unclear how Timeless Agency could ensure that.

These two problems, respectively, of *Historical Agency* and *Timeless Agency* are connected insofar as they involve the concern that human agency is understood in terms of divine agency: like God *qua* creator, we would be causally responsible for historical series leading up to the present time, and our agency would be atemporal. These problems have loomed large in the literature and been responsible for the fact that for many, Kant's conception of freedom is not tenable. The apparent implausibility of Kant's account of freedom, together with the metaphysical cost of abandoning the transcendental realism of naturalism to enable such an account (see Rosefeldt 2012: 81f), provides strong motivation for considering incompatibilist ways of addressing the naturalist compatibilist problem of the Homeless Agent (Chapter 1).

That is, it might seem metaphysically less costly to find a place for the agent – and thereby meet the sourcehood requirement – by identifying some *natural* non-deterministic causality creating the space for a possible home for the agent's will in nature. This is the option chosen by contemporary libertarians who have Kant as a precursor insofar as their approach is characterised by an endorsement of the leeway requirement, whether they take it as required for sourcehood as Kant did or as the primary characteristic of freedom. That is, the libertarian takes it that the only way to represent an agency that does not fall foul of the Argument from Manipulation involves endowing it with the leeway required for regulative control. I examine this disputed leeway requirement and contemporary libertarian proposals in Chapter 3.

F. The Historical Agency and Timeless Agency problems

Meanwhile, without going into the detail of Kant's solution, which I start examining in Chapter 4, it is already possible to provide responses to the two problems I flagged.

Contemporary responses to the Historical Agency problem

As regards the Historical Agency problem, there have been attempts in the Kant literature to defend it (Wood 1984; Rosefeldt 2012). Rosefeldt (2012: 98ff) distinguishes two aspects of the problem: the claim that we can alter the past and the claim that we are responsible for it, the latter of which is the nub of Walker's problem. On the second issue, Wood (1984: 92) argues that the agent need not be responsible for all states of nature that feature in the causal regress to his intention/action but only those that are *required* as causal determinants of it.[49] Bennett (1984: 103) points out that, however one wants to understand that,[50] it still leaves us as implausibly responsible for a number of historical events.

To address both issues, Rosefeldt (2012: 99) proposes rather that we have an *ability to alter the past* when this is understood in counterfactual terms. I'll introduce his proposal by starting with some non-modal statements. First, it follows from causal determinism that

(D1) If events $\{Z_1, Z_2, \ldots,\}$ occur (i.e. the events of a causal series) then L (e.g. a malicious lie, A554-5/B582-3 at time t) occurs.

leads, by contraposition to

(C1) If L had not occurred, (at least some of) events $\{Z_1, Z_2, \ldots,\}$ would not have happened.

To this, we must add the claim that through my transcendentally free agency, which Kant characterises by my 'intelligible character', I am nevertheless responsible for the lie (2012: 99):

(R) Because of my adopted intelligible character (IC), L occurs.

The temptation for the altered-past theorist is to think of (C1) in causal terms by appealing to probability-raising theories of causation (Reichenbach 1956; Skyrms 1980): (C1) would amount to a claim that L caused $\{Z_1, Z_2, \ldots,\}$ because this series is more likely to have happened if L happens than if it does not. Then, because of (R), insofar as I have adopted my IC, this would lead to the implausible claim that I, through this adoption, am responsible for these past events.

Rosefeldt (2012: 99) indicates that such a reading is not forced upon us. To explain this, it is important to introduce modal considerations at this point[51] and make explicit the role of the laws of nature. That is, determinism is in fact the stronger claim:

(D2) Given that events $\{Z_1, Z_2, \ldots,\}$ occur, and given the laws of nature $\mathcal{L}$, necessarily L occurs.

The idea now is to obtain some statement like (C1) which could realistically be taken to represent my ability to alter the past without resorting to causality. Bennett (1984)[52] argues that this can be achieved in terms of 'backtracking counterfactuals'. He claims, plausibly, that if one considers the nearest possible worlds *with the same laws of nature* $\mathcal{L}$, then (C1) will be true in all those possible worlds. That is, we will have:

(C2) If L had not occurred, necessarily (at least some of) events $\{Z_1, Z_2, \ldots,\}$ would not have happened.

This counterfactual dependence of events $\{Z_1, Z_2, \ldots,\}$ upon L and therefore – because of (R) – upon my free agency (IC) is then taken as definitive of the sense in which I am able to alter the past (and thereby bring about L). Rosefeldt (2012: 101–2), however, adds that there are no reasons for claiming that such counterfactual dependence implies responsibility and notes that Bennett, Walker and Wood provide no argument for implicitly assuming this; hence, he takes this to define a possible solution to the Historical Agency problem.[53]

Scholten (2021b: 151) has argued, correctly in my view, that Kant's theory of freedom involves a *causal* rather than a merely *counterfactual* dependence of the lie and the empirical causal nexus that brings it about as appearance upon the agent's freedom (*IC*). Rosefeldt (2012: 103ff) had anticipated one such type of objection. That is, he takes the objection that counterfactual dependence is not adequate as an interpretation of the agent's bringing about L, as identifying a lack of sufficiency that would be remedied by having L depend causally upon the *IC*. He objects, however, to this by drawing upon the fact that, for Kant, the intelligible character alone is in any case not sufficient to bring about the decision/action (L): other empirical factors are required (e.g. the agent's 'temperament', Rel AA06: 38, and various 'cooperating causes' A549/B578). He concludes that since there is no sufficiency problem, a causal link is not required.

But the issue is not one of sufficiency. Rather, without a causal account, just as Rosefeldt argued that the agent need not be made responsible for the events $\{Z_1, Z_2, \ldots,\}$ leading up to L, what are the grounds for claiming then that he is responsible for L other than Kant's stipulation? It is puzzling that the agent should be said to have altered the past that leads to her action, but in so doing, is only responsible for her action. This is quite possibly why Bennett, Wood and Walker implicitly assumed the agent to be responsible for $\{Z_1, Z_2, \ldots,\}$.[54] I take this concern to mean, at the very least, that backtracking counterfactuals do not help provide a plausible psychological account of the agent's responsibility and thus, *pace* Rosefeldt (2012: 83), do not help the altered-past theorist solve the Historical Agency problem.

Finally, it is worth examining the evidence that Rosefeldt (2012: 97) adduces for interpreting Kant as espousing backtracking. He draws mainly upon this text:

> Now, in this regard [i.e., as noumenon, CO] the rational being can rightly say concerning every unlawful action which he commits that he could have omitted it, even though as appearance it is sufficiently determined in the past and is to this extent unfailingly necessary; *for, this action, with everything past that determines it, belongs to a single phenomenon of his character* – the character which he on his own imparts to himself and according to which he on his own imputes to himself, as a cause independent of all sensibility, the causality of those appearances. (CPrR AA05: 98; my emphasis)

The clause which, following Rosefeldt, I highlight might prima facie seem to support his altered-past interpretation. However, on a proper understanding of causality, what determines an event, e.g. an action, is not another event but a causality. It is therefore past manifestations of a certain causality that determine the action. The phenomenon of the agent's character is then simply the appearance of the intelligible character (which Kant calls empirical character) which he 'imparts to himself'. And to make this clear, Kant adds that it is through this intelligible character that the agent 'imputes to himself (. . .) the causality of those appearances'. That is, it is by determining this causality that imputation ensues, which suggests an 'altered-law' interpretation of Kant's compatibilism.

Kant's engagement with the Historical Agency problem

Kant had already, in the early stages of his critical thought on the matter, proposed a way of mitigating the Historical Agency problem which, although unsatisfactory, helps us understand how he was led to his mature solution of the Resolution. Following the set-up of the Third Antinomy, Kant does indeed endorse the idea that leads to Walker's problem, namely that the agent (solution-thing) must, through her freedom, initiate the causal series (Thesis) which would, at the same time, be infinite since each cause in it must have a further cause (Antithesis). But, in line with Wood's interpretation of Kant's later position, he does not view this causal series as having to be the whole phenomenal series of the world up to my intention/action. Rather, we find him explaining that while a causal series in appearance which is defined in terms of inclinations determines an intention/action, 'it is possible that the intellectual power of choice (. . .) intervenes', whereby an 'alternative course of sensibility' is determined (Refl. 5611 AA18: 252). This intervention, which provides completion to the causal series leading to the action/intention, is connected with the intention/action 'through an infinite intermediate series of appearances' (Refl. 5611 AA18: 252). So, the required infinite series is located between the agent's intervention and the intention/action. What this achieves is that, for the events in this series, the requirements of the Antithesis are fulfilled: every event is causally determined.[55] There is, however, a discontinuity that is created at the moment where the intervention happens: whatever natural causality was about to produce as effect, this is somehow no longer operational.

Interestingly, this is not directly a problem of an event without a cause but rather a problem in the other temporal direction, of a causality without its lawfully determined effect: some causal law must thereby be infringed, since, without the intervention, another causal series would have followed. This is allowed on a weak interpretation of the Second Analogy, which suggests that Kant may, at this stage in his thought, have been unclear about this principle of causality.

In any case, on the required strong reading, the solution is unsatisfactory. But it is instructive to see in what way it would need to be amended: what is needed is for the agent's intervention to have an impact *on the causality* of some natural cause. I would suggest that realising this must have been part of Kant's thinking in developing his mature altered-law solution in the Resolution.

What is also implausible in this early critical solution is the need to have an infinite series of psychological states separating the agent's intervention from the intention/action. While this solution is motivated by the Antithesis' claim, it is not in fact required in the light of Kant's understanding of causality. As Kant spells out in his mature presentation of the Antinomy, what the Second Analogy requires is that the manifestation of some causality in producing an effect should itself have a cause or as he says in the Thesis:

> the causality of the cause through which something happens is always something that has happened, which according to the law of nature presupposes once again a previous state and its causality. (A444/B472)

Kant's early solution was to seek the complement of sufficiency as what causally initiates the infinite series such a partial finite one belongs to. Transcendental idealism, however, as I have interpreted it, together with a proper understanding of the notion of causality, creates the conceptual space for a different way of achieving completeness for any such partial finite series. That is, much as the manifestation of the causality of a cause defines an event, as I explained earlier, it is actually an indeterminate ground producing determinate effects. Consequently, such a partial finite series can be completed by moving from the causality of its source term (i.e. the first term temporally) to the ground of this causality in reality in-itself. That is, rather than seek *the cause of an event, i.e. the manifestation of some causality*, which defines the regress in appearance, the partial series can move to *the ground of this causality* and thus achieve completeness since this ground has no further causal conditions. This means that my freedom would consist in my grounding a causality that produces my intention/action as effect. In Kant's terminology, this will be the grounding of the agent's empirical character in her intelligible character.

To summarise, in terms of Kant's response to the Consequence Argument, I have argued

- that during the formulation of his critical position, Kant, as evidenced in his Reflexionen, considered a version of an 'altered-past' interpretation, a version that one might call a 'limited-altered-past' interpretation since it only requires that the agent's noumenal causality ground a temporally limited causal series;
- that the critical Kant's considered position must be a version of an altered-law interpretation of the impact of the agent's freedom (intelligible character) upon appearances, a position also propounded by Watkins (2005: 134–6) and Vilhauer (2004: 727, 2010).[56]

This interpretation will, however, require proper anchoring in Kant's text of the Resolution, a task I tackle in Chapter 4. For now, it is important to note that an altered-law proposal comports with my interpretation of transcendental idealism as involving a grounding of all empirical causality in reality in-itself: what is proposed is that *the agent be able to contribute to this grounding.*

The Timeless Agency problem

Turning now to the other worry about Kant's proposal, i.e. the Timeless Agency problem, it is important to recall that the solution-thing of the Third Antinomy does not define a distinct noumenal existence. Rather, it is something (the agent) that has a noumenal dimension but is also an appearance that belongs to the deterministic causal flux of nature. This might seem to shift the worry towards a concern that what we end up with is a rather schizophrenic notion of an agent straddling the domains of reality in-itself and appearances.

Allison (1990: 49, 53) takes this as grounds for rejecting a metaphysical interpretation of freedom as causality (e.g. Allen Wood's) while noting that '[m]uch of the language in the texts appears to support' it. Allison's solution involves considering how the subject must understand herself as practical agent. While this only makes sense within a deflationary conception of transcendental idealism I have already criticised, I shall indicate specific problems this interpretation gives rise to in Chapters 4 and 5.

On the contrary, the way I interpreted transcendental idealism enables us to understand that what is at stake is nothing more than the dual-aspect characterising all things that are manifested as appearances. That is, from our perspective, we must understand the agent, like any substance, to exist insofar as she has a noumenal dimension, i.e. belongs to reality in-itself, which is just one aspect which grounds her aspect as appearance in the causal flux of nature.

While these considerations address the cogency of Kant's conception of agency as temporal (volitional account), they do not explain how the agent could be said to have any leeway in time. This Temporal Leeway issue must be addressed, e.g. for the possibility of moral improvement (psychological account). To do so, and to further infill Kant's conception of free agency and provide a justification for the altered-law interpretation, it will be necessary, in Chapter 4, to examine how Kant argues for the compatibility of the real possibility of transcendental freedom and determinism in the Resolution. As explained earlier, the next chapter will first examine whether an apparently metaphysically less costly alternative solution to the Problem is conceivable by examining contemporary libertarian proposals.

3

Libertarian theories of free will

This chapter focuses upon the options available to the naturalist who is convinced by the arguments against (source) compatibilism in Chapter 1 but who does not see how she could follow Kant in making the move away from naturalism, in particular in the light of the problems flagged in Chapter 2 for Kant's proposal. That the solution must now involve a libertarian approach follows from the importance of the leeway requirement, i.e. the availability of alternative possibilities, which I shall examine in the light of the discussion around Frankfurt-style examples. Whether she takes this as more fundamental than the source requirement or not, the libertarian requires this condition to be fulfilled.

As the Consequence Argument (Chapter 1) shows, this naturalist libertarian is an incompatibilist who must seek to make sense of a notion of free will in the context of an indeterministic nature. This chapter examines the main contemporary libertarian options: event-causal, agent-causal and non-causal. The Infinite Regress Argument is then presented as a challenge to all such options. The chapter concludes by drawing upon a contemporary libertarian approach to show how Kant's transcendental idealism provides the framework required to address this challenge.

A. The leeway requirement

Leeway constitutes one of the two requirements of our self-conception as free agents. The ability to do otherwise directly informs the first-person and second-person versions of the Problem (Chapter 1). I take my act of voting to be free insofar as I understand myself as able to choose between candidates. And if I vote for one, I shall be praised by some and blamed by others. Such leeway is not available on source compatibilist proposals and, at least in the case of the reasons-responsive approach, we have seen that this is key to the Homeless Agent problem insofar as it is required for regulative control.

When considering the third-person version of the Problem (Chapter 1), the situation is arguably a little different. My culpability in exceeding the speed limit after celebrating my victory in the Grand Prix only makes sense insofar as I could have done otherwise. My legal/moral responsibility does not, however, seem to require that I could have done otherwise when I act lawfully/morally, as Susan Wolf (1990: 79) has argued.[1]

Frankfurt-style examples

It has, however, also been argued that these worries about satisfying the leeway requirement need not trouble the source compatibilist, at least insofar as the third-person version of the Problem is concerned: in a seminal paper, Harry Frankfurt (1969) describes a series of thought-experiments designed to show that it is possible to have moral responsibility without alternative possibilities being available to the agent.[2]

An immediate response to this might be in line with Widerker's so-called W-defence when discussing the case of an agent (Jones) who broke a promise but could not have done otherwise: 'Still, since you, [Harry] Frankfurt wish to hold him blameworthy for his decision to break his promise, tell me *what in your opinion, should he have done instead*?' (Widerker 2000: 191). Although this seems like a knock-down argument, it is useful to look into Frankfurt-style examples to see why things are not necessarily that clear-cut. Specifically, for our purposes, this will shed light upon the respective roles of the sourcehood and leeway requirements for free will.

The typical thought-experiment from Frankfurt (e.g. 1969: 835–6) against the leeway requirement is presented by Pereboom (2014b: 87) as follows. Consider a neurosurgeon, Black, who unbeknownst to Jones, in carrying out surgery on him, inserts a device into his brain that enables Black's computer to control Jones's brain activity. In so doing, Black is keen to ensure that Jones does what he wants him to do, i.e. kill Smith. If Jones shows an inclination not to kill Smith, the computer triggers a mechanism in Jones's brain that ensures that he does. If he shows no such inclination, there is no intervention (see also the example in Fischer 2006: 38).

Consider the action of Jones deciding to kill Smith and therefore needing no intervention by Black. Our intuitions tell us that Jones's action was free insofar as no intervention occurred. But since Jones did not have any alternative possibilities, it seems that there are cases where an agent is morally responsible although he had no alternative courses of action available (Frankfurt, op. cit., 839). Moreover, what makes Jones responsible in such cases is purely the fact that Jones was the source of the action.

Frankfurt's paper triggered a series of responses and counter-responses, which I summarise here. First, Fischer (1994: 134–40) points out that in Frankfurt's examples, there is in fact a 'flicker of freedom' insofar as Jones could have formed the intention to act otherwise. Fischer (1994: 140–7) himself provides a reply to such a critique of Frankfurt's argument by elaborating the above example through the inclusion of a separate event, Jones's blushing, whose absence triggers the intervention of the device in his brain. This example requires a link between the blushing and Jones's action: it is assumed that Jones would only decide to kill Smith if he (Jones) blushes beforehand. With this set-up, the flicker of freedom, which is Jones's having the option of not blushing, is arguably not *robust* enough to ground any 'leeway' moral responsibility (see Fischer 1994: 140–7). An alternative is robust if the agent's availing herself of this alternative involves her being willing to act so as not to be blameworthy. Clearly, this is the type of alternative course of action that is relevant to the leeway requirement. In Jones's case, the absence of blushing does not seem to fulfil this condition, however.[3] So Jones is responsible if he kills Smith (after blushing), even though he had no *robust* alternative possibilities (Pereboom 2014b: 88).

However, such examples as provided in Fischer's paper rely upon a deterministic link between the sign whose absence triggers the intervention (e.g. here, the blush) and the action. But, as Kane (1985: 51) and Widerker (1995: 247–61) point out, that begs the question for a libertarian who would counter that, after the sign, Jones should still have the option of acting either way (i.e. killing Smith or not). However, if the thought-experiment were altered to accommodate a non-deterministic link, the example would no longer work because Jones could have done otherwise than kill Smith after blushing.

Pereboom (2014b: 90–2; see also Hunt 2005) counters, however, that it is possible to construct cases resilient to such criticism. As he explains, the key is to have, as trigger for the intervention, some sign '*for the agent's availing herself of any robust available possibility*' (2014b: 90) if the device is not in place. In Pereboom's thought-experiment, Joe, whose actions are often driven by self-interest whatever the cost to others, is considering evading the taxes he owes. The only grounds he would have for not evading taxes are moral reasons, which means that he would have to reach a certain level of moral attentiveness to do so. If he did reach this level, he would have the option of evading or not evading paying his taxes, depending on the outcome of his deliberation. The device that, unbeknownst to Joe, is implanted by a neuroscientist in his brain would be triggered by Joe's attaining the right level of moral attentiveness so as to ensure that he evades paying his taxes. In fact, it turns out that Joe does not raise his level of moral attentiveness: he evades paying his taxes. And although he could not have done otherwise, he clearly seems morally responsible for his action, i.e. this would seem to be a case of free agency without alternative possibilities.[4]

One might first ask although the Kane/Widerker objection does not apply here, whether this conclusion is warranted. Indeed, what are the grounds for thinking that the action is free? Presumably, these grounds must lie in the fulfilment of the other key requirement for free will, i.e. sourcehood. And now, the question is, what will ensure that the agent is the source of the action? Pereboom's own Argument from Manipulation has shown that source compatibilist options will not do. But Pereboom's Frankfurt-case example must deliver an answer to this question if he is to be able to conclude that Joe's act is free. As it stands, his argument against the leeway requirement is incomplete.

And the objection to its completion will be that a possible free course of action requires no deliberation *only insofar as* Joe has already vetted this type of action as that which he wills to carry out. In Joe's case, this would require that he be the source of his supposed self-interested behaviour or maybe something more specifically tailored to the issue, e.g. general intentions about whether to obey certain laws or not. Pereboom cannot be assuming that these features of the agent's character are out of his control because the Argument from Manipulation would mean the action is unfree. This leaves his argument vulnerable to the leeway theorist's claiming that Joe must have had in the past (and will again have in the future) deliberations on such issues for which alternative possibilities must be available and has thereby come to form certain general policies (in this case, reflecting the agent's self-interest). So when a Frankfurt-style case shows an absence of deliberation, one cannot conclude to the absence of alternative possibilities *in the run up to the decision/action*.[5]

But now, second, it may be countered that this Frankfurt-style case is designed to show that, just for the individual action in question, no leeway is required. This assumes, however, that a reference to the availability of alternative possibilities is only made when the level of attentiveness is raised. But it is highly questionable that, when the situation encountered does not require any such deliberation, the action somehow flows without any leeway. Again, to explain that requires looking at the source of the action in some broader general 'policy' decision or a similar specific past decision: what is involved in going ahead with the action of tax evasion is a recognition of this action as falling under the *type* about which the broader decision has been made, or being sufficiently similar to one about which a past specific decision has been made. This recognition, when unproblematic, will not lead to any raising of the level of attentiveness. But it only makes sense insofar as alternative possibilities are available. And indeed, if it is not an unproblematic case, e.g. because of my revised general policy or because of a feature that makes it sufficiently novel and requiring deliberation, this availability is made manifest.

This can be understood in terms of the presence of inclinations to act similarly to how one acted in the past: often, the agent acts on this inclination. But there is a (tacit) endorsement of this inclination, an endorsement which, at some point, may not happen. For instance, Joe may come to change some of his views after finding out more about how his tax money is useful to good causes, and override this inclination when it next manifests itself. So leeway is necessary for the individual action as well, or at least it has not been shown that it is not.[6]

For our purposes, it is useful to note that, in these two responses to the Pereboom example, what is at stake are the requirements for Joe to be the source of his action: this sourcehood requires (i) that he be able to revise any general policy that is implemented at various points in time and (ii) that he be able to revise his particular actions in line with any such changes. It is therefore the satisfaction of the sourcehood requirement that requires leeway. This entails that, of the two requirements introduced at the outset in Chapter 1, sourcehood is primary as a condition of free agency. Leeway is secondary, *qua required for the possibility of sourcehood*. This, as we have already seen in Chapter 2, is a key feature of Kant's understanding of free will.

Leeway and libertarianism

Whether or not they endorse it as primary or as a requirement for sourcehood, libertarians typically see the leeway requirement as essential grounds for compatibilism's failure and therefore, in a naturalist context, according to the Consequence Argument (Chapter 1), as grounds for adopting incompatibilism (O'Connor and Franklin 2019: 18). Here, I examine various libertarian proposals, which take either leeway or source incompatibilism as more fundamental.

The Homeless Agent problem in compatibilist proposals was, I argued, encapsulated in their inability to derive a volitional account explaining how the agent is in control of her action, from a psychological one purportedly exhibiting an agent's responsibility in a deterministic setting (Chapter 1). The naturalist libertarian no longer subscribes to such a psychological account: to satisfy the leeway requirement, the deterministic grip on the causal nexus must be relaxed. Once all past causal determinants are taken into account, more will be needed to determine the action. This 'more' is where the libertarian proposes to define a home for the agent's will.

Since libertarianism thereby immediately addresses the leeway requirement, the main questions will centre around whether the conceptual space that is created by introducing indeterminism is able to accommodate the agent's will as source of the action.

B. Event-causal libertarianism

The event-causal approach takes the conceptual space created by introducing indeterminism as sufficient of itself to address the Problem. There is then the option of locating the indeterminacy prior to the agent's deliberation through which she makes a decision or within the deliberative process. The former option is *deliberative libertarianism*. Dennett (1978: 295) and Mele (1995: 214; 221) argue that it is indeterminate which reasons will be appealed to in making an evaluative judgement defining a decision to act. Alternatively, Ekstrom (2000: 137) proposes that the formation of the agent's preferences is indeterministic. But preferences (Ekstrom) or an evaluative judgement (Dennett and Mele) are not the outcome of a free action, and once they have been formed, the agent is determined to act according to them. So what is missing is a place for the free agent as source of the action (Clarke 2003: 63) and who thereby controls the course of events (Clarke 2003: 64).

Agent-centred libertarianism: Indeterministic causality and luck

The typical event-causal theorist adopts the second option of *agent-centred libertarianism*. This seeks to create a place for the agent's will within the indeterministic causal process connecting his reasons to this decision. The problem with this was already spelled out by Hume (1978: 407), who equated such a conception of 'liberty' with 'chance'. Throughout his career, Kant (see Allison 2020: 72–8; 212) echoed this complaint in his rejection of a conception of freedom as 'liberty of indifference'. In a contemporary setting, this defines the *Luck Objection* (Mele 1999 and Haji 2000): the outcome of such an indeterministic process is random, and randomness cannot be understood as control by an agent. In other words, the Luck Objection is that the introduction of indeterminism in itself does not create a suitable home for the agent's will: the agent's free will and control are absent from such an indeterministic picture.

This is aptly described as the *problem of the disappearing agent* by Pereboom (2014b: 102). It can be illustrated by supposing that the choice is between decisions φ_1 ('vote for Tweedledum') and φ_2 ('vote for Tweedledee'), with the decisions motivated by Alice's awareness of corresponding beliefs/desires, say $\{B_1, D_1\}$ and $\{B_2, D_2\}$.[7] These stand for the beliefs that each candidate is likely to improve living conditions in Wonderland in certain ways, namely more freedom (B_1) and more equality (B_2), while D_1 and D_2 are respectively the desires to have more freedom and more equality. Indeterministic causality, on a 'probability pool' interpretation[8] of it (Hitchcock 2004:

407), leads the pool of reasons, here $\{B_1, D_1\}$ and $\{B_2, D_2\}$, to determine probabilities of the agent opting for φ_1 or φ_2. But the agent's 'role in producing a decision is exhausted by antecedent states or events in which she is involved' (Pereboom 2014b: 102): it thus terminates with the determination of these probabilities which reflect her psychological make-up. She cannot thereby be said to be controlling the decision that is made when either φ_1 or φ_2 is activated, since it lies beyond the causal process itself and is random.

Drawing upon such a probability-pool model, Kane develops what is probably the most sophisticated event-causal proposal in the literature by invoking a 'movement away from thermodynamic equilibrium' (2011: 387) to explain how quantum indeterminacy can play a role. A 'combination of chaos and quantum physics' (2014: 29) thus enables quantum indeterminacies to be amplified so as to have 'large-scale effects on the activity of neural networks in the brain as a whole' (2014: 29). Kane fills in his account by drawing upon the phenomenology of efforts directed at bringing about certain outcomes which he sees as characterising the process of deliberation in cases of fundamental decisions ('self-forming actions', Kane 2014: 26). He argues that 'the effort and the indeterminism [are] fused' (Kane 2014: 31) so that for the agent, 'the whole process is her effort of will and it persists right up to the moment when the choice is made' (Kane 2014: 32). This account is interesting as it shows an appropriate concern for the first-person perspective required by a volitional account of decision-making. But when Kane then concludes that luck plays no role in his account because '[t]here is no point at which the effort stops and chance 'takes over' and that the agent chooses as a result of the effort' (Kane 2014: 32), Kane is confusing two issues. It may well be the case that there are some currently unknown reasons for the collapse of the wave function in quantum physics, and some believe consciousness may have a role to play here (e.g. Wigner 1983; see also Chapter 6). But this does not entail that choosing one of the available courses of action, however much it is manifested as an effort, has thereby been shown not to rely ultimately upon a random selection, so that Kane's account falls short of the Luck Objection (see Clarke 2003: 86–92).

Clarke (2003: 73) and O'Connor (2000: 96–7) conclude that this probability-pool conception of indeterministic causality is not what the libertarian needs. Clarke (2003: 73) proposes that, instead of the probability-pool model which reduces indeterministic causation to the determination of probabilities governing a random outcome, indeterministic causation 'has causal relations between causes and outcomes'. It should link types of events such that when an event of a certain type happens, it brings about an event of a second type with a certain probability (Clarke 2003: 33). Conditional upon the plausibility of this 'probability-fork' type of indeterministic causality, Clarke can be said to avoid the above Luck Objection (Clarke 2003: 77–82; see also Pereboom 2014b: 106). This is because the causal process goes all the way from the agent's reasons $\{B_1, D_1\}$ and $\{B_2, D_2\}$ to decision φ_1 or decision φ_2 (this disjunction defines the 'fork'). As Clarke insists, e.g. *contra* Mele (1995: 195), this type of indeterministic causation features no '"break" at any point in the process leading to a directly free action' (Clarke 2003: 72), unlike the probability-pool interpretation.

Indeterministic causation

This kind of non-deterministic causation is well established in the philosophy of science (Clarke mentions, among others, Anscombe 1981; Armstrong 1997: 237–40; Dupré 1993: chs. 8–9; Mellor 1995: ch. 5). There is a certain immediate plausibility to this conception of indeterministic causation, which is that one can establish causal links, e.g. that between being exposed to someone who is contagious and getting a disease (Anscombe 1981), without thinking of this as involving necessitation. What we thereby understand is, arguably, that exposure to a contagious person will increase the probability of our falling sick.

This plausibility is what informs the *probabilistic interpretation* of causality according to which the occurrence of event C or the obtaining of fact C (see Mellor 1995: ch. 11) causes event/fact E if and only if the occurrence/obtaining of C raises the probability of the occurrence/obtaining of E (Reichenbach 1956); or the probability of E conditional upon the occurrence/obtaining of C is larger than the same conditional upon C's absence (see Skyrms 1980). This theory has experienced a number of refinements (e.g. Dupré 1984, in response to the problem of making probabilistic claims that work for all contexts), but the core idea of causality being captured by probability-raising abilities defines one of the most influential theories of causal connection in contemporary philosophy.

It is widely held, however, that this probability-raising intuition about causal connections does not define sufficient conditions for causality (see Schaffer 2000; Koutsoyannis et al. 2022). Nevertheless, the upshot of the popularity of this probabilistic approach to causality, is that it makes *indeterministic causation* appear not only possible, but in fact the paradigm case, with deterministic causality as a mere limiting case (O'Connor 2011: 323). There are two reasons for resisting such an inference, however. The first is that the problem with the sufficiency claim of probabilistic theories of causality severely weakens the support they can provide to the claim that indeterministic causation exists. If there is more to causal connections than probability-raising, it is likely to be connected with physical processes which (quantum indeterminacy aside) are deterministic. The second is that, even if such probabilistic theories are still claimed to provide such support, this link is itself questionable: the fact that C leads to the raising of the probability of E, leaves it entirely open whether other causal factors can be found which further raise this probability above any desired level, so that it is as close to 1 as required.

Precisely, this last point is ignored in Anscombe's (1981) famous paper. She claims that once we have found a probability-raising cause C of event/fact E, we have no warrant for assuming that there are further causes which explain whether event/fact E happens/obtains or not. So, for instance, if one person gets the disease and another not, we typically assume that there was a further causal explanation of why that is the case; her aim is to question this assumption. In claiming that this is wrong, she is making the false inference from the validity of a probability-raising account of causality to the existence of indeterministic causation (see also Honderich 2011). I would argue that, *pace* Anscombe, it *is* the case that '[i]f an effect occurs in one case and a similar effect does not occur in an apparently similar case, there must be a relevant further difference' (Anscombe 1981: 133).[9]

Now it could be claimed that, by arguing in this way, I show that I am 'in the grip of the Principle of Sufficient Reason', as O'Connor (2011: 322) puts it. Indeed, in a naturalistic framework where fully determined objects are given to the cogniser, my argument entails that there must be a causal determination of the totality of the object's properties, which amounts to subscribing to that principle. My motivation, however, is different. It is merely the belief that a rational cogniser who, when confronted with what had been assumed as causal regularity (e.g. my laptop switching on when I press the power button) turns out to be infringed on one occasion (e.g. my laptop does not switch on today), understands this as calling for further investigation into the relevant difference between the two situations. This describes what one might call a *causal task principle*. This principle is seemingly implicitly endorsed by agents in their practice, and is also essential to the progress of science.[10]

While this principle entails the principle of sufficient reason in a naturalistic setting, this is not the case if transcendental idealism is assumed. As Kant claims in the Second Analogy (see Chapter 2), any (further) determination of an event entails that a corresponding cause of this particular determination be identifiable (B233–4). It follows that, determining one patient as the only one of two patients who is infected, entails that there is a cause of her being infected, while the other is not. Because of transcendental idealism, the empirical object is an appearance, i.e. something to be determined by a possible cogniser (see Chapter 2). There is no requirement that such a determination could be completed, so the principle of sufficient reason does not follow.[11]

For the purpose of the further examination of libertarian theories in this chapter, I temporarily shelve my misgivings about indeterministic causality and my claims about the causal task principle. As we shall see, the problems that arise from indeterministic libertarian proposals are closely connected with the plausibility of such indeterministic causality. Aside from the Luck Objection as presented in the form of the problem of the disappearing agent, there are other issues besetting event-causal determinist proposals. I examine two of them.

Agent-centred libertarianism: Proper control

The first problem is captured by the so-called No Choice Argument (Clarke 2003: 97ff). It is a stronger version of the Luck Argument. O'Connor (2000: 29) argues that the kind of control which one could concede that it allows, is such that the action is 'an "outflowing" of the agent'. It is not, however, '"up to the agent", something he "has a choice about" (. . .) which action will actually occur' (2000: 29). Or, as Clarke puts it, the sense in which the agent exercises 'ultimate control' on an event-causal picture is 'wholly negative: it is just a matter of the absence of any determining cause of a directly free action' (Clarke 2003: 105). What is therefore missing is the agent's having any positive control, i.e. the ability to influence which of the alternatives φ_1 or φ_2 will actually occur: this influence defines exactly the way in which leeway is required for sourcehood. This positive control is required for a proper volitional account of the action, i.e. of the control of the action being that of an agent's pursuit of her purposes. The absence of positive control characterises all versions of event-causal libertarianism examined earlier, including Clarke's probability-fork-based and Kane's probability-pool-based proposals (see Pereboom 2014b: 107–10).

Agent-centred libertarianism: Rational control

Next, recall that in distinguishing psychological and volitional accounts in Chapter 1, I indicated that their compatibility should be ensured. Since the first presents action as resulting from the agent's reasons and the second as controlled by her will, compatibility will amount to ensuring that this control is rational.[12] This compatibility can be considered

- in terms of the first and second-person versions of the Problem: the rationality of an agent's control involves my ability to provide a *contrastive explanation* of my action to myself or others. Alice should be able to explain why she voted for Tweedledee rather than Tweedledum, else one would question the kind of control she had of her action.[13]
- in terms of the third-person version of the Problem: rational control is required for *ascriptions of responsibility* (Haji 2000). My responsibility for exceeding the speed limit is diminished if I did not have a reason for doing this rather than not (i.e. no desire or belief relevant to the action). This would suggest a lack of awareness of the importance of the issue of the speed at which I was driving which I would have chosen in the same way as I pick a shirt to wear.

Nagel (1986: 116) argues that one of the features of the indeterministic causal picture is that, when the agent opts for φ_1, no explanation can be provided of why she did this rather than φ_2. This is, in effect, another type of Luck Objection, hereafter the Rational Luck Objection. Recourse to the probability-fork model does not dispel this problem: there is nothing in it to explain why the agent chose one branch of the fork *rather than* the other. Note that if the agent's control is not fully rational, it entails that she has *less* control, hence the Rational Luck Objection is also about control tout court.

So the introduction of indeterminism leads to a reduction of *rational control*, since the agent is not able to provide certain volitionally relevant contrastive explanations. One way of addressing the stronger Luck Objection ('No Choice' Argument) and the Rational Luck Objection would seem to lie in introducing a *direct controlling role for the rational agent* into the picture. This would require that a *metaphysical account* take centre stage.

C. Agent-causal and non-causal libertarian approaches

Some libertarians view the Luck Objections faced by event-causal libertarianism to have a metaphysical root: what is required is a metaphysical account enabling a satisfactory volitional account addressing Luck Objections, which is compatible with the psychological account, and therefore addresses the Rational Luck

Objection. Since event-causal libertarianism is not able to fulfil both desiderata, the introduction of a direct impact of the agent's free will into the picture seems called for.

These libertarians thus argue that the agent is in control of the choice between alternatives φ_1 and φ_2 if she directly intervenes upon the process leading to either alternative. This impact could be causal, in terms of a causality that is no longer event-causality since this does not allow for such control, but is referred to as *agent-causality*; alternatively, it could be non-causal. Both options, insofar as they no longer draw upon event-causality, involve a more radical break-up of typical compatibilist psychological accounts than that carried out by event-causal libertarians who simply introduced indeterminism into these accounts.

Consequently, we should expect these options to face problems with respect to making their proposals compatible with a plausible psychological account, i.e. problems of rational control. Additionally, the nature of such a metaphysical tool will have to be clarified. The sourcehood requirement means that agent-causality will have to be a first cause[14] but such causes, just as non-causal impacts, are metaphysically problematic, particularly in a naturalistic context.

Integrated agent-causal libertarianism

If, however, we want to retain the benefits of an event-causal psychological account, it may seem that the best way to address the Luck and Rational Luck objections is to introduce agent-causality by *adding it* to an event-causal approach. Clarke (2003) thus proposes an integrated agent-causal account. Initially, this would seem to require that the agent, endowed with a causality making her a first cause, is to be added to the probability-fork picture.

It is immediately apparent that more needs to be said about the relations between the agent and the reasons for acting, since these various causes, i.e. the agent and the agent's reasons $\{B_1, D_1\}$ and $\{B_2, D_2\}$, are apparently in competition. One possible way of dealing with the relation between agent-causality and event-causality is Clarke's (1993) proposal. The agent decides which of the set of reasons $\{B_1, D_1\}$ or $\{B_2, D_2\}$ is to be causally effective in bringing about the action. This model is not obviously vulnerable to a Luck Objection, i.e. it is not just a matter of chance which of the outcomes will happen, since it is the agent's causality that makes that choice.

This claim is, however, contested by van Inwagen (2000) in his 'Rollback' Argument. Van Inwagen imagines another Alice who has the choice between telling the truth (φ_1) or a lie (φ_2). She can exert her agent-causality to make a free decision which has a certain probability of coming out as truth or lie. But now, suppose that God 'rolls back' the universe to a time just prior to that decision and allows Alice to decide again. If God does this 1,000 times, from the law of large numbers, we would expect that Alice tells the truth approximately $1,000 \times P(\varphi_1)$ times where $P(\varphi_1)$ is the probability of telling the truth. If we pick out one of those 1,000 occurrences we would then say it is a matter of chance whether she told the truth or a lie on that occasion. Van Inwagen concludes that this introduction of agent-causality adds nothing to address the Luck Objection.

In a similar vein, Haji (2004) and Mele (2006) aim to show precisely that the same Luck Objection addressed to event-causal libertarianism applies, although agent-causality has been introduced. Indeed, much as agent-causality is distinct from event-causality, its activation does define an event, e.g. E_1 = 'the agent-causes φ_1 at time t'. Given the same conditions prior to time t, E_1 could not have occurred (i.e. the alternative E_2 could have occurred). Whether the one or the other occurs is therefore, they argue, a matter of luck.

But as Pereboom points out, this objection 'does not rule out' that the agent should play the crucial role of controlling which decision is made. And indeed, the occurrence of E_1 or E_2 is a 'logical consequence of the agent's causing a decision' (2014b: 111) that such an event should occur. In fact, what both objections fail to do is to take seriously the claim that agent-causation is 'a primitive form of control over (...) such undetermined, single-case outcomes' (O'Connor 2011: 324).

While this arguably leaves scope for a libertarian response to the Luck Objection about control,[15] let us turn to the issue of *rational control* in connection with volitionally relevant contrastive explanations. Mele (2006) points out that such a stipulation of the agent's control through his causality does not amount to endowing him with rational control. Since the reasons for the action are what the agent chooses, these reasons cannot also be appealed to in explaining why he chose φ_1 or φ_2, and therefore one rather than the other. So, if our original Alice chooses her belief that Tweedledee's election will contribute to a more egalitarian society (B_2) and her desire to see more equality in society (D_2) as reasons for deciding to vote for him (φ_2), she cannot appeal to these as reasons for this choice. As such, this proposal fails to explain how the agent's control might be rational (for further discussion, see O'Connor 2000: 78 and Ginet 2002: 397–9).

Could Clarke's proposal be amended by resorting to further reasons for the agent's choice? The problem is that these would have to be reasons for the agent's causality enabling $\{B_2, D_2\}$ to be the active reasons. If reasons are causes (Davidson 1963), then this defines causes of agent-causality, but such causes are excluded since the latter is a first cause, so no such amendment would help.

Clarke (2003) proposes a second integrated account. Here, 'as a matter of nomological necessity' (2003: 136), the decision is (non-deterministically) caused by an event only if the agent causes it. So the agent acts as a necessary condition for the causal effectiveness of the agent's reasons. Conversely, and directly addressing the problem of explanatory dearth flagged earlier, the agent can only cause the action if there are reasons that (non-deterministically) cause it. This dependence, however, apparently restricts the agent's leeway. Further, there is no metaphysical account of the possibility of such mutual dependence of causalities. Clarke (2003: 136) himself considers this proposal unsatisfactory because Mele's Rational Luck Objection is not addressed satisfactorily: there is no explanation of why the agent acts on some rather than other pre-existing reasons, so that certain (volitionally relevant) contrastive explanations are unavailable.

Although these integrated event/agent-causal proposals thus fail to address the Rational Luck Objection satisfactorily, it is worth noting the intuitively appealing way of connecting the agent's will (here represented by agent-causality) with reasons. As we shall see further, this is at the heart of Kant's approach to the Problem: Kant's idealism creates the conceptual space for agent-causality to play a grounding role with respect to the psychological causality that connects reasons $\{B_2, D_2\}$ to the intention to φ_2, but also thereby grounds their connection with prior reasons for endorsing them, and so on (see Chapter 2): it follows that there will be no problem of rational luck insofar as the choice of φ_2 is rational in the light of all these reasons.

The problem of 'pure' agent-causal libertarianism

The problems faced in attempting to combine event- and agent-causality in a naturalistic setting suggest constructing an account drawing exclusively upon the latter, i.e. a 'pure' agent-causal libertarianism.[16] However, while, as with the integrated account, the original Luck Objection which works against the event-causal libertarian can be countered here along the lines of Pereboom and O'Connor's replies examined earlier, the disconnection between agent-causality and reasons for action would seem to make agent-causal proposals fall foul of the Rational Luck Objection: what is at stake is their ability to provide not just contrastive explanations but *any* reasons for action. The agent-causal libertarian must therefore clarify the role played by reasons for action in his account. Below, I examine an important agent-causal theory addressing this issue. First, it is useful to consider the third option flagged earlier, i.e. non-causal libertarianism.

Non-causal alternatives

I briefly examine this option here insofar as it provides a useful tool that the agent-causal libertarian can avail himself of in addressing the dilemma just described. Non-causal libertarians attempt to solve the Problem by replacing the causal link of the psychological account by a non-causal one which therefore allows for the agent to be said to act freely because her action is not causally determined. Ginet's (1990: 13) proposal involves defining certain basic actions, i.e. what we might call volitions or willings, in terms of their having a certain phenomenological 'actish' quality. As Clarke (1993: 21) argues, such a characterisation of free action (whose volitional account is defined in terms of the phenomenology) is not compatible with a satisfactory psychological account since it fails to distinguish between the two following possible scenarios: because 'an agent may have a reason R to A, she may A' and 'it may be that she A-s not for reason R but for some other reason'.

McCann (1998: 163) proposes rather a notion of basic action, whose intrinsic intentionality is characterised as follows: an agent acts for reasons $\{B_1, D_1\}$ when she produces an intention, the content of which is the satisfaction of the desire D_1 on the assumption of the truth of belief B_1. The control an agent exercises in free agency is then characterised (i) by the fact that the act is directed at some objective (it is intentional in the way just described), and (ii) it is spontaneous. This defines McCann's volitional account. Clarke (1993: 19–21) observes that the first condition does not ensure that there is any control since an act with the appropriate intentional content could have its origin elsewhere than in the agent (e.g. if the agent's brain is manipulated). So it is the spontaneity condition that must ensure that the agent controls the act. But McCann does not further explicate what such spontaneity involves.[17] Although a notion of spontaneity will play a key role in Kant's volitional account, this is made possible by transcendental idealism; it is not clear how room can be found for such spontaneity within a naturalistic setting. While there is no space to further discuss these options, we shall see further that McCann's notion of intrinsic intentionality of volitions/willings will be a useful tool.

A 'pure' agent-causal libertarian option

O'Connor (2000, 2011), whose agent-causal libertarian theory of free will is probably the most fully developed such account in the contemporary debate, in effect substitutes McCann's teleological account of willings for the role played by event-causality in event-causal libertarianism, and supplements this with (i) a role for agent-causality that is meant to overcome the limitations of McCann's non-causal approach, and (ii) a theory of the causal account linking the intention and the action.

Suppose that, prior to the action, the agent has a desire D_1 and a belief B_1 that, in so acting, he would satisfy desire D_1. According to O'Connor (2000: 86), 'the agent's action was initiated (in part) by his own self-determining causal activity, the event component of which is the coming-to-be-of-an-action-triggering-intention-to-act-here-and-now-to-satisfy' desire D_1. So, the agent's decision is the bringing about of an intention which triggers an action (and further conditions are introduced to ensure that the corresponding action follows from this intention). Because of this key role of the intention, $\{B_1, D_1\}$ can be involved by defining its purpose.

O'Connor's volitional and psychological accounts

Leaving aside for now any difficulties raised by O'Connor's metaphysical account of agent-causality, his proposal ensures that the agent controls the action: through this agent-causality, the agent freely decides to pursue a purpose, i.e. the satisfaction of a desire, when the agent believes the circumstances are appropriate. This is the core of his volitional account.

O'Connor's psychological account features a non-causal role for the agent's reasons. O'Connor (2000: 29) thus seeks to avoid the Rational Luck Objection. O'Connor's proposal is that the agent *takes* reasons to be valid ones for her decision: reasons are not just tagged on to the account. For this to be true, it is necessary for the agent to select a reason upon which to act and for that selection to be rational. O'Connor's (2011: 317) theory precisely addresses this. The rationality of this process is ensured by the fact that there are further reasons $\{B_{11}, D_{11}\}$ and $\{B_{22}, D_{22}\}$ explaining her adoption of reasons $\{B_1, D_1\}$ and $\{B_2, D_2\}$ respectively. To pursue the earlier example, these might be beliefs about the primacy of, respectively, freedom (B_{11}) and equality (B_{22}) as a societal value and the desires D_{11} and D_{22} to live in a society that promotes these values. These explain why Alice would want to elect a candidate who promotes respectively freedom (desire D_1) or rather equality (desire D_2) in society, and therefore, given her beliefs about Tweedledum (B_1) and Tweedledee (B_2), intend to vote for the first (φ_1) or the second (φ_2). So, prior attitudes $\{B_1, D_1\}$ and $\{B_{11}, D_{11}\}$ and the agent's character are all relevant to the agent's selection of φ_1. It follows that O'Connor's proposal can meet a central challenge of the Rational Luck Objection insofar as it enables contrastive explanation. Indeed, in choosing to vote for Tweedledum (φ_1), Alice will be aware of reasons $\{B_{11}, D_{11}\}$ which account for her acting on reasons $\{B_1, D_1\}$ rather than $\{B_2, D_2\}$ (O'Connor 2011: 320).

While the appeal to non-causal explanations is, I think, a strength of O'Connor's proposal, it is a two-edged sword when we consider how the volitional and psychological accounts mesh. This meshing would be ensured if the desires upon which the agent acts (psychological account) were the desires which the agent's will intends to satisfy (volitional account). Insofar as O'Connor in effect breaks up the causal link of a belief-desire model by introducing agent-causality, for actions φ_1 and φ_2 that follow causally from the intentions to φ_1 and φ_2, it is no longer the case that they need be viewed as the effects of reasons $\{B_1, D_1\}$ and $\{B_2, D_2\}$. So who is to say that there are not unconscious desires (and beliefs) that are not manifested in the intentions' purposes, but are causally responsible for the formation of these intentions? (see also Clarke 2003: 140–1). To this, O'Connor can reply that it is at least possible that the agent's free will should be involved in the way he proposes, which is all that is needed for the psychological account.

But a related problem arises. As Clarke (2003: 142) points out, there are many cases where the (conscious) reasons for which an agent decides on a course of action are not represented in the intention to act that is acquired through this decision. So, for instance, Arthur may decide to be particularly focussed when playing a piece on the piano because he wants to impress Gwen. Arthur's intention may thus be to bring about that the dynamics be well defined, the tempo sustained even in difficult passages, etc. It is this intention that guides how he performs this action of focussing on his playing and therefore his decision is to bring about an intention to act in such a way as to fulfil his desire to play in this focussed manner. The reason for which he does this, i.e. to impress Gwen, does not, however, feature in this account. Such event-causal worries cast doubt over the compatibility of O'Connor's volitional account, with a satisfactory psychological one; note that the latter's inadequacy in this 'pure' agent-causal libertarian proposal results from its abandoning the causal role of reasons characterising compatibilism, event-causal and integrated agent-causal libertarianism. Still, O'Connor's theory presents the best attempt in the contemporary literature at addressing the Problem to mitigate concerns about Rational Luck.

I must now return to the issue of causal indeterminism since it casts further doubt over whether the Rational Luck argument can be addressed properly. O'Connor (2000: 28–9) argues that 'if a causal relation of the appropriate sort can constitute a form of agent control (. . .) there is no reason why that relation cannot be non-necessitating'. But the existence of indeterminacy means that however much of the decision to plump for φ_1 is accounted for by reference to these explanatory factors, once these factors have been taken into account, it is a matter of pure chance that φ_1 rather than φ_2 was chosen.

This is the nub of van Inwagen's (1983; see also Pink 2011: 364) case against the use of causal indeterminism.

O'Connor (2000: 28) rejects this by insisting that causal relations define control, whether they are deterministic or not, and indeed agent-causality as we saw earlier, does ensure that there is full control by stipulating that it is achieved through the agent-causal power. O'Connor would complain that it is only a dogmatic attachment to the principle of sufficient reason that accounts for the worries raised by van Inwagen and Pink. As I argued previously, however, this is also called for by the broader (Kantian) *causal task principle*; while the requirements these principles define coincide in a naturalistic context, their motivations are different.

So, if Alice votes for Tweedledee (φ_2) by adopting reasons $\{B_2, D_2\}$ because of reasons $\{B_{22}, D_{22}\}$, the question is, once reasons $\{B_{22}, D_{22}\}$ have been taken into account, what further justification is there for adopting reasons $\{B_2, D_2\}$? That this question is legitimate to ensure that there is rational control, can be seen from the fact that if there is no further justification, it will be a random matter whether, of the possible justifying reasons $\{B_1, D_1\}$ and $\{B_2, D_2\}$, Alice opts for the one rather than the other.[18] That is, while one can see why a belief in the primacy of the societal value of equality (B_{22}) accounts for the desire D_2 to live in an egalitarian society, since there is no causal determination here, the explanatory power of B_{22} is limited. The issue of randomness arises because of the absence of *further reasons*[19] as required by the causal task principle.

This is the reason why, *pace* O'Connor (2011: 324), there is a lack of rational control consequent upon the luck involved in the agent's choice. This deficit of rationality is faced by any libertarian theory appealing to causal indeterminism (whether event- or agent-causal) in a naturalistic setting.

O'Connor's metaphysical account

One of the most famous objections to agent-causalism is Broad's (1952: 215) that the agent's intervention is not a datable event. To this, O'Connor (2011: 318) replies that 'the having of reasons and other [circumstantial] factors before and up to the time of the action' defines the agent's 'internal state' which causally structures the agent's 'capacity to cause action-triggering events' (intentions) and that this addresses the problem of timing.

Ginet (1997), however, questions how it is that the agent's causing an event *e* at a certain time *t* could fail to explain its occurrence at *t*. O'Connor's (2000: 74–6) response is that timing is just one feature of *e* of which one cannot provide a contrastive explanation, i.e. it occurs at *t* rather than *t'*, and he cites the similar lack of contrastive explanation in typical two-slit quantum experiments to defuse the concern. But the timing of an event is not just an accidental feature of it as is the path followed by a particle is in the case of this experiment. Its occurring at (or over) a certain time is essential to its being an event, and this is why this is a problem for the metaphysical account. Although O'Connor (2011: 318) adduces the existence of prior dispositions to explain why the agent acted at time *t*, it is clear that these would be insufficient. Assume unchanged circumstances and dispositions over a duration D: why act at *t*? This lack of contrastive explanation is also a lack of reasons for acting at *t*, i.e. a lack of rational control in relation to timing.

There are other aspects of O'Connor's metaphysical account that would warrant further discussion, but there is no space to address them here. Let us, however, note O'Connor's (2000: 97) claim that 'agent-causation [is] a *structured* capacity – structured by tendency-conferring states of having reasons to act in specific ways and more enduring states of character'. O'Connor (2011: 314, my emphasis) also states that agent-causality is '*not directed to any particular effects*, but instead confers upon an agent a power to cause a certain type of event within the agent: the coming to be of a state of intention to carry out some act'. The question of how such a bare causal power is structured must be addressed. But, while it must be free, one cannot resort to this capacity itself to explain how it is structured. It could be objected that this is a problem that affects only the genesis of this structure, and O'Connor (2011: 321) concedes that the agent's early environment has a strong influence in moulding his dispositions. He argues that this only *limits* the scope of his possibilities. So, given that certain dispositions are in place, every time the agent acts, the probabilities of acting on certain reasons are thereby updated, leading to progressive changes in the agent's tendencies.[20] But this would mean that we could only act on reasons foisted upon us in childhood and would not account for the adoption of entirely *new* reasons, which is not satisfactory as a notion of sourcehood.

In summary, O'Connor's pure agent-causal theory provides one of the most sophisticated libertarian volitional accounts in the contemporary literature, but it still falls short of what is required for the rational control of action characterising sourcehood. What this theory achieves in terms of the volitional account, i.e. a plausible theory of intention-formation which clearly provides a home for the agent's will in the production of the intention and the action it causes, comes at the cost of shortcomings in providing a satisfactory psychological account that meshes with this volitional account. The indeterminism of agent-causality lies at the heart of these problems.

D. The Infinite Regress Argument

The arguments

While the above completes this chapter's overview of libertarian accounts of free will, there is a well-known objection to the cogency of the sourcehood requirement that has underpinned much of the discussion of this and the first chapter. It is independent of whether the context is deterministic or not. As we shall see, it sheds further light upon the Rational Luck Objection, in terms of its meaning both for control and for any libertarian theory. This is Galen Strawson's 'Infinite Regress Argument' (Strawson 1994, 2002).

Strawson argues that how one acts is explained by 'how one is, mentally speaking' (Strawson 1994: 6; see also 2002: 442), which includes one's reasons, character, etc. Importantly, this claim is *about both causal explanations and other explanatory reasons*. Now, if I am to be free, it must be the case that my action is under my rational control, so how I am, mentally speaking, must therefore be something (which we can broadly call 'reasons') that I have chosen. But this choice must be based upon reasons which in turn will have to be chosen. This leads to a regress of choices of reasons for action. This regress prevents the action from happening since it would require an infinite number of choices. Whether this is in a deterministic or indeterministic context is, moreover, irrelevant. What Strawson's argument implies is that a psychological account of an action which ensures that the agent is in full rational control of it (i.e. all relevant reasons would have been chosen by the agent) is impossible.

In the original version of his argument, Strawson (1986: ch. 2) considers Leibniz's (1710/1983: 421) parody of a libertarian account in which the queen (the agent) listens to all the arguments put forward by her advisors and ministers (the reasons) and the suggestions made by her favourites (the non-rational part of her character) and then freely makes her decision which may or may not agree with this advice: it is up to her. Strawson (1986: 53-4) points out that, if all the reasons ('desires or principles of choice') that could play a role in her decision are accounted for in the form of this advice, there are no further rational grounds available for this decision. So even if a libertarian claims that the agent is in control of it, this cannot be rational control.

Lack of rational control and diminished control

This latter form of the argument generalises the last point I made about O'Connor's psychological and volitional accounts by extending it beyond the indeterministic context of his proposal: it is thus a form of the Rational Luck Objection. What the infinite regress form of the argument adds to this is that it crystallises in what sense the problem of rational control is ultimately an aspect of the problem of control. It locates the reduction of control implied by the lack of rational control in the incompleteness of the infinite regress. So, in the earlier example, the queen's decision will ultimately rely upon how she was disposed at that point in time. But even if she chose these dispositions previously, the infinite regress shows that at some point, some of the grounds upon which she made choices could not have been hers. This is *the locus of the missing control*: it lies in the past determinants of action that do not all lie under the agent's control.

Responses

An agent-causal libertarian response to this argument is Clarke's (2003: 172) who argues that although agent-causal libertarianism provides no 'full rational explanation of the action' (2003: 172), this is not needed. It is the role of agent-causality, he argues, to provide an additional input that settles the decision one way or another: 'how one is mentally speaking' (Strawson 1994) is not what is at stake in this agent-causality for Clarke (2003: 175), because '[t]he agent herself is not (. . .) a feature of herself'. But if agent-causality is unrelated to rationality, this sets an arbitrary cap upon the scope of rational explanations and does not meet the Rational Luck Objection.

Now the libertarian may want to dig in his heels by pointing out that what is not 'fully causally determined' by explanatory states ('conative and cognitive states' involving reasons for action) is not thereby 'merely a "chancy" outcome of those states' (O'Connor 2011: 320) and that there may be a cap upon how much of the determinacy of the outcome of a decision could be covered by rational explanation (Clarke 2003: 175). First, on the question of a cap, if Clarke is claiming that all aspects of a free action are not freely chosen (e.g. those connected with physical abilities, cultural habits), the point is well taken. But the issue lies with those aspects of our actions that are claimed to be freely chosen: no cap can be set upon their rationality without begging the question against the rational luck objector. As Clarke himself agrees, agent-causality cannot simply be added, but exactly how it combines/interacts with reasons is a key issue agent-causal libertarians have wrestled with (see also Pereboom 2006: 68) without successfully responding to the Rational Luck Objection.

Second, as for O'Connor's comment about 'mere' chanciness, this is meant to suggest a very limited lack of rational control. But this claim rests upon an erroneous intuition of 'degrees of chanciness'. On this picture, most of the outcome is determined by reasons and some chanciness in the agent's decision adds the final touch, thereby fully determining it. But the role of uncertainty in decision-making is not 'linear': a small contribution involving flipping a minute switch one way or another can have large consequences which are not describable as a final touch. On these grounds, I think that the Infinite Regress Argument stands and is *the* major challenge to any attempt to account for the sourcehood of free agency.

A conceptual feature of libertarian accounts of free will

Strawson's critique exhibits a fundamental tension between the libertarian ambition of identifying a clear role for the agent's will as source of his action in a volitional account and the rational requirements of a plausible psychological account of action. The Rational Luck Objection identified the event-causal libertarian's problem of running out of reasons that could explain opting for φ_1 rather than φ_2. What Strawson does is to explain why this problem is unavoidable for any libertarian account of free will. That is because the impossibility of complete psychological explanations of action in terms of reasons arising from the Infinite Regress Argument implies that whatever control the agent may have over her actions is ultimately insufficient because it is not fully rational. This inevitability is therefore a *conceptual feature* of such an account which I call the *Paradox of Self-Determination* (see Figure 3.1).

Strawson's argument works for reasons *and* causes insofar as we think of reasons, like causes, as having to exist prior to a decision. Strawson therefore claims that this argument identifies a problematic conceptual feature of the very *notion of rational choice* at the heart of our intuitions about sourcehood.[21] The problem is one of lack of justification:

(i) my being free to choose between φ_1 and φ_2 requires that reasons for choosing the one or the other option are, without my free input, insufficient to causally determine this choice;

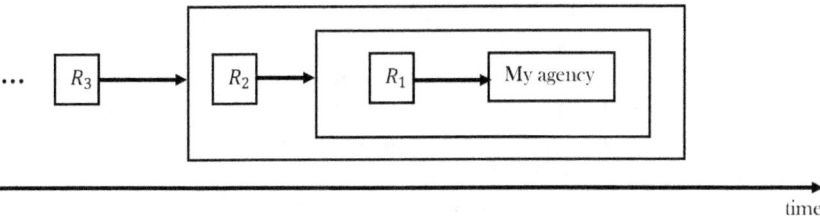

Figure 3.1 The Paradox of Self-Determination in the Infinite Regress Argument (R_i stands for a reason or reason-pair, i.e. B_i or D_i or $\{B_i, D_i\}$). 'My agency' stands for 'how I am mentally speaking' © Christian Onof.

(ii) in plumping for one option, I can no longer appeal to these reasons as justification.

Strawson (1986: 54) concludes that this amounts to filling the determinacy gap by a *'partially* reason-independent' decision, i.e. a 'flip-flop of the soul'. Strawson's critique is therefore an attack on the cogency of the notion of *free choice*.

This conclusion has implications for Kant's compatibilist proposal in Chapter 2. This proposal precisely addresses the concern raised by the infinite causal regress by identifying the logical possibility of a 'complement of sufficiency' in the causal determination of an intention/action which would be located outside the deterministic natural causal nexus. Since this location is outside time, Kant's proposal is immune to Strawson's *temporal causal* argument. However, Strawson's further claim about the lack of rational justification characterising free choice does not have to be construed temporally: it implies that any purported source of the action must make *explanatory* reference to preferences which themselves have to be chosen, etc. So, locating the source of the action outside time does not, as such, make it explanatorily autonomous.

Therefore, while Kant may have created a way out of a regress of natural causes, he is now faced with one of explanatory grounds (outside time): Strawson's argument seems therefore to imply that the logical possibility Kant's turn to transcendental idealism creates, defines no real possibility, i.e. does not define a space for a rational agent's free willings. In the next section, I examine grounds for questioning this aspect of Strawson's argument and propose a Kantian reply to it.

E. Beyond the Infinite Regress Argument

The explanatory self-sufficiency of willings

As Thomas Pink (2011: 355) is right to point out, the problem the agent-causal libertarian faces with the Rational Luck Objection is an 'intelligibility problem'. It concerns the provision of a rational explanation of action. As such, it is distinct from the 'randomness problem' (2011: 355) flagged in the original Luck Objection which concerns the action's causes; both arguments are, however, related as they deal with aspects of the agent's lack of control.

Pink argues that these two problems have erroneously been identified. He traces the source of the error in compatibilism underpinned by a Hobbesian theory of action. On such a theory, e.g. assumed in Strawson's argument, the action's explananda are necessarily *prior attitudes* (beliefs, desires) which, as in a typical belief-desire account, are explanatory of the action insofar as they are *causes* of it. Pink does not endorse this theory of action's focus upon prior attitudes. But rather than focus upon the causal claim as the traditional libertarian does (either by loosening it in event-causal libertarianism, altering it by injecting agent-causality into the picture, or by rejecting it as in non-causal libertarianism), he questions the claim about conditions of intelligibility of an action. That is, he questions that which Strawson assumes in claiming that his argument applies equally to the justification of an action and to its causal grounds.

Pink (2011: 358–9) argues that there are certain actions, those of intention-formation, i.e. what I call *willings/volitions*[22] or *decisions*, which are intelligible because of their purposive content and without reference to prior attitudes. McCann (1998) had already identified the intrinsic intentionality of willings/volitions and O'Connor (2000) used this as a key component of his volitional account. But now, *pace* O'Connor and McCann, Pink (2011: 360–1) argues that this intrinsic intentionality means that an intention to φ_1 (vote for Tweedledum) is fully explained by identifying its purpose Φ_1 (to enable Tweedledum to make this a freer society) so that specifying that this purpose is the satisfaction of prior desire D_1 (to live in a freer society) when the agent believes B_1 (Tweedledum will make society freer) adds nothing to the explanation.

What Pink identifies here is the *rational self-sufficiency* of a volitional account of an intention/action in terms of the agent's purpose, and its independence of a psychological account of the same in terms of prior dispositions.[23] The Hobbesian theory of action assumed in the contemporary debate obscures the difference between these two accounts. This analysis comports with my diagnosis that the failure of source compatibilism lies in its attempt to derive a volitional account from a psychological one (Chapter 1). Importantly, it also shows how, libertarianism's problems notwithstanding, Strawson misunderstands the reach of his Infinite Regress Argument by wrongly assuming that the dearth in a free action's causal explanation translates into an explanatory dearth.

So how does Pink use this crucial insight to address the Problem? Following Davidson (1963), Pink (2011: 360) accepts, rightly in my view, that prior attitudes are explanatory of actions only insofar as they cause them. This means that, *pace* O'Connor and McCann, there is no conceptual space for freedom in positing non-causal connections to these attitudes. However, while some intentions are caused by prior attitudes, the rational self-sufficiency of (at least some) intention-formation entails that such a causal link is not necessarily required for explanatory purposes. This leaves room for the proposal (2011: 362–5) that some intentions are brought about by a power other than causality, i.e. freedom. While this power is designed to ensure that the agent's will is the source of his action, Pink (2011) adds that it will have to be a 'multi-way power' to satisfy the leeway requirement.

A first worry is that this proposal would rely upon its being the case that the agent's explicit purpose in intention-formation is indeed the motivation for forming this intention. We have already seen, in relation to O'Connor's account, that this is questionable. This means that the psychological account may have to appeal to other causes that do not feature in the agent's intention. This problem would be limited to the issue of making psychological and volitional accounts compatible (see previous discussion) if causes are not fully determining. However, such indeterminism, in turn, would introduce worries connected with the Luck Objection in its various guises.

Second, Pink's suggestion that an intention is the product of a two-way power, freedom, is designed to dispel any such worries about luck. Indeed, he sees the problem of traditional (event or agent-causal) libertarianism as precisely that, '[s]hould more than one effect be left possible [once all relevant circumstances have been taken into account], with some chance of occurring, which effect the cause produces will be left random and undetermined, that is, a matter of pure chance' (Pink 2011: 364), a point I fully endorse. But if, as Pink suggests, the effect is brought about by a multi-way power, the randomness does not vanish for that but becomes a constitutive feature of that power. Further, would naturalism, which traditionally relies upon causal explanations, admit such powers in its ontology insofar as they are fundamental natural powers defining a limit to explanation because of their stochasticity?

A third worry is that while an intention-formation that is rationally self-sufficient is a willing/volition requiring no reference to prior dispositions, this only implies that no further explanation is required beyond specifying the pursued purpose, in the case of such a willing/volition *in isolation*. If, however, I will to pursue Φ_1 at t_1 and Φ_2 at t_2, something more must be said about the *coherence* of pursuing these purposes at those times, if the volitional account is to be compatible with the rational constraints of a psychological account. So the rational self-sufficiency with respect to prior dispositions characterising single willings/volitions does not entail rational independence with respect to one another: only a set of all of an agent's *coherent willings/volitions* possesses such self-sufficiency.

A path out of the infinite regress

In the light of the above, I will not pursue the analysis of Pink's proposed solution to the Problem but examine what his insight into the need to allow for teleological explanations of action, explanations that are not causal, implies for Strawson's argument. If Strawson's Infinite Regress is to be prevented, we must first identify something about human agency that could plausibly be said *not to depend* upon prior attitudes to explain it. As I just argued in examining Pink's insight, *the set* of all of an agent's coherent willings/volitions could play such a role. I take this set to define *the intention of having a certain nature* N, as Strawson (2002) puts it, where N is minimally characterised by the coherence of the purposes of the individual willings/volitions.

But this is not enough to address the Infinite Regress Argument, because all depends upon which explanation, in terms of prior attitudes (psychological) or of intelligibility (volitional), one has in mind. Looking again at Strawson's Infinite Regress Argument, he claims:

3.8 You must already have had a certain mental nature – call it **M** – at t_0, in the light of which you intentionally brought it about that you now have nature **N**.

Why? Because

3.9 If you didn't already have a certain mental nature, at t_0, then you can't then have had any intentions or preferences at all; and if you didn't then have any intentions or preferences at all, you can't be held to be [responsible][24], let alone [ultimately responsible], for intentionally bringing anything about, at t_0. (Strawson 2002: 446)

One can query (3.8) insofar as 'in light of which' refers to a role for intentions and preferences (3.9) as explaining the rationality of the action by drawing upon Pink's insight: there are intentions that do not require reference to previous attitudes to explain them. But while this points to how to formulate a volitional account, it does not entail that these intentions are not (at least partly) caused (psychological explanation) by prior preferences as I indicated earlier. Indeed, (3.9) makes the point that without a set of preferences already in place, it would not be possible for the agent to intend anything in time: these preferences define the beliefs and desires of a causal psychological explanation.

Since such preferences have a causal role in bringing about the intention to have nature N, the Infinite Regress Argument can proceed by showing that I must, previously, have chosen (some of) these preferences, and so on. It is therefore not threatened by any rational self-sufficiency of willings/volitions as such.

This does not, however, neutralise the utility of Pink's insight to defining a way out of the infinite regress. Rather, it points to the requirement to remove the set of willings/volitions from the temporal causal flux. Indeed, the rational self-sufficiency of willings/volitions will enable a libertarian position to avoid the pitfalls of the Infinite Regress Argument only if willings/volitions are cut loose from the causal influence of temporally prior attitudes. That is, to address the worry raised above for Kant's compatibilist solution, placing the source of free actions outside time *does* after all create the conceptual space for the real possibility of free agency if the latter is understood as intrinsically intentional willings that do not refer to other justificatory grounds. This observation, together with the metaphysical conundrums connected with O'Connor's agent-causality and Pink's multi-way power, suggests that the only way of responding to Strawson's argument is by a move beyond the natural domain: what is required is to place the intention-forming willing outside time, while its product, the intention, remains a mental occurrence in time.

This conclusion therefore chimes with that of Chapter 1's analysis of compatibilist approaches. It, however, fleshes out the mere sketch of a metaphysical account provided there. This was the identification of the *logical* possibility of a proper home for the agent's will beyond any threat of manipulation, as it arises from the transcendental idealist setting in which Kant addresses the Problem in its antinomial form. In this way, the *real* possibility of the agent's willings/volitions (whose coherence defines nature N) being located outside the temporal domain of nature has been motivated by Pink's insight.

Objection and clarification

But surely, it will be objected, a willing takes place at a certain point in time. There is no doubt that it is *manifested* in time, in terms of some more or less specific intention to act. However, the same willing could also be manifested at several points in time (e.g. the decision not to be a liar). I would argue that it is because of its atemporal nature that an agent is held responsible for an act, even long after its occurrence. Why hold someone who is truly repentant responsible for what he did before repenting unless the decision he took is in some sense a timeless feature of who he is?

This proposal's metaphysical account is in need of further clarification. So far, what we have is a strong dualism with a faculty of free will separated from the agent's temporal physical manifestation, and unlike the usual mind-body dualism, this one would place free will not only outside the physical domain, but outside time.

To further specify the metaphysical account, it is necessary to be clear about the psychological account. Recall that (i) the event-causal libertarian introduces indeterminism into the compatibilist's causal psychological account and (ii) the agent-causal libertarian more radically breaks it up with agent-causality while the (iii) non-causal libertarian breaks it up with non-causal links. It might seem that my proposal for the psychological account must also involve breaking up this causal explanation, with interventions from beyond nature in the form of the volitional account's willings. Would it be satisfactory to have actions in time explained by reference to a causal power outside time? The most obvious problem is that the temporal location of the intention and the action it causes would not thereby be accounted for, just as with O'Connor's agent-causality; further, as with the latter proposal, the absence of a rational explanation for the timing would define a Rational Luck Problem.

To understand what metaphysical account will enable volitional and psychological accounts to cohere in the case of the intention to φ, let us revisit Pink's critique of McCann and O'Connor's understanding of intention-formation. While Pink affirmed that an appeal to prior dispositions is not required for the volitional account of intention-formation, the problem he identified with McCann (1998: 165) and O'Connor's (2000: 86) theories was their attempts to provide a *non-causal* explanation of intentions in terms of prior attitudes (e.g. $\{B, D\}$), i.e. as part of a psychological account.

This leaves room for standard causal explanations of a belief-desire model, which I shall assume to be deterministic to avoid the Luck Objections. What is explained by such a model is the intention that is formed, not the act of intention-forming itself which has been removed from the time domain. So focussing first, for simplicity, upon individual willings/volitions, while the volitional account of my decision to get up and open the window is fully explained by the purpose of opening the window, the psychological account of the intention (and subsequent action) I brought about not only refers to some general preferences (e.g. for fresh air) but the specific desire D to inhale fresh air and the belief B that this could be achieved by opening the window (see Figure 3.2).

The challenge for a metaphysical account is that given that the psychological account defines $\{B\ D\}$ as causing the intention, how can it do justice to the agent's willing in the volitional account also being explanatory of this intention without assuming that this defines another causal ground of it and therefore leads to causal overdetermination?

It is, however, an open question *how* reasons are to be understood as causes if we do not adopt Davidson's (1980) anomalous monism proposal. Here, I propose that to explain *how* $\{B\ D\}$ cause the intention to φ, the agent's willing should play a role of endowing these reasons $\{B, D\}$ with the causal power to bring about the intention φ.[25] That echoes Clarke's (2003) proposed way of accounting, in his integrated agent-causal proposal, for how agent-causality *enables the activation* of event-causality. So the intention would be caused by some beliefs/desires *through* my willing, as shown in Figure 3.3.

Finally, in the light of the third criticism of Pink's proposal, this schematic should be applied not to individual willings/volitions but to the *sum total of all an agent's willings/volitions* whose purpose defines a certain nature N that is minimally defined by the coherence of these particular intentions.

This amounts to a *grounding of the agent's psychological causality* in the agent's will, while in time, each individual intention would be causally determined by prior reasons. Such a metaphysical account directly addresses Strawson's Infinite Regress Argument in its causal form, while rejecting his claim that it translates to all forms of explanation

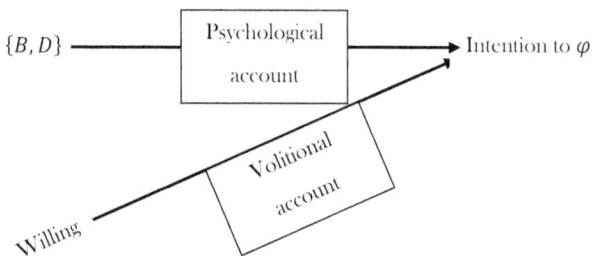

Figure 3.2 Volitional and psychological accounts of intention to φ © Christian Onof.

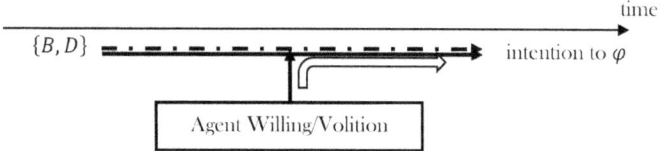

Figure 3.3 Metaphysical account (full line arrow) in which the agent's willing grounds the causal link of the psychological account (dashed-dotted arrow), thereby bringing about the effect (intention) as required by the volitional account (double arrow). $\{B, D\}$ are both causes (full line arrow) and reasons (dashed-dotted arrow). © Christian Onof.

of action. Indeed, the rational self-sufficiency of a coherent set of intentions directed at N, i.e. who the agent aims to be, does not require any reference to prior preferences: my will brings about the intention of having N (sum total of particular intentions) because my purpose is to have N, full stop.

This proposal thereby solves the conundrum faced by agent-causal libertarianism's attempts to specify the explanatory role of an agent's reasons together with agent-causality. Further, the grounding role of willings/volitions with respect to psychological causality (i) avoids the indeterminism that underpins the Luck Objections and (ii) sidesteps metaphysical problems such as those encountered by O'Connor's theory, for instance, by specifying the agent-causality's relation to reasons and avoiding the time location problem.

Outlining a plausible metaphysical account

This chapter's review of libertarian proposals has concluded that the only way to address the Infinite Regress Argument's challenge to libertarianism is by locating the agent's freedom outside the natural temporal causal flux. This conclusion was also reached in Chapter 1 when seeking a compatibilist response to the Consequence Argument that does not fall foul of the Argument from Manipulation.

While this proposal has a clear metaphysical cost, its intuitive appeal should not be overlooked. In psychological accounts of agency of the belief-desire type, it is taken for granted that some of my beliefs and desires are the causes of my intentions to act. If questions about their causal power are asked, all that is available in a naturalistic framework is an appeal to processes in the brain. These are, however, sub-personal. This therefore excludes that this appeal should explain why *my* reasons are what cause the intention, which surely was what was to be explained.

Of course, a typical (e.g. naturalist) response will be that it is insofar as they are in my brain that they are mine. What the Problem helps us focus upon is why this response is unsatisfactory. When competing sets of beliefs and desires are available, it is no longer sufficient to describe my subjectivity in terms of the possession of a certain brain: we want to say that certain reasons caused my intention *because* I made them causally efficient. It is therefore very intuitive to claim that my freedom is what endows states with causal power. This is the grounding of psychological causality in my freedom and is what makes it *my* psychological causality.

This solution amounts to addressing the Consequence Argument by considering the possibility that our free will contribute to a law of nature, if placed outside time. Chapter 4 will present Kant's own argument for his version of this 'altered-law' (Chapter 2) theoretical claim and how he fills in the metaphysical account. Chapter 5 will shed more light upon this grounding from the perspective of Kant's practical philosophy, thereby fleshing out his volitional account.

Two worries arise, however. First, as already flagged in Chapter 1, locating the agents' free will outside nature seems to leave her disconnected from the natural domain and is an apparently arbitrary metaphysical move designed exclusively to solve the Problem. And second, our knowledge that sub-personal processes in the brain are at work in bringing about the implementation of any intention to act might seem incompatible with this metaphysical picture.

The first worry is addressed, as in Chapter 1, by a move to transcendental idealism. We can now add to Chapter 2's altered-law proposal in response to the Consequence Argument, by clarifying that the agent straddles the boundary of the natural domain through the freedom of her will outside nature defining a noumenal causality grounding her (natural) psychological causality. And we now also have a teleological understanding of this free will as directed to the agent's nature as a whole.[26] These aspects of the volitional account will be revisited in Chapter 5. The move to transcendental idealism also eliminates any apparent arbitrariness of the proposed solution: the whole of nature is similarly grounded in some reality in-itself. The noumenal causality of the agent's free agency is thereby a contribution to this grounding of the whole of nature.

This move to transcendental idealism also mitigates the second worry. If the framework of transcendental idealism is adopted, sub-personal processes in the brain are similarly grounded in reality in-itself, a grounding to which the agent contributes. The agent's free will does not, therefore, have to clash with accounts relying upon sub-personal processes. More will need to be said about how Kant's solution addresses this problem in Chapter 6, where we will see that the remaining explanatory dearth is a version of the mind-body interaction problem which is thereby decoupled from the Problem.

Note finally that the proposed adoption of the framework of transcendental idealism is not *logically* entailed by having the freedom of the agent's will outside time and grounding some natural causality.[27] But if nature were real in-itself, this would make the agent the *creator* of at least one of its laws, which is implausible for any non-divine being. What transcendental idealism brings to the table is a conception of nature as a domain of appearances that are representations for a possible subject of experience. Defining a role for the human agent in determining through the noumenal causality of her free will one or more laws of appearance is compatible with a recognition of human finitude.

4

Kant's Resolution of the Third Antinomy

The dialectical situation is as follows. Chapter 1 showed the shortcomings of classical and contemporary compatibilism which were connected with the inability to find a proper place for the agent's will in the proposed solutions to the problem of free will (hereafter 'the Problem'). This absence of a satisfactory volitional account (problem of the Homeless Agent) suggested the adoption of the framework of Kant's transcendental idealism.

This option was initially explored in Chapter 2: this left us with some unanswered questions in particular around the problems of Historical and Timeless Agency. While some initial responses to these problems were given, Chapter 3 considered the alternative to the adoption of transcendental idealism, i.e. naturalist libertarian proposals, on the grounds that the leeway condition is, Frankfurt-style examples notwithstanding, a necessary requirement for free will. The Infinite Regress Argument, however, set a major challenge for such proposals. This showed that the agent's will needs to be removed from the temporal causal flux of nature and identified as ground of his psychological causality. The plausibility of such a metaphysical picture again called for a move to Kantian idealism.

The metaphysics of a Kantian solution must meet certain requirements. I argued that it must involve characterising freedom as located outside the temporal order of nature (Chapter 1) and grounding some natural causality (altered-law interpretation – Chapter 2). Further, this causality must be the agent's psychological causality (Chapter 3). The case for an altered-law interpretation, initially based upon the need to address the Historical Agency problem, as well as accounting for some textual evidence, was thus consolidated and further developed in response to the Infinite Regress Argument.[1]

In this Chapter, I want to show that the text of Kant's Resolution of the Third Antinomy (hereafter 'Resolution') provides a solution to the Problem that meets my proposed requirements for a Kantian solution and fills in the metaphysical account. In particular, as with Kant's Transcendental Deduction, I shall argue that the *structure* of the Resolution (which is mostly ignored in the literature) sheds essential light upon the nature of Kant's solution to the Problem.

After a brief reminder of the claims of the preamble to the Resolution and a clarification of the outstanding tasks, I proceed to examine each of the three sections of the Resolution, with an emphasis upon showing how the argument progresses through these sections. Among the issues this examination throws up, the relation between the two problems addressed by the Resolution, i.e. the antinomial cosmological one and the Problem (see Chapter 2), the issue of action predictability, Kant's libertarianism, the nature of the empirical character and the relation between transcendental and practical freedom are addressed. I then take stock of the extent to which Kant addresses the psychological and volitional accounts in the Resolution, which is otherwise chiefly devoted to the metaphysical account. This will define outstanding problems to be addressed by examining other Kantian texts in the next two chapters. The chapter concludes with some reflections on the nature of the causality of freedom Kant introduces in the Resolution.

A. The structure of the Resolution of the Third Antinomy

The preamble to the Resolution

In Chapter 2, we saw that the *logical* possibility of a complement of sufficiency to be provided by the transcendental freedom (hereafter 'T-freedom') of a solution-thing for causal series of any events in appearance was established by what Kant shows in the preamble to the Resolution (A630-2/B558-60) about the nature of dynamical antinomial conflicts. In the case of the Problem (which is not the cosmological problem the Antinomy originally addresses), the solution-thing is the agent. I argued that

- this logical possibility is not sufficient for Kant's purposes, and needs to be complemented with a metaphysical account of how the solution-thing/agent's freedom relates to the causal series leading to the intention/action.
- further, it does not address the needs of the volitional and psychological accounts of free will, a problem which shows up in the Timeless Agency problem and the Historical Agency problem, which I initially addressed in Chapter 2.

The Resolution has to shore up a metaphysical account of the *permissibility* of T-freedom, i.e. the compatibility of its real possibility together with natural causal determinism (hereafter 'determinism'), which will define the framework for plausible volitional and psychological accounts.

Consequences for the structure of the Resolution

What the metaphysical account must do is lay the foundations enabling the Homeless Agent problem to be addressed by 'locating' the solution-thing/agent's freedom with respect to the causal series determining his intention/action.[2] In Chapters 2 and 3, I proposed an outline of a solution to this problem in response to the Historical Agency Problem and the Infinite Regress Argument. Here, we focus upon Kant's text to confirm this outline and show how Kant fills it out. The task can be broken down into two parts.

(T1): The compatibility of the real possibility of T-freedom together with the causal determinism of appearances *in general* must be established.

This will play the important role of moving the solution to the Problem beyond the mere logical possibility of a first cause of causal series in appearance, by drawing upon the metaphysics of transcendental idealism.

The remaining metaphysical task is that of addressing the compatibility of the real possibility of T-freedom and causal determinism *within* the same solution-thing/agent. This second task itself has two components. First,

(T2): The compatibility of two co-existing causalities – a really possible intelligible causality of T-freedom and an actual empirical causality – within the solution-thing/agent must be established.
Second,

(T3) The relation of these two causalities must be specified to complete the proof of permissibility.

The metaphysical account therefore has three stages which, as we shall see, map onto the three sections of the Resolution. I thereby aim to disprove the claim made by some commentators (e.g. Adickes 1889: 437) that the Resolution must be read as a *patchwork* from ideas and claims made by Kant at different stages in the development of his critical philosophy, a claim that is hard to defend in the light of the absence of changes between the A and B editions as Wolfgang Ertl (1998: 158) points out.

Aside from the metaphysical account which is the focus of the Resolution, Kant shows an awareness of the need to address the psychological and volitional accounts if he is to be said to have provided a solution to the Problem. The third section of the Resolution directly addresses the psychological account by specifying how freedom can be causally responsible for what is also determined by reasons, and Kant will make a point of stressing the latter determinism. This is where it will become clear that Kant's solution is an altered-law interpretation where the law is that of the agent's psychological causality: this interpretation will therefore emerge from a structured argument, rather than simply being one of the options available to address van Inwagen's Consequence Argument (see Chapter 2).

As for the volitional account, Kant makes a point of focussing upon the first-person perspective at the very outset in the Resolution by introducing the notion of practical freedom (hereafter 'P-freedom'). As we shall see, the nature of this freedom is the topic of much controversy. It is, however, generally agreed that the concept of this freedom concerns the agent's experience of their freedom, which entails that it will contribute to the volitional account.

The Resolution's two tasks

Before moving on to examining Kant's text in detail, I have deliberately referred to a 'solution-thing/agent' to remind the reader of the problems that the Resolution is meant to address, an issue that has not been given much attention in the literature. The original antinomial problem is the cosmological one of a first cause for 'all appearances of the world' (A444/B472) or the 'origin of the world' (A448/B476). The problem which Kant, however, spends much time discussing, particularly in the second and third sections of the Resolution, is the Problem. How should we make sense of this apparent ambiguity between solving this *cosmological problem* and solving the Problem?

The Problem is introduced in both the Remarks on the Thesis (A450/B478) and on the Antithesis (A451/B479): insofar as T-freedom is allowed to account for the origin of the world (Thesis), then one can enquire whether it could not also be effective 'in the course of the world' (A450/B478). It may well be that the situations with respect to the claims of real possibility of solution-things for the cosmological problem and the Problem are different because of what is distinctive about agents, e.g. their rationality, and indeed, such a distinctiveness is claimed in Kant's ethics (GMM AA04: 448).

Nevertheless, the issues of *compatibility* of these real possibilities with determinism do not define two distinct problems. In both cases, once the real possibility of a solution-thing is assumed, the question is whether this is compatible with determinism: the specific nature of the solution-thing, i.e. agent or not, must be irrelevant here. What is relevant is that it is, *qua* appearance, subject to causal necessitation, and *qua* real in-itself, endowed with T-freedom.

This is why Kant's text is, as we shall see, at first uncommitted as to which problem it addresses. This is possible because in presenting T-freedom, Kant only refers to a non-specific noumenal cause, so there is no need to distinguish between the problems. There are two interrelated reasons for the progressive shift to a focus upon the 'rational agency' problem, i.e. the Problem, in sections two and three of the Resolution. First, Kant examines the role of T-freedom with respect to ethical concepts such as the moral 'ought' and shows that the assumption of T-freedom is necessary for judgements of imputation, as we shall see further. The central role of Kant's ethical concerns therefore justifies the shift. But second, the solution-thing of this problem, namely the rational agent, is the only thing in nature that we are acquainted with, and of which 'we can at least represent' (A547/B575) that it has T-freedom because (i) it is endowed with non-sensible faculties (see further), e.g. 'pure apperception' (A546/B574), and (ii) it recognises 'oughts' (A547/B576).

I now turn to a detailed examination of Kant's text in the Resolution. I shall follow the order of the text, only leaving out the discussion of P-freedom for later.

B. The Resolution: First section (A532-7/B560-5)

The initial cosmological problem

There are three titled sections in the Resolution and a short concluding non-titled section summarising the results. The first has the word 'resolution' in the title. Should we therefore understand the first section as the Resolution proper and what follows as further explanations and clarifications? A brief glance at the sentence opening the third section suggests not: there, Kant describes the work done in the second section as 'sketch[ing] the silhouette of a solution to our transcendental problem' (A542/B570). So the title of the first section is a higher-level one, and indeed the first section will prove a result that is at the core of Kant's strategy in addressing the Problem.

From the title ('Resolution of the cosmological idea of the totality of the derivation of occurrences in the world from their causes', A532/B560), the problem addressed in the Resolution is initially presented as the *cosmological* one because the Antinomy chapter deals with cosmological problems. And this is confirmed by Kant's two introductory paragraphs, which present the terms generating the antinomial conflict, namely determinism and T-freedom.

Why transcendental idealism and only transcendental idealism can solve the antinomial problem

The last and most extensive paragraph of section one of the Resolution is prefaced by Kant's describing it as a 'remark, to determine more closely [transcendental philosophy's] procedure in dealing with this problem' (A535/B563). This, together with the modest disclaimer at the end of the paragraph ('[h]ere I have only wanted to note (. . .)', A537/B565), makes it clear that this section of the Resolution will not deliver the solution to the antinomial problem. It will, however, provide a key to this solution.

Why no solution is possible under transcendental realism
In the paragraph, we find that Kant (1) explains why no solution can be found assuming transcendental realism and (2) provides two reasons for thinking that transcendental idealism can indeed crack the problem. The proof of (1) is short: under transcendental realism, 'nature is the completely determining cause, sufficient in itself, of every occurrence' (A536/B564). Consequently, there is no conceptual space, within determinism under transcendental realism, for the possibility of T-freedom. This is what van Inwagen's Consequence Argument (Chapter 1) concludes. This is also what I have argued for as a result of considering the available compatibilist solutions in a transcendental realist (naturalist) framework. Although the rejection of transcendental realism (empirical objects are things in-themselves) implies the endorsement of transcendental idealism (empirical objects are appearances, not things in-themselves), the fact that no solution to the conflict can be found assuming transcendental realism by no means entails that one can be found assuming transcendental idealism. Kant thus produces two reasons for claiming that transcendental idealism is useful.

First reason why transcendental idealism could provide a solution to the antinomial conflict
Turning therefore to (2), Kant's first reason draws upon general considerations about the dynamical antinomies. Kant does not just repeat the point made in the Preamble about the heterogeneity of the dynamical series but draws our attention to the fact that the mathematical antinomies deal with magnitude, and that they could not be resolved because the 'series must unavoidably turn out to be either too large or too

small for the understanding' (A535/B563), i.e. either the series goes to infinity, which is too large (Thesis), or it artificially stops at some boundary which the understanding must, however, overstep (Antithesis). This mathematical problem does not arise with dynamical antinomies. This is because while the *mathematical* antinomies are concerned with magnitude, the *dynamical* antinomies are concerned with existence. For the Third Antinomy, the question is thus 'whether freedom is possible anywhere at all' (A536/B564), and Kant is now pointing out that, since the mathematical problem does not arise, there are grounds for thinking that transcendental idealism could address the issue of the permissibility of T-freedom.

Second reason why TI could provide a solution to the antinomial conflict
The second reason addresses the specific problem of the Third Antinomy. It also constitutes the first part of its resolution by resorting to the metaphysics of transcendental idealism. As I interpreted it (Chapter 2), reality in-itself has a *constitutive function* in that (a) it defines a different aspect of the things that appear and (b) this grounds their aspect as appearances. I also made what I shall call a *regulative claim* that this grounding is one of empirical causality. In drawing upon transcendental idealism at this stage in the CPR, Kant should only avail himself of the constitutive and not the regulative features of this transcendental idealism. That is because the latter can only be grounded in the light of the Antinomy chapter itself.[3]

As confirmation of the correctness of my interpretation of the constitutive features of transcendental idealism, we precisely find Kant appealing to reality in-itself as the 'unknown ground' of 'both outer appearances and inner intuition' (A379). What this achieves is, first, a denial of the completeness of the determination of any natural occurrence by natural causality, i.e. the denial that 'nature is the completely determining cause, sufficient in itself, of every occurrence' (A536/B564). This claim goes beyond that in the preamble which merely identified the conceptual space afforded by a reality beyond appearances: this conceptual space is now specified as one in which the ground of appearances is located.

Next, by drawing upon this grounding thesis, Kant introduces an intelligible cause. This might appear to have already solved the Third Antinomy, an impression that is reinforced by what follows:

> Thus the intelligible cause, with its causality, is outside the series; its effects, on the contrary, are encountered in the series of empirical conditions. The effect can therefore be regarded as free in regard to its intelligible cause, and yet simultaneously, in regard to appearances, as their result according to the necessity of nature. (A537/B565)

Has Kant not shown that with this intelligible cause, the Thesis is now true when understood as applying to the intelligible domain, while, since this cause is 'outside the series', the Antithesis remains true of the domain of appearances? That is, has he therefore not shown too much,[4] i.e. the truth of both Thesis and Antithesis? It would indeed appear that Kant is saying that all appearances, while determined by natural causality, have an intelligible first cause.

Such a conclusion is not warranted, however, because nothing has been said about the intelligible causality grounding appearances, and for good reason: we can know nothing about reality in-itself. It is therefore not possible to affirm that it is a first cause. But why does Kant feel entitled to say of the causal series in appearance that it '*can therefore be regarded* as free in regard to it' (A537/B565, my emphasis)? We here have another piece of evidence for my claim that the Resolution is a highly structured argument. This claim that Kant makes at the end of the first section harks back to the first sentence of the section: '[i]n respect of what happens, one can *think* of causality in only two ways: either according to nature or from freedom' (A532/B560, my emphasis). In other words, when considering events in the domain of appearances, if we think of them as caused by something else than natural causality, it must be by a first cause. Presumably the idea is that otherwise, they would be thought of as belonging to a causal series that is non-natural, which would require considering a sort of alternative nature, but that is something we cannot conceive. In any case, what this means for appearances is that with respect to the intelligible causality grounding appearances, we must think them as effects of T-freedom, i.e. as free. So all that is claimed is that *I can regard appearances in general as caused by a first cause* because they are grounded in reality in-itself.

Nevertheless, this is an important result since it establishes the first claim of the Resolution, i.e. claim (T1). That is, this metaphysical grounding claim shows that the real possibility of T-freedom is compatible with the causal determinism of appearances *in general*. And indeed, Kant notes that this general claim is 'extremely subtle and obscure, but in its application it will be enlightening' (A537/B565).[5] By that, Kant is indicating that the grounding of the whole of nature in some reality in-itself, by enabling us to consider the possibility of the causality of T-freedom, is the nub of the whole solution to the Problem.

C. The Resolution: Second section (A538-41/B566-70)

Examining a hypothesis

The title of this section unequivocally spells out the task of the Resolution as I have interpreted it, i.e. establishing a compatibility, namely that of '[t]he possibility of causality through freedom unified with the universal law of natural necessity' (A538/B566),[6] where 'possibility', as also used in the concluding section of the Resolution, can only refer to *real* possibility (A558/B586): if it were logical possibility, the result would already have been established in the preamble (see chapter 2).

The first claim Kant makes in this section is to add the other constitutive feature of his idealism to the picture he has painted so far. That is, while the first section reminded us of the grounding role of things in-themselves, here, the dual-aspect property is key: 'I call intelligible that in an object of sense which is not itself appearance' (A538/B566). Again, this amounts to an unequivocal endorsement of a dual-aspect interpretation of idealism, at least from our cognitive perspective (see chapter 2). This claim is essential in this section as the discussion now moves to a compatibility problem within the solution-thing/agent.

Kant therefore presents the hypothesis in the title as follows:

> if that which must be regarded as appearance in the world of sense has in itself a faculty which is not an object of intuition through which it can be the cause of appearances, then one can consider the causality of this being in two aspects, as intelligible in its action as a thing in itself, and as sensible in the effects of that action as an appearance in the world of sense. (A538/B566)

Here and elsewhere in this section, the grammar confirms that the examination of a hypothesis is at stake: Kant uses conditionals. The hypothesis in question is the (real) possibility of the solution-thing/agent having an intelligible aspect endowed with T-freedom while, *qua* appearance, being causally determined. This hypothesis once formulated, Kant unpacks what is contained in the concept of the real possibility being considered here. Thus '[w]e would (. . .) form an empirical and (. . .) an intellectual concept of its causality' (A538/B566) because (i) we are hypothesising that the intelligible aspect of the thing is a first cause, and (ii) this thing is causally effective within the domain of appearances, and is therefore endowed with an empirical causality.

The laws of these causalities are defined as the *intelligible character* and *empirical character* respectively. Note that the solution is general insofar as it makes no reference to rationality: the intelligible character is just the character of an intelligible first cause.[7] Together with the fact that 'object' is used a couple of times to refer to what is the 'subject' of action, i.e. the agent, in the case of the Problem, this confirms that, in presenting what he later describes as a 'silhouette of a solution' (A542/B570), Kant is outlining something that is applicable to both the cosmological problem and the Problem. Nevertheless, for reasons mentioned earlier, the focus of Kant's interest shifts towards the latter, with several references to actions and the subject.

How then is the compatibility of the possibility of a transcendentally free solution-thing/agent and determinism assessed by Kant? Two key statements in this section explain this. The first appears very early on as it requires no proof: '[t]hinking of the faculty of an object of sense in this double sense does not contradict any of the concepts we have to form of appearances and of a possible experience' (A538/B566). Here, no real possibility has yet been considered: all that is at stake is the logical compatibility of two concepts. This result however goes beyond the logical possibility claim of the preamble insofar as the two concepts are determinations of the same solution-thing.

To assess *real* possibility, Kant examines the consequences of the possession of both intelligible and empirical characters *for our actions* (A539-41/B567-9), i.e. at least in the case of the Problem, which Kant focuses upon here. First, the 'actions would have to admit of explanation in accordance with natural laws' (A540/B568), hence the need for the empirical character; but second, for the intelligible character, 'no connection with appearances as causes is encountered in its actions' (A541/B569) since they are caused by the subject *qua* noumenon. The stark contrast Kant accentuates here shows how close to a contradiction we seemingly are in claiming both free will and determinism. Nevertheless, a few lines further, Kant happily concludes, 'Thus freedom and nature, each in its full significance, would both be found in the same actions, simultaneously and without any contradiction, according to whether one compares them with their intelligible or their sensible cause' (A541/B569).

Kant clearly thinks he does not need a proof here. He is indeed directly drawing upon the result from section one of the Resolution, namely upon transcendental idealism. Indeed, Kant has already established the compatibility of the possibility of appearances being caused by some intelligible first cause (T-freedom) while being determined. So, in fact, adding that the first cause and the causal determination are both features of the same solution-thing/agent does not add any special difficulty once it is clear how the dual-aspect nature of idealism enables each of these features to correspond to an aspect of the solution-thing/agent. This means that it is relatively unproblematic for Kant to conclude to (T2), i.e. the compatibility of two such causalities in the solution-thing/agent.

The second section: Two problems

Much as the second section only presents a silhouette of a solution, it still raises some important interpretative issues. In introducing the intelligible character, Kant claims the following:

> For since these appearances, because they are not things in themselves, must be grounded in a transcendental object determining them as mere representations, nothing hinders us from ascribing to this transcendental object, apart from the property through which it appears, also another causality that is not appearance, even though its effect is encountered in appearance. (A 539/ B 567)

The argument in this paragraph draws upon that of the first section insofar as the latter has located the intelligible domain as defining the conceptual space for a causality of freedom. But now, we are considering the hypothesis of an object with two aspects, and the issue is whether the intelligible aspect could be endowed with a causality that is not that of nature and which will, further in the text, be specified as T-freedom.

The first problem is a lack of clarity as to the distinction Kant introduces here: the appearing of the intelligible aspect of an object (here, 'transcendental object') is distinguished from 'another causality'.[8] Insofar as this causality has its effects in appearance, it too 'appears' in some sense since it makes a *contribution* to appearances. Being an appearance is a property any object obviously possesses in idealism, hence Kant's introducing the subject first as an object (A538/B566). As an appearance, this is grounded in an intelligible causality as section one has reminded us. But now, additionally, we want to consider the hypothesis that it has an intelligible aspect through which it is endowed with an intelligible causality – and here Kant refers to a subject, not merely an object – through which it contributes to its appearance-aspect. This question is therefore, first and foremost, specific to the Problem, rather than the cosmological problem.

That is all well and fine, but if we now consider, as I have suggested, that the resolution of the cosmological problem must proceed along similar lines to that of the Problem, we have a difficulty which, Kemp Smith (1979: 513) argued, is fatal for Kant's solution of the Problem. Namely, if T-freedom is to provide the first cause for all appearances, thus bringing completeness to all causal series in appearance, it seems that the conceptual space for a specifically human T-freedom has now vanished. That is, it would seem that if all my actions are, *qua* natural events, grounded in the same T-freedom that brings completeness to any natural series, this apparently leaves me with no ability to exercise my T-freedom as Ertl (1998: 90) also claims.

I think rather that Kant has precisely formulated the sentence in the previous quote to show that there need be no such worry. That is, if the grounding of appearances in reality in-itself is indeed to be understood in terms of the latter being a first cause (a 'cosmological T-freedom') of these appearances to solve the cosmological problem, then it is still true that 'nothing hinders us from ascribing to this transcendental object' (A539/B567), i.e. the agent, the causality of T-freedom. Kemp Smith erroneously seeks the conceptual space for our T-freedom *beyond* that which would be the first cause of all appearances. But if we are endowed with T-freedom, we could *contribute* to these appearances, as Kant himself points out (A539/B567). That is, the solution-thing of the Problem just needs to be interpreted as part of the solution-thing of the cosmological problem.[9]

The second problem is that, in both passages where Kant presents the empirical character (A539/B567 and A540/B568), he stresses that this causality's effects, i.e. the actions, would be connected with other appearances in accordance with 'natural laws' (A539/B567 and A540/B568). Since it is the actions (not just intentions) that are at stake and bearing in mind Kant's reference to 'external appearances' (A539/B567 and A540/B568), Kant is claiming that these actions conform to the constraints of natural causality in outer sense. This, however, raises an immediate worry: Is Kant claiming that rational agents' behaviour is governed by a causality akin to that of any physical object? To clarify this issue, Kant will have to provide more detail about the empirical character in section three.

D. The Resolution: Third section (A542/B570)

An overview of the section

The reason why Kant refers to the previous section as having sketched the 'silhouette of a solution' (A542-58/B520-86), is that while it has established the important compatibility claim (T2), we have no understanding of this compatibility insofar as the real possibility that has been examined has not featured any specification of how intelligible and empirical characters are related. The real possibility which has so far been outlined thus needs to be filled in with an account of this relation, i.e. task (T3) needs to be addressed.

This will provide a metaphysical account as solution to the Problem as formulated in the Third Antinomy. However, the real possibility of T-freedom thereby remains just that, i.e. a possibility. If this solution to the Problem is going to be appealing, Kant must indicate how this possibility could be realised in the human being: this is where Kant will introduce the important connection between free agency and rationality.

Further, Kant's interest in the Problem is essentially connected to the issue of moral responsibility. He will therefore, first, provide some materials towards a psychological account of free will which exhibits how the agent's actions are both free and explained psychologically through the empirical character. This, together with the second problem I flagged in the previous section, will require clarifying how the latter notion is to be understood. Second, Kant exemplifies how we should understand the responsibility that accrues to the agent according to the psychological account by considering the case of a malicious lie. Kant will thus draw directly upon what the metaphysical account has established to shore up the outline of a psychological account.

Kant's introductory paragraph sets out a guide to the structure of this section by indicating that he here considers 'separately the decisive moments on which the solution depends' (A542/B570). This is reflected in occurrences of 'now' ('nun') defining pivotal points in the text. The first part of the text (A542-7/B570-5) is focussed upon the main component missing from the solution's silhouette, task (T3).

The relation between intelligible and empirical characters

While the first couple of paragraphs of section three look like a recapitulation of the results of the preamble and sections one and two, Kant addresses head-on the issue of how intelligible and empirical characters are connected:

> if the effects are appearances, is it also necessary that the causality of their cause, which (namely, the cause) is also appearance, must be solely empirical? Is it not rather possible that although for every effect in appearance there is required a connection with its cause in accordance with laws of empirical causality, this empirical causality itself, without the least interruption of its connection with natural causes, could nevertheless be an effect of a causality that is not empirical, but rather intelligible, i.e., an original action of a cause in regard to appearances, which to that extent is not appearance but in accordance with this faculty intelligible, even though otherwise, as a link in the chain of nature, it must be counted entirely as belonging to the world of sense? (A544/B572)

These rhetorical questions to which the answers are respectively 'no' and 'yes' under the assumption of transcendental idealism, spell out how the hypothesis of T-freedom in an agent could be made compatible with natural causality, namely if the first were the cause of the second.[10] By referring to the causality of a cause, Kant is using the same vocabulary as in the proof of the Thesis. Kant's point is that the question about the cause of the causality of a cause which triggers the regress as described in the Thesis, leaves it open that there be an intelligible *ground of this causality itself* (Kant refers to it as a 'transcendental cause'[11] A546/B574), which would thereby provide a completeness of the causal determination of this cause's effects, i.e. all that follows from this cause's activity. That means that the empirical character would thereby be grounded in the intelligible character, thus bringing completeness of causal determination to all the agent's actions which the empirical character effects. Watkins (2005: 335–6) describes this as a sort of 'grounding thesis' whereby 'personal agents freely choose (. . .) their own natures'.

Now it is true that Kant does not present this grounding of the empirical in the intelligible character in the same way as he presented the rest of the examination of the possibility of T-freedom in section two. There, the modality of conditional necessity (conditional upon the hypothesis of real possibility of T-freedom being true) was reflected in the prevalence of expressions such as 'would have to' in relation to the intelligible and empirical characters (A539-41/B567-9). Here on the contrary, Kant asks whether something (grounding of empirical in intelligible character) might not be possible. But to say that an action is determined by the empirical character is to say that any determination of the action is causally accounted for through the empirical character (together with other laws of nature) according to the Second Analogy.[12] Therefore, if the possibility of T-freedom and determinism are to be compatible, i.e. if the causality of the empirical character is 'not so determining that there is not a causality in our power of choice' (A534/B562), it cannot be through T-freedom *adding* determinacy to what the empirical character contributes (see Chapters 2 and 3). It can only be through T-freedom causing the empirical character. So, while this causal link between intelligible and empirical characters is not immediately found to be part of the concept of the real possibility of T-freedom, it is the only way in which the required compatibility with determinism could be achieved.

We must therefore have a *causa noumenon* grounding a *causa phaenomenon* (A545/B573). The text of the Resolution confirms what was argued for in Chapters 2 and 3, namely that the move to idealism must involve an *altered-law interpretation* of the impacts of free will among appearances.[13]

Application to rational agents (1)

Having, by addressing (T3), thus completed the bare metaphysical account that is the key to the solution to the Problem, Kant now wants to fill in this account so that the real possibility of T-freedom is no longer just an abstract construction but is related to the nature of human beings who are the agents in this account. Kant expresses this by saying of his solution that one has to 'apply this to experience' (A546/B574). And the feature of a human being that Kant singles out as relevant here is that she is *rational*. As a result, Kant will now 'assume it is at least possible that reason *actually* does have causality in regard to appearances' (A548-9/B576-7, my emphasis).[14] What was a mere (real) possibility could be actual if reason has this property[15] and Kant examines the consequences of such an assumption in the light of determinism.

Insofar as the structure of the Resolution is not considered by most commentators, the important fact that the rationality of the agent had not yet been drawn into the picture is overlooked. This suits a methodological reading which seeks to reinterpret all of Kant's references to causality which are most plausibly understood as having metaphysical meaning (e.g. Wood 1984), in terms of the self-conception of a rational agent (e.g. Allison 1990: 49, 2020: 267).

Aside from its exacerbating the problem of accounting for immoral action as we shall see later, this methodological reading is questionable on other grounds (see also Guyer 2022: 375). Allison (2020: 275) accepts that T-freedom represents a 'complement of sufficiency' (from R 5611 AA18: 252) with respect to the empirical conditions in time. Since these are causal determinants, the complement must itself be the missing causal determinant needed for the full causal determination of the action. Allison, however, introduces a volitional account in terms of Kant's Incorporation Thesis (see Chapter 5). That is, Allison uses the agent's understanding of herself in acting freely – here, as taking some incentive for action as sufficient – to make sense of T-freedom (Allison 1990: 51–3).

While Allison insists that this 'taking as' involves spontaneity, what this means is unclear without any metaphysical commitment. What, for instance, does it add to something like Fischer and Ravizza's (1998) reasons-responsive compatibilist claim that the agent must take ownership of the causal mechanism leading to the action (see Chapter 1)? This spontaneity needs to be clarified just as it does in the case of McCann's (1998) contemporary libertarian proposal which seeks to avoid causal claims (see Chapter 3). This conflation of metaphysical and volitional levels of explanation is not accidental, as we shall see again in Chapter 5: it is a key feature of the methodological interpretation which understands metaphysical claims as indicating how the agent conceives of herself. But, as we shall see further, such a self-conception characterises P-freedom, not T-freedom.

The 'appl[ication] to experience' (A546/B574) first involves reminding the reader about what the CPR tells us about rationality, namely that the agent possesses non-sensible cognitive faculties (understanding, reason) and specifically 'pure apperception' (A546-7/B574-5), indicating that rational agents have an intelligible aspect, with the aim of motivating the hypothesis of an agent's being endowed with T-freedom. Reason is singled out as the faculty involved in acting on imperatives (i.e. as practical rationality), which he discusses in the following paragraph.[16]

With the first pivotal occurrence of 'now' (A547-8/B575-6), Kant expands upon the reasons presented in section one for which T-freedom is important for our practice, namely the role the concept of T-freedom plays with respect to P-freedom (see further), thereby introducing the all-important practical dimension of the Problem into the clarification of its solution. The practical focus this introduces will culminate in the discussion of a practical application, the example of the malicious lie at the end of the section (A554-5/B582-3).

This introduction of rationality at this stage of the Resolution and not before has four noteworthy features. First, it is further evidence that Kant is keen for the bare metaphysical account to be applicable to both the cosmological problem and the Problem since it does not appeal to features specific to human agency. Second, it involves a clear conceptual distinction between the causality of T-freedom and the causality of reason. While the latter is introduced to show why the human being might be endowed with T-freedom, these are distinct concepts and we shall see why their identification (e.g. Allison 2020: 262) leads to an interpretative impasse.

Third, the introduction of the causality of reason points to a *positive* content for the theoretical concept of freedom in which T-freedom is given a practical determination as capacity for autonomy (see Chapter 5) while the Resolution had so far focussed upon the *negative* concept of T-freedom (see also CPrR AA05: 42), i.e. independence of external causal determination.

Fourth, with the first reference to an act of willing (A548/B576) which is not further explicated but will involve acting or not on an 'ought' (A548/B576), Kant addresses the volitional account and clearly spells out the *leeway requirement* of free agency. But its occurrence at this point in the text shows that leeway is not what defines free will. Kant privileges *sourcehood*, expressed in terms of the possession of an intelligible character which is a first cause. Leeway is a requirement which arises when considering the human agent who is endowed with reason but not purely rational so that rationality is expressed in terms of imperatives for the agent's will. Kant then states that reason 'presuppos[es] of all such actions [conforming with an 'ought'] that reason could have causality in relation to them' (A548/B576). This is a form of the 'ought implies can' principle,[17] which implies that sourcehood for such actions requires leeway. The structure of Kant's text in the Resolution thus substantiates my claim (Chapter 2) that for Kant, leeway is a condition for sourcehood which is the primary mark of free will.

Insofar as leeway is a condition for sourcehood for Kant, his theory of freedom fulfils an essential condition that characterises it as *source libertarian* (Chapter 3). Now it will be argued that libertarianism is defined as a form of incompatibilism in all standard classifications (Fischer et al. 2014: 3; Griffith 2017: 2) and that therefore, if we want to take this aspect of Kant's theory of freedom as definitive of it as libertarian, then we must also characterise it as incompatibilist; and then we have the problem that he is both a compatibilist and an incompatibilist. Wood (1984: 73) is right that Kant's theory does not fit into 'the customary pigeonholes', but he nevertheless accepts them and is thus logically led to the conclusion that Kant's aim is to show 'the compatibility of compatibilism and incompatibilism' (1984: 74).

This is a valid argument, but it leads to what looks a lot like a logical contradiction, which opens the floodgates to many self-contradicting statements about Kant's theory as we saw in Chapter 2 (e.g. Xie 2009).[18] This means that a premise leading to this conclusion must be rejected. Given that Kant's compatibilism is not in doubt, this has led some to dispute the use of the epithet 'libertarian' to characterise his position (e.g. Scholten 2022).[19] The fact that many nevertheless view Kant as a libertarian of sorts suggests that the problem lies rather in the use of the vocabulary. What has not sufficiently been flagged is that the classification we use, just like van Inwagen's Consequence Argument, has a *default naturalist, or at least (transcendental) realist, premise*. It is therefore not fit for purpose when non-realist theories are considered. Rejecting transcendental realism must therefore also involve rejecting this classification.

I have claimed that source libertarianism (Chapter 3) is essentially characterised by leeway as a condition of sourcehood. It seems that it is because Kant's theory fulfils this criterion that free will theorists like Kane and Pereboom, and Kant scholars like Allison, are inclined to call Kant a libertarian. I therefore take it as more informative to *define libertarianism independently of incompatibilism*; one can then infer that, in a realist setting, a libertarian is an incompatibilist. Taking the essential characteristic of source libertarianism I have just flagged, I therefore claim that Kant is a source libertarian: Ertl (1998: 82) is therefore exactly right when he describes Kant as a *compatibilist libertarian*.

Application to rational agents (2)

Having introduced rational agency into the presentation of his solution (A547-9/B575-7), a second pivotal 'now' announces the point at which the text proceeds with a thorough exploration of what is entailed by the joint possession by a rational agent of intelligible and empirical characters. Although section two tells us that no inconsistency is to be found in such a duality, Kant now sheds light upon what this duality means for the nature of the rational agent's actions. Kant does this by, in effect, 'stop[ping]' (A548/B576) to start afresh an argument for the compatibility of T-freedom and determinism. This involves initially restating the antinomial conflict in its starkest form, now focussing explicitly upon the Problem. This is characterised by a clear asymmetry since we *do* know we are determined but not whether we are free. So in presenting the non-empirical side of the account, all that can be said is that 'perhaps everything that has happened (. . .) ought not to have happened' (A550/B578), i.e. nothing new. What is novel in this application to experience characterising this restarted argument is that Kant adds that we 'believe we have found that the ideas of reason have actually proved their causality' (A550/B578). This is not much, but together with the reference to 'reason in a practical respect' (A550/B578), it is a pointer to Kant's argument in the *Groundwork of the Metaphysics of Morals* (GMM) proof (see chapter 5), where he establishes that this belief functions, for practical purposes, as though it were knowledge.

As opposed to the tentativeness of the language in this depiction ('perhaps', 'believe'), the certainty of determinism on the other hand allows Kant to paint a very striking picture of the practical consequences of our actions being determined by the empirical character. The key claim is that these actions would be 'predict[able] with certainty' (A549-50/B577-8). This is certainly a strong statement which seemingly excludes any role for a free will.

The nature of the empirical character

Before examining it in more detail, we need to have an initial conception it: What kind of law is it? So far in the Resolution, the reader might have assumed that this law governs both occurrences in inner (for intentions) and outer (for physical actions) sense. Kant now makes it clear that what is at stake are the 'effects in the appearance of inner sense' (A551/B579). Further, as Wolfgang Ertl (1998: 145-6) notes, Kant's claim (A549/B577) that an observer could infer the subjective principles upon which the agent acts can be compared with his assigning such a task to empirical psychology (GMM AA04: 427). Consequently, it makes sense to view the empirical character as a psychological law. As to how this gives rise to actions, Kant just notes that the empirical character is that *through which* actions are related to other appearances according to natural laws (e.g. A539/B567; A552/B580). I shall say more about the need for a *physical account* in Chapter 6.

We shall also see in Chapter 6 that this focus upon inner sense is a key strategic feature of Kant's solution to the Problem. But it does raise two immediate issues. First, Kant famously denies the status of science to empirical psychology (MGNS AA04: 471) so that talk of psychological laws is problematic.[20] However, the laws which are excluded by this claim about empirical psychology are, *qua* laws, rules applying *universally* to all agents. While (Chapter 4) the Second Analogy justifies the claim that occurrences are governed by laws, in the case of inner sense, the scope of such a law, i.e. its domain of applicability, would be the particular inner sense in question, i.e. of a particular agent. Collections of such laws for each particular inner sense *do not* constitute universal laws, i.e. a science of empirical psychology.

Second, one might query the very applicability of the Second Analogy to inner sense. Friedman (1992b: 184f) argues that B291 and §15 of the Prolegomena show that the principles of the understanding are only applicable to matter. As Ertl (1998: 68–72) shows, these passages do not have to be interpreted in this way, while Prol. (AA04: 295) clearly states that science should include an investigation of the laws of inner sense phenomena. Recently, Markus Kohl (2014: 317–8n3) has claimed that the temporal locations of events of inner sense (A33–6/B49–52) could, like any other event, only be determined causally. Further, Kant unequivocally refers to the 'necessity of events in time according to the natural law of causality' after indicating 'whether this nature is regarded as an object of inner sense merely in time, or also of outer sense' (CPrR AA05: 97).[21] So clearly, Kant thinks that nothing needs to be added to his argument of the Second Analogy to prove his claims of psychological determinism (A549–50/B577–8), i.e. claims about our representations of inner sense, at least those representing our intentions as related to our beliefs/desires.

But further, we can see why practical rationality requires that the Second Analogy apply to inner sense by examining the nature of the subjective principles defining psychological laws. Kant characterises subjective practical principles (CPrR AA05: 19) as practical rules 'regarded by the subject as valid only for his will' (see also GMM AA04: 421n).[22] The determination of the will is the agent's intending to φ (e.g. Alice's voting for Tweedledum); the agent will take this as appropriate under certain circumstances $\mathbb{C}$ that are valid only for her, hence I rename the intention $\varphi(\mathbb{C})$. These circumstances are defined by the representations the agent has in inner sense (perceptions, sensations, desires, cognitive states, etc.; e.g. Alice's evidence about the state of the economy; her beliefs about monetarism; her desire to see the economy improve). The subjective principle takes the form:

[E] In circumstances $\mathbb{C}$, I shall $\varphi(\mathbb{C})$

Kant's formulation of this *psychological account* of action, as I interpret it, is thus consistent with a belief-desire model (Chapter 1; see Allison 1990: 33–4), since it amounts to claiming that the agent has a desire:

D = to bring about a state-of-affairs $\Phi(\mathbb{C})$

where $\Phi(\mathbb{C})$ is the state-of-affairs brought about by action $\varphi(\mathbb{C})$, and that she acts on the belief:

$B = \varphi(\mathbb{C})$ is the action needed to bring about state-of-affairs $\Phi(\mathbb{C})$ in circumstances $\mathbb{C}$

As in the example of the occurrence of an event of outer sense, e.g. the observation of the ship moving downstream on the river in the Second Analogy (B237/A192 – see Chapter 2), the order of the sequence of representations of reasons (B,D) and intention to $\varphi(\mathbb{C})$ is necessary. The necessity here is not that of empirical succession in outer sense, but of practical rationality as manifested temporally in inner sense. As with the ship in outer sense, this succession must therefore be determined 'in accordance with a [causal] rule' (B240/A195). Hence, the representations in inner sense of our reasons for acting and intentions to act must be governed by causal determinism, i.e. the Second Analogy applies to inner sense.[23]

Are our actions predictable?

With this characterisation of the empirical character in terms of subjective principles, we can now evaluate Kant's claim that the possession of an empirical character entails the predictability of our actions. To predict what the agent will do, means to know the action $\varphi(\mathbb{C})$ he will carry out given all relevant information about present circumstances $\mathbb{C}$. Since the agent acts on subjective principles of type [E], this is only possible, Kant claims, if one knows all such rules, i.e. all the sets of circumstances and accompanying actions $(\mathbb{C}, \varphi(\mathbb{C}))$. And indeed, Kant's predictability claim is a *conditional* one: we could only predict the agent's action 'if we were to investigate all the appearances of his power of choice down to their basis' (A549/B577). The translation 'basis' is ambiguous and could suggest the intelligible ground of these appearances. In fact, the German 'alle Erscheinungen seiner Willkür bis auf den Grund erforschen' means exploring *thoroughly* (*gründlich*) all these appearances: that it cannot mean going *beyond* appearances is confirmed by the next sentence which indicates that only observation is required. Although I think he misinterprets 'Grund', Ertl (1998: 164) usefully notes that Kant uses a subjunctive type 2, which implies the unreality of the condition. And indeed if the proposed investigation involves examining all the agent's appearances throughout her life, this could not be achieved by non-atemporal cognisers prior to that life's termination. I examine the grounds for Kant's claim that *all* appearances need to be investigated in Chapter 6.

Kant makes another claim in characterising the nature of the empirical determinism in question, namely that 'this empirical character itself must be drawn from appearances as effect' (A549/B577). This would seem blatantly to contradict Kant's key claim that the empirical character is causally determined by the intelligible character (A544/B572; A546/B574; A551/B579).[24] To address this worry, first note that the translation is ambiguous insofar as it is not clear what 'effect' refers to. This ambiguity lies in the original German: 'Weil dieser empirische Charakter selbst aus den Erscheinungen als

Wirkung (. . .) gezogen werden muß.' Further, the very idea that empirical causality should be an effect of other appearances conflicts with Kant's understanding of causality as temporally indeterminate ground (Watkins 2005: 296).

In fact, what precedes and follows this problematic passage in the text of the Resolution indicates that it is the appearances that are the effect. In the preceding sentence, Kant explains how 'insofar as in [the] effects [of a certain causality of his reason] in appearance this reason exhibits a rule (. . .) one could (. . .) estimate the subjective principles of his power of choice' (A549/B577). It is the same rule which Kant refers to again just after the problematic clause: 'this empirical character itself must be drawn from appearances as effect, and from the rule which experience provides' (A549/B577). The drawing from appearance is the process of inferring of a causal law from the regularity (rule) displayed in experience (appearances), as in any scientific enquiry into causes (A766/B794; see Ertl 1998: 194–5), which dispels the worry about A549/B577.

The practical perspective

Having shown that the stakes are high by setting up this stark opposition between the possibility of T-freedom and certainty of determinism, at a third pivotal 'now' Kant alters the hypothesis about the causality of reason by assuming that one could say that 'reason has causality in regard to appearances' (A551/B579). In terms of possible worlds, I take this as a move from the previous indefinite factual or counterfactual status of the possible world in which reason has causality, to a definite factual status, i.e. the consideration of a possible world as actual (see Chalmers 1996: 60–2).

Kant argues that such a stance is characteristic of our practice. He expresses this in terms of a regulative role for T-freedom (A554/B582). Much as it seems to be a novel claim in the Resolution, it in fact follows from his characterisation of P-freedom as I show further.

The Antinomy gives rise to no theoretical regulative role for the idea of T-freedom (see A566/B594), unlike the Paralogisms and the Ideal of Pure Reason which are associated with regulative functions, respectively of the ideas of soul and God (A671-3/B699-71): the regulative role of freedom is exclusively practical.[25] As with the other claims about the practical context of freedom , this one is given a proper justification in the *Groundwork of the Metaphysics of Morals* (hereafter GMM) when Kant examines the grounding of morality (see Chapter 5).

In what follows Kant puts the accent upon what enables idealism to provide a solution to the Problem,[26] namely the existence of a first cause that is 'outside the series of appearances' and restates the key claim of the grounding of the empirical in the intelligible character (A552/B580). Kant reconstructs his argument by setting out the contrast between a rational agent being determined and being free: while the agent's action is fully determined by 'series of natural effects' so that 'no given action (. . .) can begin absolutely from itself' (A552/B580), '[i]n regard to the intelligible character (. . .) no before or after applies' so that 'every action (. . .) is the immediate effect of the intelligible character' (A553/B581).[27] We know from section two, that there is compatibility between these two explanatory perspectives on the action, but here

Kant shows what this means practically. The role of reason as cause entails the action's imputability, while the temporal embeddedness in determinism entails that it can be explained in terms of past causal determinants, a contrast Kant then illustrates with an example of malicious lie (A554-6/B582-4) in which a liar's behaviour is both explained in terms of prior causal determinants and imputed to the agent.[28]

Some commentators (e.g. Rosefeldt 2012: 93) argue that in particular in this example, Kant claims that the empirical character is completely empirically determined, on the grounds that, e.g. in the case of the malicious lie (A554–6/B582–4), Kant talks of the 'sources of the person's empirical character' that lie in 'a bad upbringing, bad company (. . .) the wickedness of a natural temper', etc. He appears to be saying that the agent's background (education, influences, etc.) fully explain the empirical character.

The error here, however, is to assume that this provides any completeness of determination. Rather, Kant indicates that '[h]ow much of [the empirical character] is to be ascribed to mere nature and innocent defects of temperament or to its happy constitution (merita fortunae) this no one can discover' (A551/B579n). This clarifies that the intelligible character is not the only cause of the empirical character, and the empirical causes that contribute to it can be subsumed under the notion of 'temperament' so that 'actions are sufficiently (practically) determined by character and temperament' (Refl. 4441 AA17: 548), whereby 'character' here describes what makes the agent morally responsible and so can stand for 'intelligible character'.

Kant concludes that the antinomial conflict is thus resolved (A557/B585) after noting the unknowability of how reason determines our actions (A556/B583). As I hope to have shown, it is by means of a carefully structured argument that the Resolution is achieved.

E. The Resolution: Practical and transcendental freedom

Kant introduces P-freedom in the early part of the first section of the Resolution. It is defined as independence from causal necessitation by 'impulses of sensibility' (A534/B562). Kant further expands upon this notion by saying that P-freedom 'presupposes that although something has not happened, it nevertheless ought to have happened' (A534/B562). So P-freedom can be described as involving abilities (p1) to do otherwise than we are inclined to, and (p2) to act on an 'ought', i.e. on rational determinations so that the claim that an agent has P-freedom presupposes the truth of 'ought implies can' (in some sense). The leeway at stake here is the ability to act on an imperative, not the ability not to act upon it. In the case of moral imperatives, this is the ability to do what is good, as the reasons-responsive theorist Susan Wolf also contends (see Chapter 3).

The problem and some proposed solutions

The issue of the relation between P-freedom and T-freedom is a controversial one in Kant scholarship. Kant indicates that the concept of P-freedom is grounded in T-freedom and that the latter constitutes the 'real moment of the difficulties' of the former (A533/B561). More specifically, Kant shows that, if realism were true, then 'the abolition of transcendental freedom would also simultaneously eliminate all practical freedom' (A534/B562). Kant offers a short proof of this claim which I examine further.

The problem with P-freedom lies in that this strong dependence upon T-freedom contrasts sharply with Kant's claim in the Canon chapter of the CPR. There, Kant claims that the problem of T-freedom 'can [be] set aside as quite indifferent if we are concerned with what is practical' (A 804/ B 832). Moreover, in contrast with Kant's very modest claims in the Resolution about what we can achieve with respect to T-freedom, he says in the Canon that '[w]e thus cognize practical freedom through experience' (A803/B831). Together with the claim that the abolition of T-freedom would eliminate P-freedom, this cognition claim thus seemingly licenses the further claim that we cognise our T-freedom. This is, however, incompatible with the outcome of the Resolution which only shows the permissibility of T-freedom. How can these claims be reconciled?

A typical response to this type of exegetical problem involves appealing to the persistence of pre-critical doctrines during the critical period. That is, P-freedom in the Canon would be a leftover from Kant's earlier compatibilism and, as such, unrelated to libertarian T-freedom (e.g. Kemp Smith 1962: 69–70; Schönecker 2005). As Allison (1990: 56-7) explains, this 'patchwork theory' makes the erroneous assumption that such a compatibilist account of freedom would have suited Kant's ethical theory around the time between his Dissertation (1770) and the first edition of the CPR (1781). Additionally, why did Kant not amend this in the second edition (when his ethical theory was the critical one of the GMM)? There is also strong textual evidence against ascribing such a compatibilist theory of freedom to Kant (e.g. A798/B826) as Kohl shows (2014: 321–3).

Beck (1960: 190) avoids such a patchwork account by claiming that Kant's statements in the Canon should be read as merely indicating that theoretical issues such as the reality of T-freedom are of no relevance to the practical context of the Canon. So when Kant claims that '[p]ractical freedom can be proved through experience' (A802/B830), this is no metaphysical claim about our possessing a certain capacity, but rather a claim about the notion of freedom characterising our practice.

With this proposal, Beck is paying due attention to Kant's clear statement in the Canon (A804/B832) that theoretical issues can be set aside here. But there remains a tension with the Resolution which, on this reading, only deals with theoretical issues. That is, in the Resolution, P-freedom is still understood as a concept that describes a state-of-affairs, namely the 'independence of the power of choice from necessitation by impulses of sensibility' (A534/B562). And on Beck's reading, this is the same as T-freedom although the latter, *qua* first cause, is not just, like P-freedom, an independence of causal *necessitation* but an independence of all causal *determination*.

Beck's account has little to say on this crucial matter. As the Canon explains, it could be that 'that which with respect to sensory impulses is called freedom [is] in turn with regard to higher and more remote efficient causes (...) nature' (A803/B831): this would amount to an independence of necessitation but not of determination. This leads to the worry that the Argument from Manipulation (Pereboom 2014b: 94ff; see

Chapter 1) raises for compatibilism, i.e. whatever theory may seem to account for the agent being the source of her free agency, the agent's situation is akin to that of one manipulated by a cause 'causally upstream' of this putative source, thus robbing the agent of proper sourcehood. Beck could well answer that this is not relevant to the agent's practice, but then how can this be squared with Kant's claim in the Resolution that the 'abolition of transcendental freedom would also simultaneously eliminate all practical freedom' (A534/B562)?

Allison (1990) exploits this distinction between absence of necessitation by sensuous impulses and independence of all causal determination, and connects this with a shift in Kant's ethical theory during the early critical period. Allison thus views the Canon as referring to the earlier weaker 'semi-critical', but still, as he calls it, 'incompatibilist', i.e. meaning rather 'libertarian' (see above) conception of freedom, with the Resolution referring to the later one that is equivalent to T-freedom. Allison (1990: 57–66) plausibly interprets the Canon's account as a form of libertarianism that does not require T-freedom. That is, the agent would be endowed with the limited spontaneity of Sellars's (1974: 21–2) *'practical automaton spirituale'*: the agent could act on imperatives, but only when incentives are available as motivation (e.g. fear of divine retribution as a remote cause for acting morally). This weaker form of libertarianism would be the agent's freedom to pick between inclinations.

But Allison's interpretation must also explain how it is that the Resolution claims that 'the abolition of transcendental freedom would also simultaneously eliminate all practical freedom' (A534/B562). On this issue, Allison argues that this dependence of P-freedom upon T-freedom should be understood conceptually: 'it is necessary to appeal to the transcendental idea of freedom in order to conceive of ourselves as rational (practically free) agents' (Allison 1990: 57), a claim endorsed by Bojanowski (2006: 201f). Markus Kohl (2014: 315 n. 1) disagrees and argues that this does not do justice to Kant's claim about the consequences of 'the abolition of transcendental freedom' (A534/B562). Indeed, Allison's contention seemingly relies upon the kind of insulation of the practical context from the objective (metaphysical) one that Pater Strawson argued for in his compatibilist proposal (Chapter 1) while Kant's claim must be designed to show the error of assuming such an insulation.

A second issue with Allison's (and most other interpreters, such as Schönecker and Kohl) interpretation is that it would appear that the Canon's practical context *does not clearly enable us to decide* between non-libertarian compatibilist and libertarian metaphysical accounts. Indeed, the situation Kant describes in which a relative spontaneity is combined with more remote causal determination could be understood as Allison proposes (weaker libertarianism) but also would, *practically*, be indistinguishable from contemporary compatibilist proposals (see Chapter 1). So, for instance, on Frankfurt's theory, I am not compelled to act on a lower-level desire if a higher-order desire (which corresponds to what I rationally endorse) makes me resist it. This would enable the situation to account for a sufficient sense of independence of causal necessitation by impulses meeting requirement (p1) of P-freedom while, as in Kant's scenario, these higher-order desires are ultimately causally determined. As far as requirement (p2) is concerned, the survey of contemporary compatibilism in Chapter 1 suggests that action on imperatives could, practically, be emulated by action on higher-order desires (Frankfurt), a valuational system (Watson) or policies of practical reasoning (Bratman), and possibly also in terms of the agent's reasons-responsiveness (Fischer and Ravizza). So, when the valuational system, higher-order desires, etc., are in place, practically, it would be as if (p2) were fulfilled.[29] Note that I am not, unlike many commentators (Schönecker 2005: 98; Ameriks 1982: 194–6), claiming that the Canon's text assumes any such compatibilist theories of freedom, but merely that the practical context cannot enable us to decide between such a compatibilist and a libertarian account.

Third, the plausibility of Allison's overall interpretation is questionable. Is it really likely that the CPR, in both the editions of 1781 and 1787, should contain material that relies upon two distinct conceptions of freedom, connected with distinct ethical theories? Given the centrality of the topic of freedom for Kant, and the fact he had written the GMM in 1785, the Canon, which focuses upon the practical context, would surely have been revised in the second edition.

Finally, while it is correct that Kant does not develop a theory of moral motivation or, relatedly, of autonomy in the CPR (Bojanowski 2006: 181ff), the essential features of Kant's critical ethics relevant to the metaphysical account are in fact found in the CPR. The Canon thus clearly upholds Kant's doctrine of the purity of the moral incentive: 'the moral disposition, as a condition, first makes partaking in happiness possible, rather than the prospect of happiness first making possible the moral disposition' (A813/B841).[30]

Recently, Markus Kohl (2014) has proposed to understand P-freedom as a particular type of T-freedom, namely one that involves independence of psychological causes but not necessarily other causes, because of the way he reads the requirement of 'independence of the power of choice from necessitation by *impulses of sensibility*' (A534/B562, my emphasis). This interpretation brings out an important aspect of the relation between practical and transcendental freedom: while the notion of P-freedom refers to something that is also T-freedom, there is an important conceptual space for other instantiations of T-freedom that are not manifested practically, as Kohl (2014: 318) indicates, e.g. God's T-freedom.

In addressing the compatibility between the Resolution and the Canon, Kohl then claims that Kant resorts to a particular type of proof to show that we are practically free. He interprets Kant's claim that our intentions/actions may be determined by 'higher and more remote efficient causes (…) nature' (A803/B831) as referring to the possibility of non-psychological causes affecting the agent. This would mean that the agent's P-freedom is not threatened (no necessitation by 'impulses of sensibility'), but, Kohl argues, he would not possess T-freedom (independence of any causal determination). This is puzzling because it is seemingly inconsistent with his contention that P-freedom is a type of T-freedom.

Kohl (2014: 328) avoids this inconsistency by saying that '[w]e can then read the Canon passage as emphasizing that for *practical purposes* we can assume that we are practically free' (even when not transcendentally free). This does not, however, do justice to Kant's contention that practical freedom *can be proved* (not just assumed) though experience (A802/B830).

What is missing in Kohl's interpretation, I think, is that he does not fully exploit the role of the practical context in which, in the Canon, Kant proves that the agent has P-freedom: this is, as Kohl argues, a practical, not a theoretical, proof. But he overlooks the fact that what is shown, i.e. P-freedom, is itself a practical, not a theoretical, characterisation of freedom. As a result, he has to introduce *a way of understanding P-freedom for practical purposes*. While Kohl recognises that P-freedom characterises us insofar as we are endowed with a will, it is still essentially a theoretical concept for him, describing the kind of freedom possessed by beings endowed with such a will, which leads to the above problem in his reading of the Canon and, as I shall show, in the Resolution. By a practical concept, I mean that which governs the way the agent understands herself in her practice, i.e. the kind of conception Allison's methodological interpretation proposes for T-freedom.

With this corrective, Kohl's interpretation would enable him to claim that the agent in the Canon's hypothetical scenario of determination by more remote causes does not possess T-freedom but has P-freedom *qua* practical concept, which involves the claim that practically, the agent takes herself to be free. I use these ideas to propose an alternative interpretation building upon the above proposals.

An alternative proposal

The starting point for a solution to the problem of compatibility between the Resolution and the Canon must therefore be the explicitly stated practical context of the latter, which Beck correctly places at the heart of his interpretation, rather than any appeal to a 'semi-critical' ethical theory. The concept of P-freedom is therefore directly relevant to the volitional account. However, the claim that the Resolution's context is, by contrast with the Canon, entirely theoretical, is not tenable. The Resolution itself considers the practical context, as is clear from Kant's discussion of the malicious lie (A555/B583) and his description of our practice as involving imperatives (A547/B576).

This practical context is introduced in the Resolution with the notion of P-freedom which, as the text clearly states, is *not a concept of a freedom distinct from T-freedom* but 'the practical concept of' (A534/B561) this freedom in human agents. Indeed, first, it is a concept that is only relevant to practical contexts: the definition of P-freedom (A534/B562) refers unambiguously to how freedom features in our practice for Kant. This is in terms of the ability to act on imperatives (p2) which thereby requires independence from necessitation by inclinations which in turn, practically, is experienced as an ability to do otherwise (p1). Statements about P-freedom are therefore about *how freedom is understood in a practical context*.[31]

That such a context must be at stake here[32] can clearly be seen from the overlooked claim Kant makes immediately after introducing P-freedom: '[t]he human power of choice is an *arbitrium* (...) *liberum*, because (...) in the human being there is a faculty of determining oneself from oneself, independently of necessitation by sensible impulses' (A534/B562). Such a claim that we are not pathologically affected, i.e. are practically free, *cannot be a theoretical claim* .[33] Indeed, combined with the claim in the following paragraph that 'the abolition of transcendental freedom would also simultaneously eliminate all practical freedom' (A534/B562), it would, by contraposition, entail a claim about transcendental freedom's possibility or even actuality,[34] which is stronger than what the whole of the Resolution sets out to show. Therefore, P-freedom refers to the subject's self-understanding *qua* rational agent engaged in practical agency.

Second, that the same freedom is referred to through the practical concept (P-freedom) and the theoretical concept (T-freedom) can be seen from Kant's short proof of the claim that 'the abolition of transcendental freedom would also simultaneously eliminate all practical freedom' (A534/B562). In terms of the contents of the concepts of T-freedom and P-freedom, the proof turns upon Kant claiming (1) that insofar as she is practically free, the agent would, in her practice, understand herself as able to do otherwise (from p1). This is taken to imply that (2) she conceives herself as able to act independently of natural causes which, in turn, is supposed to entail that (3) she conceives herself as endowed with the power to 'begin a series of occurrences entirely from itself' (A534/B562). Now the claim in (2) requires that *áll* natural causes be at stake, if the further inference to (3) is to succeed: this is where Allison and others see a distinction between a weaker conception of freedom involving independence of causal necessitation (P-freedom) and T-freedom which requires independence of all causal determination.

If the imperatives that P-freedom requires we can act upon (p2) are only hypothetical, T-freedom is not obviously required: I can choose to act on the desire to drink another pint according to a hypothetical imperative which tells me I ought to go and order it at the bar, while thereby requiring that some desire be available to act upon.[35] *If*, however, categorical imperatives exist, then the inference from (2) to (3) is valid.[36] Now this assumption is explicitly made when Kant considers our practice in the CPR: 'I assume that there are really pure moral laws (. . .) by appealing (. . .) to the moral judgment of every human being' (A807/B835). This practical context includes what Kant will, in the GMM, refer to as our 'common rational knowledge of morals' (GMM AA04: 392) which includes categorical imperatives. So, while the sense of the concept of P-freedom is that of the notion of freedom characterising our self-understanding *qua* practical beings, when its theoretical implications are unpacked, we find that it must refer to the same freedom as the concept of T-freedom. This is what justifies Kant in talking about freedom defining a 'regulative principle' (A554/B582) of *practical* reason.

The claim that such a libertarian conception of freedom (Chapter 2) is presupposed in our practice is common among contemporary libertarians (e.g. Keil 2018: 18–19). Kant's endorsement of this view (e.g. see Willaschek 2018: 109–10) is reiterated in the GMM (AA04: 448) and goes hand in-hand with his clear rejection of classical compatibilism which he famously refers to as a 'wretched subterfuge' (CPrR: 95–7).[37] While P-freedom *refers* to the same freedom as T-freedom, it is with a different *sense* attached to it, one that characterises *practical contexts*, by which is meant the freedom we take ourselves to enjoy *qua* agents or *qua* moral judgers.[38] This context is relevant to the volitional account of freedom (note the reference to the 'power of choice'), and P-freedom will therefore be at the heart of that account (see Chapter 5).

How do these clarifications of the concept of P-freedom help defuse the tension between the Resolution's claim that the abolition of T-freedom would eliminate P-freedom, and the Canon's claim that theoretical issues are irrelevant to it. To understand this, we first need to interpret exactly what Kant has in mind with the 'abolition' of T-freedom (A534/B562). To do this, note that further in the Resolution, Kant explains that the experience of the 'ought' central to P-freedom 'presuppos[es] (. . .) that reason *could* have causality in relation to' actions on these imperatives (A548/B576, my emphasis). This implies that by 'abolition' of T-freedom Kant has in mind a situation in which T-freedom has been shown to be *impossible*.

Importantly, given the practical context, this 'abolition' can only be relevant if the agent knows it. Further, it could only be from a theoretical demonstration of the (real) impossibility of free will that this 'abolition' is established: no empirical evidence can conclusively prove that there can be no contribution of an agent's freedom to her actions.[39] What Kant has in mind is therefore an *a priori* proof of the impossibility of T-freedom (e.g. because of the truth of transcendental realism). Such knowledge would disturb the agent's practice since he could no longer act on the assumption of freedom except in a fictional sense, in line with what I argued against Peter Strawson's compatibilism (Chapter 1).[40]

This, however, crystallises the Resolution/Canon tension: this need for a revision of our practice apparently contradicts the Canon's claim that we need not be concerned with metaphysical issues in practical contexts (A803/B831). To address this tension, consider a clause that commentators have not paid sufficient heed to at the beginning of Canon's discussion of P-freedom: 'the first thing to note is that for the present I will use the concept of freedom only in a practical sense and set aside *as having been dealt with above*, the transcendental signification of the concept' (A801/B829, my emphasis). First note that by referring to the same concept of freedom with a different 'signification' Kant is indicating, as I have argued, that P-freedom and T-freedom have the same referent but with different senses (see also Bojanowski 2006: 203–4). Second, I have claimed that the Resolution shows there is no contradiction in entertaining the real possibility of T-freedom together with determinism. This will entail that *there cannot be any proof of the impossibility of T-freedom*: since we cannot know anything about the intelligible domain, the only possible proof would be one establishing that there is a contradiction in entertaining the possibility of T-freedom together with determinism, and precisely this is excluded by the Resolution.[41]

This means that the abolition of T-freedom considered in the Resolution is no longer a possible scenario after it, e.g. in the Canon. And indeed this abolition is considered in the Resolution *before* Kant has achieved his aim of showing the compatibility of the possibility of freedom with determinism: after that, it is no longer a concern. This does not mean that T-freedom itself does not remain 'a problem' for reason as Kant reminds us at A802/B830 and A803/B831. But that concerns the theoretical conception of freedom, not what is contained in our self-conception as free agents. So it may well be that we are in error in thinking that we can act on a categorical imperative[42] because some more remote cause always plays a role in determining our action (A803/B831) but that does not alter our self-conception as agent who can so act, which refers, practically, to T-freedom. That is why Kant can state that we 'cognize practical freedom through experience' (A803/B831): it is part and parcel of our practice as rational agents acting on imperatives that we understand the reasons we are acting upon (i.e. our psychological causality which is 'one of the natural causes') as 'a causality of reason in the determination of the will' (A803/B831). The claims of the Canon are therefore not only fully compatible with the Resolution, but reliant upon them.

This therefore enables Kant's conception of P-freedom itself to be rescued from claims of inconsistency within the CPR (Schönecker 2005) because P-freedom always refers to the practical context. Further, P-freedom can also be rescued from claims of inadequacy in comparison with the practical conception of freedom in the GMM (Allison 319ff): as we shall see in Chapter 5, the GMM works with the same concept of P-freedom, the difference being that the normativity of the moral law is no longer taken for granted, but under examination there. This investigation will address not only the existence of a moral law, but also the claim that we are endowed with the kind of power of choice, or will, that Kant assumed in the CPR (GMM AA04: 448–9).

A further consequence of this interpretation is that it shows in what way transcendental idealism is required for our self-conception as agents expressed in P-freedom: it is insofar as it shows that T-freedom is permissible, i.e. not a real impossibility in the light of determinism. This addresses a much-debated issue, namely that of whether transcendental idealism is needed for blameworthiness (see Kohl 2015b; Vilhauer 2004 and forthcoming).[43] On the basis of the Resolution one cannot conclude that the reality of T-freedom is required, but any claim that transcendental idealism is irrelevant (e.g. Scholten 2021a) is exegetically implausible (see Ertl 2024): if the example of the malicious lie is presented in the Resolution, that can only be because what has been achieved there is relevant to it. And that relevance can only be as an account of why one is justified in considering the liar to be blameworthy. Specifically, Kant says that 'blame is grounded on the law of reason, which regards reason as a cause' (A555/B583), and the Resolution has precisely shown that this is a stance that does not conflict with determinism only because of the adoption of transcendental idealism: this ensures that there is no incoherence internal to reason, i.e. between theoretical and practical rationality.

F. The Resolution: Achievements and problems

Achievements

The Resolution has established the following:

- Section one of the Resolution has made the case for the move to transcendental idealism as the only way of solving the Problem, in line with what I contended in Chapters 1 and 3 by considering, respectively, classical/contemporary compatibilism and libertarianism.
- Section two confirms that Kant is solving the Problem by showing that the real possibility of T-freedom is compatible with determinism.
- Section three confirms the contention first made in Chapter 2, that Kant's solution to the Problem must be an altered-law compatibilist theory to address the Consequence Argument.
- Section three confirms that Kant's is a libertarian proposal of the type I proposed at the end of Chapter 3 to address the Infinite Regress Argument, in which the agent's free will grounds her psychological causality.

This provides a fairly complete metaphysical account sufficient to develop a volitional account locating the agent's free will in relation to determinism, i.e. the Homeless Agent problem. Further, it

- addresses the first-person perspective of the volitional account by presenting the notion of P-freedom and its dependence upon T-freedom.
- sketches a psychological account by presenting the empirical character as defined in terms of the agent's subjective principles of action.

These accounts will need to be further filled in to provide a satisfactory solution to the Problem.

Problems

The metaphysical account itself leaves us with two problems that have the same origin: while Kant is a libertarian insofar as he understands sourcehood to require leeway, the leeway presented in the Resolution is not obviously sufficient. Kant has presented it as the ability to have a different intelligible character and thereby cause another empirical character. However:

- in 'applying his solution to experience' the human being's intelligible character has been presented in terms of rationality so that it is unclear how the agent could act otherwise than according to the dictates of reason which, for Kant, define the moral law (categorical imperative);
- the leeway available to the agent of causing another empirical character does not seem to enable him to act otherwise in time since this character is a law that is timeless, so that his behaviour would seem temporally fixed by the determination of this empirical character.

I shall call these issues those of *Moral Leeway* and *Temporal Leeway* respectively. The first problem arises essentially because Kant's solution to the Problem adds a *normative* dimension insofar as it characterises freedom as a capacity to act according to the dictates of reason, i.e. morally. It is important to note that this normative dimension is not forced upon us to solve the Problem: it goes beyond the other features of the Resolution listed earlier which I have argued for in previous chapters. For now, I shall assume that this is a desirable feature of a theory of free will, and I return to this issue in Chapter 7.

This normative dimension involves a claim about the very nature of the Problem. The latter, in its third-person formulation, was defined (Chapter 1) as that of accounting for the coexistence of determinism with the kind of freedom required for moral responsibility. I thus accepted a widely held view that the focus should be on freedom that enables moral imputation. Kant goes further in *defining* freedom in terms of morality, i.e. as an ability to act according to the dictates of reason which are determined by the law of our rationality, i.e. the moral law for Kant (GMM AA04: 458;

CPrR AA05: 30). This clearly makes it difficult to understand how the agent could be said to act freely if her action is immoral, a problem which was raised for Kant by his contemporaries (e.g. Reinhold 1975) and more recently in particular by Michelle Kosch (2006: 43ff; see also Allison 1990: 35ff, 2020: 456ff; Ertl 1998: 149). While some commentators have concluded that, for Kant, immoral action is due to some form of malfunction, and therefore is not imputable (Korsgaard 1996b: 159–87; Wood 1999: 172ff), this is hardly compatible with Kant's claims about imputability, starting with the example of the malicious lie in the Resolution (A555/B 583).[44] This has led other commentators to argue that there may be two distinct notions of freedom in play, freedom *qua* rationality and freedom of choice, as Sidgwick (2005: 185) contends (see Allison 2020: 469ff). This, in turn, is related to Reinhold's (1975) claims that, to make sense of the possibility of evil choices, the spirit of Kant's conception of freedom must be understood in terms of an ability to determine oneself *as good or evil*.[45] Kant, however, rejected the notion of a freedom of choice defined in terms of symmetric leeway (MM AA06: 226), an issue I examine in the next chapter.

Some, e.g. Wood (1984: 81), have attempted to solve the problem by describing evil as 'not a lack of freedom but (. . .) a failure of execution'.[46] As Courtney Fugate (2012: 361) shows, this involves an equivocation on what exactly freedom is, since there is apparently a distinct power to act freely which must, however, also be freedom. Michelle Kosch (2006: 44) agrees that there is a genuine problem in accounting for the possibility of freely acting immorally. Kant addresses it in the *Religion within the Bounds of Reason Alone* and the *Metaphysics of Morals*, not by distinguishing two independent types of freedom, but rather two aspects of the will (*Willkür* and *Wille*) which broadly map onto the two types of freedom Sidgwick proposes.

Whether Kant's strategy is successful is questionable: Reinhold, for instance, argued that it does not address the possibility of a free choice of evil (see Allison 2020: 456–60). This Moral Leeway problem will be addressed in Chapter 5 as part of the task of explaining how the metaphysical account makes it possible to understand our action as the result of the agent's will controlling her action in such a way that he can choose to act morally or not. This will involve filling in the volitional account.

The Temporal Leeway problem is a further feature of the issue flagged in the initial examination of Kant's theory of freedom in Chapter 2, namely that of Timeless Agency. Insofar as there would seem in fact to be only one atemporal act of freedom, i.e. the choice of an agent's character (e.g. Schopenhauer 1960: 26–64; see also Beck 1987), the agent apparently has no alternative possibilities available in time (Pereboom 2006: 551), which appears to make moral change impossible (Indregard 2018: 663). Aside from this absence of leeway that the agent seemingly requires (Chapter 3), his action is apparently predictable, a worry left over from the discussion of predictability in this Chapter: I contended that such predictability would not be possible for a non-atemporal cogniser before the end of the agent's life, but a justification of that claim is outstanding.

The Temporal Leeway problem will be addressed in Chapter 6 where the psychological account is further specified. This will show how, much as the empirical character, *qua* law of nature, is timeless, it is nevertheless possible for the agent to act differently in the future.

The other aspect of the Timeless Agency problem (Chapter 2) was the worry that atemporal noumenal agency does not seem to reflect the way I understand my agency as the pursuit of purposes (in time). I want to conclude this chapter by pointing out that Kant does connect his conception of freedom as causality with that of agency as teleological which at least addresses some of this worry.

G – Intelligible causality of freedom as teleological causality

Freedom can be grasped in teleological terms

When Kant distinguishes the causality of freedom from that of nature (A532/B560), the distinction is between a causality that requires a further cause to account for its activity, and that which is a first cause. In the *Critique of Judgement* (CJ AA05: 372), Kant introduces another distinction, between 'efficient' and 'final' causes. The CPR's causality of nature, i.e. which is thought 'through our mere understanding' (CJ AA05: 372), is of the first type.

Kant notes that the second is found 'in the practical sphere' (CJ AA05: 372) and insofar as we are free,[47] we are the only kind of beings with such 'a causality that is teleological' (CJ AA05: 435). Kant thus points to the fact that P-freedom is teleological. Since it refers to the same freedom as T-freedom, it provides one sense in which we are able to refer to freedom, that which characterises the volitional account. This therefore enables us to connect the intelligible character of the metaphysical account with the pursuit of purposes, which is what was required.

The teleological understanding of freedom

Kant explains that natural causality, which Kant also calls *mechanism*, is characterised by causal explanations of wholes in terms of parts; teleological causality on the other hand proceeds in the reverse direction (CJ AA05: 408–9). A brief examination of why the first proceeds in that way will shed further light upon Kant's understanding of (i) the notion of psychological causality, (ii) the requirement to endorse the explanatory self-sufficiency of willings, and (iii) his account of why we cannot understand the causality of freedom.

The key feature of a mechanism is that the effect is *external* to the mechanical cause, a claim that Kant held throughout his career (e.g. PND AA01: 410; see Watkins 2005: 113–18; 138–40).[48] Causality in outer sense (i.e. in space) thus involves 'bring[ing] about passive determinations in a distinct substance' (Watkins 2005: 296).

While this characterises causality in outer sense in terms of spatial externaltiy (what is physically outside us), psychological causality is a causality of inner sense. Inner sense, for Kant, is the locus of our sensations, representations, intentions, etc., i.e. a broad notion of empirical consciousness. In inner sense, *psychological causality* (whose law is the empirical character) is therefore, similarly to the case of outer sense causality, just a bringing about of determinations (e.g. intentions) at times following the time at which the causality is manifested, i.e. in an interval temporally external to it.

Second, while psychological causal explanations in terms of beliefs/desires thus always refer to the past, teleological explanations are not constrained in this way. A teleological explanation is a type of causality, but one in which the purpose is brought about by its representation (CJ AA05: 180). Since this explanation does not refer to anything external, this amounts to an explanatory self-sufficiency of the pursuit of a purpose: the cause of the purpose is just the representation thereof. Insofar as the causality of freedom is grasped as purposive causality, this suggests that Kant implicitly subscribed or at least should have subscribed to the *explanatory self-sufficiency of willings* (when considered in isolation), which I took as the key to addressing the Infinite Regress Argument in Chapter 2.

Third, it is not just because freedom is located in the merely intelligible unknowable domain of reality in-itself that it cannot be understood. Rather, it is, more fundamentally, because it is not mechanistic: it is grasped merely as a whole-part ('top-down') causality from the agent as cause to the various intentions/actions that are the practical 'parts' of her life. So, even if transcendental idealism ensures the permissibility of T-freedom, there can be no further understanding of the possibility of this causality. Similarly, organisms behave in a way that is grasped teleologically and that we cannot further explicate, however much we understand its mechanistic underpinnings (see Onof and Schulting 2023). When compared to van Inwagen's 'mysterianism' (Chapter 1), the major difference with Kant's claim is, of course, that van Inwagen thinks that freedom is impossible but nevertheless real. Kant's position avoids the quasi-incoherence of this position: the possibility of freedom is compatible with determinism, but this freedom is a causality that we could not understand.

5

Freedom in Kant's practical philosophy

The previous chapter's examination of the text of the Resolution of the Third Antinomy (hereafter 'Resolution') confirmed Kant's compatibilist theory of freedom to be a libertarian one insofar as leeway is required for sourcehood. Further, it is also normative in that freedom is characterised for Kant as the capacity to act morally, i.e. according to the dictates of reason. The conclusion of the Resolution is, however, metaphysically weak in that it only shows the permissibility of transcendental freedom (hereafter 'T-freedom'), i.e. the compatibility of the real possibility of freedom and natural causal determinism (hereafter 'determinism'). This real possibility is that of the agent's grounding his psychological causality.

In the *Critique of Pure Reason* (hereafter 'CPR'), Kant assumed the moral law, which enabled him to make certain claims in the Resolution about our practical conception of the same freedom (hereafter 'P-freedom'). In his practical philosophy, he aims to ground the moral law. In so doing, he will therefore be shoring up these claims about P-freedom and make stronger claims about T-freedom which need to be evaluated carefully. In this and the next chapter, the focus will be upon interpreting Kant's texts: while commenting on the plausibility of Kant's claims, I leave it to Chapter 7 to review what we need to take from Kant's theory of freedom to address the Problem.

In this chapter, an examination of Kant's practical philosophy will enable outstanding questions about the volitional account which Kant addresses through P-freedom in the Resolution to be answered. These are aspects of the problems of Timeless Agency and Moral Leeway. That is, first, while I concluded Chapter 4 by showing that Kant understands an agent's possession of a causality of T-freedom in purposive terms, I shall now show that this can be understood as the pursuit of the various purposes characterising the agent's will (the specifically temporal issue is examined in Chapter 6). And second, while this causality is characterised in terms of a causal power of reason, Kant's theory of freedom does make room for immoral action, but there is an asymmetry in the leeway that is necessary for sourcehood. Aside from these specific problems, this examination of Kant's moral philosophy will, more generally, help enrich the volitional account by showing how Kant develops a *Theory of Choice*.

The chapter is organised as follows: I devote the first part to an overview of what Kant's ethical writings add to the Resolution. This will show in what respect the volitional and metaphysical accounts of free will, as they stand, are not properly integrated.

Moreover, this integration is the key to addressing the Moral Leeway question, and this will involve considering one form of Kant's 'ought implies can' principle. I explain how Kant goes about further infilling what is needed for the volitional and metaphysical accounts and their proper integration. Next, I turn to the *Religion with the Boundaries of Mere Reason* (REL) and the *Metaphysics of Morals* (MM): these texts show how, by providing a *Theory of Choice*, Kant addresses the question of making sense of an agent's willings as manifestation of spontaneity, and thereby address aspects of the Timeless Agency problem. This will provide the necessary evidence to support my interpretation of how the integration of the two accounts is achieved and, thereby, of how to solve the Moral Leeway problem. This interpretation is then applied to understanding degrees of evil and the possibility of a moral conversion.

A. Free will in Kant's ethical writings

The *Groundwork of the Metaphysics of Morals* (GMM)

Given that Kant's central concern with freedom is closely tied up with its being a necessary condition of imputability (e.g. A555/B583), it is to be expected that the topic of free will should loom large in his critical ethical writings. Kant devotes GMM III to grounding the normativity of the moral law and the categorical imperative (CI). To do so, he establishes what Allison (1990: 201–13) calls the *Reciprocity Thesis* (GMM AA04: 446–7) according to which the reality of T-freedom and the normativity of the moral law mutually entail one another. The moral law is what GMM I identified as doing what is unconditionally good because it is unconditionally good, i.e. acting out of duty (GMM: 397) which Kant identifies as acting on the CI (GMM: 401–2; 416).

Because of the Reciprocity Thesis, the strategy Kant follows to prove the bindingness of the moral law consists in finding grounds for showing that human agents are transcendentally free. To this strategy, the first response must surely be one of surprise: the Resolution (note that the second edition of the CPR was published two years after the GMM) makes it clear that no such grounds can be found: one cannot even show the possibility of T-freedom.

However, the GMM's focus is practical and Kant's aim is to show that T-freedom is a *necessary presupposition* of our agency. This is nothing more than the Resolution's claim that freedom has a practical regulative role (A554/B582; Chapter 4), but in the Resolution, moral normativity was *assumed* (Chapter 4; Gardner 1999: 308). The problem Kant faces now is that the grounds for showing this regulative role cannot be the normativity of the moral law: this would involve a *petitio principii* (Allison 2020: 325–6) since, in the GMM, T-freedom is *to provide the ground* for morality; or as Kant points out (GMM AA04: 450), it would mean that we are going round in a circle (see Quarfood 2006: 288). What is needed is a 'third term' (GMM AA04: 447; Ameriks 2003: 174).

The constraints upon the proof of T-freedom as necessary presupposition of our agency are (1) that it cannot be theoretical and (2) that, although practical, it cannot appeal to morality. That is, Kant must find some evidence in our practice that requires this presupposition, irrespective of the moral worth of the actions in question. The problem seems insurmountable (see Bittner 1989) since all we can get from considering action irrespective of moral considerations, i.e. action on hypothetical imperatives, is evidence for the need to presuppose a weaker form of libertarian freedom identified by Allison (1990: 57–66) and discussed in Chapter 4, namely the freedom to choose between inclinations.

Kant's attempt to establish T-freedom as necessary presupposition is generally viewed as a failure (see Allison 2020: 330–1; Bittner 1989: 83–5). The problem is that Kant appeals to our membership of the intelligible world as the required third term, allegedly without providing a satisfactory justification (Henrich 1975: 67; Guyer 2009: 177–8; Ameriks 2003: 174–5). As Allison (2020: 331) explains, even with a deflationary methodological understanding of such a membership, the grounds for it would seem to rest precisely upon the assumption that reason has causality and therefore upon the possession of T-freedom.

I propose that, while Allison (2020: 331) correctly identifies Kant's appeal to a 'generic conception of reason' encompassing theoretical and practical capacities, this move *does* entitle him to some such assumption. What is not sufficiently appreciated by commentators is Kant's ingenious way of meeting requirements (1) and (2). While no *theoretical proof* of T-freedom is possible, I shall argue that a certain type of theoretical activity[1] can provide us with an example of a *practice* (hence fulfilling constraint (1)) which, because of its characteristic features, in line with constraint (2), enables us to take up the intelligible perspective from which we view ourselves as transcendentally free.

As in the Resolution (A546–7/B574–5), Kant appeals to our intelligible nature *qua* rational cognisers. In the Resolution, this merely served the purpose of motivating the hypothesis of the actuality of our being endowed with T-freedom (i.e. a possible world considered as actual – see Chapter 4). Here, Kant wants to make full use of this observation: he claims that the fact that a rational being is endowed with the 'pure spontaneity' of reason implies that there is another standpoint from which he can consider his powers and thereby 'recognise the laws of all his actions'. From this intelligible standpoint, 'man cannot think of the causality of his own will except under the idea of freedom' (GMM AA04: 452).

But what entitles Kant to introduce the causality of an agent's will as one of her powers? Unlike the Resolution, where Kant made use of claims based upon our common pre-philosophical conception of ourselves in our practice (e.g. we are an *arbitrium liberum*, A534/B562), the GMM is in the business of shedding philosophical light upon our common practical conceptions. And indeed, this is why Kant is, at first, only able to derive the weak claim that 'we must ascribe to each being endowed with reason and will, the property of determining himself to action under the idea of freedom' (GMM AA04: 449), where, by will, Kant means a 'consciousness of [one's] causality with respect to actions': this claim just spells out what is implied by the assumption of being endowed with reason and will. It is only after introducing the consideration of the epistemic spontaneity of reason that Kant makes a claim about agents having a causally efficacious will.

While this seems to rest upon unsupported metaphysical claims, Kant is here considering a certain employment of our theoretical/epistemic spontaneity *from a practical point of view*.[2] Kosch (2006: 33) observes that there are reasons for not taking Kant to be claiming that theoretical spontaneity requires T-freedom (e.g. the Paralogisms).[3] But in so doing, she does not consider theoretical activity from the practical point of view, i.e. as goal-directed activity. A significant difference[4] between this passage and the corresponding one introducing epistemic spontaneity in the Resolution (A546–7/D574–5) is that here, Kant's focus is exclusively the spontaneity of reason as it is completely independent of anything sensuous.

As Kant reminds us in the Resolution, 'reason determines the understanding', 'in accordance with' ideas (A547/B575). But the fact that the subject has a faculty that spontaneously regulates the employment of the understanding through ideas is not obviously sufficient to exhibit a role for this subject *qua* agent, i.e. as engaged in voluntary epistemic activity. And Kant is aware that he needs to do more here, hence his prefacing these considerations about reason's spontaneity with more general ones about the common understanding grasping that appearances are grounded in some reality in-itself. This somewhat surprising claim[5] is, however, tempered by the observation that, whatever insights are thereby gained, 'such an understanding soon spoils it by trying to make the invisible again sensuous' (GMM AA04: 452). The negative assessment Kant is led to, that our 'common understanding becomes not in the least wiser' (GMM AA04: 452), defines a *task*. It is in addressing this task that the spontaneity of reason which Kant then introduces can be utilised: it 'shows its chief occupation in distinguishing the world of sense from the world of understanding, thereby prescribing limits to the understanding itself' (GMM AA04: 452). This task is that of *critique* which addresses the common understanding's confusion.

This pursuit of reason has a well-defined *purpose*, i.e. overcoming the error which hampers the common understanding and therefore negatively impacts our common understanding.[6] This is something that it is up to the agent to engage in, and it therefore defines a *practical activity*. The activity of the critique of our cognitive powers is therefore a case in which agency is manifested in the use of the theoretical spontaneity of reason.[7] This activity is primarily intelligible. It is arguably also empirical (in inner sense) since Kant claims that any thinking is always accompanied by what has been termed 'self-affection', i.e. the imagination's determination of inner sense through the figurative synthesis (B154–5),[8] but this is not important for the point made here.

By identifying this intelligible practical activity of reason, Kant creates a standpoint from which the agent can consider herself.[9] From Kant's language from that point onwards in the text, it is clear that he no longer hesitates in talking about the agent's will. This is because even though it is intelligible, the epistemic activity of critique is a *bona fide* activity which therefore involves the agent's will in choosing to engage in it. Insofar as the agent is now considered as endowed with a will at least from the intelligible standpoint, the result established at GMM AA04: 449 can be applied: she must conceive of herself practically from the intelligible standpoint as transcendentally free,[10] and therefore, assuming the Reciprocity Thesis (which I examine later), as autonomous in an intelligible world governed by the moral law. Hence, *qua* sensible beings, we are obligated by the moral law (GMM AA04: 452–4).

The key point in this deduction is therefore the consideration of a type of epistemic activity that characterises subjects as agents from the intelligible standpoint. Although this does not exclude the possibility that we should be *automata spirituale* (Sellars 1974: 81–2; Allison 1990: 65, 2020: 337), i.e. our will should not be able to bring about intentions to act in the outer sensible domain, this is not a problem here because all we need is to have to consider reason to be practical at the intelligible level.

The GMM and the CPrR

The details of Kant's full derivation of the moral law in GMM need not detain us here. It is enough to point out that *assuming the Reciprocity Thesis*, Kant can claim that, as agents having to conceive ourselves as transcendentally free, we 'transport ourselves into the intelligible world (. . .) and know the autonomy of the will together with its consequence, morality' (GMM 453):[11] Kant has thus provided a grounding for the *practical regulative role of T-freedom* proposed in the Resolution (Chapter 4), which no longer relies upon the merely hypothetical status of the moral assumptions in the CPR. He can conclude that we are 'really free in a practical respect' (GMM 448) i.e. *practically free*.[12]

Why then did Kant resort to a different approach to grounding the moral law in the CPrR? The standard view is that he was dissatisfied with the GMM proof although this is a controversial issue (see Allen Wood 1999: 174ff). First, some consider the GMM proof too weak as it only shows freedom to be a necessary presupposition of our practice (Allison 2020: 329–30). If freedom and moral normativity are reciprocally related as the Reciprocity Thesis claims, then the bindingness of the moral law is also such a presupposition: this means that in acting *we have to take it* that the moral law is binding.

On a methodological interpretation of transcendental idealism, it is, however, unclear why there could be anything more to being free than our having to conceive ourselves as such when engaged in practical activity (see Onof 2021b): a consistent methodological interpreter is not able to explain how Kant could make a stronger claim than that in the GMM. On a metaphysical interpretation, there is obviously a further step involved in showing that we are actually free. This is moreover required for imputability.

Second, the GMM proof perhaps does not meet the requirements Kant set out for himself in writing the GMM, namely that this work is capable of 'adaptation to common understanding' (GMM AA04: 391) since clearly the common understanding, as we saw, is confused about what lies behind appearances. Specifically, Kant might be thought to want a proof that does not rely upon the metaphysics of transcendental idealism.

To address these issues Kant adopts a simple strategy in the CPrR, namely that of arguing that one of the terms of the circle identified in the GMM derivation, the bindingness of the moral law, is a 'brute fact' characterising rational agency. This is the Fact of Reason (CPrR AA05: 31–2). That is, rather than conclude that we have to presuppose that we are free *and therefore* have to presuppose that we are bound by the moral law, Kant cuts out the middleman: it is a fact about practical rationality that the moral law is binding. As Willaschek (1992: 174–93) and Franks (2005: 260–336) explain, Kant claims that the authority of the moral law manifests itself in our practical reasoning. This is the consciousness that forms the content of the deed ('Tat') that is the Fact of Reason.

And with this, Kant takes himself now to have shown *the reality of T-freedom*, but in a practical sense. That is, we know a fact, that we are transcendentally free (CPrR AA05: 33)[13] although we cannot understand it, since such understanding is beyond the powers of our theoretical faculties (CPrR AA05: 94). This claim might seem to be equivalent to that of the GMM proof, i.e. we are 'really free in a practical respect' (GMM 448). However, in the CPrR Kant is addressing the issue, not of how we should think of ourselves in a practical context (P-freedom) but how the practical context gives us access to a theoretical truth about freedom, hence T-freedom is at stake (see also Hogan 2021: 424 and n. 72).

Kant thus introduces a notion of *practical cognition* as alternative to our theoretical access to reality and thereby delivers a stronger result than the GMM proof. This stronger result is possible because Kant can now, on practical grounds, exclude the possibility of our being '*automata spirituale*' (see above) or even '*practical automata spirituale*' (whose reason is practical but whose agency requires an external stimulus – see Chapter 4) insofar as the Fact of Reason establishes that *pure* reason is practical (see Allison 2020: 362).

This understanding of the achievement of the CPrR has been challenged by Willaschek (2018: 113–15), who claims that all that has been shown is that the concept of T-freedom has received some objective reality. But otherwise, the epistemic relation to it is, as for all Postulates of Practical Reason, belief. Without going into the details of the motivation for Willaschek's investigation (see Onof 2019a), in support of his view,[14] he first seeks to extend a distinction in theoretical philosophy between cognition and knowledge (Willaschek and Watkins 2020) to the practical domain though these authors indicate that this is a complex issue (Willaschek and Watkins 2020: 3196n.6). He draws upon the fact that the Jäsche Logik's (Jäsche AA09: 66) characterisation of knowledge is in terms of a 'kind of *assent* that requires *consciousness of epistemic warrant*' (Willaschek 2018: 114), while cognition is a representation and does not involve such consciousness. What this removes is the knowledge relation to a justified truth. That we should not have access to any warrant in the case of practical cognition is unsurprising though: the Fact of Reason is a given feature of our consciousness.[15] What Willaschek wants to claim is that cognition gives no access to a truth.

But from the fact that this is not knowledge of a truth, it does not follow that what is represented in cognition does not have to be a truth. And indeed, in theoretical cognition, the cognition of an object gives access to a true representation of this object, so there are grounds for thinking the same should be true of practical cognition.[16]

Further, Willaschek contrasts the reality of T-freedom that Kant establishes with its actuality which, Willaschek claims, has not been shown. While Willaschek's point about Kant's distinction between reality and actuality is well taken, what does he mean by the actuality of freedom? In the practical context at stake, the modal category of actuality would seem to have to apply to judgements about the objects, and these practical objects are actions (CPrR, AA 5: 104). But Kant does not claim to have shown the actuality of any free action.

Willaschek rather wants to drive a wedge between the actuality and reality *of freedom as capacity*. But the actuality of this capacity is just the (real) possibility of an agent acting freely, which is just what the reality of freedom is. In the same way, the actuality of the electromagnetic force is just the (real) possibility of electromagnetic causal effects. Just as it would be wrong to say that the latter possibility is merely the (real) possibility of (the existence of) the electromagnetic force, there are no grounds for Willaschek's implicitly equating the (real) possibility of an agent acting freely, with the mere (real) possibility of (the existence of) freedom.

In fact, Kant makes clear that the actuality of freedom is at stake in claiming 'that unconditional causality and its faculty, freedom, [. . .] are determinately and *assertorically* known' (CPrR AA5: 105, my emphasis): *pace* Willaschek (2018: 114–16), this is not a matter of mere possibility. Finally, note that, while P-freedom suffices for the moral law to be binding for our practice, the mere possibility of T-freedom would be insufficient for the objectivity of imputability.

The *Critique of Practical Reason* and the Problem

In the Elucidation of the Analytic (CPrR), having established the reality of T-freedom, Kant returns to the Problem (CPrR AA05: 94–100) to rebut those 'who believe they can explain (. . .) freedom with empirical principles' and 'to expose empiricism in its naked superficiality' (CPrR AA05: 94). As in the Resolution, Kant first shows that transcendental realism would not be able to solve the Problem, but here, explicitly stressing the key role of time: if the whole of reality were in time, causal determinism would mean that what happens next is 'predetermined' (CPrR AA05: 95). In arguing this, Kant first appeals to the fact that 'the past is no longer in my power' (CPrR AA05: 94), a key assumption of van Inwagen's Consequence Argument. Then he shows that it is not determination by outer causes that is the problem but the very temporality of reality, as I claimed in Chapter 3, in constructing a response to the Infinite Regress Argument: 'if I assumed my entire existence were independent of any external cause (. . .) I still stand under the necessity of being determined to act by what is not in my power' (CPrR AA05: 95), i.e. the past. Further, he summarises the spirit of the Luck Arguments against contemporary libertarians (Chapter 3) and the need to move outside the order of time by indicating that for 'a being whose existence is determined in time, (. . .) an exception' to the 'law of natural necessity (. . .) would be equivalent to delivering this being to blind chance' (CPrR AA05: 95). With transcendental idealism, Kant explains that, to save freedom, we must consider the possibility of a thing that is determinable in time as appearance, also being free *qua* thing in-itself (CPrR AA05: 95), i.e. the *solution-thing* (Chapter 4) at the core of the hypothesis of section two of the Resolution.

Kant then turns to compatibilist approaches to the Problem and their 'comparative concept of freedom' (CPrR AA05: 96), which ascribes freedom to anything as long as 'the determining natural cause is internal to the acting thing' (CPrR AA05: 96). This general description addresses traditional compatibilism (e.g. Hume, Leibniz and the pre-critical Kant), but Kant would thereby also be in a position to attack contemporary forms of compatibilism examined in Chapter 1. Indeed, for instance, mesh theories amount to identifying certain features of an agent (higher-order desires, evaluation system, policies of practical reasoning) which can be taken as essential characteristics of this agent so that their role in bringing about action by controlling agency is precisely an instance of an internal cause driving this entity's deterministic development. The same goes for the mechanism characterising the reasons-responsive approach. Kant calls this 'the freedom of a turnspit' (CPrR AA05: 97) and famously describes these strategies which try and pass off a notion of 'psychological freedom' for the real thing (T-freedom) as a 'wretched subterfuge' (CPrR AA05: 95–6).

Kant next turns to what he has achieved in sections two and three of the Resolution. In line with what we saw in Chapter 4, he emphasises that once transcendental idealism is in place, the key to the resolution of the Problem lies in the fact that the agent 'creates' his 'character' through 'his causality as a noumenon' (CPrR AA05: 97–8). He also echoes what he wrote in section three of the Resolution to explain how our actions would be predictable, were the empirical character to be known down to its very basis (CPrR AA05: 99). This is then immediately contrasted with the intelligible point of view from which they are free, a contrast he illustrates by an example of sorts, much as in the Resolution.

In this passage (CPrR AA05: 98–9), we have an amendment to the vocabulary of the Resolution. What Kant refers to there as the agent's empirical character is here described as a 'phenomenon of his character' or 'appearances of character' (CPrR AA05: 98–9). This amounts to a short version of the intelligible grounding of the empirical character which is at the heart of the Resolution (Chapter 4). The account Kant formulated in the Resolution, which, as I explained in Chapter 4, spelled out what was required by the assumption of the possibility of T-freedom in conjunction with determinism, is now taken, on practical grounds (because of the Fact of Reason), as a truth entailed by that of the reality of T-freedom. It would therefore be mistaken, as Wood (2008: 137) contends, to describe this account of intelligible grounding of the empirical character of the Resolution, as a mere story.

It is interesting to note that there is no use of the word 'intelligible' to describe this character. Relatedly, Kant introduces a reference to the agent's *disposition* (*Gesinnung*), of which the character's appearance (the empirical character) is the appearance (CPrRAA05:98-9). This could also be thought to refer to the intelligible character, and this is indeed what is standardly assumed in the literature (e.g. Allison 2020: 402). Loosely speaking, this identification is warranted. After all, Kant does refer once to the empirical character as the appearance of the intelligible one in the Resolution (A541/B569), and since here the empirical character is described as appearance of the *Gesinnung*, there are grounds for making such an identification and indeed of extending it to include the notion of 'character'.

However, I shall resist any such a straightforward identification because the account that Kant is sketching here has a different emphasis: the notion of '*Gesinnung*' is novel and the use of 'character' here is different from that in the Resolution. There, 'character' was defined as a 'law of (. . .) causality' (A539/B567). By contrast, in the CPrR, Kant appeals directly to a practical understanding of character and *Gesinnung*, one found in a Reflexion from the 1770s. He there describes it as what is explained by the 'special cause' that is describable as freedom. Importantly, he distinguishes it from 'temperament', since the first is explained by 'freedom' as a cause 'of intelligence' and the second by 'the influence of sensibility' (Refl. 4441 AA17: 548). Allison (2020: 202) interprets the acquisition of character as the adoption of 'ends and values' by the agent. Thus, 'character' is apparently here connected with *choice(s)*, while temperament is not.

However, Allison (2020: 402) denies that agents could be responsible for their character. This is puzzling in the light of the requirement of imputability of the character (as opposed to the temperament). What leads Allison to deny this is the worry that choosing one's intelligible character would amount to 'a choice without a chooser' (2020: 402). I think that Allison is right to make this point: the intelligible character is not chosen, but having an intelligible character is what characterises the making of certain choices. But if *Gesinnung* has to be chosen by the agent for the sake of imputation (more on this further) while, as Allison correctly argues, the intelligible character cannot be, the *Gesinnung* cannot straightforwardly be identified with the intelligible character.

The implication is that Kant is filling in the *volitional account* he provided in the Resolution, which means showing how to reconcile a voluntaristic account in terms of the choice of *Gesinnung* with a deterministic one. While the Resolution indicated that agents act on 'oughts', the CPrR is drawing the reader's attention to what this means for the individual agent's choices. Since the Fact of Reason has established that there is one CI valid for all agents, this leaves it open (i) to what extent the agent acts on it and, (ii) when acting on a hypothetical imperative, i.e. an imperative of skill or of prudence (GMM: 414–15), *which ones* she acts upon. The *Gesinnung*, for Kant, refers to 'the disposition which is of concern to the moral law' (CPrR AA05: 99): it therefore characterises the agent with respect to the first issue.[17]

The examination of the text of the REL will provide further evidence for this understanding of '*Gesinnung*'. For now, what this focus upon the volitional account brings to the fore is the Moral Leeway problem. Indeed, the further infilling of the volitional account would seem to allow for any type of choice, so that an evil *Gesinnung* is possible. However, the metaphysical account of the Resolution left us with an explanatory gap with respect to immoral actions.

So addressing the Moral Leeway problem must involve reconciling the metaphysical and volitional accounts of free agency. Since this problem looms large in theology, it is not surprising to find that the issue is only addressed explicitly in the REL text. Insofar as this is also a question that is both metaphysical and practical, Kant's MM also has relevant textual material. Before examining these sources, there is further textual evidence in the Resolution, the GMM and the CPrR of what is needed for this reconciliation.

B. Reconciling volitional and metaphysical accounts (1): Further evidence from CPR, GMM and CPrR

Textual evidence from the Resolution

The practical importance of the Problem led Kant, in the third section of the Resolution, to consider what had so far been described simply as the hypothesis of an intelligible first cause, to be specified as the hypothesis of a causality of reason (A547/B575). As indicated in Chapter 4, most commentators overlook the fact that the focus upon the causality of reason only happens ten pages into the Resolution and straightforwardly identify the intelligible character with the law of the causality of reason.

But the textual evidence for such an identification is problematic. Indeed, once Kant has introduced the causality of reason, he only refers to the intelligible character four pages later. Crucially, when he does, he refers to '[t]he causality of reason *in* the intelligible character' (A551/B579, my emphasis). This does not suggest a straightforward identification.

Further, consider the way Kant concludes his interpretation of the example of the malicious lie in the Resolution. After pointing out that reason could act on its own without any other causes, he judges the case of the lie as one in which 'the action is ascribed to the agent's intelligible character (. . .); hence reason, regardless of all empirical conditions of the deed, is fully free, and this deed is to be attributed entirely to its failure to act' (A555/B583). While the action is ascribed to the intelligible character, in line with the hypothesis Kant examines in sections two and three of the Resolution, reason is accused of failing to act.[18] So the intelligible character cannot just be the causality of reason, otherwise, it would be a causality that simultaneously brings about the action and fails to act (in some sense).[19] It is because these issues have been overlooked that many commentators have claimed that Kant's accounts in the Resolution and CPrR are unable to solve the Moral Leeway problem (e.g. Kosch 2006: 9; Guyer 2009: 186–9).

Now it is certainly not the case that the distinction I am drawing attention to between the intelligible character and the causality of reason implies that only the first, and not the second, was causally active in bringing about the malicious lie. Indeed, the further explanation Kant provides clarifies this: 'reason, is present to all the actions of human beings in all conditions of time, and is one and the same' (A556/B584). So the question posed by immoral action is rather 'Why has [reason] not determined appearances *otherwise* through its causality?' (A556/B584, my emphasis): this is reason's 'failure to act' (A555/B583).

This clarification suggests an important distinction between reason as one *and the same* for all rational agents and reason *as it is used* by a particular agent. A role for the agent in using the spontaneity of reason was already identified earlier in her involvement in the theoretical activity of critique. But further, there are systematic grounds for thinking that this distinction will shed light on the relation between the intelligible character and the causality of reason. Indeed, now that in the CPrR, the Fact of Reason has identified the law of the causality of reason with the moral law, if the intelligible character were the law of the causality of reason, this character would be the moral law. Aside from, again, the impossibility of accounting for immoral action, it would mean that there is nothing distinguishing the intelligible characters of different agents.

It would therefore not be an agent's character but one shared with all rational beings. Since the intelligible character defines the intelligible cause of the agent's free actions and reason is always involved, it is if and only if we take this character to be *the law of the agent's use of the causality of reason* that this problem is avoided. Aside from its being compatible with Kant's referring to '[t]he causality of reason *in* the intelligible character' (A551/B579, my emphasis), it follows directly from a statement Kant makes in a Reflexion: 'Freedom is the determinability of the power [of choice] through mere reason (. . .) the *use* of reason is itself freedom' (Refl. 5613 AA18: 254, my emphasis). Since the law of the causality of freedom is the intelligible character, this entails that this character is the law of the agent's use of (the causality of) reason. The GMM and CPrR will provide further support for this interpretation.

Textual evidence from the GMM

Insofar as it deals with practical philosophy, the GMM contributes to the volitional account by introducing the will.[20] This is characterised as 'a kind of causality [*eine Art von Causalität*] of living beings so far as they are rational' (GMM AA04: 445–6). The concept of freedom is then introduced here, not itself as a causality but as 'that property of this causality [i.e. the will,] by which it can be effective independently of foreign causes determining it' (GMM AA04: 446). This is an important alteration from Kant's definition in the Resolution of freedom as a causality. But insofar as Kant is addressing the volitional account here, while the Resolution's definition was relevant to the metaphysical account, there is no incompatibility in describing what is, metaphysically speaking, a causality, as a property of the will in volitional terms. The question which Kant turns to next, is that of shedding light upon the causality of this freedom from a practical (volitional) perspective, with the aim of making the connection between freedom and morality which, in this section of the GMM, will ground the moral law (in the sense discussed previously).

While freedom (T-freedom) is here introduced in *negative* terms, i.e. independence of foreign causes determining it, Kant tells us that a 'positive concept of freedom flows from it' (GMM AA04: 446). This *positive* concept is, according to Kant, what reveals the true essence of freedom. Kant then claims that, since the causality of the free will must have a law, the question of the nature of that law arises. Kant asks, apparently rhetorically, what else could then the law of freedom be but the law of a cause that determines itself, i.e. the law of *autonomy*? This law is the moral law since the principle of autonomy is one formulation of the CI (GMM AA04: 446–7). At this point, we apparently have an identification of freedom with autonomy, but, mystifyingly, Kant then announces that 'the proposition that the will is a law to itself in all its actions', however, only expresses the principle *that we ought to act* from the CI (GMM AA04: 447).[21] This result defines a key connection between morality and freedom which forms part of the Reciprocity Thesis (Allison 1990: 202ff, 2020: 312–14).

What is puzzling is the apparent slide from a *descriptive* understanding of the law of freedom to a *prescriptive* one (see Kosch 2006: 50) that amounts to an equivocation over how this law is to be understood. Only through this equivocation is it possible for Kant to conclude to the bindingness of the moral law for a free will. Kosch settles for a descriptive understanding of autonomy, one that describes the 'operation [of rational beings] only under ideal circumstances (the frictionless plane of intelligible agency)' (Kosch 2006: 50). While it is not entirely clear what is meant by the parenthetical clause since the locus of T-freedom is in the intelligible domain anyway, these ideal circumstances presumably correspond to what is prescribed by the moral law, so that Kosch's solution is in effect to suggest presenting what Kant claims is prescriptive, as descriptive under certain ideal circumstances. She concludes that a proper prescriptive result applying to all circumstances is not derivable from Kant's argument.

Allison's (1990: 94–9) solution to the conundrum is to propose a notion of autonomy that is 'morally neutral' (and *descriptive*)[22] in one sense (as property of the will) and, at a deeper level, not morally neutral as only the moral law 'gives it any standing', so that there is a deeper *prescriptive* dimension. This is justified by Allison's viewing autonomy more generally as involved in our giving ourselves our own 'maxims' of action, together with the possibility (and moral requirement) that this be independent of any other causal influence. The 'standing' that this notion of autonomy would receive from the moral law is, for Allison (1990: 202–7, 2020: 315–17), grounded in the requirement for justification of any choice made by a transcendentally free agent: ultimately, he claims, it is only through unconditional justification that such a requirement can be met, and this must amount to reason's giving itself the law. Is this the only way of satisfying the requirement for justification (see Onof 2009b) and is there such a requirement anyway?[23]

My purpose here is not to address all the exegetical problems this passage raises or to examine thoroughly the validity of the Reciprocity Thesis but just to take from the text what is useful to inform the understanding of freedom. I start with three observations. First, Kant clearly characterises freedom at the outset as a causality through which the will 'can be effective independently of foreign causes determining it' (GMM AA04: 446); this contrasts with the causality of natural causes whose efficiency is determined by other causes. But when he then asks whether the causality of freedom could be anything else than one which is a law to itself (GMM AA04: 447), this seemingly ignores the intermediate option of a causality that is not *determined* by foreign causes, but nevertheless *may draw upon* other causes in the way, for instance, that a skipper draws upon the wind by trimming his sail.

Second, when Kant asks 'What else, then, can the freedom of the will be but autonomy' (GMM AA04: 447), is this really a rhetorical question? The previous remark suggests not taking it as such but as claiming that *we are only able to understand the freedom of the will as autonomy*. Insofar as Kant has not yet, in his moral works, provided an account of how free action could be immoral, it is plausible to assume that he takes it that immoral actions are incomprehensible.[24]

Third, while the positive conception of freedom has the same referent as T-freedom, the richer content it defines suggests that it is perhaps not through a mere description of T-freedom that it refers.

These three observations lead to the following interpretation of GMM: 445–7. There is a type of freedom whose law is that of autonomy, i.e. the moral law for Kant, the concept of which captures what is *essential* about T-freedom. This is, for Kant (at least at the time of writing the GMM), the only concept of freedom whose law we can make sense of. Because it captures what is essential about T-freedom, it is prescriptive for agents who are transcendentally free. An agent's T-freedom can, however, involve foreign causes when the agent does not act autonomously.

This interpretation agrees with Allison's emphasis upon a deeper aspect of freedom that is revealed by autonomy, as well as with Kosch's idea that the freedom in question corresponds to some ideal. But while Kosch's response is to plump for a descriptive understanding of autonomy (of a rational agent 'under ideal circumstances'), and Allison analogously privileges the morally neutral version of the notion of autonomy with the prescriptive dimension arising from an explanatory requirement, I argue that we should take the claim that the law of freedom is autonomy, i.e. the moral law, as inherently *prescriptive*, i.e. what is at stake in this claim is not what T-freedom *is* but what T-freedom *ought to be*. This prescriptive nature of autonomy is, after all, that which Kant introduces in GMM II. It defines a form of the CI, i.e. the principle of autonomy which Kant describes as the 'supreme principle of morality' (GMM: 440) and as such spells out how one *ought to* act if the moral law is binding. T-freedom is then characterised essentially as the will's *capacity for autonomy*.[25] This corroborates a conclusion from Chapter 4, i.e. the claim that freedom is defined normatively as capacity to do the good, and adds a characterisation of the latter as autonomy.

While the law of an autonomous (good) will is the moral law, we do not know what the law of the will *qua* causality is in general (including when it acts heteronomously). That is, we have no insights into the *descriptive* law of such a will. We can, however, connect the volitional account which Kant presents in GMM III in terms of the will, with the previous section's further development of the metaphysical account in terms of the intelligible character being the law of the agent's use of the causality of reason. Since the agent's will is essentially characterised through its capacity for autonomy, and since the law of the causality of reason is the moral law, the two accounts are compatible if and only if *we take the intelligible character to correspond to the (descriptive) law of the will*. This is the law of the agent's use of that causality through which she *can* be autonomous, i.e. of the causality of reason whose law is the prescriptive moral law. This identification means that Kant's volitional account of freedom meshes with the metaphysical one, insofar as the distinction between the causality of reason and the capacity to use the causality of reason is here mirrored in the distinction between the prescriptive moral law that the autonomous agent gives herself and the descriptive law of her agency.

In terms of leeway, the normativity of autonomy accounts for an important asymmetry:

> the faculty [*Vermögen*] for actively willing the known good that is in our power is freedom, but the faculty for willing the known evil the hindrance of which is within our power does not belong equally necessarily to freedom. (R 3868 AA17: 318, see Allison 2020: 465)

This asymmetry[26] echoes Susan Wolf's claim of an asymmetric 'leeway' in her account of free will (Chapter 3). But unlike Wolf, Kant is not claiming that there should only be leeway to do what is right/good. Rather, he refers to different types of necessity. Similarly, he also refers to the ability to deviate from the moral law as an 'incapacity' (e.g. REL AA06: 29).[27] Let us clarify the different modalities at stake here.

The normativity of freedom, which is defined as a faculty to act autonomously (morally), implies that it is essential to freedom that there be leeway to intend to act morally (here I do not consider the physical action). Consequently, the latter necessity could be taken as logical since freedom is defined as the capacity to act autonomously (see Timmermann 2003: 45–65). Kohl (2015b: 705) has provided a careful evaluation of the necessity of this form of 'ought implies can' principle: it is the requirement that our 'volitional powers' are suited to the 'normative demands' that arise from our 'self-legislation' (2015: 705). This would make it a requirement of internal consistency of the will whose legislative and executive powers must be attuned in such a way that the latter can implement what the former necessarily dictates because of its rational nature. This necessity could then better be described in terms of what is logically necessitated by having a self-legislating will.

Kant says little about why there should also be leeway in the other direction. In the REL, Kant takes as a given 'the possibility of the maxims'[28] deviating from the moral law' (REL AA06: 29). One reason is therefore the empirical evidence of human moral transgressions (MM AA06: 226). Such immoral actions would not qualify as free without such leeway, so that the agent would not be responsible for them. The modality at stake for such leeway would then be empirical.

I think, however, that this leeway is best seen as part of a symmetric leeway that is not connected to the morally normative aspect of freedom.[29] As I argued in Chapter 3, the control required for ascriptions of responsibility must be regulative control, which requires the ability to do otherwise. Kant is committed to this principle as a libertarian: his rejection of the 'psychological freedom' of the 'turnspit' (CPrR AA05: 97) is a rejection of any attempt to define freedom without the required kind of regulative control. He thus indicates that we possess 'the capacity for *doing or refraining from doing what one pleases*' (REL AA06 MM: 213).

The reference to inclinations here is important because it indicates that the agent's humanity is now essential. To understand the kind of modality this defines, it is useful to note that what Kant adds to this general libertarian stance is that freedom is a rational power. Acting on inclinations is acting on hypothetical imperatives (otherwise it is not free action). Freedom is then only possible if the human agent has the leeway to act in a way which a hypothetical imperative determines as required to further whatever purpose she pursues: if this is to be true for any possible purpose, symmetric leeway must be available. This seems to be the leeway that Kant alludes to when, in the Resolution, he refers to the imperatives (not specifically moral) agents act upon and says that an "ought" expresses a possible action'[30] (A547/B575). Although Kohl's (2015b) focus is upon moral imperatives, the requirement that our volitional powers be suited to our legislative ones can be extended to non-moral imperatives, i.e. imperatives of prudence which all human agents endorse, or various hypothetical imperatives of skill which individual agents endorse. The necessity at stake here is that of what is logically required for having a human will at all.

So we have two practical modalities in play here: a symmetric leeway is required insofar as I am endowed with a human will, while asymmetric leeway is necessary for the will of any rational being's self-legislation. The latter necessity is more fundamental to freedom since it is defined as capacity for autonomy, hence Kant's claim in the above citation (R 3868 AA17: 318).

From my interpretation of GMM III (445–7), Kant in the 1780s does not think that we can make sense of the law of a heteronomous will, so it is only by looking at later works, namely the REL and MM, that we might find material to understand this law and thereby provide a full response to the Moral Leeway problem.[31] But first, one more piece of textual evidence from the CPrR needs to be examined for its relevance to the interpretation of the intelligible character as law of an agent's use of reason.

Textual evidence from the CPrR

In the CPrR, Kant identifies a second problem of free will, i.e. a second threat to free agency aside from that of (natural causal) determinism. This is the role of God as creator. Although this is not the topic of this book and recent thorough treatments of how Kant deals with this problem are available (e.g. Insole 2013; see also Brewer and Watkins 2019), it will shed useful light upon the interpretation of Kant's theory of free will.

As Kant puts it, the worry is that, if 'it is assumed' that human agents are created by God, 'the actions of man have their determining ground in something completely beyond his own power' which would seem to turn the human agent into an 'automaton' (CPrR AA05: 100–1).[32] As with the Problem, Kant argues that he cannot see how, if appearances are in space and time, a solution could be found. After a short discussion which touches upon other issues which need not concern us here, Kant announces that '[t]he difficulty mentioned above is resolved briefly and clearly as follows' (CPrR AA05: 102).[33] The solution involves the claim that God can only be said to create noumena, because 'creation does not belong to the sensible mode of conceiving of existence': it would be 'contradictory to say God is the creator of appearances' (CPrR AA05: 102). As a result, Kant concludes that God cannot be said to be 'the cause of actions in the world of sense' (CPrR AA05: 102) and therefore that the agent's responsibility as free cause of his actions is not impeded.

There are many problems with this solution, but two stand out as relevant here. First, the agent's freedom is, we have been told repeatedly, a feature of her intelligible aspect. So it is unclear why excluding God from having an impact among appearances should be relevant if moral responsibility pertains to this intelligible aspect. Second, even if we go along with Kant's account, the question must be: Why is there not transitivity? If, plausibly, we assume that God creates human agents' intelligible character which, in turn, via their respective empirical characters, cause their actions in time, does this not make God the ultimate determining ground of these actions?

Starting with the second issue, if Kant thinks his solution is clear, it must be because this transitivity does not in fact hold. I claim that this is directly related to the problem we examined in revisiting the argument of the Resolution, namely that of too hasty an identification of the intelligible character with the law of the causality of reason. Importantly, Kant does not refer to the intelligible character in this CPrR passage. Rather, he claims that creation concerns only beings 'as noumena' and specifically 'concerns their intelligible (. . .) *existence*' (CPrR AA05: 102; my emphasis). And the feature that Kant repeatedly presents in the Resolution and GMM as characterising our belonging to the intelligible world is our rationality, of which the CPrR has shown that it is endowed with causality. So it is a being endowed with the causality of reason, that which 'is present to all the actions of human beings in all conditions of time, and is one and the same' (A556/B584) that is created by God.

If there is to be no transitivity, i.e. if this is not to make God responsible for our actions, this must be because God does not create the intelligible character which brings about these actions, although He does create the causality of reason. This is plausible insofar as the intelligible character is a *determination* of our nature as noumena, while our *existence* as noumena is that of our faculty of reason. The intelligible character is therefore not identifiable with the causality of reason. Rather, since the intelligible character is the individual agent's character, it is then plausible to suggest, as proposed earlier, that it is the law of the will, i.e. of the individual agent's *use* of the causality of reason. And it is because agents are not purely rational that this character is not (necessarily) the causality of reason. The first issue is thereby also addressed since it is indeed at the noumenal level that the problem is resolved.[34]

As indicated earlier, these interpretations of passages from the CPR, GMM and CPrR leave us with the problem of making sense of a descriptive law governing the free agency of a non-perfectly moral agent, i.e. the intelligible character *qua* law of the agent's capacity to use the causality of reason. The clue as to how Kant will, in the REL and MM, tackle this issue and thereby further develop his volitional account, lies in viewing the duality of descriptive law (intelligible character) and prescriptive law (law of autonomy, i.e. the moral law) as reflecting a dichotomy within the will.

C. Reconciling the volitional and metaphysical accounts (2): The nature of the will

While the GMM and CPrR focussed upon the conception of an agent giving herself the law, i.e. autonomy, with the REL, Kant attends to the issue of the freedom of the agent who is bound by the law of autonomy, a focus that will bring the issue of the possibility of evil centre stage.[35]

Willkür and maxims

Kant addresses head-on the problem of making sense of the agency of a non-perfectly rational being by further refining his volitional account in line with the duality of normative and descriptive laws of the will. He introduces a dichotomy within the will. The first 'component' of the will is the *Willkür* or 'power of choice' (REL AA06: 21). The notion of *Willkür* as source of our willings seems precisely to be what is needed in a volitional account.[36] Unlike the willings discussed in chapters 1 to 3 *Willkür*'s acts are not defined by Kant as issuing in intentions, but as the adoption of 'maxims' (REL AA06: 21). This follows from Kant's more general characterisation of the will as 'capacity to act *in accordance with the representation* of law' in the GMM (AA04: 412). This characterisation is germane to the definition of the freedom of the will as the capacity to act morally, i.e. from the moral law.

Willkür's acts are therefore atemporal in the sense that they concern maxims that guide our action,[37] i.e. the rules governing our actions. Of course, it is important to note that although the adoption of a maxim is an atemporal feature of the agent's will, i.e. merely intelligible, it will be manifested at one or more points in time by defining intentions to act. Similarly, the deliberation leading to adopting a maxim is also temporally located. These are not problems for the intelligible/empirical duality characterising an agent whose reality in-itself appears temporally. Rather, they raise the issue of the compatibility of the temporality of the agent's empirical appearance with an unchanging empirical character, which is part of the Timeless Agency problem I examine in Chapter 6.

Maxims (GMM AA04: 401n) are, for Kant, always defined as 'subjective principles'. These can be represented in the following form:

(M) 'I shall φ with purpose Φ.'[38]

For instance, I shall develop my talents (φ) so as to be more useful in helping others (Φ), in line with Korsgaard's (1996b: 57–8) claim that action φ's purpose must be included. I take this to be faithful to what Kant means when he says that a subjective principle 'is determined in accordance with the subject' (GMM AA04: 412n).[39] I do not make any reference to circumstances as O'Neill (Nell 1975: 34–9) suggests, because this would introduce a misleading hypothetical form (if circumstances $\mathbb{C}$ obtain I shall φ). Correspondingly, φ is not thereby determined specifically but is a *type* of action.

This amounts to interpreting maxims as 'underlying principles (. . .) by which we guide and control our more specific intentions' (O'Neill 1989: 84). Aside from being what I understand Kant as intending, it avoids problems with specific rules that cannot be universalised for non-morally relevant reasons (O'Neill 1989: 87; Timmermann 2000: 44–5), and with immoral forms of action that can arguably be made universalisable in the will through proper specification of the maxim (Illies 2007: 315).

By characterising the will in terms of various adoptions of maxims with the purposes they define, Kant's account of *Willkür* addresses one aspect of the Timeless Agency problem, i.e. the worry that all of our agency is defined by a single choice of empirical character. In Chapter 6, I shall propose a way of understanding how these adoptions are manifested in time.

The Incorporation Thesis

If *Willkür* is the locus of the agent's willings which Kant interprets as the adoption of maxims of action, and since willings can only be understood as purposive, this means that *Willkür* chooses a purpose Φ and a type of action φ that will contribute to achieving Φ.[40] What makes φ and Φ appropriate choices for the agent depends upon the agent's interests, and this is manifested in the existence of *incentives* that function as determining grounds of the choice (GMM AA04: 413). An incentive or 'drive' is defined as 'subjective determining ground of the will' as contrasted with the objective law, i.e. the moral law that the agent ought to adopt as ground (CPrR AA05: 72). More specifically, it therefore seems that a primary incentive is required as ground for the decision to bring about Φ and a secondary incentive as ground of the decision to φ.[41] The latter is secondary in the sense that our agency's purposiveness necessarily gives pride of place to an action's purpose.[42]

As Jens Timmermann (2009: 55) points out, in the case of dutiful actions 'the action itself is commanded by the moral law', which would seem to exclude a role for the action's purpose. Kant certainly distinguishes between duties of right and virtue (MM A06: 395) whereby only the latter are directed at the action's end, but it does not imply that the end should be ignored in other actions out of duty. The end belongs to the very notion of what it is to be an action (GMM AA04: 227): the moral law does not command actions without purposes; it is rather that in the case of narrow duties such as keeping one's promise, the end just is the completion of the action. So the end prescribed by the Formula of Ends (GMM AA04: 428–9) determines my purpose which in turn defines constraints on the action which either leave room for several or only one type of action depending upon whether the duty is broad (e.g. duty of charity), or narrow. In the case of the latter, no distinct secondary incentive is in principle required, but it may be needed in practice (see further).

How do these determining grounds function in terms of the adoption of a maxim of action? Although he interprets the term 'incentive' merely methodologically, Allison provides an illuminating account of what he calls the *Incorporation Thesis*, i.e. Kant's explanation of the role of incentives in the adoption of maxims. As Kant spells it out,

> the power of choice has the quite peculiar characteristic that it cannot be determined to an action by any incentive *except insofar as the human being has admitted the incentive into his maxim* (has made this a universal rule for himself, according to which he wills to conduct himself). (REL AA06: 24)

The text unambiguously refers to an incorporation of an incentive into the maxim. Allison explains that this is an act of self-determination defined by how the agent *takes* herself 'qua engaged in a deliberative process' (Allison 1990: 38) and through which 'the inclination or desire is deemed or *taken as* an appropriate basis of action' (Allison 1990: 39, my emphasis), whereby the action is the object of practical philosophy.[43]

But Kant's notion of incentive or drive, i.e. *Triebfeder*, is, as the name (*Triebfeder* = spring) indicates, a causality whose motivating force is the conative factor (Beck 1960: 76)[44] endorsed by the agent's act of *Willkür*, i.e. the adoption of a maxim.[45] While a volitional account is distinct from a metaphysical account and does indeed represent how the agent conceives of herself, it has to be integrated with the metaphysical account. Consequently, this conception is best couched in causal terms.[46] So *Triebfeder* are causalities that the agent uses by 'admit[ting them] into his maxim' (AA06: REL 36): they will contribute to making sense of the causality of freedom.

What are these incentives? They are the moral incentive ('respect' for the moral law, GMM AA04: 400) and 'the incentive of self-love and its inclinations' (REL AA06: 36). From the point of view of the morality of our action, it is the '*subordination* (in the maxim's form)' of these incentives that is relevant. That is, morality requires that the incentive of self-love be subordinated to that of respect for the law. I take this subordination as evidence that more than one incentive can be present, *pace* Allison (2020: 277) and most other commentators. So, on the interpretation I propose, a morally obligatory maxim has a form that is characterised by respect for the law determining Φ, while self-love can contribute to further determining φ.

Before continuing, the nature of the incentive of self-love requires clarification. It encapsulates the inclinations the agent experiences from her nature as animal and human. These inclinations are, for Kant, all traceable to natural causality. Indeed, although he differentiates a *predisposition to animality* and, with the involvement of our rationality, a *predisposition to humanity*, Kant characterises both predispositions as having a *physical* nature (REL AA06: 26–7; see Palmquist 2015b: 113–18).

This apparently creates a problem for the volitional account of free will, and therefore *Willkür* (REL AA06: 39), insofar as I argued that it is located in the intelligible domain (*pace* Allison 2020: 453) outside causally determined appearances. In the intelligible domain, it must therefore be *the agent's appropriation of the ground of natural causality* (hereafter 'Ground'; see Chapters 2 and 4)[47] that defines the causality manifested in the incentive of self-love.[48] By 'appropriation', I refer to the agent's endorsing the manifestation of the Ground in terms of natural inclinations of self-love characterising his pursuit of happiness by defining purposes corresponding to these inclinations.[49] Practical rationality is involved here in the instrumental role of determining these purposes.

What I now propose so as to shed light upon the law of the causality of freedom *qua* the agent's capacity to use the causality of reason, is to provide a causal interpretation of the Incorporation Thesis, which will draw upon Kant's crucial distinction between *Wille* and *Willkür*.

Wille/Willkür

Kant describes an incentive's incorporation into a maxim as a contribution to its matter. But there is more to the matter of the maxim. The latter is a (subjective) principle, and as such has a structure defined by formula (M). The maxim acquires this structure insofar as the choice of the primary incentive is simultaneously a choice of how rationality is to structure the maxim. If motivated by self-love, as we shall see, it plays the role of determining how to serve the agent's interests; if motivated by respect for the law, it defines my action's purpose (e.g. keeping a promise) and constraints upon how to achieve it. In so doing, the role of practical reason is prescriptive in its relation to *Willkür*. This function of practical reason defines the other core 'component' of the will, which Kant refers to as *Wille*. This translates as 'will', but to avoid confusing it with the whole faculty of the will with its internal duality *Willkür/Wille*, the German term is generally used.[50] It is in the MM that Kant first clearly spells out the *Wille/Willkür* dichotomy:

> The capacity for desiring in accordance with concepts, insofar as the ground determining it to action lies within itself and not in its object, is called the capacity

for *doing or refraining from doing what one pleases*. Insofar as it is joined with one's consciousness of the capacity to bring about the object by one's action it is called the *capacity for choice (Willkür)*; if it is not joined with this consciousness, its act is called a *wish*. The will (*Wille*) is therefore the capacity for desire considered not so much in relation to action (as the capacity for choice is) but rather in relation to the ground determining choice in action. The will (*Wille*) itself, strictly speaking has no determining ground: insofar as it can determine the capacity for choice, it is instead practical reason itself. (AA06 MM: 213)

Willkür is here characterised as the capacity for adopting maxims, in line with its definition in the REL.[51] Further, *Wille* is introduced as playing a role 'in relation to the ground determining choice in action' (AA06 MM: 213). Now in the REL text, we saw Kant referring to incentives as determining grounds. The role that *Wille* plays in relation to these incentives is different depending upon the incentive. Let us examine this more closely.

Kant is primarily thinking of the case of obligatory moral action. If the incentive is respect for the moral law, the determining ground is just the law of the causality of reason, i.e. the moral law: the role of respect is to mobilise the causality of reason whose law is the moral law so that practical reason determines the maxim; this will be clarified further. The will in this case is therefore *autonomous* since *Willkür* acts upon the law given by *Wille*.

Kant does not indicate what role *Wille* plays in relation to the incentive when this is self-love, but we can reconstruct this from the REL's claim of a reversal of the order of subordination of the incentives involved in immoral action. *Wille* plays a subordinate role of defining the purpose to be pursued for my happiness, as required by this incentive, so that the causality of reason plays a role here, as 'instrumental rationality' (Timmermann 2009: 46). The incentive's requirements define the determining ground of action, so the will is here *heteronomous*: it gets its law from outside itself, from the causality of the incentive of self-love.

While this provides the elements of the causal story enabling the volitional account in terms of *Willkür* to mesh with the metaphysical account in terms of the intelligible character, I next need to further clarify the prescriptive role of *Wille*. This is expressed in terms of *oughts* first introduced in the Resolution with the concept of P-freedom and further expounded in the GMM and CPrR: the role of *Wille*, whether the action is autonomous or heteronomous, is to provide *imperatives*.

Indeed, maxim M ('I shall φ with purpose Φ') can be adopted by the capacity for choice (*Willkür*) through one of two processes. First, if M is obligatory, *Wille*'s prescription is to pursue purpose Φ on moral grounds through action φ compliant with moral constraints. Since this prescription is defined in general by the CI (GMM AA04: 421), it has the form:

(C): Bring about the realisation of purpose Φ by means of φ on the grounds that you can simultaneously will that this act[52] be universal law.[53]

The primary incentive determines Φ (e.g. to be helpful to others in need), which is morally required as a task, and thereby sets constraints upon possible actions φ (e.g.

to donate money which I lawfully own to a relevant charity) contributing to it. Further determination of φ would then involve the incentive of self-love; it will involve practical reason through a *hypothetical imperative of prudence* (GMM AA04: 416), namely 'among the moral types of action, select those types φ which are most "convenient" to fulfil Φ' (e.g. to donate an amount of money that leaves enough to pay my utility bills). The determination of action-tokens (e.g. which charity shall I donate to) is a further issue I examine in Chapter 6.

Second, if M is not a moral maxim, the incentive of self-love is in the driving seat, but practical rationality has a role to play since this incentive does not directly determine purpose Φ.[54] What is required is a hypothetical imperative of prudence:

(H): Pursue purpose Φ (through some action φ).

For instance, Φ may be to become rich. As Kant indicates in the REL and MM, morality also defines the aim of being *merely* virtuous, i.e. acting so as to *comply* with morality, not on moral grounds, but rather because it is convenient, e.g. good for one's social standing or selfish interests, as in the case of the honest shopkeeper (GMM AA04: 397) who chooses actions φ complying with the moral law to secure his reputation as honest. This defines a secondary role for the moral incentive: as Kant says (REL AA06: 28-30), even in the highest form of evil Kant considers, namely '*wickedness*', the moral incentive is present, but just not in its rightful position as primary incentive. This means that the type of action φ would receive further specification for compliance, either partial or complete,[55] with the moral law.[56] While this compliance is defined by the CI, the subordinate role it plays is defined by an *imperative of skill* (GMM AA04: 415) (e.g. for the shopkeeper, specifying that honesty pays off).

The volitional account's causal story so far

The previous discussion enables us to better understand in what sense the intelligible character is the law of the agent's *capacity to use* the causality of reason, i.e. corresponds to a descriptive law of the will and therefore, more specifically, how this can be the law of an immoral will.

From what has been said, there are two possible ways in which the agent can adopt a maxim, which I shall examine by focussing upon the primary incentive. First, in the case of moral action, through respect for the moral law, the agent acts on the CI and the law describing her action is this moral law, i.e. the fundamental prescriptive law of practical reason (*Wille*).[57] We already knew this, but Kant's theory of the will has now added an account of how the intelligible character, which corresponds to the law of the will, is the law of a causality that, even in this moral case, is not (as implicitly assumed earlier) just the causality of reason. This causality is the agent's use, on the grounds of respect for the law, of this causality as determining cause.[58]

This suggests that there are two components to this volitional account of the intelligible character, which can be thought on the model of the cause of the light in an electric bulb: the switch may be called an *enabling cause* and the power source the *driving cause*. This echoes Clarke's (2003) proposal (Chapter 3) for integrating the causal power of reasons (driving cause) with the agent's will which he understood as agent-causality (enabling cause). In the moral case therefore, the choice made by the *Willkür*'s incorporation of her respect for the law into her maxim is the enabling cause triggering the activity of the driving cause which is the causality of reason, i.e. the causal power of *Wille*. The latter features here in its *unrestricted* form, characterised by a categorical imperative (C). Since I (*Wille*) give myself the law, my agency is *autonomous*.

Second, in the case of immoral action, the agent incorporates an incentive of self-love into his maxim. This act of incorporation again defines an enabling cause. The incorporation of self-love is the agent's appropriation of the Ground, an appropriation which, as we saw earlier, involves a role for the causality of reason: it determines the act's purpose Φ through an imperative of prudence (H). This means that the driving cause is the causality of reason thus conditioned by the Ground. This causality is thus *used* by the agent in a *restricted* form (ignoring the morality of pursuing Φ) serving only to direct the Ground towards purpose Φ. Since the agent thus co-opts the Ground for his purposes, he is not giving himself the law of his agency (he does not even know the law of the Ground): his agency is *heteronomous*.

The secondary incentives, which I cannot examine here, add to this picture in terms of a contribution to the enabling causes. As illustration of my interpretation of the volitional account, consider Alberich's theft of the Rhinegold at the beginning of Wagner's Ring (Wagner 1900: 38–9; 1918). The story starts with Alberich's failure to satisfy the demands of his animal and human self-love with either of the three Rhinemaidens.[59] We could assume for the purpose of this example, that this pursuit is morally permissible. Then, upon hearing of the Rhinegold and its power-bestowing properties, he decides to acquire that power by stealing it, even though the price is the cursing of love. That is, he opts for a self-love-driven strategy characterised by a hypothetical imperative of prudence which commands to aim for power to satisfy his animal (mechanical) and human (comparing) self-love: he will be able to gratify his animal needs and lord it over others. His act of *Willkür* is the enabling cause that uses the causality of reason conditioned upon the appropriated Ground (this defines the driving cause) thereby implementing an imperative of skill defining a purpose (to steal the Rhinegold). Its temporal manifestation should not detract from its timeless nature as manifested in the reappearance of the leitmotiv of the Renunciation of Love[60] throughout the whole Ring.[61]

Figure 5.1 summarises the *volitional account* (primary incentives only) in the two cases. As explained earlier, they represent a different ordering of the incentives, with respect for the moral law and self-love taking pride of place in each case.

The dual-causality enabling/driving cause thus provides an understanding of the causality of freedom as the agent's capacity to use the causality of reason by showing how *Willkür* draws upon the latter in its acts, i.e. the adoption of maxims.[62] The role of *Willkür* in this causal story needs further clarifying, however, if it is not to be reduced to some random choice, thereby letting the concerns of the Luck Arguments (Chapter 3) rear their head again. Indeed, this spontaneity of which Kant says that '[o]nly choice can therefore be called free' (MM AA06: 226) would precisely seem not amenable to being described as law-governed and hence appears random. To examine this requires understanding Kant's Theory of Choice.

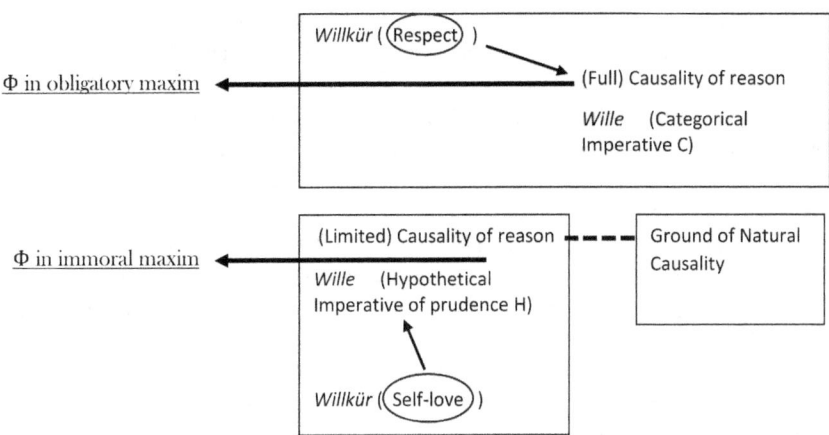

Figure 5.1 The volitional account for the primary incentive (the thin arrows represent the enabling causes; the thick ones the driving causes; the oval shapes are the incorporated primary incentives and the large rectangles the agent's will; the dashed line represents conditioning) © Christian Onof.

D. Reconciling the volitional and metaphysical accounts (3): Kant's Theory of Choice

Willkür and *Gesinnung*

The evolution of Kant's conception of freedom, as Allison's (2020) comprehensive study reveals, is characterised by a move away from Leibnizian/Wolffian compatibilism under the influence of his reading of Crusius and Rousseau. Crusius interprets freedom as liberty of indifference, which thereby injects leeway into the account of freedom. While Kant came to understand that alternative possibilities are crucial to freedom insofar as I ought to φ only if I can φ, he never embraced the Crusian characterisation of freedom for reasons similar to those spelt out in the contemporary Luck Arguments (Chapter 3). Kant fully subscribes to a rejection of the idea of creating space for freedom by introducing a gap in the deterministic process. And, as we saw in Chapter 4, this is why the key to his solution to the Problem lies in his claim that the agent's freedom can only consist in her determining the law governing her actions in appearance (the empirical character).

But this rejection of freedom as liberty of indifference means that even a choice, i.e. an agent's act of *Willkür*, must, for Kant, be law-governed. Insofar as our common understanding of choice, which also informs libertarianism, involves the thought that choice is *not* rule-governed, Kant's account implicitly questions this. On this common/libertarian understanding (Keil 2018: 18–19), the freedom to do otherwise must be understood as the absence of a full predetermination of whether I shall decide to φ_1 or to φ_2. Against the objection that this amounts to letting the outcome of a random process do the deciding, the common/libertarian understanding of choice will counter that there are *grounds* for the choices we make. But the point of the (rational) Luck Objections is that, since these grounds are not fully (rationally) determining ones, once we have taken into account the partial determination they define, we are again left with pure (rational) luck/randomness (Chapter 3). Kant produces a version of this objection throughout his career. Thus, of Crusius's notion of a liberty of indifference, he points out in 1755 that it implies that '[a]ctions are the product of chance; they are not determined by grounds' (ND AA01: 402).

As we saw earlier, in the GMM (1785) and CPrR (1788), Kant argues that there are determining grounds of the will, i.e. *interests* accounting for the availability of *incentives* the agent acts upon (GMM AA04: 413; CPrR AA05: 79). This means that, in adopting maxim (M), the agent pursues purpose Φ which, insofar as it is an interest, accounts for this maxim-adoption. This is consistent with the claim of rational self-sufficiency of a willing/volition insofar as it is the pursuit of an interest/purpose (Chapter 3).[63] This means that this purposive pursuit is governed by a law it simultaneously defines.

But, as I indicated in Chapter 3, while this is sufficient for a volitional account of a single such act (here a maxim-adoption), when several purposes are pursued in different acts, the volitional account must ensure their rational coherence: only with this coherence in place do we have willings/volitions that can define the atemporal ground of psychological causality as required in response to the Infinite Regress Argument. Allison (2020: 347, 386) usefully refers to the agent's interests as what binds the agent's purposive activities, but this does not explain why they cohere.

This is why Kant introduces the notion of 'subjective basis' (REL AA06: 21), i.e. the basis for making determining grounds of the will (i.e. interests/incentives) the agent's own: only if the *maxim-adoptions* have a subjective basis, can they cohere. It is noteworthy that Kant understands 'subjective basis' as a 'cause' (REL AA06: 21): as I argued, although a volitional account is here at stake, it is designed to fit in with the metaphysical one of the intelligible character causing the empirical character, so a causal story in terms of subjective bases is apposite.[64] But in what sense is it a cause? Since the objective basis of maxim-adoption is the law that *ought* to guide any agent's acts of *Willkür*, i.e. the moral law, it is reasonable to interpret the subjective basis as the law that *actually* governs the particular agent's actual maxim-adoptions: it is the law of these choices (REL AA06: 21).

The subjective basis Kant proposes lies in the adoption of a *Gesinnung*. This is characterised as an 'attitude [(*Gesinnung*)] to the moral law' (REL AA06: 24) and defined as 'the first subjective basis for the adoption of maxims (...) it applies universally to the entire use of freedom' (REL AA06: 25).[65] So individual acts of *Willkür* through which maxims are adopted, are referred to the adoption of a *Gesinnung* or 'supreme maxim' (REL A06: 36)[66] defining one's whole moral disposition. Since Kant is a moral rigourist, there are only two options: a good or an evil *Gesinnung* (REL AA06: 22–6; see Pasternack 2014: 89–93). Importantly, Kant indicates that this supreme maxim 'must also have been adopted through a free power of choice' (REL AA06: 22–6), i.e. is imputable.

Problems with the *Gesinnung*

This proposal for the subjective basis of maxim-adoptions has intuitive appeal if it amounts to what Steve Palmquist (2015a: 236) describes as 'a one-off decision to dedicate one's life in one direction or another'.[67] Why, however, is Kant only focussing on one's attitude with respect to the moral law? Because all that is relevant for Kant is how I use the causality of reason, whose law is the moral law, i.e. (i) how I stand with respect to its prescriptions; further, (ii) the scope of moral choice for Kant, insofar as it is intelligible and non-empirical (REL AA06:: 39), concerns only whether I opt for what is morally required or not.[68] But this leaves us with two problems.

First, it appears that the *Gesinung*-adoption is not sufficient[69] to ensure that the various maxim-adoptions cohere. Indeed, suppose, for instance, that a good *Gesinnung* accounts for an agent's implementing his duty of beneficence (MM AA06: 393) by devoting all his resources (within limits defined by perfect/narrow duties) to charity work. This is not compatible with his devoting all these resources to fulfilling his duty of self-improvement (MM AA06: 391–2). Kant may well claim that there are no conflicts of duties (MM AA06: 224), but he is at pains to convince in his insistence that one ought not lie to the murderer at the door, even to protect a friend (AA08: 424).[70] Consequently, Kant's notion of *Gesinnung* would seem to fall short of providing the required subjective basis. Discussing these issues at length would take us too far into Kant's ethics and away from our purpose. We can, however, conclude that, while Kant's own stipulation of the notion of *Gesinnung* may not be sufficient as subjective basis, *a notion of Gesinnung could be stipulated as fundamental decision ensuring the coherence* of maxim-adoptions insofar as it defines the law governing these adoptions. A further worry arises, however, namely the apparent determination of all acts of *Willkür* from the single *Gesinnung*-adoption. This would seem to amount to a resurfacing of an aspect of the worry about Timeless Agency that this chapter claimed to have addressed.

A second problem concerns the notion of *Gesinnung*-adoption insofar as Kant's answer to the question about the subjective basis of *maxim-adoptions* may seem like kicking the question into the long grass. Indeed, since the *Gesinnung* is freely chosen, the question now is: What is the basis for the *Gesinnung*-adoption? Kant says that 'it must not be possible to go on asking about the subjective basis, in a human being, for the adoption of this maxim rather than the opposite one' (REL AA06; 21). This important statement is in line with the outline of the solution to the Problem in Chapter 3: in both real causal[71] (metaphysical account) and explanatory (here, the volitional account) terms, placing coherent willings/volitions outside time addresses the challenge of the Infinite Regress Argument. So, the volitional account must be compatible with the metaphysical account's appeal to a *first* cause, which would seem to require some act of the will that is rationally self-sufficient, i.e. requires no further justification, and thereby steers clear of the Rational Luck Objection.

But, while Kant's claim is what is needed, how can he justify it? Kant offers a short argument: "[f]or if ultimately the basis itself [of the *Gesinnung*-adoption] were not a maxim anymore but a natural impulse, then the use of freedom could be reduced entirely to determination by natural causes – which, however, contradicts freedom' (REL AA06: 21, my amendment). This does not obviously address the question. What Kant does not explain is his rejection of the other option, namely that the basis is another maxim. A *reductio* argument could be provided here: if another maxim were identified, it would itself have its basis in the *Gesinnung*-adoption since this is the basis for the adoption of *all* maxims. So this maxim would both be the basis of, and based upon the *Gesinnung*-adoption. It can therefore not be a maxim, but since it must be free, and thus not the effect of any external cause, we cannot make sense of any further cause/basis of this adoption.

What is at stake here are *limitations of our understanding* of volition as Kant makes clear in his alternative argument that points rather to a regress: the 'subjective basis or cause of this adoption [of *Gesinnung*] cannot again be cognised (. . .) because otherwise one would in turn have to adduce a maxim into which this [*Gesinnung*] has been adopted and this maxim must likewise have its basis in turn' (REL AA06: 25; see also 21n). By claiming that we can only think of the basis of the *Gesinnung*-adoption in terms of a regress, Kant can claim that the first basis for the *Gesinnung*-adoption is 'inscrutable' (REL AA06: 25) as a result of our cognitive limitations.

What these arguments show, however, is not what needed to be shown, namely why one cannot go on *asking* about the subjective basis of the *Gesinnung*-adoption: Kant shows why one cannot *answer* the question about this basis. This is sufficient to block a Luck Objection which would claim that there is no subjective basis. But what about the Rational Luck Objection? If the agent chooses a good *Gesinnung*, the choice is to act from the CI as required by rationality, so the objection is addressed insofar as the agent *can* make the rational choice of such a *Gesinnung*. The Rational Luck objector might still complain about the inexplicability of the alternative choice, however. I return to this issue later.

Kant's Theory of Choice therefore amounts to a complete determination of one's free agency through a suitably stipulated *Gesinnung*-adoption and maxim-adoptions based upon it, thereby combining with the metaphysical account to provide an answer to the Infinite Regress Argument (Chapter 3). But the two problems with the concept of the adoption of a *Gesinnung* which I have flagged will need to be addressed.

Volitional/metaphysical account compatibility and causality of freedom

Leaving aside these problems of Kant's conception of *Gesinnung*, what does the appeal to the *Gesinnung*-adoption mean for our attempt to make volitional sense of the causality of freedom. It means that the law of *Willkür*'s enabling cause(s) is determined by the *Gesinnung*-adoption and there is no further understanding of this adoption to be had. As for understanding what this law is in the case of immoral action, Kant is at pains to reiterate the point that inclinations do not explain evil doing (e.g. REL AA06: 21, 34). This lack of understanding is hardly surprising, given the noumenal picture. The agent opts for a key contribution of the Ground in adopting his maxim: he co-opts the Ground (that he experiences as drives) which conditions his practical rationality to the pursuit of some goal Φ thereby defining his choice's driving cause. The agent thus opts for a driving cause whose law he is necessarily ignorant of, rather than the driving cause of the moral law that characterises his predisposition to personality: he thus accepts a law (heteronomy) rather than giving himself the law (autonomy).[72]

Further, according to Kant's doctrine of the propensity to evil (REL AA06: 32), all human agents have a propensity leading them to choose an evil *Gesinnung*.[73] Of this, Kant claims that 'we are unable to indicate a further cause for why evil has corrupted precisely the supreme maxim in us' (REL AA06: 32). The two issues are linked: if we could understand the law of the *Willkür*'s enabling cause in adopting non-moral maxims, we would make some headway in understanding why an agent opts for an evil *Gesinnung*. So, while this explanatory dearth is familiar in dealing with the theological problem of evil (e.g. Augustine 1993 book II.20; see Insole 2013: 129–34), Kant's account has the advantage of tracing this inexplicability to the nature of our cognition.

As far as the issue of compatibility of volitional and metaphysical accounts is concerned, *Willkür*'s maxim-adoption is based upon *Gesinnung*-adoption which, by defining a supreme maxim, determines the law of maxim-adoptions. With a suitably stipulated notion of *Gesinnung* (see earlier discussion), the integration of the two accounts has been achieved by filling in the volitional account with a causal story of how the agent's will makes use of the causality of reason when adopting a maxim of action which is the practical perspective upon the causality of freedom whose law is the intelligible character. In both the moral and non-moral cases, the causality of reason plays a role as driving cause, unconditioned or conditioned by the Ground, thus spelling out how the intelligible character is the law of the agent's *capacity to use* the causality of reason. No *assertions* are made here about (the possibility of) 'noumenal acts': *pace* Wood (1984: 97–9), Kant makes no extravagant metaphysical claims but proposes a volitional account, i.e. an account of how an agent can understand herself as controlling her agency. However, this proposal's causal nature enables it to shed light upon the metaphysical account's causality of freedom in terms of enabling/driving causes.[74]

The integration of the volitional and metaphysical accounts therefore clarifies the law governing the agent's capacity to use the causality of reason as

- *qua* law of an enabling cause, defined by the *Gesinnung*.
- *qua* law of the driving cause, practical reason, either pure (defined by the unconditional moral law: autonomy) or conditioned by the appropriated Ground (heteronomy), whereby a subordinate role is played, through the secondary incentives, respectively by the Ground and rationality.

The answer to the Moral Leeway problem

As we saw earlier, this question could only be answered by showing the *real possibility* of acting immorally. This in turn first required that we be able to provide an account of the law of the causality of freedom which covers cases of immoral action. I have shown that in immoral action, the agent uses the causality of reason improperly by having it play a mere role of channelling the Ground to define the driving cause of my agency. The choice to adopt maxims that are not permissible involves the enabling causal factor that is *Willkür*, whose law is defined by an evil *Gesinnung* whose adoption lies beyond our ken.

This amounts to answering the question about the real possibility of a free choice of evil which, as I indicated in Chapter 4, was raised in related forms by a number of Kant commentators both early (e.g. Schmidt in 1790; Reinhold in 1790–2) and recent (e.g. Ertl 1998: 149; Kosch 2006: 44ff; Allison 1990: 35ff, 2020: 456ff; Fugate 2012). I have argued that this problem does not threaten Kant's contention that there is a single notion of freedom in play, namely the causality whose law is the intelligible character, as long as this is understood as the law of the agent's use of the causality of reason.[75] This causality carries a prescriptive connotation: the proper use of the causality of reason is autonomy. However, immoral action requires freedom just as much as moral action: I have shown this by providing a causal interpretation of the Incorporation Thesis enabling an integration of volitional and metaphysical accounts. By thus shedding light upon the law of the causality of freedom, this interpretation has solved the Moral Leeway problem.

E. Application: Types of evil and the change of heart

In this section, I show how the above interpretation can be applied and further specified by addressing two important features of Kant's Theory of Choice.

Types of evil

Kant distinguishes three 'levels' of the propensity to evil, 'the frailty of human nature', its 'impurity' and 'the wickedness of human nature' (REL AA06: 29).[76] Taking these in reverse order, the latter two are direct examples of the subordination of the moral incentive to self-love. Wickedness involves the adoption of an evil maxim (REL AA06: 30). For instance, this is the case when I adopt the maxim of not keeping my promises when it is not convenient and it will not endanger my reputation. Impurity is a case of such an inversion defining a non-purely moral maxim, which aims to fulfil a moral duty but conditionally, such as the maxim to provide help to people in need when I happen to have some time available.

The case of frailty is different: here, Kant claims that the maxim is moral, but the moral incentive is 'weaker (by comparison with inclination)' (REL AA06: 29). So in this case, the action, not the maxim, is evil. So, for instance, I may have adopted the maxim to improve certain talents but fail to act upon it out of laziness. This distinction maxim/action is too often ignored in contemporary Kantian ethics. It is problematic if it implies a new level of free agency in choosing the maxim to act upon.

It might seem that the action can only be free if another, non-moral maxim accounts for it.[77] To explain why this is not the case, consider the role of the circumstances in which the agent formulates her intention to act. These circumstances can be understood as determining the nature of the maxim that will be acted upon without requiring a further free choice if maxim-adoption is manifested in time by identifying the circumstances of application of the maxim. So frailty would be a case where the circumstances seldom or never identified the moral maxim in question as that to be acted upon. This introduces a useful representation of a *hierarchical order* of maxims,[78] which is reflected in appearance in the frequency of action upon them. I explain these issues in detail in Chapter 6.[79]

The possibility of a new *Gesinnung*

This hierarchical ordering of maxims will help address the thorny issue of a change of heart or conversion in which the agent adopts a new, good *Gesinnung* (REL AA06: 44ff). On my metaphysical interpretation, this amounts to having a different law for *maxim-adoptions*. But (1) how could the law change? Further, (2) if this new law accounts for the adoption of moral maxims, what about those other maxims the agent was previously acting upon? How does this new *Gesinnung* stand in relation to them?

To address these issues, first note Kant's radical claim that a conversion involves the agent 'put[ting] on a new human being' (REL AA06: 48). The change involved must be understood as a new noumenal identity, thereby directly addressing (1). The previous *Gesinnung* is no longer relevant: what appears post-conversion in time are actions governed by the new *Gesinnung*.

This is, however, problematic for a metaphysical interpretation in which the agent's noumenal aspect introduced in the Resolution (A538/B566) has been interpreted volitionally in terms of maxims adopted under an (initially) evil *Gesinnung* because of the propensity to evil. How could a 'new human being' define a different noumenal identity? In his careful analysis of the conversion, Lawrence Pasternack (2014: 156–7) points out that, while 'punishment cannot be considered appropriate' for this new human being who is 'well-pleasing to God' (REL AA06: 73), 'it does not follow from this that the debt is forgiven' (Pasternack 2014: 157). If this is right, the agent's 'old' maxims still characterise the subject's noumenal identity as required by a 'metaphysically determinate' noumenal identity.

This leaves us with question (2). How can such a combination of old and new maxims be understood as governed by the new *Gesinnung*. To answer this, it is useful to consider Pasternack's (2014: 142–3) analysis of Kant's doctrine of salvation. He identifies a shift in soteriological requirements from CPrR to REL. In the first, salvation requires (endless) struggle[80] towards 'complete conformity with the moral law' (CPrR AA05: 122), i.e. towards an unrealisable state. In the second, something achievable is at stake, namely the conversion. Leaving aside for now the appropriateness of Pasternack's interpretation, this suggests that the agent does not have to be (and in practice is not) perfectly good after the conversion.

But, it will be objected, surely a good *Gesinnung* would not govern the adoption of non-moral maxims. While this is true, as we saw above, if the old human being's debts are not forgiven, the new human being thus takes responsibility for the old one. Consequently, while no non-moral maxims will be adopted under the new *Gesinnung*, the old maxims must somehow fall under it too. I want to propose that my interpretation of maxims as hierarchically ordered allows precisely for an understanding of a good *Gesinnung* as law to all the agent's *maxim-adoptions*, moral or not. The idea is simply that if a maxim finds itself at the bottom of the ranking, it will seldom be definitive of the agent's intention to act: a low-ranking maxim means few circumstances in which it is acted upon.

But how is it that even only a few actions on a non-moral maxim could be understood as emanating from an agent with a good *Gesinnung*. This is where I would query Pastnernack's strong claim of a soteriological shift from CPrR to REL. Indeed, this leaves him claiming both that we are to be judged by God upon our change of heart and simultaneously having the CPrR duty (also MM AA06: 446) to strive endlessly towards perfection. This is an uneasy combination: Why strive in this way if one's good *Gesinnung* is the real measure of our moral worth (in God's eyes)? The interpretation I have given earlier suggests rather that the adoption of a good *Gesinnung* can be completely integrated with the CPrR requirement, and I claim that this is *required* by the REL which, like the CPrR, argues that there is a 'progress, advancing *ad infinitum*, from the bad to the better' (REL AA06: 51). Under a good *Gesinnung*, the circumstances in which the agent acts on non-moral maxims are few in the sense that they define a finite set, which over an infinite period of time is negligible, equivalent to zero: this is exactly the asymptotic convergence to moral perfection of the CPrR. In other words, for any such maxim, after a (finite) time the agent will no longer act on it.

This resolves the above conundrum: the actions of a good *Gesinnung* are good in the sense that there is a convergence towards moral perfection (the finite time during which non-moral maxims are acted upon is negligible over an infinite duration). In the next chapter, I examine the temporal manifestation of a conversion.

F. Concluding remark: Amending the notion of *Gesinnung*

The exegetical investigation work in this chapter has proposed a resolution of the Moral Leeway problem which arises specifically from Kant's theory of freedom, a theory that has a normative dimension that, it must be noted, is not forced upon us to address the Problem.

Assuming that some such normativity is endorsed, Kant's volitional account, which involves a Theory of Choice that I analysed in detail, presents us with the two problems arising from the concept of the adoption of a *Gesinnung* which I discussed earlier. First, with this notion, all individual acts of *Willkür* are grounded in a single act of *Gesinnung*-adoption, apparently without any further available leeway than the choice between good and evil, since any such further leeway would be left to a freedom of indifference that Kant rejects. This picture is germane to Kant's moral rigourism (Rel AA06: 23; see Palmquist 2015b: 109ff) insofar as the freedom to do otherwise is exclusively required in relation to the only moral choice that we have to make for Kant, namely a choice between good and evil. Kant's moral philosophy might suggest that we have more leeway than that, e.g. insofar as it is open to us how to implement broad imperfect duties of virtue (MM AA06: 446). However, Kant never says that how these duties are implemented calls upon any further choice and for good reason: What would be the ground of such a choice? Rather, it would seem to be a matter of various inclinations. So, aside from the fact that this picture arguably ignores issues of conflicts of duties, it lets an aspect of the Timeless Agency problem resurface, namely the reduction of all leeway to a single choice, much as the volitional account in terms of various maxim-adoptions had seemingly addressed this worry. Second, the adoption of a *Gesinnung*, while not random, cannot be further understood if it is evil, thereby generating a Rational Luck worry.

I think that the way to address these two worries is to revise the notion of *Gesinnung* so that it defines a choice encompassing the multiplicity of individual choices made in adopting individual maxims. The proposal is that the way the *Gesinnung*-adoption acts as subjective basis for individual maxim-adoptions is no longer to be thought in causal terms. In Kant's picture, there is in any case a tension between his acceptance that the causality of freedom can only be thought in purposive terms (Chapter 4) and his attempt to represent it volitionally in causal terms without any explicit appeal to final causes. My proposal is that the *Gesinnung* is a choice of the whole of my (morally relevant) agency understood in purposive terms, and provides a basis for individual choices of maxims by defining a goal that ensures their coherence:[81] This satisfies the condition defined in Chapter 3 for a notion of free agency that addresses the Infinite Regress Argument (Chapter 3).

Aside from the teleological nature of this Gesinnung-adoption, the major differences with Kant's theory[82] will therefore be the way that it (i) will not just be the adoption of a good/evil *Gesinnung* but incorporate more detail of the kind of moral or immoral choices I thereby make and (ii) the *Gesinnung*-adoption cannot be said to be manifested temporally from birth as Kant claims (REL AA06: 22, 25) but will rather be manifested progressively over time.[83]

This temporal process necessarily requires that we accept that randomness will be involved in aspects of individual choices at least at the process' inception. This is an aspect of O'Connor's libertarian proposal that I criticised in Chapter 3, i.e. his agent-causality would involve some randomness in the role of past determinants of the agent's choices, and it is a randomness that seemingly falls foul of the Infinite Regress Argument insofar as some aspects of the past that are out of my control determine who I choose to be.

Given the atemporal setting underpinning this temporal process, however, this randomness does not have to 'infect' my whole agency. Rather, I take a stance on all such determinants by endorsing or rejecting them on the grounds of how they fit into my overall purpose of unification of my agency: such endorsements/rejection will be manifested temporally as aspects of my agency in appearance which I examine in Chapter 6.

What grounds are there for claiming that free agency involves the adoption of such a *Gesinnung*? First, this *Gesinnung* need only be defined very minimally as the very purpose of coherence itself. Second, the constraints of practical rationality, which govern both immoral and moral action, require such coherence (whatever conception of moral normativity is assumed): for instance, I would not simultaneously deliberately pursue a purpose and its opposite. These two points are all that is needed to claim that all my actions can be understood as the pursuit of a certain minimal conception of myself as a unity, i.e. to have 'nature N' (Strawson 2002: 446 – see Chapter 3) and thereby conform to the understanding of my freedom as lying in this explanatorily self-sufficient willing that grounds my nature. The unifying role of the *Gesinnung* implies that my individual choices will be justified in relation to it as overall purpose which itself requires no further justification because of its explanatory self-sufficiency, thereby addressing Rational Luck worries.[84]

Such a conception of my *Gesinnung* leaves room for it to be a motley collection of the pursuit of various interests that are unrelated aside from their coexistence not infringing the constraints of practical rationality. In particular, it apparently leaves room for the pursuit of immoral purposes in certain contexts while moral ones are pursued in others.

In Chapter 7, I shall propose a normative dimension of freedom defined by the requirement that my *Gesinnung* be the pursuit of an *integrated unity*, something that could be described as a fundamental project, to use a Sartrean term:[85] it would involve an awareness of what defines the unity of one's agency.

6

The temporal dimension of free agency

Chapter 5 examined how Kant's ethical writings provided the material to reconstruct a volitional account with a Theory of Choice at its core. Kant's volitional account is essentially that of a normative theory of freedom and relies upon a fundamental notion of adoption of a *Gesinnung*, which I discussed critically. Of the problems flagged in Chapter 4 which arose from the limited material provided in the Resolution concerning the volitional and psychological accounts of free will, Chapter 5 addressed the Moral Leeway problem and one aspect of the Timeless Agency problem, namely the apparent reduction of all our agency to a single choice.

The other aspect of the latter problem is its essential temporal dimension. This is the question of how we are to understand the temporal manifestation of that which, in metaphysical terms, is the possession of an intelligible character, and which, in volitional terms, is the adoption of maxims. The latter will have to be manifested in time in such a way that this is compatible with the determinism of nature.

In metaphysical terms, this compatibility is achieved by Kant's theory of the determination of an empirical character. But how does this unchanging law of nature represent my temporal agency, i.e. my pursuit of various purposes at different points in time? This is an aspect of the volitional account that needs clarification.

Related to this, and perhaps more pressing, the Temporal Leeway problem arises from this doctrine of the empirical character: How could I have the ability to act otherwise in time if my character is unchanging? The leeway that, I claimed in Chapter 3, is required for sourcehood, must also be manifested in time. Indeed, without such temporal leeway, the agent's action would in principle be predictable, which would clash with the control I understand free will as involving. This question must be addressed by further examining the nature of the empirical character, i.e. the key concept at the heart of the psychological account.

I have already indicated that this character is the law of the agent's psychological causality, but one might well wonder about the agent's ability to bring about physical actions, so something must also be said about the need for and possibility of a physical account of free will.

The chapter is organised as follows. In Section A, I examine how to integrate the account of agency in terms of maxim-adoption with the possession of an empirical character as it has been defined in Chapter 4. This raises several questions, among which the determination of the circumstances in which an agent acts on a particular maxim and the impossibility of action predetermination are the two most important ones (Section B). By proposing an account of the empirical character in Section C that addresses these two related questions, a solution to the Temporal Leeway problem is formulated which completes the response to the Timeless Agency problem. In terms of textual resources, Kant's *Religion within the Boundaries of Mere Reason* (REL), the *Metaphysical Foundations of Natural Science* (MFNS) and various *Reflexionen* will provide valuable source material.

The final two sections of the chapter focus upon, first, the clarification of what is needed in terms of a physical account of freedom, as well as what Kant's conception of freedom as normative implies for the physical account, namely a requirement in the form of the 'ought-implies-can' principle. I then examine the question of further understanding *in principle* how the psychological account's intentions and physical actions can be connected without infringing the natural laws of the physical world, by drawing upon a *Reflexion*. I thereby propose a possible approach to the empirical question of this mind-body interaction required by the physical account and show how it chimes with a contemporary account of this interaction.

A. The nature of the empirical character

Maxims, actions and subjective principles

As discussed in Chapter 5, a maxim of action is defined by Kant as a 'subjective principle ()' (GMM AA04: 401n; see AA04: 421n) and can be represented in the following form:

(M): 'I shall φ with purpose Φ.'

So, for instance: 'I shall develop certain skills (φ) so as to be more helpful to others (Φ). The adoption of a maxim, *qua* part of the volitional account of what is, metaphysically, the intelligible causality of freedom, is not temporally located.

However, the manifestation in appearance of the adoption of maxims, i.e. the manifestation of the agent's intelligible character, occurs at determinate times. So, at time t the agent's will is manifested as an intention to act on maxim (M). That is, at t, the agent decides, in circumstances $\mathbb{C}$, to do $\varphi(\mathbb{C})$ (action-token of type φ) to serve purpose Φ, i.e. to realise purpose $\Phi(\mathbb{C})$ which is the state-of-affairs achieved by completing $\varphi(\mathbb{C})$; $\mathbb{C}$ includes all that the agent is aware of at t, i.e. the state of her inner sense. So, for instance, in the face of the needs of my ageing local community ($\mathbb{C}$), I shall learn to drive a minibus ($\varphi(\mathbb{C})$) to get the required licence ($\Phi(\mathbb{C})$) to drive them around.

The intention to $\varphi(\mathbb{C})$ belongs to the psychological account and is explained by Kant in terms of the empirical character which, in turn, is characterised by 'subjective principles of his power of choice' (A549/B577) and as 'the appearances of his power of choice' (A549/B577; see Chapter 4). Since the power of choice is described by the adoption of maxims, these subjective principles are the appearance of the maxims[1] which are, as noted earlier, themselves defined as subjective principles.

That Kant does not understand the empirical character's subjective principles as maxims is clear from his not using the term 'maxim' in the Resolution of the Third Antinomy (hereafter 'Resolution') when characterising the empirical character while he does use it elsewhere in the CPR in discussing ethics (A812/B840). Further, Kant's distinction between 'practical principles' (called 'maxims' when they are subjective), 'which contain a general determination of the will' and the 'several practical rules' under it (CPrR AA05: 18–19), indicates that there is a need for further specification of these maxims, a task which will have to be shouldered by the empirical character's subjective principles since they determine action.

This suggests understanding the empirical character's subjective principles as having the form (see Chapter 4):

[E] In circumstances $\mathbb{C}$, I shall $\varphi(\mathbb{C})$,

where $\varphi(\mathbb{C})$ is the action-token to be performed in circumstances $\mathbb{C}$ to bring about purpose $\Phi(\mathbb{C})$.

Since [E] must specify both the set of circumstances $\mathbb{C}$ and the action-tokens $\varphi(\mathbb{C})$ of the action-type φ to be performed therein, this is actually a short form for a conjunction of propositions:

[E]: In circumstances $\mathbb{C}_i$, I shall $\varphi(\mathbb{C}_i)$ for $1 \leq i \leq p_E$.

where P_E is the number of distinct circumstances $\mathbb{C}_i$ in which principle [E] is active, i.e. where (M) is manifested in appearance.

It is worth noting that. in this specification of the psychological account, although the action-type φ does not feature explicitly (it belongs to the merely intelligible volitional account), the specific intentions $\{\varphi(\mathbb{C}_i)\}$ for $1 \leq i \leq p_E$ define *classes* with common features. This is an instance where source compatibilism, e.g. in the form of Bratman's (2003) planning theory (Chapter 1), provides a useful formulation of the psychological account. His *general intentions* capture the meaning of these classes of particular intentions. While Bratman's theory fails to meet the challenge of the Argument from Manipulation (Chapter 1), this problem is avoided by Kant's grounding of these general intentions in the agent's intelligible causality of freedom and the maxim-adoptions it can be understood volitionally as involving.

Linking the psychological and volitional accounts

The psychological account as it has been formulated so far raises two questions that must be addressed if the volitional account in terms of maxim-adoptions is to be integrated with it. First, how are the circumstances $\mathbb{C}$ determined in which maxim (M) is acted upon, e.g. why is the state of my ageing local community viewed by me as calling for me to develop certain skills to help them? Second, given (M) is the maxim to act upon in $\mathbb{C}$, how is action-type φ specified as action-token $\varphi(\mathbb{C})$; e.g. How do I reach the conclusion that it is by getting a minibus driving licence that I should implement (M)?

Addressing the second question first, one particular worry is that the determination of $\varphi(\mathbb{C})$ does not simply follow as manifestation in appearance of the adoption of maxim (M), but that a *further choice* might seem required; this would involve a further maxim. As Talbot Brewer (2002: 560f) explains, however, the issue of how a maxim (M), moral or otherwise, is to be applied, cannot require appealing to a maxim (M') since the application of (M') would in turn involve a maxim (M"), which would lead to an infinite regress. That no further maxims are involved means that *no further free choice* is required.

Nevertheless, there is an epistemic question here as to how the agent knows to intend $\varphi(\mathbb{C})$ in circumstances $\mathbb{C}$. It seems therefore that what one might call a *practical judgement* is required. Kant refers to such judgements in the case of duty: they reflect 'the proficiency of choice in accordance with the laws of freedom' (MM AA06: 218; see also CPrR AA05: 67–8). Further, Kant is confident that we know 'how to distinguish in every case that comes up what is good and what is evil' (GMM AA04: 404). As for the non-moral practical issue of what to do, Kant refers to the need to develop children's judgement about 'what they might make their ends', and as to how to go about pursuing them, Kant refers to the acquisition of '*skill* in the use of means to all sorts of *discretionary* ends' (GMM AA04: 415).[2]

Turning now to the first question, in metaphysical terms, it is the question of why this agent's causality of freedom manifests itself in this way, by being activated (intention/action on (M)) at this time, i.e. in these circumstances. This might seem like asking why the causality of magnetism manifests itself now by attracting this object, and later by repulsing that one, to which the answer just lies in the nature of the causality in question. But insofar as the causality of freedom has been represented volitionally in terms of the adoption of *Gesinnung* and maxims, some further explanation is needed of how this volitional account is related to specific intention-formation in particular circumstances. This is an aspect of the Timeless Agency problem that, for some commentators (e.g. Ferrari 2018: 1620), provides a major obstacle to their endorsing Kant's account of freedom. I turn to it in Section B.

Duty, inclinations and Temporal Leeway

Two more worries arise for the compatibility of the volitional and psychological accounts. First, Kant's psychological account is sometimes characterised in terms of inclinations (e.g. Kerstein 2002). Among the psychological circumstances $\mathbb{C}$ are inclinations. Their function in agency is that of desires, but also beliefs: the desire to bring about $\Phi(\mathbb{C})$, and a belief that $\varphi(\mathbb{C})$ is the way to do this are both inclining factors in doing $\varphi(\mathbb{C})$. So, for instance, feeling exhausted after working on this book for ten hours ($\mathbb{C}$), I desire to switch off ($\Phi(\mathbb{C})$) and believe that this is best achieved watching a stand-up comedian ($\varphi(\mathbb{C})$). A problem arises, though, which has exercised many Kant scholars (e.g. Kerstein 2002): in the case of my acting on a maxim (M) of duty (e.g. to repay the £100 I borrowed from a neighbour), it is not clear what inclination could be involved in the psychological account in appearance. The problem here is the desire component of this inclination: How could a dutiful action be causally accounted for in appearance by a desire?

Some commentators assume that the relevant inclination is respect (Insole 2013: 130). However, respect has an 'intellectual cause' and 'is known a priori', so cannot be a sensuous inclination (CPrR AA05: 73). Further, unlike an inclination, it is always present (REL AA06: 49; see Timmermann 2003: 189–95): this is indeed essential if imputability is not to be conditional upon the assumption of its presence (Timmermann 2003: 189–95; see Köhl 1990: 123).

It is, however, the case that action from duty develops inclinations towards doing what is morally worthy, as Kant explains: 'Reason gradually draws sensibility into *habitus*, arouses incentives, and hence forms a character' (Refl. 5611 AA18: 252; see Onof 2011b: 132). Thus an inclination-to-the-good characterises dutiful action in appearance and is active as the agent forms the intention to act.[3] So, as for any type of action, the purpose Φ defined by maxim (M), which is here the purpose of fulfilling my duty, is manifested as a *desire* to achieve state-of-affairs $\Phi(\mathbb{C})$ (e.g. settle my debt with my neighbour) called for by duty in circumstances $\mathbb{C}$ (e.g. my being my neighbour's debtor). The fact that action-type φ is required by duty according to (M), is manifested in appearance as a belief that action-token $\varphi(\mathbb{C})$ (e.g. to give my neighbour £100 in cash) is the way to achieve $\Phi(\mathbb{C})$. This is perfectly compatible with the bringing about of Φ resulting from the incorporation of the incentive of respect for the moral law into (M) (see Chapter 5).

Second, the Temporal Leeway problem is possibly the most important concern raised by the concept of the empirical character. The worry is that when, in circumstances $\mathbb{C}$, my adoption of maxim (M) is manifested through the formation of the intention to $\varphi(\mathbb{C})$, this intention and the action which follows would *seem to be predetermined* insofar as it is already specified in my empirical character characterised by subjective principle [E], that I shall intend $\varphi(\mathbb{C})$. This worry threatens a cornerstone of my interpretation since it could suggest, as Indregard (2018: 665f) contends, that it is mistaken to reduce the empirical character to causal law(s).

The problem can also be spelled out in terms of a belief-desire model. My decision (maxim-adoption) is manifested in time as a *desire* for the realisation of state-of-affairs $\Phi(\mathbb{C})$, which specifies purpose Φ in circumstances $\mathbb{C}$, and a *belief* that a token of action-type φ, $\varphi(\mathbb{C})$, through which $\Phi(\mathbb{C})$ is realised, is the way to achieve this in circumstances $\mathbb{C}$. With this understanding of the empirical character in terms of reasons, the problem now takes the following form: the relevant beliefs/desires must either be in place before the agent's action, or be determined, in the deterministic psychological account, by others which are. This apparently leaves no place for the agent's will altering them at time t. I return to this question in Section B.

Further clarifications

Three clarifications are required here. First, while the Resolution has the intelligible character as transcendental cause of the empirical character, this does not mean that the agent's free willing is the only causal factor accounting for the nature of the empirical character. As Kant puts it, '[h]ow much of [the empirical character] is to be ascribed to mere nature and innocent defects of temperament or to its happy constitution (merita fortunae) this no one can discover' (A551/B579n; see Chapter 4). The full causal determination of the empirical character therefore draws upon initially non-freely chosen contingent features of the agent, namely his temperament. Elsewhere, Kant distinguishes that which pertains to freedom as 'character' (which stands here for the intelligible character) from 'temperament' as the effect of other causes: 'actions are sufficiently (practically) determined by character and temperament' (Refl. 4441 AA17: 548). The latter is determined by 'the influence of sensibility as a special cause' (Refl. 4441 AA17: 548). Character and temperament together determine the empirical character.

This does not weaken Kant's reply to the Infinite Regress Argument (Chapter 3): any aspect of temperament relevant to one's actions (i.e. of which I am conscious) is something one endorses or else strives to eliminate: the randomness of my temperament having certain characteristics does not infect the rest of my agency (see also Chapter 5).

There is also, for Kant, a normative dimension to this: there is thus a 'prohibition against depriving [oneself] of the *prerogative* of a moral being, that of acting in accordance with moral principles, that is, inner freedom' (MM AA06: 429) and therefore against endorsing any inclinations that would threaten one's ability to do one's duty. Developing inclinations counterbalancing defaults of temperament is also required. Thus, against an 'evil will (...) in him', an agent has a duty to 'develop the original disposition to a good will' (MM AA06: 441), namely the inclination-to-the-good . This involves cultivating 'disposition[s] of sensibility that () promote (...) morality' (MM AA06: 443). For instance, there is 'an indirect duty to cultivate the compassionate natural (...) feelings in us' (MM AA06: 457).[4]

Second, a requirement for the compatibility of psychological and volitional accounts is that the empirical character reflect the hierarchical organisation of maxims (Chapter 5). This must be satisfied through a greater frequency of action upon of higher-ranked maxims, which in turn will correspond to stronger or more prevalent inclinations to act on those maxims.

This result sheds light upon an agent's conversion to a good *Gesinnung* (Chapter 5). Kant describes the process of the agent's carrying out dutiful action as an infinitely long progression towards holiness (REL AA06: 48), and we can now see what it involves in time, i.e. at the psychological level. In the case of frailty, by acting more frequently on a maxim of duty after the conversion, the strength of inclinations opposing my duty decreases. With impurity, the growth of the inclination-to-the-good which ensues will progressively render otiose the need for a sensuous inclination for me to act in accordance with duty. In the case of perversity, this growth relative to other inclinations will mean that a diminishing number of circumstances will be found in which the agent acts on non-moral maxims, as explained in Chapter 5.

Third, according to what I have said, it would seem that maxim-adoption is only manifested when a specific intention is formed to act on this maxim. In distinguishing between inner and outer actions (MM AA06: 214, 218–19), Kant could be interpreted as pointing to the first, i.e. acts of *Willkür*, as being manifested at temporal locations independently of any action. I think that this is quite plausible and would just involve adding to the proposed picture the manifestation of the outcome of some general act of deliberation at some point in time in terms of the acquisition of a belief and a desire reflecting the content of the adopted maxim. The possibility of such an acquisition will follow from the possibility of my free will producing any intention (and determining corresponding belief and desire) to act in time, which I examine further.

While this initial examination of the empirical character has shed light upon the formal integration of volitional and psychological accounts, the two questions about the temporality of agency still need to be addressed: (i) Why does the agent act on maxim (M) when circumstances $\mathbb{C}$ arise? and (ii) how is it that our actions are not predetermined by the empirical character?

B. Determination and predetermination of action

Spelling out the Temporal Leeway problem

I am going to assume for now that question (i) has been addressed, i.e. I have an account of why maxim (M) is that which the agent acts upon in circumstances $\mathbb{C}$. I therefore turn to question (ii) about predetermination. With the empirical character as I have interpreted it earlier, this Temporal Leeway problem takes on the following form.

If circumstances $\mathbb{C}$ reoccur at time t, I should have alternative possibilities available to me. But my empirical character (A539/B567) is, like all natural causality, a power that is an unchanging ground of temporal determinations, here, of mental states, e.g. of intentions. So if circumstances $\mathbb{C}$ have already occurred, it is therefore the case that it is already determined that I shall bring about state-of-affairs $\Phi(\mathbb{C})$ by doing $\varphi(\mathbb{C})$. This can be formulated in terms of a belief-desire model: I already have a desire to bring about $\Phi(\mathbb{C})$ and a belief that $\varphi(\mathbb{C})$ is the way to do this; or in terms of Kantian inclinations: I have an inclination to $\varphi(\mathbb{C})$. So it would seem that my action is predetermined and that I have no alternative possibilities in time.

To be clear: this does not take away the leeway I have that is expressed in terms of my ability to either cause a different empirical character (metaphysical account) or adopt different maxims (volitional account), which would have led to different actions $\varphi(\mathbb{C})$. This leeway is certainly manifested in time in this sense that, the first time that circumstances $\mathbb{C}$ arise, my maxim-adoption is manifested temporally as the determination of an intention to $\varphi(\mathbb{C})$. But the issue flagged by the Temporal Leeway problem is that, once these circumstances have occurred, I seemingly no longer have any leeway in time when they next occur: my action is predetermined, and in principle, predictable.

On this latter point, let us briefly revisit Kant's predictability claim in the Resolution:

> if we could investigate all the appearances of his power of choice down to their basis, then there would be no human action that we could not predict with certainty, and recognize as necessary given its preceding conditions. (A549–50/B577–8)

My interpretation of the empirical character sheds light upon the meaning of investigating 'the appearances of the power of choice down to their basis'. What is needed for action prediction is knowledge of the subjective principles [E] that constitute this character. They represent this basis insofar as they define general intentions which include all particular intentions (see previous discussion). Knowledge of these principles would not infringe the Kantian prohibition upon knowledge of merely intelligible reality, namely the underlying maxim (M) as feature of the agent's intelligible character. I interpreted Kant's epistemic requirement for predictability as unrealisable even in principle, however, because all appearances over a lifetime would have to be thoroughly investigated (Chapter 4), implying that Kant is here making a clear distinction between determinism and predictability. But what justifies Kant's claim that *all* the appearances of the power of choice need to be thoroughly investigated? From what we have just seen, *if circumstances* ℂ *reoccur*, I do not need to know the whole of subjective principle [E] (which, as we saw earlier, specifies the agent's intentions for a range of circumstances), or indeed any other such principle to predict what the agent will do: I just need to look at what she did last time these exact same circumstances occurred.

Now one response to this problem would be to accept the consequence, i.e. actions can be predetermined, and argue that the leeway available in the adoption of maxims is all that is needed. I think this response is not satisfactory in volitional terms. Much as the law that predetermines my actions has been chosen by me, it still remains the case that I find myself lacking temporal control of my action. If in circumstances ℂ of a busker boarding the commuter train and playing a certain tune on his fiddle, I have in the past given him one pound, my control of my agency implies that I should have the leeway, next time the same busker plays the same tune on the same train, with all other aspects of the spatial setting identical, not to donate that pound.

Determination and predetermination: Textual evidence

Some Kant scholars argue that accepting a strong claim of psychological determinism commits Kant to endorsing the possibility of predetermining action (e.g Irwin 1984: 38), hence the need to espouse a weaker deterministic claim (e.g. Ertl 1998: 83). Others, like Allison (1990: 43), view Kant's predictability claim in the Resolution (A549–50/B577–8) as a threat to the possibility of free will, and so rejects it as incompatible with his views on psychology. But is there any evidence that Kant himself understands the agent as having alternative possibilities in time?

Kant does make a clear distinction between determination (implied by determinism) and predetermination of action (which entails predictability in principle) in the *Reflexionen* (n° 5611 to 5620), which Adickes dates back to 1776–9 and which were famously analysed by Heimsoeth (1973). The distinction predetermination/determination is flagged in Reflexion 5619. Kant indicates that 'everything is *quoad sensum* necessary and can be explained in accordance with laws of sensibility' (Refl. 5619 AA18: 257). He then argues that, since 'reason is a *principium* that does not appear and is thus not given among appearances', predetermination of action, i.e. 'determination to *actu* cannot be' (Refl. 5619 AA18: 257).

This certainly in line with the Resolution claim as I have interpreted it, but the argument is problematic[5] insofar as, while reason does not appear, it is an open question, as discussed with respect to the text of the Resolution, whether the empirical character is itself inferable, at least in part, from these appearances. This text, together with that of the Resolution strongly suggest that Kant must be *assuming something* about psychological causality which enables him to conclude that, however much we could infer from the past about the empirical character, it still is not the case that actions are predetermined. To understand the covert assumption in these claims from Kant's texts therefore requires looking at his views on empirical psychology. Examining this in the next subsection will shed light upon what is distinctive about laws of inner sense such as the empirical character.

That the nature of inner sense is crucial here is generally overlooked in the literature. However, it is worth noting Benjamin Vilhauer's (2010; see also 2004) important proposal for dealing with the problem of making sense of an altered-law interpretation of the causal impact of freedom upon appearances. Vilhauer actually addresses a problem that would arise if we accept that the empirical character is determined by causal antecedents in time as Walker (1978: 148–9) contends: in this way the same problem that the altered-past interpretation (see Chapter 2) gave rise to rears its head again. That is: it would seem that to be the first cause of my empirical character, I must be the first cause of the causal regress determining it. I do not consider this as a problem insofar as I showed in Chapter 4 that what is caused by antecedent appearances is merely my temperament, leaving plenty of aspects of my empirical character that are not so determined.

Nevertheless, Vilhauer's proposal to avoid this problem, i.e. the laws of nature that free will has control over are 'limited-instantiation-scope' laws (2010: 59) whose manifestations are 'rare enough' (2010: 70), is interesting. Importantly, he argues that inner sense (2010: 66–9) is the locus of limited-instantiation-scope laws. The spirit of this proposal is correct, I think, insofar as it is useful for making actual predictability very unlikely because of the absence of sufficient plurality of instantiations from which to infer laws by induction.

However, Vilhauer's proposal does not address the metaphysical problem of predetermination (predictability in principle): he does not show that such laws do not constrain the agent in the future. I shall argue further that this issue must be addressed by drawing upon specific features of psychological laws that are instantiated *once only*. Further, Vilhauer relies upon the *contingent* diversity of mental events which ensures the limited instantiation of laws in inner sense. What is needed to prop up Kant's claim are *necessary* features of such laws.

C. The determination of the empirical character

Kant and empirical psychology

I have already indicated in Chapter 4 that there is no contradiction in claiming that every agent has an empirical character, i.e. a law of his practical rationality in appearance, although there are no psychological laws. Indeed, a psychological law, *qua* law of a presumed science of empirical psychology, would apply universally to any agent's inner sense. But the empirical character, defined in terms of subjective principles, is singular, characteristic of *a particular agent*, since it is the effect of this agent's intelligible character. Still, a law such as the empirical character is valid for all time in the agent's domain of inner sense, i.e. when she is alive and conscious, and this is the nub of the problem giving rise to the Temporal Leeway problem of predetermination.

In the MFNS, Kant explains that empirical psychology, or 'the empirical doctrine of the soul', is, like chemistry, not a 'science' (MFNS AA04: 471). The reason is that it is not mathematisable because it deals with the one-dimensional domain of inner sense: the only mathematical properties that could be assigned to phenomena of inner sense would pertain to the continuity of time. What exactly is the issue Kant is referring to?

The ability to determine the content of the senses mathematically is explained in transcendental idealism by their having an *a priori* form (e.g. B40–1; B47). For outer sense, a plethora of determinations are thus available. Position in space and shape are determined through the three spatial dimensions of an object's boundaries and/or the positions of its parts, colours are definable by reference to wavelengths, the material content of space is characterised in terms of physical properties that relate its changes over time and space[6], etc. So the three dimensions of space and the evolution of spatial properties over time enable the rich content of outer sense to be represented mathematically.

By contrast, for two distinct states of inner sense (see A22/B37; A34/B50; A38/B55),[7] we can only determine mathematically their relative positions within the one-dimensional form of inner sense, time. That means that we can determine the times of their occurrence and judge, for instance, that, in continuous time, an infinity of other time-points separates them. We cannot represent mathematically anything about the contents of these states and how they might be related, because one-dimensional time affords no formal structure in which this content could be determined quantitatively.[8]

If this debars empirical psychology from being granted the status of a science, Kant claims that even as 'systematic art' or 'systematic natural doctrine', psychology is much poorer than chemistry (MFNS AA04: 471). The reason is that, unlike the spatial case, 'the manifold of internal observation is separated [from the observer] only by mere thought, but cannot be kept separate and be connected again at will' (MFNS AA04: 471). So, while the object of introspection is immediately present in awareness, when I seek to determine it objectively, I have to distance myself from it *in thought*. But such distancing is not based upon any given objective criteria as in the spatial case. Consequently, when I claim that I am thinking of the same object, no re-identifiability criteria are given to support this claim.[9]

A science can rely upon mathematical criteria (e.g. quantities such as position coordinates). A systematic natural doctrine can draw upon looser criteria that have not been given mathematical expression, such as classification criteria. These criteria all ultimately rely upon spatiality. In the case of empirical psychology, the nature of time does not allow for objective criteria to be given to introspection. It is not only the one-dimensionality of time that is at stake here: if this one dimension were spatial, it would be possible to keep an objective distance from the object. What is different with time is the way the subject is *in* time:[10] while I can alter my spatial position at will, I am constrained to be in the present: I am carried along one-dimensional time together with all that is present. As a result of this *temporal embeddedness*, I cannot distance myself objectively in inner sense from the object of introspection which is present to me.

Further, 'the observation itself alters and distorts the state of the object observed' (MFNS AA04: 471). Since time does not provide the means of defining objective re-identifiability criteria, if the subject determines the manifold of inner sense, this determination will partly be a result of the subjective perspective from which the object is kept at a distance in thought. That entails that the determination will involve a contribution of the subject which alters the object.[11] In terms of the aims of empirical psychology, this is a distortion. Again, the embeddedness of the subject in time is the issue: insofar as both subject and object are not separable on the basis of given objective criteria, the subject alters the nature of the object in determining it from its subjective perspective. This comports, at least for objects of inner sense, with a central tenet of hermeneutical phenomenology: namely, phenomenological description is always interpretation (Heidegger 1962: 61–2).[12]

Finally, note that what I have just claimed about objects of inner sense does not apply to perception. While my perceptual states are states of inner sense, in perception, their content in outer sense is what is at stake: this is determined objectively. This is important because it provides one aspect of the circumstances I am in that is determined objectively without further ado.

The practical interpretation's metaphysical role as complement of sufficiency

What are the implications of these features of objectivity in inner sense for the determination of the empirical character and the question of predetermination? In discussing the Temporal Leeway problem, I have so far assumed that circumstances $\mathbb{C}$ are given. However, these are circumstances of the agent's inner sense: while perceptual circumstances in isolation could straightforwardly be identified objectively, the determination of the other circumstances of inner sense is, as we have just seen, itself a problem. That is:

1. There is no objective method applicable to the determination of the whole of $\mathbb{C}$[13]
2. The determination of the whole of $\mathbb{C}$ has no independently given criteria.
3. The determination of the whole of $\mathbb{C}$ must be an interpretation in which I make sense of $\mathbb{C}$.

These features of the content of inner sense are not only of epistemological import. To say that the object can only be determined with a subjective contribution reveals both an epistemological shortcoming and, *metaphysically*, the inevitability of a contribution of the subject to the object of inner sense.[14] In terms of psychological causality, this means that something (e.g. state-of-affairs) is a reason for action only insofar as the subject makes that something into such a reason. We will see the consequences of this in the following section.

Having established these features of the determination of circumstances of inner sense, I now want to return to question (i) which I left aside at the outset of this investigation into the Temporal Leeway problem. This is the question of how I determine the maxim (M) to act upon in circumstances $\mathbb{C}$. This will shed light on how to solve this problem.

The first point to make in addressing this question is that, to decide what to do in the circumstances the agent is in at time t, the agent must determine them since she needs determinate circumstances $\mathbb{C}$ for her decision as to how to act. From what has just been said about this determination, it amounts to *interpreting* $\mathbb{C}$: let us call this a *practical interpretation*. What this interpretation has to work on are the determinate perceptual circumstances and some indeterminate contents of inner sense. In the light of these, the agent will judge what practical attitude to take towards them.[15]

So we find that, to determine the object of inner sense in question, i.e. to determine the circumstances at t as circumstances $\mathbb{C}$, a *decision* is required. From Kant's Theory of Choice (Chapter 5), this must involve a maxim. But our problem is that determinate circumstances are needed to identify the maxim (M) to act upon. A vicious circle would seem to emerge here since determinate circumstances are required to identify the relevant maxim, but a maxim is required to determine these circumstances.

It can only be avoided if the present manifestation of the act of *Willkür* of adopting maxim (M) involves my taking the current circumstances, as circumstances $\mathbb{C}$ of application of (M). That is, on the basis of the already objectively determined perceptual circumstances and the other indeterminate contents of inner sense, the agent decides through this act that maxim (M) is to be applied and thereby determines these non-perceptual aspects of the circumstances of inner sense as circumstances $\mathbb{C}$ to which (M) applies.[16]

This has intuitive appeal. So far, maxim-adoption has been discussed in terms of its providing a volitional account of what is, metaphysically, the causality of freedom; but to adopt a maxim (M) must also be to determine when it applies, otherwise, it would be pure theory and not what defines my actual free agency. So the temporal dimension of maxim-adoption must be the determination of circumstances $\mathbb{C}$ of application. What characterises this determination is that, for the non-perceptual aspects of $\mathbb{C}$, because of the nature of inner sense, this amounts to determining them as circumstances of application of (M).

To illustrate this, consider perceptual circumstances that are objectively determined as the presence of a person standing in my way as I go to a party, a person who is struggling to carry a heavy item. What is not determinate is my attitude towards these objective perceptual circumstances. The determination of this mental state (which will fully determine the circumstances of action as $\mathbb{C}$) can, for simplicity,[17] be reduced to determining: (i) a desire D that is required to define what I aim to do ($\Phi(\mathbb{C})$) with respect to this obstacle, and (ii) a belief B about what action $\varphi(\mathbb{C})$ I shall take to achieve this aim. Both B and D are required to determine my intention as causally determined by my psychological causality (empirical character).

Two such available options for me to choose might be:

- I determine $\mathbb{C}$ as the presence of an obstacle to be avoided to minimise the time I waste in getting to the party according to a maxim of being efficient in pursuing my goals. This decision is made on the basis of self-love and defines my purpose $\Phi(\mathbb{C})$. A secondary moral incentive (see Chapter 5) enjoins me not to infringe any narrow duties to the obtruding person: this will define action $\varphi(\mathbb{C})$. My desire D is to get around the obstacle as quickly as possible, and the content of my belief B is how to achieve this within these moral constraints.
- I determine $\mathbb{C}$ as the presence of another agent in need of help. The incentive here is the moral one and defines the provision of help as my purpose $\Phi(\mathbb{C})$. A secondary incentive of self-love motivates me not to waste too much time in so doing since I am on my way to the party: this will define the action $\varphi(\mathbb{C})$. My desire D is to provide help, and the content of my belief B is how to achieve this most efficiently given my other purposes.

The formation of my intention to act corresponds to the *manifestation at this time t of my incorporation of a maxim (M)* defining a purpose Φ and a type of action φ. The timeless act of maxim-adoption of *Willkür* examined in Chapter 5 (Incorporation Thesis) has a temporal manifestation: it is manifested at the times at which the adopted maxim is applied.[18] This manifestation is the temporal locus of the 'complement of sufficiency' (Ref. 5611 AA18: 252; see Ref. 5612 AA18: 253 and Chapters 2 and 4) that Kant identifies as the conceptual space for freedom: it provides the complement that is sufficient to determine the state of inner sense as *circumstances $\mathbb{C}$ of application of maxim (M)*. This is the temporal manifestation of the Incorporation Thesis (Chapter 5): my taking these circumstances as circumstances of application of (M) is the temporal manifestation of my incorporation of the relevant incentives in (M).[19] The practical spontaneity of an act of *Willkür* is thus manifested in a particular type of theoretical spontaneity, i.e. involved in making judgements about the nature of circumstances as circumstances of application of a certain maxim.

Alternative possibilities in time and the nature of the empirical character

The above proposal addresses the question of the determination of maxim (M) to act upon in circumstances $\mathbb{C}$ by showing that it is the temporal aspect of my decision (maxim-adoption). While it furthers the integration of volitional and psychological accounts, let us see how this addresses the Temporal Leeway problem. My ability to act differently in the future would be the effect in appearance of my ability, through acts of *Willkür* mediated by my practical interpretations, to choose different maxims.

But how could I have such an ability to act *differently over time*? The key here is the arrow of time. It implies that *circumstances of inner sense will never be replicated exactly in the future*. Indeed, even if all the perceptual information is identical (i.e. same spatial circumstances), *I* am not: I have new contents of inner sense (and maybe some that are no longer available, depending upon what I remember) due to what I have experienced since the last time identical perceptual circumstances occurred. For instance, one content of inner sense that is always different, is a representation of how and how often I acted previously in otherwise similar perceptual circumstances.[20]

The non-identity of circumstances of inner sense at a future time implies that it is up to me to interpret them as circumstances $\mathbb{C}$ of application of (M) even if in the past, identical perceptual circumstances were interpreted as such circumstances. As illustration of acting differently in identical *perceptual* circumstances, consider the following. I may judge that now that I see a homeless person in the same place for the third day running, it is appropriate for me to spare some cash, hence my acting on a different maxim (M), all perceptual circumstances being equal. Also, while a year ago one pound seemed like a big donation, this now seems rather stingy in the light of my understanding of the changing cost of living (which features as representation in inner sense and is therefore part of $\mathbb{C}$), hence this alteration of $\mathbb{C}$ does not yield a new action-token of the same type as previously, but of a different action-type φ because a different maxim is applied here.

So the unchanging nature of the empirical character does not impose any restrictions upon the agent's actions in the future. The agent's free will, which is her freedom to adopt maxims of action, is manifested in the absence of any predetermination in appearance of what the agent will do in the ever-new circumstances in which she acts. At any time t, a certain subjective principle [E] will be updated to include new circumstances $\mathbb{C}$ under which the agent acts on the corresponding maxim (M), and how to do so ($\varphi(\mathbb{C})$); or a new principle (implementing a different maxim) will first be manifested.[21]

This suggests that, strictly speaking, the 'appearances of [the] power of choice' (A549/B577) should not be equated with the empirical character but understood as temporally evolving, constituting *the progressive activation of the unchanging empirical character*.[22] This suggestion is supported by Kant's explaining how '[r]eason gradually draws sensibility into *habitus*, arouses incentives, and hence forms a character' (Refl. 5611 AA18: 252) where he is here not referring to the character *qua* law, i.e. the empirical character,[23] but the moral character in a more general sense. This unfolding of the empirical character over time and its constant requirement of the agent's free input (complement of sufficiency) is a feature of it *qua* law of causality of inner sense: it is the particular nature of its form, one-dimensional time, and the subject's embeddedness in it, which account for the difference between such a law and a law of causality of outer sense. This difference explains the oft-overlooked[24] *strategic role* of the division inner/outer sense in Kant's resolution of the Problem: the empirical character is an appearance over time of the intelligible character, thus allowing for open futures.

Further, let us return to Kant's statement in the Resolution about the need to explore *all* the 'appearances of the power of choice' (A549/B577) to predict her actions (see also CPrR AA05: 177). This requirement is clearly necessary because the empirical character as manifestation of the intelligible character, is always only partially manifested at any point in time. Hence the impossibility, even in principle, of inferring the agent's empirical character at any time before the agent's passing.[25] The covert assumption in Kant's argument is therefore the nature of inner sense and its causal laws. The latter also explain Kant's grounds for claiming the impossibility of predetermination in the *Reflexionen* examined earlier. This therefore solves the problem of Temporal Leeway.

Plausibility of the appeal to interpretation

A first objection to my proposal is that the agent seems to be required to constantly make free decisions to be able to act. In fact, the practical interpretation required to determine $\mathbb{C}$ as circumstances of application of (M) is most often nothing but a mere endorsement of the inclinations (or belief/desire) that present themselves (i.e. inclinations based upon how I acted in similar circumstances) as also applying here.[26] This endorsement ensures that some principle [E] is updated to include these new circumstances. This mere endorsement is, however, an act of free will, and this is why the agent is morally responsible for the action.

A second objection is that my account's reliance upon issues of interpretation arguably makes it non-Kantian. Earlier, I indicated in what ways Kant's account of the problem of objective determination in inner sense is, however, strikingly in tune with a basic insight of hermeneutics. But I want to adduce a further consideration, namely Kant's repeated claim that we never know if we act morally (GMM AA04: 406–7).[27] Given that it would not make sense for the volitional account to include any uncertainty in principle about the maxims I adopt, the problem can only lie in the uncertainty about the maxim I act on at any particular point in time. The lack of transparency of an interpretation accounts for this uncertainty and creates room for self-deception. Note that noumenal ignorance requires such uncertainty.[28]

The fact that the determination of the maxim to act upon involves the practical interpretation of $\mathbb{C}$, allows room for self-deception as to which maxim is really involved here. I may thus convince myself that I am interpreting $\mathbb{C}$ as circumstances of application of maxim (M), when in fact I identify action $\varphi'(\mathbb{C})$ called for by (M'). It is arguably only this lack of transparency in interpretation that makes such self-deception possible.

D. What is needed for the physical account

The physical account and the mind-body problem

Since Kant's solution to the Problem goes only as far as explaining how free will could impact the deterministic domain of appearances in inner sense,[29] we are left with the further question of how it impacts outer sense by causing an action,[30] which is the question at the heart of the *physical account* of freedom. Kant's strategy of focussing upon inner sense in the Resolution enables him to view the further problem of how inner impacts outer sense as a separate one lying beyond the Problem *stricto sensu*: it is an aspect of the broader *mind-body problem*, specifically, that of mind-body interaction.

During his critical period Kant does not say much about mind-body interaction. He does argue that the mind-body problem, understood as the problem of the coexistence of both physical and mental properties of the same entity, vanishes within the framework of transcendental idealism. This follows because both are appearances and what is at stake is merely a 'heterogeneity of the appearances of substances' with 'those we ascribe to inner sense' (A385), as Kant puts it in the Paralogisms. This is no longer a problem since there is 'nothing that makes the community of both modes of sense appear strange' (A386): what is at stake is the 'conjunction of representations in inner sense with the modifications of outer sensibility' (A386). Kant no longer needs something like his earlier physical influx theory to account for interaction: the problem has disappeared (Ameriks 1982: ch. 3).

That one can nevertheless talk of interaction is clear from Kant's further indicating that representations of inner and outer sense will therefore 'be conjoined with one another according to constant laws, so that they are connected into one experience' (A386). So, if there is still a question here for an account of the possibility of free will in a deterministic world, it is an *empirical* one. Kant's idealism enables him to defuse any philosophical worries about this interaction since all appearances, whether of inner or outer sense, are not real in-themselves, but ultimately are our representations: representations (manifold in intuition) grounded in the underlying reality in-itself and object-referring syntheses thereof (see Schulting 2017: 10–17).

While the Problem is transcendental (Third Antinomy), the mind-body interaction issue is therefore, because of transcendental idealism, empirical. From what has been said, the core of the physical account therefore consists in the claim that the agent's intelligible causality of freedom, whose law is the intelligible character, can be understood as ground of effects both in inner sense (in terms of the empirical character) and in outer sense (physical actions). Inner→outer sense interaction enables us to interpret this in terms of the determination of inner sense having a causality impacting outer sense. We know that the intelligible character is manifested in inner sense through the formation of the intention to $\varphi(\mathbb{C})$ in circumstances $\mathbb{C}$. The interaction is therefore this intention's causality with respect to outer sense, i.e. the causality of a representation of the purpose $\Phi(\mathbb{C})$ of completing $\varphi(\mathbb{C})$. As Kant puts it: 'real movements of the body arise whose causes lie in the soul's representations' (CJ AA05: 457).[31] This causality of the intention *qua* representation is, like any natural causality, grounded in the intelligible domain, here, in the intelligible character. This interpretation is faithful to the meaning we give to an intention, namely that it triggers an action (assuming no change in $\mathbb{C}$ before the action's inception).[32]

An important additional requirement

More is, however, required of a physical account in the case of a normative theory of freedom such as Kant's. Insofar as freedom is defined for Kant as the capacity to act morally, it must be possible for the agent to act on the moral imperatives that apply in the various situations he may find himself in. Kant thus states unequivocally in the Resolution that 'of course the action must be possible under natural conditions if the ought is directed to it' (A548/B576). This is the 'ought implies can' principle (hereafter OIC), which we have already come across in some form in Chapters 4 and 5.[33] What is not clear in this principle is *the nature of the modality* it involves.

To start with, note that in terms of the framework I have proposed for the volitional and psychological accounts, a maxim (M) does not refer to empirical conditions, so the issue is rather that of defining constraints upon the practical interpretation which determines the current circumstances ℂ as calling for action according to (M).

Markus Kohl (2015b: 691–2) shows that the OIC principle does not entail 'that a valid prescription to aim at some effect implies that the agent's capacities actually suffice for producing that effect' (Kohl 2015b: 691). Indeed, if that were the meaning of the OIC principle, since we have limited knowledge of what we are physically able to do in particular circumstances, all imperatives would depend upon 'the unforeseen vagaries of the empirical world' (Kohl 2015b: 692) so we could not recognise the validity of the imperatives we act upon (which is particularly problematic for the moral 'ought').

Kohl (2015b: 693) then considers Kant's notion of real possibility (A220–3/B267–70).[34] If this is the modality at stake, I must have the kind of powers that would enable me to carry out an action if I ought to do it. So, if I am relevantly disabled, it cannot be required of me that I try and save a drowning child. That the principle is now taken to refer to my general abilities rather than what I can actually do has, as explained earlier, been motivated by epistemic considerations: it might therefore seem that what is relevant is what I take myself to be able to do.

Kohl (2015b: 694) realises this but rejects an interpretation of OIC as 'merely subjective'. That is, it cannot just be a matter of what I happen to believe/know: 'for Kant practical rationality requires theoretical knowledge of facts that fundamentally constrain the efficacy of agency' (Kohl 2015b: 695). This seems right: if that were not the case, I could make a point of avoiding knowledge-acquisition so as to reduce the demands the moral law makes on me. And indeed, Kant's statements are about actual abilities (e.g. AA08: 276–7).

Kohl (2015b: 696) concludes that what is at stake must be real possibility for the agent in terms of her general abilities, and he resists on practical grounds the epistemic alternative which often coincides practically with this, namely the modality of what is foreseeably possible. In decision-making, (i) I must first draw upon what I know about 'general capacities, laws and inductive truths' (2015: 696) before considering what is foreseeable, so these general capacities, etc., have 'epistemic priority' (ii) time-constraints will often not permit me to explore what is specifically foreseeable, and (iii) predictability is limited so that in effect, it is mainly my knowledge of these general capacities that is the only reliable knowledge to draw upon.

This seems prima facie reasonable, but focussing upon general capacities might not be enough. Is it not relevant to know that a certain pill, although generally useful to alleviate pain, can cause a heart attack in special cases? There is something artificial in restricting oneself to general capacities and laws of nature. And further, this restriction is really motivated by our epistemic limitations: these are implied in all of Kohl's arguments I just listed.

I therefore propose that it seems more appropriate[35] (a) to claim that empirical possibility is what is at stake (i.e. real possibility in the particular empirical circumstances ℂ), and (b) to recognise the epistemic dimension for what it is without falling into the trap of describing OIC as merely 'subjective'. This is also called for by the way I consider the agent's grasp of circumstances ℂ as calling for an implementation of a maxim (M), as relying upon an interpretation by the agent of these specific circumstances which will depend upon what the agent knows.

Now Kohl (2015b: 695) points out that we have a moral duty to acquire the knowledge necessary to satisfy our duties (AA09: 43), and he takes this as grounds for not interpreting OIC as 'subjective' in any way. But the existence of such a duty does not imply that other duties assume its fulfilment. Rather, they give rise to this indirect duty of knowledge-acquisition, a duty that will not be fulfilled instantly. So what of the agent's duties who is engaged in thus increasing her knowledge but still has considerable gaps? Does she have imperatives hanging over her which she does not know how to obey?

To answer that, it is important to distinguish between the intelligible and empirical levels. That is, morality requires that we incorporate the maxim of charity (GMM AA04: 423) for instance. But this intelligible act only defines circumstances $\mathbb{C}$ in which the maxim ought to be implemented, *conditionally* upon what the agent knows about the perceptual circumstances that the agent recognises as those of an agent in need of help. That is, the 'ought' goes all the way down to actual intentions in specific conditions that are dependent upon what the agent knows.

Further, the indirect duty of knowledge-acquisition precisely makes sense because without any knowledge, our general moral duties may well define maxims that we ought to adopt, but would not define any circumstances in which we ought to implement them. If I do not know how to recognise someone's needing help, I cannot be blamed for not providing it and therefore what I know is relevant to what I ought to do. But now, since this defines epistemic limitations in identifying circumstances of applicability of a moral maxim, it is my duty to reduce them by acquiring more knowledge to find out how to implement it, and I can be blamed if I am not doing this.

I think this interpretation would be faithful to Kohl's (2015b: 695) essential point that this is not *merely* a subjective matter: knowledge implies truth and it is the truth of a certain state-of-affairs (e.g. someone's needing help) that is at stake in my duty to help in specific circumstances *but only* insofar as I know it. Also, it captures Kohl's important distinction between the OIC principle as applied to 'inner' and 'outer' actions (MM AA06: 214, 218–19; see previous discussion) – the first of which I examined briefly in Chapter 5 – in terms of the intelligible/empirical levels at which free will is manifested. I think that Vilhauer captures this nicely in his claim that the OIC principle with respect to the physical realisation of imperatives should be interpreted as the claim that we know we ought to act in certain ways when and only when we know that we can act in those ways (Vilhauer 2023).[36]

E. Some speculations about further infilling of the physical account

Drawing upon Kant's earlier *Reflexionen* on the Problem

While there is no further material in Kant's critical publications that is directly relevant to the physical account, I want to show that Kant's *Reflexionen* (from 1776–9) on freedom provide textual resources which can be used to suggest an outline of a plausible account of the impact upon outer sense of the formation of intentions in inner sense.

As I noted in Chapter 2, Kant's early critical thinking about the Problem reveals a 'limited-altered-past' understanding of how free will impacts appearances. Kant describes this impact as a transition that occurs in the causal flux 'in sensibility'. This transition arises when 'the intellectual power of choice () determines () an alternative course of sensibility' (Refl. 5616 AA18: 255).[37] It is a transition between the 'first given condition' at time t and this 'alternative course' which is the 'determined action' (Refl. 5616 AA18: 255) at time t'. Kant handles this 'through an infinite intermediate series of appearances' (Refl. 5616 AA18: 255). It is useful to visualise this proposal as in Figure 6.1.

The infinite series separating t and t' (see Figure 6.1) can be called a Zeno series insofar as it is constructed in a way that is analogous to the first of Zeno's paradoxes of motion (Aristotle 1995:Z 9, 239b(11)). That is, the action starting at t' can, according to the determinism of natural causality, only start if an event prior to it but posterior to t causes it. If this event happens at t_1, then in turn, this event can only happen if a further event prior to it but posterior to t causes it, which leads to identifying a time t_2 and so on.[38]

As I indicated in Chapter 2, this proposal, as it is, can only be claimed to preserve the unity of experience (Refl. AA18: 256) on a weak reading of the Second Analogy. All the events in the series follow upon other events according to the law of cause and effect, as the Second Analogy requires (B232/A189). However, the causality that would have been operative at time t had the power of choice not intervened has been prevented from producing its natural effect by the intervention of the power of choice. That means that some law of nature has been infringed here, which is incompatible with the Second Analogy on my strong reading.

Applying this early proposal to mind-body interaction

My reason for looking again at this early critical Kantian solution to the problem is that it would seem well designed to fill in the physical account by providing a model for inner→outer sense interaction. What needs explaining is how the causality of interaction grounded in the intelligible character brings it about that, after time t, the course of physical events is altered insofar as the agent does $\varphi(\mathbb{C})$. The first part of this alteration

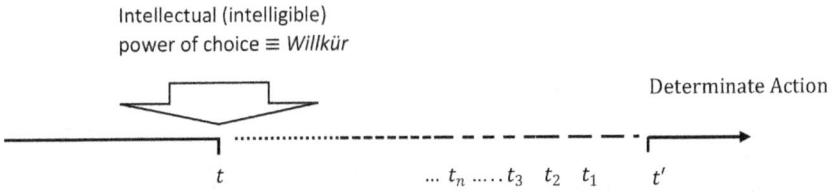

Figure 6.1 The infinite (Zeno) series from decision to action © Christian Onof.

of events through the agent is a neutralisation of the causality/ies of outer sense that would have been activated in certain ways at t had the agent not acted. For example, my intention could alter/neutralise the manifestation of the causality of neurons in the medulla part of the brain stem that were about to trigger a reflex response of sneezing, by delaying/preventing this from happening as I stand on stage at the Royal Albert Hall on graduation day. So the triggering of $\varphi(\mathbb{C})$ can reasonably be thought to involve inner sense determining new circumstances $\mathbb{C}$ [39]in which the course of physical events is altered: this is possible insofar as the domain of outer sense is not a causally closed totality.[40]

Second, the intention must trigger the Zeno series of causally interrelated events, but now, unlike in Kant's *Reflexion* 5616, these are events of outer sense. As in Kant's *Reflexion*, though, the key point is that the events are causally linked through natural laws. This means that the impact of the agent's intention is to trigger an alternative causal series, while the unfolding of this series is ensured by laws of outer sense. All that is therefore required is that inner sense define circumstances that ensure that the various natural causalities involved in producing this causal series are manifested in such a way that they do so. As with the first part of this causal interaction, the idea is that the openness of outer sense can allow for alterations of circumstances in which the causality of outer sense is manifested.[41]

On this picture, therefore, the inner→outer sense causal connection is realised by having the *causalities of a non-causally closed outer sense* feature clauses in their causal laws[42] that define their effects when the circumstances include the presence in an agent's inner sense of the intention to $\varphi(\mathbb{C})$.[43] These extensions refer to single-instantiation circumstances for a given agent. Indeed, as explained earlier, the circumstances $\mathbb{C}$ defined by the state of a particular agent's inner sense when the intention to $\varphi(\mathbb{C})$ is produced, are unique in that agent's life. They could in principle perhaps be reproduced in another agent, but that is irrelevant to an agent's free agency.

The key to the causal interaction must be the relevance of the state of an agent's inner sense when intentions to act are formed, to laws of outer sense causality, through its defining part of the circumstances under which certain causalities of outer sense are manifested in certain ways and others are not. It is this relevance that is properly described as the *causality of inner→outer sense interaction*, a causality partly grounded in both the ground of natural causality in general[44] and the agent's causality of freedom (the intelligible character). Empirically, one would expect it to be (components of) neural nets of the brain's motor cortex whose causality can be represented by laws that feature clauses involving intending-circumstances of inner sense. Below, I examine a contemporary proposal to account for this process.

But what about the infinity of events that follows the discontinuity in circumstances of inner sense? In outer sense, in contrast with Kant's use of this account for inner sense (*Reflexion* 5616), such an infinity of events is arguably more plausible: the infinite divisibility of space would allow causal links to be broken down into infinite series as a causal effect is transmitted through the matter of a substance (as in the motion of an electric current).[45] Further, such an infinity enables us to understand inner-outer sense causality in purposive terms which are consistent with its being a series of events required for the realisation of $\Phi(\mathbb{C})$. To achieve $\Phi(\mathbb{C})$, I need to start $\varphi(\mathbb{C})$ after t', which, as in Zeno's paradoxes, requires that I get half-way to this start, which in turn requires that I get a quarter of the way there, and so on.[46] Such a series has no beginning (Refl. 5616 AA18: 256) insofar as 'we cannot observe () [its] commencement'.

Finally, note that once the dependence of physical laws upon the circumstances of inner sense $\mathbb{C}$ is in place, the above picture could be simplified by doing away with the discontinuity, and rather having circumstances that allow a causal link to connect events at time t and some time t_i of the series that brings about the inception of action $\varphi(\mathbb{C})$ at t'. So, while the previous discussion suggests how it would be possible to bring this about by showing the possibility of such an infinite series, in practice, one might hope that it need not be infinite. With this in mind, I turn to a contemporary account of mind-body interaction.

A related contemporary theory

Although this is only the outline of a proposal, it comports with a contemporary theory of mind-body interaction which provides a plausible physics-based story of the dependence of an outer-sense law upon the contents of inner sense. Insofar as the issue is the causal relevance to outer sense of inner sense, therefore of awareness/consciousness, the obvious place to look is in quantum theory, since certain interpretations of it (e.g. Wigner 1983) argue for such a role. More recently, the quantum-Zeno effect has been proposed to address the mind-body problem. This effect is observed in quantum systems when a sufficiently large number of observations or other perturbations of this system are carried out during a fixed time interval $[0,T]$, so, for instance, at times $T/n, 2T/n, ..., T$. The theoretical result is obtained at the limit as $n \to +\infty$: the high-frequency perturbations ensure that the system remains in a particular state, i.e. the probability of being in that state converges to 1 (Itano et al. 1990; Itano 2009). In that way, a deterministic state of an indeterministic system is brought about.

Henry Stapp (2011: 33-6) proposes this as a mechanism by which an agent, through conscious effort, can force the occurrence of certain quantum states of the firing of calcium ions in nerve terminals, which will lead to the release of neurotransmitters in the brain (2011: 29-32), i.e. in the motor cortex, for instance in the cerebrum.[47] Stapp adds an important phenomenological dimension to his proposal (2011: 41-5): the effort involved in bringing about an action (the effort involved in intending) is exactly what is experienced through the high-frequency perturbation of brain states.

In discussing Clarke's (2003: 181) libertarian proposal, Pereboom (2014: 112) argues that any such interventions in the physical causal account would be incompatible with the statistical law determined by quantum theory (i.e. the Schrödinger equation). But it is the law of large numbers which leads us to expect a certain frequency of outcomes in identical situations. Strictly speaking, such a law is never infringed in an indefinitely long-lasting universe. One might well argue that the law should nevertheless hold approximately over finite durations. But to show that the law is infringed would require having samples of sufficient size where the sample average statistic differs significantly from the value of this statistic according to the statistical law in question. But now, the likelihood of reoccurrence of exactly the same neural configuration in the brain is low as it evolves over time, so that sample sizes will not be large enough for meaningful results to emerge from standard statistical tests.

It might be objected that, with this introduction of an 'intervention' in the physical causal process, this account, like any libertarian account, appeals to causal indeterminism and therefore falls foul of the Luck Arguments discussed in Chapter 3. This is not the case, because in its role of only infilling the *physical* account, the causal indeterminism of quantum theory is not invoked to find a place for *freedom* in the physical domain. Quantum theory is only used to address the question of the possibility of any action based upon a conscious representation whatever its causal origin might be (free or not), a question belonging to the mind-body problem. As explained earlier, Kant has strategically separated this issue from the Problem.

I am not claiming that Kant's proposal is a precursor to this theory, but, if Kant's idealism can be extended to accommodate quantum phenomena (see Strohmeyer 1995; Pringe 2007),[48] Stapp's theory provides a ready explanation for exactly what, empirically, the Zeno series might turn out to be, namely the unfolding of a causal sequence in a neuronal quantum system, which causal sequence experiences a forcing in the form of the subject's intention (experienced as conscious effort) to bring about the action. This forcing will ensure that a particular brain state which corresponds to the triggering of the action, is realised.[49]

F. Concluding remarks

This chapter has clarified how Kant's volitional account of free agency in terms of *Gesinnung-* and maxim-adoption is to be integrated with a psychological account in which free will is manifested in the constant updating of the laws of an agent's power of choice in appearance, which is just the progressive temporal activation of an unchanging law of inner sense, the empirical character. In so doing, the remaining aspects of the Timeless Agency problem, in particular the problem of Temporal Leeway, have been addressed by focussing upon the particular nature of inner sense and its laws.

The further issue of the physical account raised one philosophical question, namely that of how to understand the relation between the normativity of freedom and the agent's ability to implement its imperatives. Otherwise, once mind-body interaction is endorsed in the framework of transcendental idealism, the physical account is an empirical issue for which I proposed the outline of a solution that resonates with a contemporary approach to this issue.

As I indicated in the Chapter 4, the normativity of freedom is not a feature that is required to address the Problem, although it may be a desirable one. The other aspects of the psychological and physical accounts in this chapter are, as I have argued, plausible ways of addressing the Problem; but they do require, apart from transcendental idealism, a conception of inner sense (consciousness) that does not supervene upon outer sense (the physical domain) but has its own causality that interacts with the latter.

With these last three chapters, Kant's metaphysical, volitional, psychological and physical accounts have been interpreted and reconstructed, and the questions of Moral and Temporal Leeway, as well as broader worries about Timeless Agency have been addressed. In Chapter 7, I examine what aspects of Kant's solution we need to retain to address the Problem. I also consider the concern about endorsing transcendental idealism, which I take to be the main stumbling block to finding such a Kantian solution plausible, and I revisit the issue of the normative dimension of freedom.

7

The Kantian solution and its requirements

In Chapters 1 and 3, I argued that the review of contemporary compatibilist and libertarian theories of freedom pointed to the need to adopt transcendental idealism to solve the problem of free will (hereafter the 'Problem'). The Argument from Manipulation called for the need to adopt transcendental idealism to remove the agent's will from the temporal causal nexus of nature, and the Infinite Regress Argument called for a further refinement of this picture characterising freedom as a non-natural causality grounding the agent's psychological causality.

Kant's theory of freedom was presented as a proposal that fits these requirements as a, respectively, source compatibilist (Chapter 2) and libertarian (Chapter 4) solution to the Problem. To this, a normative (Chapter 5) dimension was added as one of its essential features for Kant, although not required to solve the Problem.

The previous three chapters have mainly focussed upon exegetical and systematic issues raised by the interpretation of the details of Kant's metaphysical, volitional and psychological accounts. In this Chapter, in Section A, I draw the consequences for the central aim of this book by examining how Kant's proposal defines an alternative to the naturalistic compatibilist and libertarian proposals available today. This will involve, first, summarising the main features of Kant's proposal and clarifying what is and what is not essential to addressing the Problem. Since I have argued that this Kantian approach appears to be the only solution to the Problem,[1] I consider the implications of the alternative of hard incompatibilism, which enjoins us to accept that there is no solution to the Problem.

Thereafter, I turn to the metaphysical stumbling blocks posed by this proposal, chiefly the adoption of transcendental idealism. I shall thus argue for transcendental idealism on grounds independent of the Problem (Section B), which will lead to some reflections upon the parallels between the problems of free will and of naturalism (Section C). I then discuss various concerns: first, those connected with the adoption of Kant's idealism, and second, some further concerns for naturalism (Section D). Before providing some overall conclusion summarising the claims made in this book, I offer some thoughts about grounding the third essential feature of Kant's proposal, i.e. the normative dimension of freedom, in a way which goes beyond Kant's theory and comports with the outline of the notion of *Gesinnung* I proposed in Chapter 5 (Section E).

A. Kant's theory of free will as the basis of the Kantian solution to the Problem

Kant's conception of free will in a nutshell

From the interpretation of Kant's texts and discussion of the relevant literature carried out in the three previous chapters, Kant's conception of free will can be summarised as follows. Kant's theory does away with the opposition between compatibilism and libertarianism through a radical metaphysical shift through which nature is a domain of appearances grounded in reality in-itself, which requires the adoption of transcendental idealism (Chapters 2 and 3).

The presentation of the *metaphysical account* (Chapter 4) clarified that freedom in its transcendental sense is a noumenal capacity that is a causality (intelligible character) independent of natural causality (transcendental freedom in the negative sense). This causality of freedom grounds a natural law, namely the agent's psychological causality (empirical character) thereby enabling this causality of freedom to be manifested in the deterministic natural domain of appearances. Kant is thus an 'altered-law' source compatibilist.

No theoretical proof of even the real possibility of transcendental freedom can be given, but Kant shows that this real possibility is compatible with causal determinism. Our practical conception of ourselves as free agents under the moral law is of beings endowed with transcendental freedom.

Chapter 5 showed that transcendental freedom is defined by reference to the causality of reason as the capacity to use the latter. The proper use of the causality of reason (transcendental freedom as positive freedom) is action guided by the causality of reason, whose law is the moral law. Since this law is one the agent gives herself, this positive conception of transcendental freedom is autonomy. Kant's doctrine of the Fact of Reason implies that we have practical knowledge of the reality of this freedom.

As far as the *volitional account* is concerned, Kant has shown the reality of practical freedom, i.e. we act under the idea of transcendental freedom. Further, to represent the causality of freedom in terms of a free will exerting its control through making choices, the duality of enabling/driving cause is useful. The agent's *Willkür* is his freedom to adopt a maxim of action and is represented as the agent's incentive (enabling cause) determining the use of the causality of reason (driving cause) characterising *Wille*. Depending upon the nature of the incentive, the latter will either be used properly, in the role of determining the maxim's purpose, or just in a secondary role of defining constraints upon the action governed by this maxim: this is my causal interpretation of the Incorporation Thesis. The *Willkür*'s maxim-adoptions have a law that is the agent's fundamental choice of attitude to the moral law, the *Gesinnung*. The ground for the adoption of the latter cannot be understood given our cognitive limitations.

According to the *psychological account* (Chapter 6), the causality of freedom is manifested in time through the progressive activation of the empirical character, thereby causing the various intentions leading to physical actions. The empirical character can be characterised in terms of subjective principles or of beliefs and desires specifying the circumstances in which to act on the agent's adopted maxims; these principles or reasons causally determine intentions from which actions follow. The progressive unfolding of the empirical character involves an updating of these subjective principles. The circumstances are those of the agent's inner sense (consciousness) which, aside from perceptual circumstances, comprise the agent's perspective upon the latter. A maxim-adoption thus appears in time through a practical interpretation of the circumstances which determines them as circumstances of application of a maxim (practical interpretation).

The further issue of the implementation of the agent's volition as physical action is compatible with the normativity of freedom insofar as Kant endorses an 'ought implies can' principle. No further philosophical concerns arise for this implementation insofar as transcendental idealism defuses any specific concerns connected with mind-body interaction. What will be needed is to endorse the existence of single-instantiation clauses in certain natural laws (e.g. governing neural processes) through which mental circumstances (intentions) are relevant to the determination of the effect brought about by physical causality.

What is needed for a complete Kantian solution to the Problem

The metaphysical account in terms of the grounding of the empirical in the intelligible character, which is the law of a first cause, transcendental freedom, defines the core of the Kantian compatibilist response to the Consequence Argument, and libertarian response to the Infinite Regress Argument. Since such a grounding of a natural law is only plausible in transcendental idealism, the latter is essential to a Kantian solution.

Although in the Resolution of the Third Antinomy, Kant connects this first cause to the concept of the causality of reason, this is required neither by the Consequence nor by the Infinite Regress Argument. This connection is part of the outline of what Kant develops, in his moral writings, into a full volitional account of freedom which has at its core the third essential characteristic of his theory of free will, namely its normativity.

While this normative feature is not required to address the Problem, it allows for an explanatorily more powerful theory of freedom. For, with this feature, the characterisation of an agent's freedom as what makes an agent morally responsible is no longer a merely contingent feature with respect to the existence of moral norms. Rather *freedom is essentially the capacity to act morally*.

I have not, however, endorsed the Reciprocity Thesis' claim (Chapter 5) that the prescriptive law of transcendentally free agency has to be Kant's moral law: the claim that action ought to be motivated by universalisability is questionable, I would argue (see Onof 2009b). I here set aside the issue of what this means for the content of morality and the characterisation of autonomy[2] and will only, further in this chapter, outline an alternative grounding of moral norms motivating the normative conception of freedom as capacity for moral agency. Insofar as Kant's doctrine of the Fact of Reason is questionable, I also do not endorse his claim that we have practical knowledge of transcendental freedom.

However, Kant's consideration of the theoretical use of reason as practical activity shows that the agent always acts under the idea of freedom. Further, Kant's volitional account in terms of maxim-adoption and the Incorporation Thesis is a useful model of choice. I have already commented on the fact that Kant does not, ultimately, draw upon the explanatory self-sufficiency of willings in shoring up individual acts of maxim-adoption in the choice of a *Gesinnung* as he understands it. To address the Infinite Regress and Rational Luck objections, a notion of *Gesinnung* is required that is a fundamental choice defining a purpose for the whole of agency.[3] Minimally, this purpose is the coherence of this agency.

Kant's strategy of drawing upon the specific nature of inner sense as the locus of a law of nature is another key pillar of his theory of freedom that is generally not sufficiently appreciated. The fact that the circumstances of inner sense are always novel implies that the causality of inner sense always requires a complement of determinacy. The progressive appearing of the intelligible character (the law of the agent's freedom) as empirical character (the agent's psychological causality) is an essential feature of the psychological account which enables atemporal leeway and choices to be manifested in time. Finally, the intentions that are thereby defined must be able to cause physical actions.

The two major metaphysical requirements of a Kantian solution to the Problem are therefore (i) the truth of transcendental idealism and (ii) the plausibility of Kant's conception of inner sense. As far as this second issue is concerned, inner sense for Kant is the locus of all manner of conscious mental states (A357-8), including representations (imaginary or perceptual), among which there are also intentions (A358-9). This would have been familiar to his contemporaries from Tetens's (1777) empirical psychology. Although we no longer use the term 'inner sense' today, much of what is needed for the purpose of a Kantian theory can be accommodated by characterising the contents of inner sense in terms of a type of consciousness of them.[4] The notion of awareness is useful here when defined as 'an object in the environment, a state of one's body, or of one's mental state, among other things' (Chalmers 1996: 28). Inner sense, however, cannot be a candidate for reduction to (functions instantiated in) physical processes.[5] There is no space to discuss this further here other than to note that this reducibility is an open issue in contemporary philosophy of mind, with at least phenomenal consciousness arguably not supervening upon the physical (e.g. Chalmers 1996).

Before turning to an argument and various considerations supporting transcendental idealism, I want to emphasise the intuitive aspects of Kant's theory and, by contrast, consider the implications of the only remaining alternative reply to the Consequence Argument once naturalistic compatibilism and libertarianism have been eliminated (Chapters 1 and 3) but such a Kantian theory is not endorsed.

The intuitive appeal of the Kantian proposal

It might be objected that Kant's account is a fairly complex one, as the presentation of the past three chapters suggests.[6] Much of the complexity arises, however, out of the need to address questions of detail. It seems rather that the essential features of Kant's theory have strong intuitive appeal as a theory of that which makes agents morally responsible for their actions, i.e. free will.

The intuitive appeal of Kant's metaphysical solution lies in the following consideration. When we impute responsibility to an agent for some misdemeanour, we take it that what is reprehensible is not just the act that is now in the past but the agent himself. If we reprimand the agent now it is because the misdeed is symptomatic of something about the agent that is blameworthy. Kant's metaphysical account perfectly captures this by presenting the misdeed as a manifestation of some feature of the agent's psychological causality (empirical character) that the agent is responsible for having chosen. This choice should not be temporally located if the misdeed is punishable at any time (once it is known, i.e. after its occurrence), and this is reflected in its involving an intelligible causality, i.e. the agent's freedom (intelligible character). Further, this type of causality is beyond the reach of our cognition, which reflects our sense that the possibility of freedom in the light of determinism is incomprehensible.

The volitional account has two important features that chime with our intuitions. The first is that it assigns a central role to acts of *Willkür*, i.e. the agent's willings as purely spontaneous, which echoes our common conception of what a willing amounts to. Nevertheless, these willings are not random: I do not, for instance, make a decision departing from previous ones in similar circumstances without justifying this to myself. A notion of *Gesinnung* (Chapter 5) ensuring the coherence of my willings through the identification of a goal for my agency reflects these characteristics of my practice.

The second feature is, after the adoption of transcendental idealism, the second pillar of Kant's theory. This is that my freedom is a capacity to act autonomously. My ability to choose to act upon a law *whose origin lies in me* defines a stronger value-laden conception of sourcehood than is typically found in contemporary sourcehood accounts, namely that of autonomy. Nevertheless, the emphasis of the contemporary debate about free will around the requirement to ensure the agent's control of her actions (Chapters 1 and 3) reveals our intuition that control is valuable. This issue I return to later, echoes Kant's identification of *autonomy* as defining (through the moral law) the good will as norm for free agency.

The psychological account's intuitive appeal lies first in its presenting the agent as endowing the reasons she acts upon with causal power through her freedom as transcendental cause of her empirical character. Further, this account reconciles the lawful regularity of my behaviour (e.g. as encapsulated in the causality of a belief-desire model) and my sense that I develop my character over time. This is made possible by the third pillar of Kant's theory, namely his focus upon inner sense, thereby (Chapter 6) separating the Problem from the mind-body problem which, in the context of transcendental idealism, is no longer a metaphysical problem.

I now turn to the one remaining possible response to the Consequence Argument that has not yet been discussed.

Hard incompatibilism

Hard incompatibilism is the consequence of fully endorsing the validity of the Consequence Argument and the truth of all its explicit and implicit assumptions (e.g. naturalism), while rejecting the plausibility of mysterianism (Chapter 1). The absence of free will it entails, would require alterations of our first-, second- and third-person attitudes. This is a vast topic to which some (e.g. Pereboom 2004, 2014a) have devoted extensive investigations; here, I can only briefly address a few aspects of it.

Pereboom (2004) argues that blaming practices would be altered insofar as agents cannot be deemed ultimately responsible for their actions. Importantly, the way they would be altered involves the disappearance of second-person reactive attitudes, such as resentment and gratitude, and with the disappearance of third-person characteristics that depend upon them, such as blameworthiness and praiseworthiness. Pereboom (2014b: 118–22) argues that the inappropriateness of resentment might be 'good for interpersonal relationships' (2014: 119). This may well be true, but the same cannot be said for gratitude. When Pereboom (2014b: 121) invites us to consider the kind of gratitude we display towards young children for some kindness as the kind of thankfulness that 'could be retained if one gave up the presupposition of praiseworthiness', I do not share Pereboom's optimistic take upon what would be lost if we effectively treated others similary to children in this respect.

Peter Strawson's (1974: 11) concern about how we would cope with such attitudes disappearing is justified.[7] Is the watered-down praiseworthiness Pereboom proposes not, after all, just the same as that which we would display towards individuals brainwashed to please us? The comparison with our attitude to kind children is moreover misleading: the gratitude I express to the latter is, on the contrary, at least partly an expression of my (perhaps subconsciously) taking the child to have exhibited a modicum of free will in so acting, not just an expression of pleasure at the outcome of the deed itself.

Consider now the attitude of forgiveness. Pereboom claims that, while the attitude as we know it today would be undermined, key features thereof would not. He mentions that it would still be appropriate in the presence of (i) signs that the apology indicates a *recognition* of having been in the wrong, and (ii) indications that the agent who did wrong is now *committed* to improvement (2014b: 120). But the very notions of recognition and commitment can no longer have the same meaning without free will.

The notion of *commitment* without free will is just the existence of a causally efficient reason for action that is likely to have a long-lasting impact upon the agent's behaviour: this is hardly something that warrants forgiveness. Rather, it would warrant *relief* that whatever harm was done will likely not reoccur. As with Pereboom's own concern with the disappearing agent (Chapter 3) in event-causal libertarian theories, here the agent who has wronged me does not feature *qua* agent in this attitude: Why should she, since all I should be interested in are the causal determinants of her behaviour and how this impacts the future?

Further, our first-person understanding of ourselves as acting on the basis of deliberations would be impacted. Pereboom (2014a: 104ff) argues that rational deliberation is compatible with determinism. The argument hinges on the claim that the uncertainty we have about what we will do after deliberation is epistemic: there is an epistemic openness of the outcome of the deliberation and a further epistemic uncertainty about its efficacy. In addressing the problem in this way, Pereboom is assuming that the reason why the belief that my actions are determined beyond my control threatens the practice of rational deliberation, is that when I deliberate, I must believe that the outcome of the deliberation is not certain. That is, we 'presuppose that we have more than one distinct option for which action to perform [such that] we can or could perform each of these actions'; the key to the solution that is developed lies in the claim that 'the sense of "can" or "could" featured in such beliefs might not always or even typically be metaphysical' (Pereboom 2014a: 107).

The plausibility of this claim is, however, questionable. To be sure, let us consider mundane deliberative cases such as that of whether, given that I feel tired and given the other beliefs about the time I have available for my task and how my output is affected by my tiredness, I should stop working for one hour or continue. In such cases, all that is at stake is arguably my finding out, on the basis of all my existing beliefs, what I really think it is best to do (epistemic openness) and whether that, combined with all the relevant desires, will lead me to act in this best way (epistemic uncertainty about efficacy).

But, I no longer have the intuition that this is a valid analysis of the situation when the issue is whether I choose to shave my beard, change jobs, etc. The reason is that I take it that I am the *source* of some new belief that is acquired through the deliberation. The issue of sourcehood looms as large here as it does elsewhere in the Problem. And further, the issue of the efficacy of this new belief in bringing about an intention to act is settled in the way in which I endorse the newly acquired belief, e.g. that it would be sensible not to change jobs. I will at that point either commit to doing just that or, on the contrary, may have a conflicting desire (new to me), to take the risk of trying something new.

I would argue that novel beliefs and desires are in fact present in the most mundane cases because the situation we are in is always novel: acting the way we would have done in the past involves extending the scope of the belief we have about the appropriateness of the proposed action and consolidating the inclination to act in this way (Chapter 6). This is not compatible with our deliberation being determined beyond our control.

Finally, if our deliberations no longer had the meaning we assign to them, our sense of our selves would be severely impacted. This brings up the issue of the meaning of life under such a scenario. Pereboom follows Ted Honderich (1988: 382) in arguing that while some aspect of our 'life-hopes' would be undermined, they would mostly remain intact. Pereboom considers the case of a teacher and argues that if she 'hopes that her efforts will result in well-educated children' (Pereboom 2014b: 137), this will indeed give her life meaning. But in the absence of free will, the sense to be given to 'her efforts' has to be watered down to referring to the causal sequence of mental events with a phenomenal effort-like quality that led to her behaviour and the consequent good education of the children. It is hard to see how the hope in question could be more than interested *speculation* about a future outcome, e.g. will the coin fall heads or tails when only heads delivers a reward. That is not a notion of hope that will ensure a meaningful life. There is no space to discuss this in more detail, but I at least hope to have shown that hard incompatibilism is an option that involves radical shifts in our self-conception as agents with substantial impacts upon our second- and third-person attitudes.

B. An argument for transcendental idealism

Transcendental idealism is contrasted with transcendental realism which claims that objects are things in-themselves. Kant 'understand[s] by the transcendental idealism of all appearances the doctrine that they are all together to be regarded as mere representations and not as things in themselves' (A369). Insofar as objective appearances are constitutive of nature, this contains two claims:

(TI1): natural properties and natural objects/events are just the possibility of objective representations.[8]

(TI2): natural properties and natural objects/events are not real in-themselves.

The positive metaphysical claim (TI1) will be derived once the negative claim (TI2), which is the denial of transcendental realism, has been established. I shall also show that we can enrich the characterisation of transcendental idealism with the following two claims:

(TI2'): natural objective properties (and hence natural objects/events) are not real in-themselves but grounded in a non-spatio-temporal reality in-itself.

(TI2"): natural objective properties are, from our cognitive perspective, an aspect of a non-spatio-temporal reality in-itself.

The further specification of the grounding claim (TI2'):

(TI3): natural causality is grounded in reality in-itself.

is then proven in a final part of the argument.

Some definitions

A first consideration is that arguing against transcendental realism in general would be to pitch the argument at the wrong level. While transcendental idealism provides conditions for objectivity (this is what the CPR examines), transcendental realism does not. As a result, a general doctrine of transcendental realism is not constrained as to what might count as objective, and more specifically, as real natural object or event. Criteria of metaphysical commitment will have to be formulated; typically, these will be tied to a theory, as Quine (1948: 33) proposes: 'A theory is committed to those and only those entities to which the bound variables of the theory must be capable of referring in order that the affirmations made in the theory be true.'

The transcendental realist theory that is perhaps most likely to meet with a broad consensus today is that of the natural sciences: the metaphysical commitments this theory defines are those of naturalistic realism which I take to be what is referred to as naturalism. Although I shall focus upon this theory, space permitting, I would argue that the argument could be adapted to the theory-related metaphysical commitments of any are form of transcendental realism.[9]

I now need working definitions of nature and naturalism. This is surprisingly not a straightforward matter, but there is a broad consensus around what Danto (1967) proposes for the latter: 'naturalism is polemically defined as repudiating the view that there exist or could exist any entities which lie, in principle, beyond the scope of scientific explanation'. As for the notion of 'scientific explanation', there is some consensus around the deductive-nomological model according to which a phenomenon is explained scientifically if (i) there is a deductive explanation of it in terms of true sentences from which the explanandum logically follows, and (ii) among the sentences of the explanans, there is at least one law of nature (Hempel and Oppenheim 1948).

The second requirement, since it involves a law of nature, would seem to entail that the explanation must be *causal*: although there is some disagreement on this issue, for my purposes, the generality of the types of scientific explanation relevant to the argument will not suffer from assuming with Salmon (1984) that this is the case.[10] Further, any causal explanation will not do: an appeal to an omnipotent God, for instance, is here excluded – since the natural domain is spatial and temporal, this means that the causal factors should be *spatio-temporal*. For simplicity, I shall characterise this by saying that the causal explanation must be spatio-temporal.

The next question is, what should we accept as true sentence to fulfil the deductive-nomological model's requirement for the explanans? Presumably, this could contain truths that have already been ascertained on the basis of previous explanations of phenomena. But ultimately, it will have to be *observational truths* which enable the scientific theory to be validated: while Quine (1996) holds on to an ideal of theory-free observation sentences, a looser notion of evidentially basic sentence is sufficient as observational truth.

On the basis of these brief considerations, it seems reasonable to claim the following characterisation of nature:

(N1) All objects/events that are either (i) amenable to being observed, or (ii) which feature in spatio-temporal causal explanations of observable phenomena[11] belong to nature, and nothing else does.

Naturalism is then the claim that

(N2) All that exists belongs to nature.

In what follows, the characterisation (N1) of objects/events is assumed true throughout. (N2) on the other hand will be proven false in a first part of the argument, which will lead to denying the truth of naturalistic realism and affirming that of transcendental idealism. The question the argument addresses is whether *the world*, either *qua* sum total of all existing natural objects, or *qua* sum total of all natural events, itself defines a natural object/event.

Preliminary claims

Below, I present the argument in numbered steps, with short proofs/comments following each claim. A long chapter could easily be devoted to discussing the steps in more detail and considering possible objections, but given the constraints of this book, concise supporting arguments and comments will have to suffice. I start with three preliminary claims.

> (P1) The possibility of observation characterising natural objects/events is a physical possibility for an ideal observer.

The possibility cannot be merely logical since it is logically possible that I should observe a unicorn, but there are no grounds for including unicorns in a scientific theory. On the other hand, (i) it need not be the case that the conditions of observation be suitable to accommodate a human being, and (ii) a specification of the observational instruments is not required. We are therefore not dealing with a full notion of physical possibility. Rather, all that is needed is that a human could, *in principle*, carry out the observation. The notion of possibility at stake is therefore physical possibility for an ideal observer.[12]

> (P2) Things[13] (e.g. objects/events) are real in-themselves if and only if they have intrinsic properties.

For the purposes of this proof, I use Langton's (2006: 173; see also Lewis 1983) characterisation of intrinsicality as the feature of a property, namely that it is 'compatible with loneliness'. Some thing (e.g. object/event) is real in-itself, if and only if it has properties in virtue of what it is independently of anything else, i.e. if and only if it has intrinsic properties. Note that on such a characterisation, the relational property of being a causal power is intrinsic (2006): while relationality is a conceptual issue, intrinsicality is a metaphysical matter (see Langton 2006).

> (P3) For any thing that is real in-itself, the properties of being a natural object/event, or of not being a natural object/event, are *intrinsic* properties it may possess.[14]

This is the *transcendental realism* characterising naturalism: if some thing (object/event) is found to fulfil the criteria defined in (N1), and is thus identified as natural, this property characterises it as the thing that it is in-itself: it would be natural in any other physically possible circumstances. This transcendental realism could be motivated by the conception of this property as a causal power (the power of being causally related to an observation or to other observable phenomena). If something were found to be a non-natural object/event, it could not be natural in other possible circumstances, because according to what has just been said, it would then have to be natural in all circumstances.

> (P4) The world *qua* totality will not feature in a causal explanation of observable phenomena.

Causal explanation by the totality of all existing objects (hereafter W_s) or all past and future events (hereafter W_t) would be irreducible downward causation; this is not found in the natural sciences.

The argument (part A): Refuting naturalism

With these preliminaries in place, the argument proceeds to show that the conditions of observability of the object or event 'world' (W_s or W_t)[15] are incompatible with its being grasped in its totality and to draw the consequences thereof for the objects/events of nature.

(1) Any observation of the totality of objects/events requires that the observer (with instruments) be located beyond this totality in space/time.

For W_t, it will be necessary for an observer to be already in place before any putative first event, otherwise she cannot report that she has observed the whole of this event. For W_s, the observer needs to be able to report observing the totality of the world and will therefore need to be located outside this totality.[16] These requirements follow from the modality defined in (P1).

(2) There are no possible locations for a putative observer of the totality of a finite world.

If the world is a finite W_s or a W_t with a beginning, the required location in space/time of the subject carrying out the observation according to (1), is such that what is observed is no longer the totality of objects/events. A further observer would need to observe the first observer plus the original totality, but the same problem arises that what she observes is no longer the totality. This defines a regress leaving no possible locations for an observer of the totality.

(3) There are no possible locations for a putative observer of the totality of an infinite world.

If the world is infinite in extent (in at least one some spatial direction/in the past), there is no location that is beyond the infinite in space or prior to an infinitely long time in the past, hence, according to (1) no possibility of observation. This could be described in terms of the same regress as in (2), with the difference that here what is observed is never a totality even if, at each step, more of the world is included.

(4) *Paradox of Observed Totalities*. (2) and (3) can be summarised as the claim that the world as a totality is not observable (see Figure 7.1).

(5) W_t is not a natural event and W_s is not a natural object.

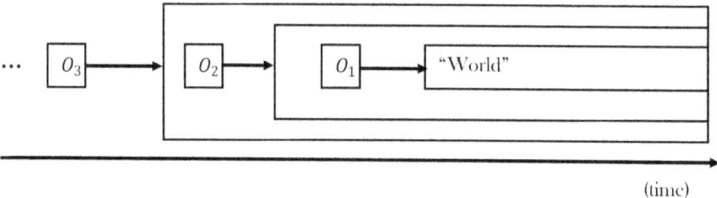

Figure 7.1 Paradox of Observed Totalities arising from the infinite regress in steps (2), (3) (O_i stands for observer number i). 'World' stands for W_s/W_t observed by O_1 in the 'finite' case; in the 'non-finite' case, it is some part of the total world and more gets included at each step. The schematic covers the spatial and temporal cases. © Christian Onof

Since the world is not observable ((4)) and cannot causally explain observable phenomena ((P4)), this follows from (N1).[17]

(6) *Conclusion A*. Naturalism is false

The existence of something that, according to (5), is not a natural event (W_t) and of something that is not a natural object (W_s) invalidates (N2).

This conclusion however concerns an aspect of the theory of naturalism that seemingly does not affect its useful core, so could easily be dismissed as unimportant by the naturalist.

The argument (part B): Nature, natural objects/events and reality in-itself

I now examine the type of reality of W_s/W_t and its implications for natural objects/events. I shall focus upon whether, in possible counterfactual scenarios,[18] W_s/W_t could be a natural object/event. In so doing, I take it that the definitions of W_s/W_t as totalities identify something that can now be considered in various possible counterfactual situations.[19]

Consider a scenario that does not infringe the laws of physics and that is identical to actuality in all respects apart from the fact that an additional object is located outside W_s and an additional event happens before W_t (see the following remark).

(7) In that possible scenario, W_s/W_t would be a natural object.

Indeed, the locations defined by the additional object/event allow for the possibility of an observer of W_s/W_t.[20]

(8) If W_s/W_t is real in-itself, it is a non-natural object/event in all physically possible scenarios.

The property of being non-natural is intrinsic for an object/event that is real in-itself according to (P3), which entails that it is independent of, however, anything else is.

From (5), W_s/W_t is actually non-natural. It follows that it would be non-natural in all such possible counterfactual scenarios.

(9) W_s/W_t is not real in-itself.

This follows from (7) which states that there is a possible scenario in which W_s/W_t is non-natural, while (8) excludes this being the case if W_s/W_t is real in-itself.

Remark: The scenario assumed in (7) requires a finite W_s/W_t. For simplicity, I confine the case of W_s/W_t infinite to this remark. Consider a finite subworld W'_s/W'_t. That subworld is a natural object/event because there are locations for possible observers outside it, but there is a possible scenario in which it is not, namely when it is isolated with a boundary replicating the causal forces exerted by the rest of the world upon it. The physical plausibility of doing this will depend upon the sufficient causal isolation of this subworld.[21] From (8), it follows that it is not real in-itself. Now all parts of something with intrinsic properties have intrinsic properties inherited from those of the whole, so if a part of the world is not real in-itself, then neither is the totality of the world: (9) therefore follows from this.

(10) If X is not a real object in-itself or a real event in-itself, it follows that its constituent parts, respectively in space and in time, are not real in-themselves.

By *reductio*: if any part of X were real in-itself, it would have intrinsic properties. These would define intrinsic properties of X, namely the properties of having some part with the properties in question. X would therefore be real in-itself which contradicts the assumption.

(11) Natural objects/events are not real in-themselves.

This follows from (9) and (10).

(12) *Conclusion B.* (TI2) is true

Since, from (11), natural properties are not real in-themselves, transcendental realism about nature is denied.

The argument (part C): The basic grounding claim

I now take this a little further to establish (TI2'):

(13) Natural objects/events depend upon some other reality-in-itself for their existence. This reality grounds that of nature.

Insofar as a natural object/event X is not real in-itself from (11), it follows from (P2) that it has no intrinsic properties. Extrinsic properties are instantiated in virtue of how something else X_1 is (Lewis 1983: 197). If how X_1 is, is an extrinsic property of it, this is in virtue of the way something else X_2 is. This leads to a regress which can only be stopped by reaching some property of a thing X_n that it has in virtue of how it itself is, i.e. an intrinsic property of it. According to (P2), X_n is a thing in-itself.

> (14) The natural world is grounded in a more fundamental non-spatio-temporal reality in-itself.

This follows from (13) plus the following considerations: if the grounding reality were spatio-temporal, it would be a spatio-temporal causal factor of observable natural objects/events. This, however, would mean that is belongs to the domain of nature according to (N1). It follows that this reality in-itself cannot be spatio-temporal.[22]

> (15) *Conclusion C*. The grounding claim (TI2') is true.

This follows from (14).

Comment

The argument shows that the spatiality/temporality of nature is incompatible with its being real in-itself. The reason lies in the property of space/time (see Section C) according to which the objectivity of a natural thing in space or event in time lies in its possible relation (either directly or through a causal link) to a subject (observer/perceiver) that is *external* to the thing: this is the *externality requirement*. The impossibility for such things to be real in-themselves is manifested when one notices the non-objective status of a particular thing, i.e. the totality of all things in space or of all events in time. This cannot be an object since the subject guaranteeing its objectivity must both be a part of the totality and fulfil the externality requirement. This impossibility is the Paradox of Observed Totalities (Figure 7.1).[23]

The argument (part D): Transcendental idealism and its consequences

What is missing so far is an argument for characterisztation (TI1) of transcendental idealism. This claim will follow from the previous assumptions by answering the question:: What is it that accounts for the appearance of a natural world?

> (16) A natural property is an appearance of reality in-itself for a possible subject of experience.

From (11), a natural property is not real in-itself. However, insofar as a causal impact of it can be observed, it is real for a possible observer. From (13), the ground of such a property lies in some reality in-itself. It follows that this property is an appearance for a possible observer, of this reality in-itself. The grounding in reality in-itself thereby defines the relation of 'appearing' and this possible observation defines what is possible experience for a cognising subject.

> (17) *Transcendental idealism.* (TI1) is true, and nature, as domain of appearances, is transcendentally ideal.

Insofar as, from (16), the reality of a natural property, *qua* appearance. is nothing more than its defining the content of a possible experience for an observer, i.e. a cognising subject, there is nothing more to it than the content of such a subject's possible representations of it.

This is what Kant expresses by saying that an object[24] is nothing more than a possible subject's *representation* of it (e.g. B235/A190). This has, since the publication of the first edition of the CPR (see Gardner 1999: 271), often been misinterpreted as a version of Berkeley's idealism. However, the 'is' in this claim refers to the properties of an object and does not characterise its existence (e.g. Prol. AA04: 292–3; see Gardner 1999: 274–5, Schulting 2017: 328–9, Onof 2019b: 206–7; see Chapter 2). The next claim specifies this 'ontological situation':

> (18) *Perspectival dual-aspect.* From our cognitive perspective, reality in-itself is the grounding aspect of what appears as natural objects/events.

From (13) and (16), it follows that objects/events exist outside the mind insofar as they are grounded in reality in-itself. That means the existence of these objects/events is nothing but that of their grounding reality in-itself. It follows that, since knowledge is here excluded,[25] we should conceive of reality in-itself as one aspect of something that appears as natural object/event.

> (19) *Conclusion D.* (TI2") is true.

From (18), we should conceive of the duality appearance/thing in-itself as two aspects, one of which is non spatio-temporal ((14)), while the other are the spatio-temporal natural properties of our possible experience, which establishes the perspectival dual-aspect claim (TI2").

The argument (part E): The causal grounding claim

Finally, I now turn to the more specific grounding claim (TI3) of empirical causality in reality in-itself. This section of the argument goes over material presented in Chapter 2 but without referring to Kant's arguments here.

> (20) Sensations are caused by something outside the subject of experience.

This is fairly uncontroversial, barring scepticism about the external world.
This, however, means two things:

> (21) Something independent of my cognition causes my sensations.

(22) I can in principle determine an object in space that is causally responsible for my sensation through perception,[26] either directly or indirectly of an effect it brings about.

For the transcendental realist, these two statements refer to the same object. Not so for the transcendental idealist for whom they entail the following two assertions:

(23) Some reality in-itself is causally responsible for my sensation.

This follows from (21) since the required independence of our cognition denotes a reference to something real in-itself. This is a metaphysical claim of transcendental affection by reality in-itself (see Chapter 2).

(24) In perceptual knowledge, I determine an empirical, i.e. natural, object that causes my sensation.

Statement (22) entails that my sensation is (empirically) causally linked to the object I determine. This is a metaphysical claim of empirical affection by appearances (see Chapter 2).[27]

(25) My sensation is caused by both a thing in-itself and an empirical, i.e. natural, object.

This follows from the conjunction of (23) and (24).

(26) A satisfactory conception of reality in-itself cannot entail a causal overdetermination of my sensation.

Given that knowledge of reality in-itself is excluded, the question is how, from our cognitive perspective, we should conceive of it. Clearly, a conception that implies causal overdetermination of sensations is excluded.

(27) Statement (25) does not amount to overdetermination if and only if the grounding of appearances in reality in-itself ((14)) refers to a grounding of empirical causality in appearance.

Causal overdetermination will be avoided in (25) if and only if empirical and transcendental affection define the same cause impacting our sensations. Given the grounding of nature in reality in-itself, this can only be achieved by having empirical causality grounded in it. This requires that this grounding define a causal link between reality in-itself and empirical causality, as illustrated in Figure 7.2.

(28) The grounding of the objective domain of nature in reality in-itself should be thought of as one of empirical causality in reality in-itself.[28]

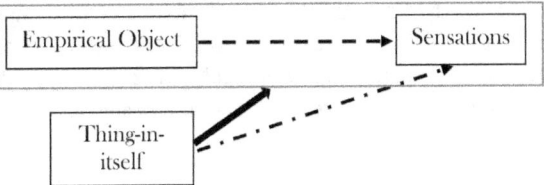

Figure 7.2 The causal origin of my sensations. Empirical affection (dashed arrow) results from an empirical causality grounded in reality in-itself (thick arrow). This leads to the latter defining the transcendental cause of sensations, i.e. transcendental affection (dashed-dotted arrow) © Christian Onof.

Since a satisfactory conception of reality in-itself does not feature any causal overdetermination ((26)), it follows from (27) that we should think of it as grounding empirical causality, from which (28) follows.

(29) *Conclusion E*. (TI3) is true.

This follows from (28).

(30) *The metaphysical picture.* From our cognitive perspective, reality in-itself is an aspect of what appears as natural objects/events which grounds these objects' empirical causality.

This follows by putting together (TI3) (from (29)) and (TI2") (from (19)) and summarises the metaphysical picture defined by transcendental idealism as it emerges from the above argument. This is the metaphysics called for by a plausible conception of freedom, as I have argued in this book (see Chapter 3).

Diagnosis

The paradoxical situation this argument for transcendental idealism reveals is reflected in the way empiricist and realist intuitions (in the non-Kantian sense) interact. According to the first, our empirical knowledge arises from the impact things outside us make upon our senses. The second, which are grounded in the first, are of the existence of a world that is completely independent of my conscious experience.

While this second claim is motivated by the first, this does not license the inference to the further claim that this world independent of my conscious experience is that of which I have empirical knowledge through the senses. The transcendental idealist denies the validity of this inference because space and time are *a priori* conditions of cognition: the spatio-temporality of what I cognise is contributed by the subject.

The proposed argument for transcendental idealism draws upon the need for such an implicit inference from some *epistemological* fact (e.g. the possibility of an observation in the case of naturalism) to ground the transcendental realist's *ontological* claim about our thereby cognising some reality independent of us, a claim which otherwise would be purely speculative. It then exhibits a spatio-temporal topological requirement upon the epistemology (e.g. objects' being *outside* the observer in the case of naturalism) that is incompatible with the ontological claim (e.g. initially, that of the totality of nature as object) as discussed in the comment above.

Arguments for transcendental idealism

The argument I proposed draws directly upon the properties of space/time (see Section C) and its implications for the dependence of objects upon some possible subject external to them. In that respect, it differs from Kant's two approaches to proving transcendental idealism in the CPR. With the mathematical antinomies, Kant's focus was not directly upon the intuitive (spatial/temporal) dimension of cognition but on its conceptual dimension. Indeed, the problem they raise is the determination of a putative object, the totality W_t/W_s, and the validity of claiming it is both finite and infinite.

Unlike the mathematical antinomies, my argument is concerned directly with the notion of totality itself, rather than with the problems arising from its infinity or non-infinity. Rather than show the incoherence of the conception of the size of this totality, it can thereby use this totality to infer the non-in-itself status of the natural objects/events within it.

Kant's main argument for transcendental idealism in the CPR is in the Transcendental Aesthetic, where he establishes that, insofar as the representations of space/time are shown to be *a priori*, the spatial/temporal objects of our cognition are not real in themselves (A26-30/B42-5; B49-53/A32-37). That approach relies upon the claim that space/time could not *also* be a feature of things in-themselves. Trendelenburg (1862: 184), however, argued that this 'neglected alternative' is a possibility, as Vaihinger (1881–92: I-134–50) reports. Allison (1983: 113–14) argues that this alternative would require that there be a qualitatively identical space/time for things in-themselves and for appearances. Since the latter are mind-dependent and the former not, Allison (1983: 113–14) concludes that it is a vacuous idea although he stops short of saying that it is self-contradictory.

To get a stronger result, it is necessary to change strategy and consider the features characteristic of the *intuitive* nature of space-time.[29] In the case of space, Kant resorts in other writings (e.g. *Prolegomena*) to arguments from incongruent counterparts, i.e. the chirality of spatial objects such as right and left-hand gloves.[30] I use the topological mereology of space, but the broad strategy is the same:[31] it avoids the problem of the neglected alternative that plagues Kant's appeal to the a-priori status of space/time by establishing the impossibility of things in-themselves being spatio-temporal.

C. Time/space, paradoxes and transcendental idealism

The analogies between the Paradox of Self-Determination (Chapter 3, Figure 3.1) and of Observed Totalities (Figure 7.1) call for further examination to shed more light upon the argument for transcendental idealism and the Problem.

Two paradoxes with isomorphic structures and solutions

In both cases, a paradoxical situation was exhibited in the attempt to determine a totality:

- Galen Strawson's Infinite Regress Argument defines the Paradox of Self-Determination, i.e. of the attempt to practically determine the totality of my agency.
- The above argument for transcendental idealism defines the Paradox of Observed Totalities, i.e. of the attempt to observe the totality of the world in space/time.

These paradoxes have the same structure because the main features that generate them are isomorphic. First, the regresses of both paradoxes exist because of the nature of time/space. That is, observability requires that the possible observer stand *outside* what is observed in time/space which defines a larger region of time/space which contains the observer as well,[32] and the same goes for the possibility of self-determination in the Infinite Regress Argument in relation to time. This dependence upon what is outside is what is crucial to the two arguments: for the Infinite Regress Argument, it reveals the impossibility of self-determination as a temporal occurrence/process, and for the argument for transcendental idealism, it is a dependence that reveals the impossibility for spatio-temporal regions to be real in-themselves.[33] This dependence of parts of space/time upon what lies outside them is the key characteristic of the topological mereology of space/time (see Onof and Schulting 2015; Onof 2023).

Since this dependence condition also applies to collections of (finite) regions of space/time, it follows that the topological mereology of space/time requires (i) that there be a unique space/time containing all such parts; and since there should be enough space/time to define some region completely outside any finite region, (ii) space/time will have to be infinite in magnitude. These are the two characteristics of unicity (B39/A25; B47/A31–2) and infinity (B39–40/A28; A32/B47–8) of space/time that Kant singles out as essential features of the representation of space/time insofar as it is a intuition rather than a concept.[34]

Second, what is common to both determination of one's agency and observation of the world is a causal relation. The arrows in Figure 7.1 link the observer to the observations in the same way as those in Figure 3.1 relate the determining agent to her determined agency. The observer must be observing the world prior to its beginning in the same way that the determining self must be determining agency prior to its manifestation. So it is not the topological mereology alone that generates the paradoxes, but *the way that causality is manifested in space and time characterised by these mereological properties*.

The identical structures of these two paradoxes explain why naturalism is unable to solve the Problem. This is because naturalist metaphysics has it that reality in-itself is spatio-temporal: this creates the problems these paradoxes identify, because of the way causality is manifested in space/time. For this reason, as I indicated earlier, the Problem was at the heart of Kant's preoccupations in his critical turn, as the lengthy focus upon the idea of freedom (as contrasted with those of God and immortality) in the B Preface of the CPR attests (Bxxvii–xxix).[35]

The isomorphism of these paradoxes calls for solutions with the same structure. The Paradox of Observed Totalities can only be solved by denying spatio-temporal reality the status of reality in-itself while identifying a ground for its causality in some unknowable reality in-itself. The Paradox of Self-Determination could only be resolved by placing the source of free agency beyond the natural domain where it grounds the agent's psychological causality.

Kant's critical philosophy was largely motivated by the problem of free will because it involves an apparent conflict between the norms of empirical objectivity and of moral responsibility. This called for an investigation into the conditions of possibility of such norms (B19; CPrR AA05: 45). Kant's investigation shows that there is no conflict between the conditions of possibility of these two types of norms. The structural similarity of paradoxes they give rise to if transcendental realism is assumed accounts for the parallel approaches to their resolution which involve the adoption of transcendental idealism.

There is a difference in the modalities of these paradoxes' resolutions, however.

- Free will could be an illusion, which means that the solution to the Paradox of Self-Determination only defines a really possible metaphysical state of affairs that is compatible with the determinism of the natural domain. While I have argued that it is *required* if we are not to radically revise our self-conception, this is a weaker requirement than that of the grounding of nature in reality in-itself.
- Indeed, the solution to the Paradox of Observed Totalities *necessitates* a metaphysical account of the reality of nature as transcendentally ideal, i.e. as defining appearances for a possible subject of cognition.

D. Transcendental idealism: Further considerations

In this section, I want to address, necessarily briefly, the concern that contemporary natural science is incompatible with Kant's idealism, and indicate a worry that arises in a naturalistic framework, and is relevant to the concern about transcendental idealism's defining a more fundamental level of reality.

Scientific worries for transcendental idealism

Kant's understanding of space and time is of course dependent upon the physics (and geometry) he was acquainted with. This defines a concern insofar as transcendental idealism defines space and time as *a priori* conditions of objectivity of a nature that is, today, described by non-Newtonian physics and draws upon conceptions of space and time that Kant could not even have imagined (see Friedman 2008). Thus, special relativity (SR) requires conceptualising space and time together as space-time. This supplants a conception of space containing all that is simultaneous at any given time and of time independent of velocity. With general relativity (GR), spatial metric properties (e.g. curvature) are determined by the distribution of matter. This clashes with a conception of space (space-time) as containing objects (events) it is independent of.[36]

To respond to these worries, let us observe that while Kant lists, among the objectives of his critical philosophy, that of securing the foundation of pure physics (B20), exactly what this means is open to interpretation. Minimally, it means to secure basic principles of the application of the understanding to the manifolds given in intuition. Here, the Analogies (A176-218/B228-265) governing the application of the categories of substance, causality and interaction are key.

Kant's broader project of grounding Newtonian mechanics, which he carries out in the *Metaphysical Foundations of Natural Science*, involves an important move beyond transcendental philosophy insofar as Kant identifies matter as defining substance (MFNS AA04: 470). We need not follow Kant in this, and can rather take the concept of a field of force, manifested as energy or matter, as more congenial to SR's principle of the equivalence of mass and energy ($E = mc^2$). And rather than follow Kant who now assigns to the pure space of the CPR the function of absolute space required by Newton's universal gravitation theory (MFNS AA04: 481-2), we should satisfy the requirements of GR which rather calls for the distribution of this mass to be taken, through Einstein's field equations, as what determines the metric of space-time.[37]

But, it will be argued, the required alterations of the conceptions of space and time are incompatible with their being *a priori* forms of sensibility (see Friedman 2008). A first reply is that the forms of spatial and temporal intuition are not concepts and define rather minimal topological features of space-time.[38] Crucially for the Problem, these define the notion of externality of spatio-temporal locations with respect to a possible observer (and to one another). Such a topological structure of space and time can be understood as represented, in GR, by the four-dimensional pseudo-Riemannian manifold in which events are located.[39]

Still, the worry is now that this is very minimal: objective determinations of manifolds in space and in time according to the categories apparently require knowledge of the state of motion according to SR; and GR requires knowledge of the distribution of mass.

But here, we must surely distinguish the objectivity of our common experience of the world from scientific objectivity. The grounds for this lie in understanding what is involved in Kant's characterisation of the reality of appearances as that of 'possible experience'. As with naturalism, this involves what is either observable or causally related to possible perceptions which Kant expresses in terms of the 'empirical progress of experience' (B521/A493).

Now Kant indicates that in considering what, in the past, is causally related to possible perceptions, we represent to ourselves that 'in accordance with empirical laws', a 'regress series of possible perceptions (. . .) leads to a time-series' that is the condition of the present time (B533/A495). But how should we understand this reference to empirical laws? The Marburg school of neo-Kantianism has distorted our understanding of Kant's project by understanding objectivity in terms of the empirical laws discovered by science (Natorp 1981). But when Kant discusses how a judgement of experience is produced on the basis of perception, what Kant refers to as the 'law'

(Proleg AA04: 296ff) that is involved in the principle of causality, is some universal 'rule' that we assume holds without necessarily knowing what it is, rather than an empirical law, as I argued in Chapter 2. The examples he considers confirm this: to claim that the 'air is elastic' requires no appeal to scientific theory. Rather, while Kant indicates that we represent that there are indeed empirical laws connecting what is real to some possible perception, we actually operate 'under the guidance of history or in the footsteps of causes and effects' (B523/A495).

Although Kant himself did not go so far, I suggest that this calls for a distinction between two notions of objectivity with different scopes. There is scientific objectivity which requires identifying empirical laws to establish the reality of some phenomenon. But there is also an objectivity of experience which does not refer to scientific theories: it is based upon the common knowledge of mankind that is useful to our daily practice over time and thus includes historical knowledge. This might be called the *objectivity of intersubjective experience*. Now it is certainly the case that, over time, this type of objectivity will incorporate more and more of scientific objectivity as it becomes common knowledge. But it is only over a limited range that this scientific objectivity permeates the objectivity of intersubjective experience. It is, for instance, of no relevance to our common experience that at speeds that are non-negligible with respect to the speed of light, we have to substitute Minkowski's four-dimensional space-time (SR) for our usual three-dimensional Euclidean space and one-dimensional time. It is equally not relevant that space-time is curved according to the presence of gravitational fields (GR).

One might object that some of the technology we use does rely upon relativistic effects being taken into account. This is obviously the case, for instance, for a physicist reading off some measurement instrument the evidence of the deviation of light rays produced by a gravitational field. Such a situation requires a guarantee of *continuity* between the two types of objectivity because ultimately there is only one domain of appearances so that these two types are just ways of distinguishing between different types of objective determinations. Thus, while the physicist treats his instruments as part of intersubjective objectivity, what they measure requires appealing to scientific objectivity. And it is only through such measurements that scientific theories are validated. This defines a *continuity* requirement between these two objectivities. Further, the scientific theory will include some account of the observer and the objects of his perception: this must somehow be *compatible* with the observer's common experience.

These continuity and compatibility issues can be understood as addressed in GR by the facts (i) that a possible observer and her perspective define a coordinate system in the pseudo-Riemannian manifold of space-time events, and (ii) that this perspective can be encapsulated, locally, as that of a tangent space to the manifold. This space is flat, i.e. has no curvature, and, given the relatively modest speeds at which an observer could ever move, they can be represented as a Euclidean space together with a decoupled temporal dimension.[40] So the observer's intersubjective objectivity finds its place in this tangent space (compatibility) and the observer can use the coordinate transforms of GR to carry out objective determinations further afield in space and time (continuity).[41] Much more would need to be said about these issues: here I only sought to indicate how one might proceed to allay such scientific worries.

Worries for naturalism

Having considered worries for transcendental idealism, I want to show that the concern about an inaccessible more fundamental level of reality,[42] which many find unattractive in transcendental idealism (as I have interpreted it), also arises in naturalism, and that there, it is more problematic. I defined naturalism in terms of what is observable or causally related to it according to scientific theories. This leads to privileging material nature and, more specifically, the objects of physics. The problem is that physics only deals with relational natural properties. So, as Russell puts it: 'the only legitimate attitude about the physical world seems to be one of complete agnosticism as regards all but its mathematical properties' (1927: 270). These limits of our knowledge are comparable to those of transcendental idealism. However, insofar as naturalism has nothing to say about why they exist, they constitute a relative weakness of the naturalist viewpoint.

This issue might be dismissed as of peripheral concern, but recently, it has acquired more prominence. Indeed, while physicalism has been adopted by most naturalists (see Bourget and Chalmers 2014), the problem of the nature of consciousness, and in particular its phenomenal character, has led several naturalist philosophers to question it (even non-reductive forms thereof). They claim that there is more to the natural world than what physics deals with. This hard problem of consciousness, when not denied (Dennett 1991; Churchland 1985) or dealt with by non-reductive physicalist strategies whose shortcomings have been exposed (Chalmers 2010: 115–18 and chapter 6), was initially addressed by proposing a dualism of phenomenal and physical properties (Chalmers 2010; Robinson 2004).[43]

There is now a growing consensus among those who take this problem seriously that phenomenal properties are best thought of as defining the intrinsic nature of reality (see Onof 2009a). Following Russell (1927) and Chalmers (1996: 293–301, 2010: 133–7), Philip Goff (2017) points out that physical science can only reveal relational properties of the material world, leaving its intrinsic nature completely unknown.[44] Along with Galen Strawson (2006),[45] Goff speculates that, if we are to solve the hard problem of consciousness, i.e. account for how material entities are able to have conscious experience, we must assume that something like this experience constitutes the intrinsic nature of entities that are studied by physics insofar as they are related by physical properties. This is pan(proto-)psychism.[46]

On an understanding of nature as defined by observable phenomena and those which feature in scientific causal explanations thereof, this is problematic, however. For sure, the experiential intrinsic nature of natural entities can be claimed to ground, and therefore cause in some sense (directly or not) observable phenomena. But it is excluded that such causal relationships should belong to any scientific theory, precisely because science can only explain extrinsic relational properties of natural objects. So the naturalist is in effect required to expand his definition of what can count as natural, by including grounding relations that *cannot* be the object of scientific enquiry.[47]

What should logically follow from the requirements of naturalism and the identification of the intrinsic nature of things as grounding the physical properties of natural objects, is the recognition that this grounding relation is not a type of natural causality. This would lead to understanding nature as a domain of purely relational properties that are grounded in an unknowable reality characterised by intrinsic properties, i.e. something that is real in-itself, i.e. claim (TI2') which most plausibly leads to a transcendental idealist account. The naturalist can counter that the definition of nature should be relaxed to include grounding relations that cannot be the object of scientific enquiry. But, aside from being *ad hoc* to address the hard problem, this move is too liberal: What would then prevent supernatural entities from being included on the basis of bogus causal claims?

Further, as indicated earlier, transcendental idealism has the distinct advantage of providing an account of why reality in-itself is not knowable. For the naturalist, unknowable facts about the intrinsic nature of things are a contingent feature of our epistemology. For the transcendental idealist, they follow essentially from the nature of our cognition: this explains why the natural domain is defined by a particular kind of relations, namely spatio-temporal ones which are not properties of how reality is in-itself.

Finally, a further comment should be made about pan(-proto)-psychism. It takes what Kant rightly characterises as the essentially subjective nature of sensations (CJ AA05: 206), namely its phenomenal character,[48] and uses this to define a natural property of *the experiential* which is then taken to underpin all objective physical relations. To avoid idealism, it is claimed that the experiential has none of the subjectivity of the phenomenal properties (Goff 2017). But why should we believe that it can ground the *subjective* character of experience? It seems that the pan(proto)-psychist wants to have it both ways: the experiential is not subjective, but nevertheless must do the work of grounding what is essentially subjective: Is this not the hard problem all over again?

E. The normative dimension of free will

Before concluding the book, I offer some thoughts about an alternative conception of practical normativity to Kant's own. In Chapter 5, I outlined a notion of *Gesinnung* that is broader than Kant's and more appropriate to addressing the Infinite Regress Argument. This is the *Gesinnung* as defining the purpose of a unified agency. I want to argue that one ought to strive for an *integrated unity* defining a notion of unity that I have some conception of. This is a richer concept than that of the mere coherence of my various pursuits, which, I have argued (Chapter 5), is a purpose inherent to any agent's practice. This concept defines an alternative to Kant's understanding of the normativity characterising free will, thereby providing a different content to the concept of autonomy.

A key insight of Kant's theory of freedom is the essential connection freedom has to morality through the concept of autonomy. In Chapter 5, I indicated the shortcomings of the Reciprocity Thesis (GMM AA04: 446–7) that grounds this relation for Kant.[49] I see Kant's attempt to derive practical normativity from the presupposition of freedom as problematic. Allison (2020: 315ff) succeeds in reconstructing a valid proof by assuming a justification requirement. Although I am sympathetic to its intent, this is not a requirement that will meet with universal assent. Similarly, while I think that Guyer (1998: 22–35) is exactly right in taking the *value* of freedom as what can ground ethics, I think one can still question why this value should be endorsed. My proposal below amounts to seeking some further ground for the value of freedom that is implicitly recognised in all our agency.[50]

I want to propose drawing upon a meta-philosophical aspect of the debate on free will, namely that, issues of moral responsibility aside, in all this debate, freedom is considered as something worthwhile (e.g. Kane 1996: 100) *because* what would be lost were it to be illusory would be a sense of *control*. This key feature emerged from the discussion of compatibilism in Chapter 1 and informed the various contemporary attempts at formulating libertarian theories (Chapter 3). It therefore seems that it is implicitly recognised that *the agent values control*.[51] The reason why is that our actions are end-directed: insofar as agents take themselves to be acting towards the realisation of goals they represent, they implicitly value the ability to exert regulative control to achieve these goals.

Using this value of control, a derivation of the normativity of a conception of autonomy can be outlined. Such a conception is tied to a notion of good *Gesinnung*. For Kant, it is action on the moral law. On my alternative proposal, it is the pursuit of the single purpose characterised by a conception of integrated unity definitive of my agency.[52]

First, observe that, if I act autonomously in the latter sense, insofar as this means that, through a notion of integrated unity of my agency, I give myself the law under which I act, I am therefore in control of my action. I now want to show that any decision to act heteronomously will reduce this control.[53]

Consider the adoption of a notion of *Gesinnung* which allows for heteronomous action in some circumstances. To be clear, this means that some of my actions could not be understood as directed to the integrated unity I conceive of for my agency. The coherence that is a requirement of any notion *of Gesinnung* entails that, in certain circumstances, the agent willingly allows for something whose source is external to him, e.g. certain random inclinations[54] whatever they may be at the time, to define the driving causality of his agency (Chapter 5). This is what we might call *autonomous holidays* by analogy with the notion of moral holidays (James 1997: chapter 11). While it is the case that the agent will have decided upon the type of circumstance under which these holidays can occur and what they will consist in, this decision cannot, ultimately, be given any proper explanatory grounds. It will most probably have some rational features, such as the fact that the holidays are allowed when the negative consequences for others are minimal, but these will not be enough to provide a full satisfactory explanatory ground for it.

This lack of justification is not per se a problem as Allison would have it. Rather, the problem is that the agent has relinquished some control over her action by allowing into the decision-making process something that is not under his control as ground for the decision. By accepting this as ground, the agent deliberately endorses a reduction in the control exerted over his action. This leads to a contradiction in the will that necessarily seeks greater control.

As objection, it might be argued that insofar as the episodes of autonomous holidays are entirely under the agent's control as far as the timing of their occurrence and the tolerated type of action are concerned, there is in fact no loss of control. That is, such episodes are a far cry from any state of being 'out of control'. But that objection overlooks the way in which randomness pervades the whole of the agent's decision-making, as soon as it has been let in through the back door as it were. For since there is no ultimate justification for the restrictions the agent places upon his moral holidays, there is no reason why he should not relax these restrictions. There is thus ultimately no reason why he behaves autonomously the rest of the time: the fencing off of some behaviour as autonomous is groundless once other parts of the agent's behaviour are allowed to be heteronomous. The whole of his agency now appears unstable because it is ultimately random when he does or does not act autonomously.

If this does not directly lead to a loss of control through a slippery slope towards more and more extensive heteronomous behaviour, this will only be because of some other heteronomous ground, namely because some other inclination that the agent acts upon prevents it. This could, for instance, be an attachment to social decorum, or the avoidance of the consequences of law-breaking. And in that respect, some of the agent's behaviour when he is seemingly behaving autonomously is actually also ultimately out of his control since it is defined by inclinations he happens to have. Heteronomy will therefore infect more of his behaviour in this way, and it is unclear how far it might spread. Since any decision to act heteronomously in certain circumstances contradicts this implicit objective of free agency, i.e. to increase his control, a free agent ought to act autonomously.[55]

This short argument, first, answers the question about the normativity characterising my proposed notion of *Gesinnung*. While the very adoption of a *Gesinnung* is the decision to act in ways which exhibit a certain coherence, thereby defining a purpose uniting all my agency, greater control will be achieved if various purposes I pursue are properly integrated into a unity. Therefore, I ought to aim for an integrated unity of my agency (which requires my having some conception of it). Second, it is also a proposal to address Kant's (rhetorical?) question: 'What else can the freedom of the will be but autonomy, i.e. the property of the will to be a law to itself' (GMM AA04: 446–7). By endorsing (although on grounds that go beyond Kant and with a different specification of the concept of autonomy) the reciprocity between freedom and the requirement of autonomous action which is at the heart of Kant's attempt to ground morality in GMM III, I am providing further grounds for the claim I made earlier, namely that we should accept a key feature of his notion of freedom, namely its close connection with practical normativity. And even though the conception of autonomy is different, this amounts to endorsing an important building block of Kant's foundational argument, namely that *freedom is a capacity for autonomy*.

F. Conclusion

The systematic conclusions of this book are as follows:

- Volitional and psychological accounts are required to address the first- and third-person aspects of the Problem; the failure of naturalistic compatibilist approaches

shows that a metaphysical account is also needed to solve the Problem, and it must be shown how the physical account could in principle be addressed .
- While contemporary (source) compatibilism proposes sophisticated psychological accounts, it falls foul of the Argument from Manipulation and fails to provide a volitional account of sourcehood.
- Frankfurt-style cases fail to disprove that freedom requires the availability of alternative possibilities.
- While the introduction of agent-causality into a libertarian account enables it to address the Luck Objection that event-causal libertarianism falls prey to, its naturalistic setting makes its metaphysical account unable to fully address the Rational Luck Objection.
- If there is to be a place for free agency in a causally deterministic natural world, the Consequence Argument and the Paradox of Self-Determination defined by the Infinite Regress Argument require that the naturalistic framework be replaced by a metaphysical framework creating the conceptual space for willings characterised as follows: (i) they are outside time and define a first cause that grounds a natural law, that of the agent's psychological causality connecting beliefs/desires and intentions/actions, and (ii) together they form a coherent set that is explanatorily self-sufficient.
- The shortcomings of naturalist metaphysics stemming from the Paradox of Observed Totalities call for an analogous move to a metaphysical framework in which natural causality is an appearance grounded in reality in-itself.
- Kant presents us with a comprehensive theory of free agency covering the metaphysical, volitional, psychological and physical accounts of the Problem in this metaphysical framework, i.e. of transcendental idealism.
- A Kantian proposal that endorses Kant's theory while leaving aside the specifics of his ethics and the shortcomings of his notion of *Gesinnung* provides the solution to the Problem.

In terms of Kant scholarship, I have attempted to shed light upon the following issues:

- Kant's theory of freedom is compatibilist in its refutation of the Consequence Argument (without the implicit assumption of naturalism), and libertarian in its response to the Infinite Regress Argument.
- Transcendental idealism is a metaphysical theory in which the relation things in-themselves/appearances is one of two aspects of reality that involves a grounding of empirical (natural) causality in reality in-itself.
- Kant's is not an altered-past but an altered-law response to the Consequence Argument.
- The structure of the Resolution of the Third Antinomy is a progressive argument beginning after Kant has already shown that freedom with determinism is logically possible within transcendental idealism.
- The purpose of this Resolution is to show the compatibility between the real possibility of freedom and determinism.
- Practical freedom is not a distinct type of freedom but the practical concept of the same; as a result, the accounts of the Third Antinomy and the Canon of Pure Reason are not mutually contradictory.

- The grounding of morality in GMM III involves a particular manifestation of the epistemic spontaneity of reason which grounds the claim that we are practically free, i.e. in acting, we have to assume we are transcendentally free.
- The causality of freedom is the capacity to use the causality of reason; the distinction between these two is the key to explaining the possibility of (free) immoral action (Moral Leeway question).
- Kant develops a comprehensive Theory of Choice as volitional account; this involves assigning causal roles to reason and our free endorsement of incentives in our decisions.
- Kant's conception of *Gesinnung* blocks possible Luck Arguments, but leaves us with worries about Rational Luck and the reduction of all choice to a single one (part of the Timeless Agency problem), worries which could be addressed by broadening this conception to defining a purpose of unity of our agency.
- The agent's empirical causality is defined by an empirical character specifiable in terms of subjective principles, or a belief-desire model, or inclinations; these account for the formation of intentions that are the temporal manifestation of the adopted maxims.
- The specific nature of inner sense allows Kant to find the conceptual space for the determination of a fixed law of nature, the empirical character, which is activated progressively over time; this accounts for alternative possibilities in time (Temporal Leeway question).
- Kant's claims about free will across the critical period (CPR, CPrR and CJ) are consistent.
- The framework of transcendental idealism does away with the mind-body interaction problem, and allows for clauses of physical laws that refer to inner sense circumstances, in particular intentions, thereby ensuring the possibility of a physical account of free agency.
- Kant's theory of free will is normative: freedom is the ability to act morally, but in human agents this also implies the ability to act immorally; the corresponding 'ought implies can' principle relates our knowledge of what we ought to and can do, and thereby has factual implications.

Although the turn to transcendental idealism defines the only metaphysical framework allowing for the possibility of freedom,[56] if one does not endorse Kant's analysis of ethical obligation and the Fact of Reason, the reality of freedom has not thereby been shown. This is, however, sufficient to address the Problem by showing that the possibility of freedom is compatible with determinism. And further, our libertarian intuitions have been vindicated insofar our practice necessarily assumes freedom.

One might still bemoan these results as a meagre achievement. But they address the worry motivating this work, namely that a certain scientific picture of the world leaves no room for the freedom of these libertarian intuitions. Further, the following points should be noted. First, the framework of transcendental idealism itself provides a ready explanation for why we cannot know whether we are free or even whether this is a real possibility. Second, but independently of this framework, the requirement that the real possibility of freedom be proven theoretically is unrealistic. Indeed, what exactly would a theoretical proof of the real possibility of the causality of freedom look like? It should be a proof that there is a possible world with the same natural laws in space (and which could be the actual world) in which the agent plays a causal role as source of an action. But it is not possible to show that in such a world no natural cause beyond my control is not ultimately responsible for a certain phenomenon, i.e. my intention or my action. To be able to do that, one would have to have knowledge of all the causal forces that could be manifested at time t. This would require (a) a complete knowledge of all natural laws and (b) a knowledge of the sum total of all causalities active in the world. But since (a) is not, and could not be shown to be, true, as there may be types of causality we are ignorant of, and since (b) our knowledge of what fills the whole of space will always be limited, I cannot exclude the possibility that such a causality, whose source may be out of my epistemic reach, should have a causal impact upon my behaviour. It is therefore impossible to exclude that what I do is entirely caused by natural causality in this possible (or the actual) world.

In this book, I have argued that it is only through Kant's critical approach to natural objectivity that it is possible to solve the Problem. By failing to identify a place for free will in a deterministic world, the framework of naturalism cannot properly account for our moral responsibility and our self-conception as agents. The revision of our metaphysics involved in endorsing transcendental idealism might not be attractive to contemporary philosophers, but it is unlikely profoundly to affect the world outside the philosophical community. On the other hand, the revision of our notions of moral responsibility and conceptions of guilt and punishment required by the hard incompatibilism implied by the Consequence Argument in a naturalist framework, would compel us to revise deeply entrenched libertarian intuitions and profoundly impact our sense of self. The choice between these two metaphysical frameworks is, I have argued in this book, the choice we face in the light of the Problem. The way forward I advocate is a Kantian one. This is not a *Back to Kant* call, but rather a summons to go *Forward with Kant*.

Notes

Preface

1 Fyodor Dostoevsky (1864) *Notes from the Underground*. Reproduced with permission of Simon Powell [trans.].
2 Erasmus (1524) *On the Freedom of the Will*. Reproduced with permission of Dennis Schulting [trans.].
3 Robert Musil (1943) *The Man without Qualities, Vol II*. Reproduced with permission of Sabine Best and Chris Onof [trans.].

Introduction

1 While these chapters refer to the contemporary debate discussed in the other chapters, a reader interested purely in Kantian exegesis can focus exclusively upon them.
2 In some cases, the interpretation of scientific theory arguably calls for a form of transcendental idealism (see Bitbol, Kerszberg and Petitot 2009).

Chapter 1

1 Libertarianism is given a precise definition later.
2 Helen Steward (2012: 4–6) considers a broader notion of free will that is not connected to responsibility. This is loosely identifiable with agency and therefore also concerns non-rational animals. This leads to a distinct problem that I cannot discuss here, apart from noting its connections with the issue of teleology in biology (see Onof and Schulting 2023: 254–5 for a discussion of this in relation to Kant).
3 Depending upon one's understanding of morality, moral norms are either second-person (e.g. Hume) or third-person (e.g. Kant) ones. As we shall see later (Chapter 5), it is not just a contingent fact for Kant that there happen to be norms for free agents: freedom, for him, is essentially connected with moral normativity.
4 The status of the second-person form is more complex. It is arguably closely tied to both the first-person and third-person forms. Indeed, I treat others in ways that reflect how I understand myself, but legal and penal norms are also closely linked with second-person reactive attitudes. This issue need not be discussed further here.
5 An empirical proof of free will, just as a proof of determinism, would be impossible. One would have to exclude the possibility that a more remote cause of my action could be found for the causal role identified for free will, but how could one, e.g.,

exclude a role for action at any distance according to the phenomenon of *quantum entanglement* (Isham 1995: 147–9), for instance (see also chapter 7)?

6 I examine Bennett's use of backtracking counterfactuals against this premise in Chapter 2.

7 Until Chapter 7, I only need to characterise naturalism as a form of realism about nature according to which natural objects/events are completely independent of our cognition.

8 In Chapter 3, I shall return to the definition of free will libertarianism.

9 With the following notation:
(*NP*): S cannot change the past;
(*NL*): S cannot change the laws of nature;
the argument relies upon the so-called *transfer of powerlessness principle* (Fischer 1986: 19):
(*T*): (*NP*) and (*NL*) necessarily entail (*NA*), where (*NA*) is 'S cannot act otherwise than how she in fact acts'.
(*T*) is the most debated premise in the literature. More precisely, what has been questioned is the underlying β-principle (van Inwagen 1983) (β):
$(\Box p)$ *and* $\Box(p \rightarrow q)$ *entail* $(\Box q)$, where $\Box$ is the modal operator 'necessarily'. For instance, following Widerker (1987), the β-principle is only true under the assumption that p be made true before q (O'Connor, 1993). Other attempts have been made to find fault with the β-principle, but some version of it which ensures the validity of the Consequence Argument is widely held to be valid (Speak 2011: 118–21).

A rather more popular type of criticism of (*T*) questions the nature of the counterfactuals involved in it from the point of view of Lewis-Stalnaker possible-world semantics. For instance, Vihvelin (2000, 2013: 155–66) argues that different types of counterfactuals are involved in making sense of (*NL*) and (*NP*). The two types of counterfactuals correspond respectively to the notions of *ability* and *opportunity*. Vihvelin claims that to assess if we are able to do something, we consider possible worlds in which the laws of nature are identical to ours but in which the past could be different. To assess if we have the opportunity to do something, the relevant possible worlds have the same past, but the laws of nature need not be the same. So, while (*NL*) leaves it open that S might have the opportunity to act otherwise, (*NP*) allows for S's having the ability to act otherwise. (*NA*) does not therefore follow from these premises.

The instability which this 'finessing' of the principles defining what is unchangeable leads to has been pointed out by several authors. Thus, Helen Beebee (2003: 260) shows that on Vihvelin's proposal, (*NP*) and (*NL*) respectively commit us to claiming (a) that S is able to do things which would require a miracle *and* (b) that S is not able to do things which would amount to a miracle. Other worries have also been formulated about this Lewisian approach insofar as it appears to support only a limited notion of free will corresponding to a *conditional analysis* of it (see Speak 2011: 123). Indeed, when it is claimed that (*NL*) allows for S's opportunity to do otherwise, this amounts to saying that she could act otherwise *conditionally* upon the past having been different (because if it had not been different, together with the fixity of the laws of nature, it would have entailed a unique present). That conditional analyses of free will are insufficient is a point I examine further.

Finally, assuming this insufficiency, note that Vihvelin's interpretation of (*NP*) is also questionable. In van Inwagen's argument, this does not refer to an opportunity as opposed to an ability claim: we should require that the opportunity be brought

about through the agent's ability, so it is a matter of having the ability to create an opportunity. If that is correct, (*NP*) does not allow S a *relevant* ability to act otherwise.
10 For the sake of brevity, I omit a third strand which Clarke (2009) dubbed *new dispositionalism*, as exemplified in Vihvelin's (2004) work. Drawing upon Lewis's (1997) work on dispositions, she argues that an ability is an intrinsic property of the agent, while laws of nature are not (which is contentious). This enables counterfactual situations to be defined with distinct laws of nature when assessing an agent's ability to do otherwise (see Vihvelin 2013 and the previous endnote). Clarke (2009), however, shows that this account does not deal satisfactorily with phobic agents.
11 I thereby refer to Kant's publications from 1781 onwards (and some earlier non-published writings).
12 Compatibilism is not just a feature of the empiricist tradition (Hume 1978: 73; Mill 1963–91: X 841); there are also important rationalist strands of compatibilism. Leibniz (2007; although see Sotnak 1999) has it that actions emanate from the agent's essence (see further) but are not necessary: I could have had a different essence, i.e. if the whole of the universe had been different. Spinoza (1992) goes further in claiming that all occurrences, including human actions, are necessary.
13 This epitomises the aspirational idea of freedom pervading popular Western culture: 'A man is a success if he (...) does what he wants to' (Dylan 1967) insofar as one seeks to reduce the constraints of what is materially (physically, financially, etc.) possible.
14 Note that this argument also works against Strawson's (1974) compatibilism. Indeed, the 'manipulation-fuelled exemptions to moral responsibility' proposed in the argument are based upon moral intuitions and 'internal features of the practice of holding people morally responsible' (Pereboom 2014a: 82). Since it is also an internal feature of this practice that if the agent is exempted from moral responsibility in one case, she is in the other, the 'basic elements of the argument are features internal to the practice' (Pereboom 2014a: 82), so that determinism does, after all, impact what is internal to this practice.
15 Although much of the discussion around mesh theories has focussed on Frankfurt's proposal and the various responses he made to objections, it is possible to summarise the issues arising for the general mesh theory approach.
16 See Davidson (1963).
17 It is noteworthy that Frankfurt (2002: 27–8) and Watson (1999: 363–5) accept this consequence and embrace the counterintuitive idea that the history of the volitional structure is irrelevant to defining the agent's self.
18 Watson (1977) may in fact only be making a weaker requirement on free agency, namely that the agent should *be able to act* in accordance with his valuational system, although it is not clear how that ability is to be understood without drawing upon any ability to do otherwise.
19 I return to this issue in Chapter 3.
20 Insofar as Fischer and Ravizza accept that determinism may be incompatible with the freedom to do otherwise, their theory is a form of *semi-compatibilism*: it is compatibilist insofar as determinism is compatible with responsibility because guidance control, they argue, is all that responsibility requires, but it rejects the compatibility of determinism and regulative control.
21 I am *freely* introducing a bit of democracy into a territory governed by the colourful but despotic Red and White Queens in Lewis Carroll's (2015) classic story.
22 A related complaint about the merely subjective ownership condition was formulated by Mele (2006), who considers the case of a philosopher who becomes a hard

incompatibilist and therefore does not fulfil the ownership requirements but nevertheless seems to be morally responsible.

23 The debate around reasons-responsive theories is very rich (see McKenna 2011: 191–5): I can only touch on a couple of issues here. Another question that arises is how the mechanism's responsiveness to reasons can be assessed. McKenna (2011: 193) considers the case of an addict who acts from such a mechanism in his normal drug consumption but would react to stronger reasons not to take the drug and only to such strong reasons. This agent is therefore not responsive to weaker reasons not to take the drug and therefore on the proposed theory, not responsible for taking it.

24 See further discussion of objections in Pereboom (2004: 99ff).

25 As we shall see, this is only partly true of the reasons-responsive theorist.

26 Note that a first barrier to addressing this metaphysical question in a naturalist setting is the indexical reference to the agent. For indexicality does not supervene logically upon physical properties (Chalmers 1996: 85) and arguably also not upon natural properties more generally (Onof 2024).

27 Even within compatibilism, leeway compatibilists have raised objections to this account (see Vihvelin 2004).

28 I am *freely* introducing a bit of democracy into a territory governed by the colourful but despotic Red and White Queens in Lewis Carroll's (2015) classic story.

29 The worry that one's actions are then ultimately determined by God is dealt with by Leibniz's claiming that God did not determine me but 'discovered' me in his intellect and actualised me as belonging to the best of all possible worlds (Jorati 2017: 300).

30 This was Kant's version of the doctrine of 'physical influx' (Watkins 2005: 155–60).

31 That Kant could have adopted Boethius's conception of eternity has been proposed by Wolfgang Ertl (1998: 208–11), although here too, a move to transcendental idealism would be needed for it to provide a possible solution to the Problem (1998: 238–41; see Chapter 2, n. 56).

32 Note that the Copernican Revolution does not entail transcendental idealism. The latter is a substantial thesis involving the sensible conditions of knowledge/objectivity (see Gardner 1999: 43–4).

33 What is required is that reality in-itself should not be temporal. Transcendental idealism, as Kant understands it, also has it that it is not spatial. For simplicity, I ignore this issue since it does not impact any of my arguments about free will. I defend the claim of non-spatiality of reality in-itself on independent grounds in Chapter 7.

34 Meerbote (1984) attempted to make transcendental idealism more palatable to contemporary analytic tastes by interpreting it as a version of Davidsonian anomalous monism. However, if things in-themselves and appearances are *the same natural things* under different descriptions, then the fact that they are fully determined under one description does not create the conceptual space for free will under the other (see van Cleve 1999: 253).

Chapter 2

1 While Desmond Hogan (2009) may be right in claiming that such 'noumenal affection' is 'partly motivated by Kant's commitment to noumenal ignorance', i.e. our

inability to know things in-themselves, I see it as a pre-philosophical assumption that will have to be given support once the critical system is in place.
2. I agree with Andrew Chignell's (2017) identification of the real possibility of the cognised object as Kant's key requirement for cognition. In the case of things in-themselves and *indeterminate* cognition thereof, we have evidence of their real possibility in the possibility of being affected: it is through the actuality of sensations that we posit things in-themselves (see CJ AA05: 402).
3. These are distinct concepts, however, since the transcendental object is the same for all appearances (A109): it grounds them in an explanatory sense for the whole of our cognition. With the thing in-itself, the grounding is understood metaphysically, i.e. in causal terms. Kant is, however, not consistent in differentiating these concepts because their referents are the same unknown existence of reality in-itself.
4. The empirical object is outside me but dependent upon my cognition; the transcendental object is independent of it.
5. By adding this perspectival restriction (Onof 2019b: 209ff), I indicate that the relation appearances/things in-themselves is not, as Jauernig (2021) proposes, an ontological distinction between two levels of reality, because this would require a further level of reality to locate the relation between them. It is only from our perspective that we can interpret the relation appearances/things in-themselves.
6. The importance of the connection between reality in-itself and causality is emphasised by early twentieth-century Kant commentators such as Emile Boutroux (1926: 113).
7. I clarify the concept of causality further.
8. Prichard (1909: 71–100) adds that to save the empirical reality of appearances, Kant is committed to the confused claim that appearances are really spatial.
9. Epistemic conditions are also distinct from ontological conditions, i.e. conditions for the existence of things.
10. My proposed perspectival dual-aspect view disagrees with this statement insofar as it involves an existence claim for reality in-itself, which is in no way describable as spatio-temporal although it appears as such for us. This does not define two things because the appearance is not a thing; it is just how the thing which exists in-itself appears.
11. On what grounds can Kant postulate that judgements of actuality are justified by reference to a 'sensation of which one is conscious' (B272/A225)? It can only be because sensation is, as I claimed earlier, from the outset, taken to be caused by some existing reality in-itself.
12. One can discern an alternative to this in Korsgaard (1996b: x–xi), namely that noumena and phenomena define two standpoints on the same 'world'. But, if the way these standpoints relate is not further specified, why believe that they are standpoints on the same 'world'?
13. For further problems with the methodological interpretation, see Ameriks (2003: 22–5; 33–5; 75–9; 104–5).
14. Mathematical categories enable us to compare a token with other possible ones in terms of magnitude (quantitative or qualitative). Dynamical categories of relation define the way in which determinations of particular objects are related. Dynamical categories of modality define how such determinations are related to the whole of our knowledge.
15. For simplicity, I equate empirical object and natural object.
16. See Gardner (1999) and Buroker (2006) for clear presentations of Kant's main arguments.

17 This power, although timeless, is, of course, only manifested in this magnet so long as the latter exists as individual substance. This power could also be understood as a property of Substance through a unified account of all causal powers, i.e. of all 'fundamental forces of nature'.
18 The same is true for any causal theory of time.
19 This leads to a temporal ordering S1-S2 (see A203-4/B248-9; Allison 2004: 253–4).
20 This rule singles out a particular cause, but circumstances (e.g. referred to in a *ceteris paribus* clause) are also relevant. These are causal factors defining conditions under which the causality is manifested.
21 See Guyer's (1987) convincing reconstruction of Kant's argument.
22 See also Kant describing the rule as one under which 'the occurrence [of the effect] (. . .) *always* follows' (A200/B246, my emph.).
23 This task is not to be confused with that characterising regulative principles of reason: an analogy is a regulative principle of the understanding which is *constitutive* of experience (A179-80/B222-3; Onof 2020). So I am guaranteed to find a law (instantiated at least once).
24 This is what the Second Analogy requires, but the arguments for Thesis and Antithesis must be independent of principles established using transcendental idealism, since they assume transcendental realism.
25 The principle of sufficient reason can of course be rejected, which motivates the libertarian response (see Chapter 3).
26 I use the term 'noumenal cause' to refer to an intelligible (not knowable) ground. As I interpret Kant's idealism, this means that from my perspective, this is a ground and therefore thinkable under the category of causality. This does not entail any ontological claims as in Jauernig's (2021: 76) understanding of 'noumenal causality'.
27 Irwin (1984: 38) argues that if something is determined, it is determined in all possible worlds. But to conclude that determination among appearances therefore entails determination among things in-themselves assumes an ontological interpretation of the distinction appearance/reality in-itself as one of possible worlds. *Pace* Allison (1990: 44), the problem is not the metaphysical nature of the interpretation but the assumption that appearances are things in-themselves in another possible world: that would entail that if one of these is actual, the other is not, which is patently not what the distinction signifies.
28 As we shall see further, it is just the causality that is outside nature.
29 I therefore disagree with interpreters for whom Kant's solution is confronted by what Sorin Baiasu (2020: 8) calls the 'Paradox of Kantian Libertarianism' because my action must be both 'causally determined' and 'in principle free from causal determinism'. As I show in Chapters 3 and 4, because of transcendental idealism, Kant does not have the problem confronting standard libertarianism (which responds by rejecting such determinism).
30 Owen Ware (2023: 4) puzzlingly defines compatibilism and incompatibilism in terms of a compatibility with a 'universal determinism, according to which both appearances and things-in-themselves are subject to natural causality'. If nature is the domain of appearances, things in-themselves cannot, however, be subject to natural causality.
31 Scholten argues that since Frankfurt-style examples (see Chapter 3) address the main worry that animated classical compatibilism in respect of determinism, i.e. the absence of leeway, there is scope for compatibilism freed of this concern. This is true but is not the main motivation behind contemporary compatibilism, which is the focus on sourcehood.

32 He convincingly argues for this claim by considering a compatibilist who relies upon Lewis's realism about possible worlds and his analysis of counterfactuals but who nevertheless would not be called anything else than a compatibilist.
33 Scholten (2021b: 139ff) shows that Kant does not dispute the transfer of powerlessness required for the validity of the Consequence Argument (see Chapter 1, n.7).
34 Ertl (2024) makes the same point in a different way, i.e. by looking at determinism and free will purely at the level of appearances and noting that this defines an incompatibility.
35 If libertarianism were *necessarily* a type of incompatibilism, the issue would already be settled. However, I have also indicated that Kant's proposal, in identifying freedom with a type of causality, is a forerunner of contemporary agent-causal theories. Like Ertl (1998: 82, 2024), I shall therefore be led to question standard classification assumptions.
36 Introducing a causality outside appearances still involves an existence claim about reality in-itself. But by not involving any claim about a *distinct* substance, the Third Antinomy's solution can address the Problem: it is the agent in space/time who is endowed with a noumenal first cause.
37 For now, whether it is the intention (mental state) or action (physical event) that is at stake is irrelevant.
38 Byrd (2008) argues persuasively that Kant already abandoned the principle of sufficient reason in his *Regions of Space* (AA02: 377–83) of 1768, as a result of his analysis of incongruent counterparts (see also Onof 2024).
39 I examine this claim in detail in Chapter 4.
40 Kant himself refers to a '*mechanism* of nature' (CPrR AA05: 97).
41 Objections to the leeway requirement are examined in the next chapter.
42 I am simplifying what is found in the literature: in fact, some authors (e.g. Guyer) argue that the mere logical possibility of transcendental freedom is at stake, while others explicitly claim it is the logical possibility of transcendental freedom together with determinism (see Onof 2021c).
43 Although my interpretation in Onof (2021c) of what the Resolution achieves otherwise coincides with this one, I there overlooked what the preamble establishes.
44 I discuss this in Chapter 6.
45 Ludwig (2015), who must be credited with drawing attention to the insufficiency of logical possibility interpretations, attempts to avoid this conclusion. He claims that Kant is only saying that we cannot understand *how* we could be transcendentally free. I have argued that this interpretation is implausible (Onof 2021c).
46 This is close to Pereboom's (2006: 547) interpretation, although he translates real possibility in terms of what agrees with 'our best empirical theories about the natural world'. We shall see, however, in Chapter 4, that the real possibility of freedom is independent of the nature of these empirical theories.
47 This compatibility is itself a logical possibility. To see this, note that we have two modalities in play here. Denoting f = transcendental freedom of a solution-thing impacting appearances, and d = natural causal determinism, with subscripts L/R referring to the possibility and necessity operators $\Diamond$ and $\Box$, standing for 'logical'/'real' respectively, the Resolution has to show $\Diamond_L (\Diamond_R f \wedge d)$. Note that conditionally upon the real necessity of determinism (Second Analogy), this is equivalent to the internal coherence of the real possibility of f. This follows from: $\Diamond_L (\Diamond_R f \wedge d) \wedge \Box_R d \leftrightarrow \Diamond_L (\Diamond_R f \wedge \Box_R d) \wedge \Box_R d \leftrightarrow \Diamond_L (\Diamond_R (f)) \wedge \Box_R d$.
48 See Ertl (2020: 32–3) for three such threats.

49 Wood and Rosefeldt refer rather to the causal antecedents of the empirical character, but insofar as, on their reading, this is a mere causal intermediary between intelligible character (the noumenal ground) and action, which, just as much as the action, is causally determined by previous empirical causes, it is simpler to discuss the logical issues without reference to this character. That their interpretation involves a misunderstanding of the empirical character is an issue I address in Chapter 4.
50 Rosefeldt (2012: 100–1) offers a plausible reconstruction of Wood's point in terms of Bennett's counterfactuals.
51 Rosefeldt does not do this, but it seems essential to obtaining the desired result.
52 Rosefeldt (2012: 99–100) notes that Bennett has since retracted this theory but for reasons which do not impact upon its use here.
53 In view of Chapter 1's critique of compatibilism, it is easy to see how enlisting backtracking counterfactuals does not define a plausible compatibilist alternative in a realist setting: without the agent's noumenal ground (intelligible character), it, for instance, falls prey to the Argument from Manipulation.
54 The intuition here is that, following the logic of the Consequence Argument, it is *because* of my ability to change the past that I am free. Therefore, responsibility would seem to have to accrue to the alteration of past events too. This intuition also, however, expresses what is unsatisfactory about the use of backtracking conditionals: my ability to alter the past does not play the role it should in the Consequence Argument, i.e. of *explaining why* I am free to act although I am determined, but instead *follows from* the assumption of freedom.
55 As Heimsoeth (1973: 298) points out, Kant's thinking that such a series must exist is a consequence of his understanding of time as a continuum rather than an atomistic series of instants.
56 Wolfgang Ertl opts for altered-law compatibilism but without the agent having any causal impact on natural laws. Instead, Ertl draws upon Boethius (Ertl 1998: 246–7) and de Molina (Ertl 2014: 426) to suggest that God could have ordained the laws of nature to be such as to enable transcendentally free agency to be compatible with them. There is no space to examine this important proposal here. I shall just observe that while it seems cogent as a way of addressing the Problem, its Kantian credentials are questionable. Setting aside the issue of Kant's actually endorsing de Molina's views, it would seem to make the regulative role of the idea of God in the *CPR* a requirement for the Resolution. This does not prima facie chime with Kant's systematic organisation of the Dialectic of the *CPR*. Further, it is not clear how adequately it would address the Timeless Agency problem, in particular the Temporal Leeway problem (see further). There are also problems in the further specification of the proposal which has it that agents' noumenal agency (intelligible character) is characterised in terms of 'counterfactuals of freedom' (Ertl 2020: 39f) specifying what the agent would do in each situation: such counterfactuals have to refer to states-of-affairs of appearances and therefore cannot be purely intelligible.

Chapter 3

1 Wolf's (1990) attempt to ground the possibility of a limited form of (asymmetric) leeway compatibilism in a distinction between psychological and metaphysical determinism is problematic. She argues that since the latter does not entail the former,

it is possible for the agent to form alternative intentions; the problem is that since the action is fixed by the causal determinants that precede it, the agent's leeway role would amount to a mere ability to have a different take on what he does anyway (as in other reasons-responsive theories – see Chapter 1). This is not sufficient for blameworthiness.

2 Frankfurt (1971) himself does not abandon the view that free will requires alternative possibilities but denies that this is required for moral responsibility.

3 It is questionable that this is the case though, because the assumed deterministic link between blushing and killing Smith could be seen as making the first the inception of an action culminating with the second; in that case, not blushing would be a manifestation of the intention not to kill Smith.

4 Otsuka (1998) counters that Joe had the option of raising his level of moral attentiveness and that had he done so, since the intervention would have occurred, he would not have been morally responsible. Pereboom (2014b: 91) replies, correctly in my view, that since Joe does not believe that by raising his level of moral attentiveness, he would not be morally blameworthy, this is not, from his perspective, a proper alternative to doing the blameworthy action.

5 It might be thought that this Frankfurt-style case could be revised to be located at the point where Joe raises his level of moral attentiveness to deliberate upon these issues. But the same objection can be made to any such move: if the agent proceeds to act in a certain way without any manifest deliberation, this is because he feels that an earlier decision establishes how to proceed.

6 O'Connor (2000: 105) also argues against van Inwagen's (1989) case for restricting the scope of free will.

7 This simplistic description of a belief-desire psychological model could be upgraded to a more sophisticated account distinguishing higher-order desires, valuation systems, as examined in Chapter 1, but it is sufficient for our purposes here.

8 Thus what is caused is not an event but a probability distribution of possible outcomes (e.g. Humphreys 1989: 37) while the occurrence of the determinate effect is not the result of any further causal determination. This model is used in quantum mechanics: the Schrödinger equation enables the determination of the evolution of the wave function, i.e. a state vector characterising the probability distribution of the state of the system. Through a process of 'collapse of the wave function' a determinate state is obtained. This collapse is thought to be random on standard interpretations of quantum mechanics (e.g. see Bohm and Hiley 2003 for a review and critique).

9 This distinction between causation and necessitation is also made by Steward (2012: 217–18) although on different grounds: she endorses the claim that natural laws only *constrain* what will happen. Similarly, Stephen Mumford argues that when a, b, c and d together cause e, it may be (Mumford 2015: 4–5) that there exists an 'additive interferer' i such that a, b, c, d and i together do not cause e. And if that is the case, then a, b, c and d together do not necessitate e since there are cases when they do not cause e. But this ignores the fact that causal laws have *ceteris paribus* clauses; with these, it can be said that a, b, c, d in given sets of circumstances necessitate e. Although he argues that understanding causality as a 'dispositional modality', i.e. a power to bring about certain effects (which it will not always do because of such possible interferences), is more fundamental, and not reducible to probabilistic causality (Mumford 2015: 6–7), it creates space for free will in the same way as probabilistic causality does, defining a species of agent-causation (see further).

10 Here is a short proof that indeterministic causality is incompatible with the unity of time *if* temporal determinations are, as in transcendental idealism, dependent upon causality. Consider the following causal nexus. Cause C brings about events E_1 or $E_1{'}$ with probabilities p_1 and $1-p_1$ respectively. Conditional upon having produced E_1, it then causes either E_2 or $E_2{'}$ with independent probabilities p_2 and $1-p_2$ respectively. Additionally, event $E_1{'}$ is the manifestation of causality C' which (this time deterministically, for simplicity) causes event E_2 and thereafter E_1. The problem this causal nexus generates is as follows. First, all circumstances being equal, it is not always the case that C causes E_2 after having caused E_1. This sequence only happens with probability $p_1 p_2$. So this causality is not usable for the determination of temporal succession. But further, with probability $1-p_1$, C causes, via the causation of event $E_1{'}$ (manifestation of C'), event E_2 to occur before E_1, i.e. in reverse order from what occurs with probability $p_1 p_2$. The randomness of the temporal order of these two events shows that indeterministic causality is incompatible with the objective unity of time.
11 There is another way of grasping the problematic nature of indeterministic causation. Consider a cause C issuing in effects E_1 or E_2 with probabilities p and $1-p$ respectively. The situation is indistinguishable from a deterministic causal link from C to E_1 with a first cause intervening with probability $1-p$ to override that causal link and bring about E_2 instead. The problem then lies with the conceivability of such a first cause (see below in the context of agent-libertarianism).
12 See Aristotle (1986: iii, 10) for the need to include practical reason in accounting for voluntary action.
13 This does not concern *any* possible contrast: I may not have a ready account of why I opened my newspaper rather than took another sip of tea, but I can probably explain why I read a certain article rather than not. That is because this contrast has *volitional relevance*.
14 Clarke (2003: 153–4) is right to understand this as a first cause; if it were not, (i) either there would be some causal links to the reasons for action which would reduce this to an event-causal account where agent-causality does no real work; (ii) or the agent might cause her agent-causality, but that would lead to a regress.

A further, separate question is that of the causal status of the event agent-causing-an-intention? *Pace* Reid (see O'Connor 2000: 47), this is a mental event of which one can either claim that (i) it is not caused, (ii) it is agent-caused or (iii) it is event-caused (Clarke 2003: 153). The third option can be excluded as it would take away the control that the very introduction of agent-causality was meant to introduce. Chisholm (1971: 40–1; see also 1976) and van Inwagen (1993: 194) argue for the second option. This leads to an infinite regress since the agent's causing the event agent-causing-an-intention itself defines an event for which a cause must be found. O'Connor (2000: 55–8) shows that this is not tenable.

Thorp (1980) opts rather for the claim that these two events are identical, which avoids the regress but, if this claim is intelligible, it is in terms of its collapsing onto the first option, i.e. the claim that this event has no cause. Most agent-libertarians accept this and agree with O'Connor's (2000: 59) diagnosis: 'it is senseless to demand some further means of controlling the exercise of control.' However, the objection could be that it has not been shown that no other event, not under the agent's control, is actually the cause of this event. This is where a Kantian understanding of causality is helpful, as Watkins (2005: 415–17) points out: there need not be an event causing the event agent-causing-an-intention: it is just the agent's causality doing this.

15 Pereboom and O'Connor's response to Haji and Mele's Luck Objection also applies to the stronger Luck Argument examined earlier.
16 Although this is sometimes described as an alternative to introducing causal indeterminism into a compatibilist picture (e.g. Watkins 2005), indeterminism remains a key feature of agent-causality.
17 Further, McCann's non-causal account of how an intention and the action it intends are related is insufficient (Ginet 2000: 634–5).
18 This randomness could be illustrated in terms of an adapted Rollback Argument.
19 Such a further reason to adopt reasons $\{B_2, D_2\}$ could be that Alice thinks that Wonderland's economy would benefit from the implementation of inequality-reduction measures.
20 Pereboom (2014a: 69) assumes these probabilities are a given, which would lead to a further problem for O'Connor; but this assumption is not forced upon us since this is not event-causality.
21 Strawson (2002) describes it as the ambition to be a *causa sui*. That seems not quite right because the influence of circumstances, upbringing, etc., is not denied. What is denied is that the way they impact our behaviour should be beyond our control to reject/alter.
22 A willing is an act of intention-formation so that the intention is a product of the willing.
23 Of course, one can ask what further purpose the action's purpose serves, but this move 'beyond the action' is not required for the action's intelligibility.
24 Strawson's text has 'RD' which stands for '(truly and without qualification) responsible and deserving of praise or blame or punishment or reward'.
25 *Pace* Davidson (1980), this will mean that psychological and/or psycho-physical laws are involved.
26 I am not hereby claiming that this is Kant's understanding of free will. I return to this issue in chapters 4 and 5.
27 As I indicated in Chapter 1 (endnote 33), for simplicity I here ignore the fact that the non-temporality but not the non-spatiality of reality in-itself is necessary and return to this issue in Chapter 7.

Chapter 4

1 This response also requires viewing the whole of one's agency as directed to a purpose defining its unity, but this is not a constraint on the metaphysical account, only on the volitional one (see Chapter 5).
2 I say 'foundations' because developing the volitional account (see Chapter 5) will require explaining how this 'location' accommodates something I can understand as my free will.
3 Indeed, it is precisely on the basis of the Third Antinomy that we can justify such a regulative claim (Onof 2021a).
4 Beck (1960: 190) argues that this may also be too much in another sense, namely that this amounts to a 'pan-libertarianism' in which T-freedom is present everywhere, as Erdmann (1878: 69) understood it. But in fact, nothing has yet been claimed about T-freedom as I explain later.
5 The present interpretation differs a little from Onof (2021c) where I overlooked the role of the preamble and interpreted this first section as dealing only with logical

possibility. In fact, since the actuality of an albeit unspecifiable intelligible ground is at stake, the claim is stronger.

6 Pluhar usefully introduces a comma in his translation of 'Possibility of the Causality through Freedom, as Reconciled with the Universal Law of Natural Necessity', which I think is a more faithful translation. But, whether we consider the scope of '[real] possibility' to cover 'causality through freedom' and 'universal law of natural necessity' (Guyer/Wood translation) or just 'causality through freedom' (Pluhar translation) is irrelevant assuming transcendental idealism, since causal determinism is itself a condition of (real) possibility. Indeed, assuming $\Box_R d$ (using Chapter 2, endnote 47's notation) $\Diamond_L (\Diamond_R f \wedge d)$ is equivalent to $\Diamond_L(\Diamond_R f)$.

7 The word 'faculty' translates 'Vermögen', which does not assume a rational agent: indeed Kant talks of the faculty of an object of sense (A538/B566). So Pluhar's translation, 'power', is preferable here.

8 Guyer and Wood add the qualification 'another' which is absent from the original German ('eine Causalität'). This usefully draws attention to the distinctness of this causality but should not prevent us from viewing it as the agent's contribution to the general grounding of the whole of nature as I shall suggest further.

9 An important difference between these two problems' resolutions is that while the cosmological solution involves merely thinking of the ground of appearances as T-freedom (what is not natural causality can only be thought as T-freedom), T-freedom in the rational agency problem will be grounded practically in the Fact of Reason (see Chapter 5).

10 Commentators (e.g. Allison 2020) generally overlook that this defines a further specification of the outline of the solution in section two.

11 Kant's characterisation of the intelligible character as the 'transcendental cause' (A546/B574) of the empirical character is usually taken as primarily referring to the noumenal nature of the first. But in fact, for Kant, 'transcendental' always refers to 'conditions of possibility'. This means that it is *insofar* as it is an effect of an intelligible character that a certain law of causality in appearance is described as an empirical character.

12 *Pace* Friedman (1992b: 182), I take it that Kant must be committed to the Second Analogy as applying not only to outer but also to inner sense (Prol. AA04: 295) (see further).

13 From here on, Kant will mostly only deal with the Problem. What we do not therefore get is a regulative principle emerging from the cosmological problem unlike the practical regulative principle arising from the rational agency problem (A554/B582) and the theoretical regulative principle connected with the Fourth Antinomy (A564/B592). I would argue that one is hinted at (A672/B700) although it defines no 'hypostatic idea' (A673/B701) and apparently has no regulative function with respect to cognition. This is reality in-itself as ground of empirical causality which would regulate our transcendental knowledge (see Chapter 2 and Onof 2021a).

14 In strictly modal terms, the possibility of an actuality of p is just the possibility of p, a trivial fact Kant is no doubt aware of. The reason for which 'actually' is included is to emphasise the distinction with section two. Here it is the possibility of a state-of-affairs featuring this first cause, not just a concept of it, that is at stake.

15 So the possible state-of-affairs Kant considers is not necessarily counterfactual.

16 Kant takes it that, since there are theoretical grounds for locating a non-natural causality in the agent's reason, it must be there that it should be located, if it exists

at all. But that is a weak argument which Kant strengthens in the *Groundwork to the Metaphysics of Morals* (Chapter 5).
17 I discuss this in relation to P-freedom. I consider a justification of this form of the principle in Chapter 5 and another form of it in Chapter 6.
18 Ertl (2024) correctly indicates that *at the level of appearances*, Kant is an incompatibilist; but this is a limited sense of incompatibilism.
19 Scholten (2022: 88-9) adduces textual grounds for this, but they are in fact arguments (which I endorse) against calling Kant an incompatibilist since they are directed at the problems arising from introducing indeterminism as the contemporary libertarian does. For Kant, such indeterminism is incompatible with the unity of objective experience and turns freedom into mere chance (see Chapter 3, in particular endnote 10).
20 Vilhauer (2010: 69) argues that while such laws exist, Kant denies they could be identified because of the nature of inner sense. This epistemic point is important, but I shall argue in Chapter 6 that Kant's claims have metaphysical import.
21 Note the 'also' here: objects of outer sense are, in the sense I explained in Chapter 2, representations, and as such define contents of inner sense.
22 I distinguish between the subjective principles of the empirical character and maxims (which are also subjective principles). In that, I follow Bittner's (1974) distinction between, respectively, specific rules and rules guiding the agent's way of living (see Allison 1990: 91) and O'Neill's (1983) distinction between, respectively, rules for specific intentions and rules defining the agent's underlying intentions. As we shall see (Chapter 6), this distinction is important for the compatibility of the volitional and psychological accounts.
23 One might worry about how the notion of causality in inner sense fits with the general interpretation of Kantian causality as property of substance in Chapter 2. Julian Wuerth (2014) makes a convincing case for the claim that, the Paralogisms notwithstanding, the critical Kant allows us to *think* of ourselves under the category of substance (Wuerth 2014: 185-6).
24 Rosefeldt (2012: 93) thus takes this to mean that the empirical character is determined by appearances.
25 But see endnote 13.
26 See the grounds for moving to transcendental idealism in Chapters 1 and 3.
27 Kant here describes the empirical character as the sensible schema of the intelligible character (A553/B581), unsurprisingly, given this passage's emphasis upon the role of temporal conditions: actions are temporally determined through the empirical character *as* manifestations of the agent's causality of freedom. Allison (1990: 32 and 2020: 280-4) puzzles over the different descriptions of the relation empirical/intelligible character and claims that Kant's preferred formulation, namely that the intelligible causes the empirical character (e.g. A544/B572; A546/B574), is problematic as it would preclude the latter being a causality of reason. I do not see the problem here: if I represent to myself a map of the way to the railway station and draw it on paper so that a visitor can navigate his way there, it is knowledge (my representation) that is causally efficient by means of the drawn map. The fact that my representation is only *indirectly* causally responsible does not make it any less causally relevant: the immediate cause (drawn map) can be described as a manifestation of it. Since the empirical character is caused by the intelligible in appearance, one can also refer to the first as appearance of the latter ('appearing' is a causal relation) in line with Kant's terminology elsewhere (e.g. CPrR AA05: 99; CJ AA05: 196n).

28 Scholten (2021a: 29) wants to see this example as involving an appeal to the 'ought implies can' principle but notes that it does not feature explicitly here. In fact, this claim has implicitly been endorsed in an epistemic form in the notion of P-freedom (see below).
29 So, for instance, the agent would in effect be as though acting on some 'oughts' through the coincidence of action commanded by these 'oughts' and determined by first-order desires endorsed by the higher-order desires. Such a coincidence is not so improbable if the higher-order desires are the right ones.
30 As for Kant's claim that '[t]hus without a God and a world that is now not visible to us but is hoped for, the majestic ideas of morality are, to be sure, objects of approbation and admiration but not incentives for resolve and realization' (A813/B841), what is claimed is, arguably, a forerunner of the CPrR's Postulates of Practical Reason, which in the CPR takes the form of reason's need to 'connect with the moral law (. . .) an efficient cause' (A812/B840) of the realisation of the Highest Good: the prospect of happiness should not motivate but is bound up with moral action: '[t]his will (. . .) requires these necessary conditions [(the postulates)] for obedience to its precept' (CPrR AA05: 132). For if 'the highest good is impossible (. . .) the moral law (. . .) must be (. . .) false' (CPrR AA05: 114).
31 This is distinct from Kohl's theoretical claims about freedom that are *adopted for practical purposes*. This distinction is important since only *qua* practical concept can one understand P-freedom properly as what is involved in an agent's self-conception in acting: it is not *just* that for practical purposes, certain theoretical worries are set aside, but rather that this self-conception is *essential* to this practice. I think Kohl (2014: 328–30) comes close to agreeing on this point, but his appeal to the 'phenomenology of practical deliberation' is not quite strong enough: what is at stake are transcendental conditions of agency.
32 Kant's characterisation of P-freedom is in terms of 'necessitation' rather than 'complete determination' (independence of causal 'determination' is, by contrast, used in the definition of T-freedom), which, although equivalent, indicates that the focus is upon the modality i.e. the negation of the *possibility* of a contribution by the agent.
33 Note that here, Kohl cannot appeal to Kant's referring what is *useful for practical purposes* as he does to interpret Kant's claim about P-freedom in the Canon: Kant makes no such statement in the Resolution.
34 This depends upon how one understands 'abolition'. This is an issue I examine further.
35 This is the limited type of libertarian freedom Allison draws upon (see above). Kohl (2014: 320–1 n.7) disputes that the independence of necessitating causes could define any such weaker libertarian freedom because 'determining causes are necessitating causes'. While the latter is true, Kohl overlooks the implied completeness of the determination in 'necessitation'.
36 It is only on the assumption Kant makes (CPR, A807/B835) that morality defines a categorical imperative, that this result is obtained, so the concepts of T-freedom and P-freedom are not analytically related.
37 Because of the Argument from Manipulation, Kant would have to include contemporary source compatibilism as equally enjoying nothing more than the 'freedom of the turnspit' (CPrR AA05: 97).
38 Kant also refers to T-freedom as freedom in an 'absolute signification' in the CPrR (AA05: 3) and otherwise refers only to 'freedom', further confirming there is only one

type of freedom (the compatibilist's 'psychological freedom' is not, for Kant, a proper concept of freedom, CPrR AA05: 96).

39 With transcendental idealism, the Resolution shows that there is a conceptual space for T-freedom as ground of the agent's empirical causality: this is not an empirical matter; that there is no such space within a transcendentally realist metaphysics is also not an empirical matter. Empirical evidence such as that provided by Libet's experiments (Libet 1985) which have been taken to show that, because our consciousness of acting follows the inception of the action, these actions are not free, cannot therefore be relevant to showing free will is impossible; Bojanowski (2006: 15) reaches the same conclusion.

40 Hard incompatibilists like Pereboom (2014b: 114–24) thus analyse in what ways our self-conception, penal practices, etc., would be altered in the light of the theoretical impossibility of freedom in a deterministic world (see Chapter 7).

41 The practical context is thus for Kant reliant upon the theoretical proof of the permissibility of T-freedom, and not completely immune to theoretical worries as Peter Strawson would have it (see Chapter 1).

42 One might worry that 'ought implies can' entails that we cannot thus be mistaken. But although Kant assumes in the CPR that categorical imperatives characterise our practice, he has provided no grounds for a theoretical claim about their validity, so cannot exclude the theoretical possibility that they are an illusion.

43 The debate is typically couched in terms of moral responsibility, but what is at stake is the *practice of our holding* agents to be morally responsible, and hence also blameworthy, rather than responsibility as objective state-of-affairs. Scholten's contention that there is no 'ontological' claim (Scholten 2021a) about responsibility requiring T-freedom is correct *here*, but only because what is at stake is *holding agents to be responsible*. Actual responsibility does require T-freedom because, as shown earlier, our ability to act on the categorical imperative requires it.

44 Ware (2023: 22) argues that imputation does not require leeway freedom since the latter is only chance. Even if it were mere chance, i.e. if I had no ground for acting against the moral law, I had a ground for acting morally and did not do so: it is this choice to act otherwise that makes my action imputable.

45 See Ware (2023: 31–5) for how Fichte responded to this.

46 See also Bojanowski (2006: 258), who argues that Kant characterises evil as weakness, and Ware (2023: 24), who claims it involves a diminished power of freedom (see Chapter 5 endnote 31).

47 In the CJ, Kant can draw upon the practical grounding of freedom in his earlier critical ethical works (see Chapter 6).

48 Angela Breitenbach (2006: 707) notes that this externality condition is required by the *Metaphysical Foundations of Natural Science*.

Chapter 5

1 I differ from Schönecker (1999: 225–6) in emphasising the practical nature of (at least some of) our epistemic activity (see later).

2 *Pace* Henrich (1960: 110), Refl. 5442 (AA18: 183) does not suggest that the understanding's spontaneity could not be involved in some activity that, considered *practically*, is a manifestation of T-freedom.

3 I cannot discuss the issue here, but while I broadly agree with Kohl's (2015a) contention that freedom of thought is genuine freedom, I would argue that it involves the freedom of the will (see also McLear 2020).
4 Although this differs from Bojanowski's (2006: 220–3) interpretation, he correctly identifies the fact that Kant's argument appeals to reason as such (the genus of theoretical *and* practical reason). I argue that this arises precisely by identifying the practical dimension of a certain type of theoretical/epistemic spontaneity.
5 Kant claims in the *Prolegomena* that transcendental idealism is 'opposed to all ordinary notions' (Prol., 261)). However, Kant is not thereby necessarily claiming in the GMM that the common understanding espouses transcendental idealism: this could rather be understood as referring to a Platonic view of reality conveyed through a Christian lens.
6 I take Kant's reference to the agent not being any 'wiser' through the mistaken assumption that the ground of appearances can be intuited, as implying a negative impact upon her practice. Kant may have in mind how 'the pretensions of dogmatic authority' (A739/B767) restrict the subject's freedom. In a contemporary context, dogmatic claims about the non-existence of freedom would impact our agency (e.g. see Pereboom's revisionism). Similarly, dogmatic atheistic claims would make it impossible for us to hold that it is possible to realise the Highest Good although this is, for Kant, commanded by morality (e.g. CJ AA05: 469).
7 Puls (2016: 62) argues that Kant's focus is the theoretical spontaneity involved in practical judgements. But the text does not support this reading as I have argued. Note that one could arguably claim that all epistemic activity has a practical dimension since it is end-directed: 'that (...) at which all thought as a means is directed as an end is intuition' (A19/B33). This would bring freedom of empirical thought (Kohl 2015a) and freedom of the will under one general heading. But caution is required here as Kohl (2015a) indicates because freedom of thought is not voluntaristic in the sense that I do not will what to think and believe.
8 Our beliefs are thus arguably contents of inner sense insofar as they correspond to such representations.
9 I disagree with Allison's (1990: 227–8) criticism that Kant slides from a negative to a positive sense of noumenon: Kant's text does not refer to reality from the perspective of an intellectual intuition (the positive sense). Allison's methodological interpretation, however, prevents him from endorsing Kant's claims about intelligible reality as pertaining to a noumenon in the negative sense.
10 As Jules Vuillemin (2017: §30) puts it: 'La liberté est un devoir'.
11 'Autonomy' provides a positive concept of freedom (see further).
12 My interpretation of P-freedom (Chapter 4) avoids the complications arising from the view that there might be distinct notions of P-freedom in play in these published works (e.g. Allison 2020: 319).
13 It has seemed puzzling to many (e.g. Beck 1960: 207–8; Allison 2020: 407–10) that Kant affirms this in the Analytic of the CPrR, while claiming that it is a postulate of practical reason in the Dialectic. In fact, since Kant already refers to freedom as postulated in the Analytic (CPrR AA05: 94), there is no conflict here. While Willaschek (2018) offers a solution drawing upon a theoretical distinction cognition/knowledge (see further), I suggest that the issue is simpler: 'practical knowledge' (CPrR AA05: 31) defines necessary assumptions/beliefs, i.e. postulates, *for theoretical reason* (CPrR AA05: 121, 132). There is then only a difference of degree: freedom is postulated directly through the Fact of Reason, whereas the other postulates rely upon the postulation of freedom.

14 I do not examine a third ground which is simply an assertion that in saying that we cognise freedom, Kant is not saying that we know freedom: any argumentative work this could do would require drawing upon the distinction cognition/knowledge.
15 A discussion of the precise nature of the fact is beyond the scope of this study (but see Onof 2009b).
16 Scholten (2021a: 35) argues against Vilhauer (2023) and Kohl (2015b) that Kant's statement (in the false testimony example) that the agent 'cognizes freedom within him' (CPrR AA05: 30) only amounts to a belief about the possibility of freedom rather than a knowledge claim about freedom. This, however, relies upon the same questionable appeal to a distinction between practical cognition and practical knowledge (Willaschek 2018: 114).
17 Note that the CI arguably also leaves room for further individuated specification reflecting the agent's ends (see Onof 1998: 423–4).
18 We shall see further that reason is causally involved but in a conditioned role.
19 I am thereby rejecting the explanation endorsed by Schönecker (1999: 188–95) that immoral action could not involve the intelligible character, because that would mean it is not free and the agent not responsible for it.
20 The will does not feature in Kant's metaphysical account.
21 This is to establish that morality is necessary for freedom. The reciprocal entailment, that freedom is necessary for morality follows from the discussion in Chapter 4: the unconditional moral 'ought' requires independence from external causal determinations (see Allison 1990: 204–10).
22 Allison's decision to view autonomy as morally neutral is well motivated by the worry (shared by Bittner 1983: 151) that, if not, equating autonomy with freedom would entail that immoral action is not free. But, as I shall propose further, the error lies in straightforwardly identifying T-freedom with autonomy.
23 We shall see further that the subjective basis of a choice lies in the agent's *Gesinnung*. What Kant seems to be requiring in GMM III is that this basis should be universally, i.e. objectively, valid; but he has not shown why this requirement is imposed.
24 We shall see further that there remains something incomprehensible about evil action for Kant.
25 While Kant's assertion in GMM III that autonomy is 'the property of the will to be a law to itself' (GMM 447) suggests a descriptive meaning, it is in effect the same statement as in GMM II (GMM: 440) where it is clearly prescriptive.
26 This asymmetry is Kant's answer to Reinhold (1975) who sought to define freedom in terms of symmetric leeway.
27 See also the MM (AA06: 226–7), where Kant makes it clear that freedom should be defined in terms of what is necessary for it as intelligible capacity, not what characterises it contingently in sensibility.
28 Below, I explain Kant's account of choice in terms of maxim-adoption.
29 Owen Ware (2023: 24) wants to account for evil in terms of a diminished causal power of freedom which he interprets as governed by the moral law. This, however, involves equivocating over the assumed conception of power. He seemingly correctly understands it in the way any causal power is a capacity, but seeks to introduce some notion of magnitude. While its effects may be assigned some magnitude, the causal power itself is not augmented or diminished. Alternatively, it could be understood in the way our faculties of understanding or reason are powers. While the use of such powers admits of degrees of skill, the powers themselves do not.

30 Here, all that is at stake is the possibility of what Kohl (2015b: 700) calls an 'inner act of choice', i.e. a willing that issues in an intention (see further). I examine the issue of 'ought implies can' for physical actions in Chapter 6.
31 Ware (2023: 6) mistakes two types of inscrutability about evil: Kant thinks that we cannot understand *why* an agent chooses evil (see further). The *possibility* of immoral action, on the other hand, must be shown to be compatible with determinism: that the Resolution of the Third Antinomy does not only address this possibility for moral action is evidenced by Kant's choosing an example of lying.
32 And with this, the theological problem of evil rears its head since this makes God responsible for human agents' evil acts.
33 In Rel AA06: 143, Kant might be seen to contradict this optimism with his claim of a mystery. However, the mystery in question is rather that of making sense of creation as a causality that could produce free beings; in that sense, it is no more mysterious than the mystery of the nature of the causality of freedom.
34 This proposal raises theological issues that cannot be addressed here. Insole's (2013: 178ff) interesting account of noumenal creation defines an alternative solution.
35 Bojanowski (2006: 229–62) provides a convincing defence of the claim that this does not amount to a revision of Kant's theory of freedom in the Resolution, GMM and CPrR.
36 Noller (2021: 260–4) usefully proposes that Frankfurt and Kane's theories involve contemporary equivalents of *Willkür*.
37 Sellars's and McDowell's 'space of reasons' is useful to illustrate this idea (see McDowell 1996: 5) since, while the intelligible domain is a metaphysical reality, what is at stake here is a volitional account which concerns our self-conception as rational agents, not a metaphysical account.
38 While maxims are *understood in terms of empirical descriptions of action*, I hereby emphasise the fact that they define choices that do not refer to appearances since they are intelligible explanatory grounds of psychological causality in appearance. Thus, for instance, promise-breaking and lying refer to our attitude to the truth in relation to other agents, without needing to draw upon any empirical cultural institution. Similarly, our attitude to the satisfaction of our animal/human propensities refers to how we deal with external causal forces in relation to our duties.
39 See Allison (1990: 87). Here I differ from the account in Onof (1998: 411).
40 Note that I am using a formulation that is meant to cover what Kant distinguishes in the MM as maxims of action and of ends (MM AA06: 394–5). The purpose Φ is thus either immediately definitive of a type of action through the constraints it imposes upon φ (narrow duty of right) because it concerns the form of the maxim; or it is not, because it concerns the 'matter' of the maxim (MM AA06: 394–5). In the latter case, it is what Kant describes as an end and is the subject of the Doctrine of Virtue.
41 My controversial proposal differs from Barbara Herman's (1996) primary/secondary incentives distinction originally introduced to deal with permissibility.
42 Although this cannot be discussed here, *pace* Herman (1985), I would argue that ensuring that the purpose plays this role is as much as the Kantian can do to address the 'one thought too many' critique of Kant's ethics (Williams 1981: 18): if I save my drowning wife out of duty, it is at least true that my purpose was her rescue even if my motivation remains problematic as Bernard Williams argues.
43 Allison (1990: 37–9) relates it to the 'I think' which *takes* a manifold in intuition *as* representing an object with a conceptual determination. If (as I cannot argue for here)

epistemic spontaneity depends upon some form of practical spontaneity, the parallel is not fortuitous.
44 As such, it is contrasted with the cognitive factor, i.e. what rationality commands us to do (Beck 1960: 76).
45 It is thus perhaps best translated as 'driving mechanism' (see Herrera 2000: 395).
46 Timmermann (2022: 79–83) provides six reasons for the shortcomings of an intellectualist interpretation of Kant's ethics like Allison's, centred around the claim that, for Kant, we act upon reasons that we take to be sufficient (see also Reath 2013). Similarly, Wuerth (2014: 262ff) shows the shortcomings of Korsgaard's analogous intellectualist reading of inclinations. I agree that equating incentives with reasons (Allison) or proposals (Korsgaard) does not do justice to Kant's meaning. However, the idea of an agent taking an incentive as basis for action, in the sense of 'going for this incentive', is fruitful.
47 The agent contributes to grounding natural causality (Chapter 4), so here the Ground is understood as the whole of the intelligible ground of natural causality apart from this (or any other) agent's contribution.
48 This means that immoral action has a 'noumenal dimension': it is important that it does not simply result from the contingency of some inclination being pleasant or not to us.
49 The will thereby has an outer determining ground, contrasting with its 'inner determining ground (. . .) within the subject's reason' (MM AA06: 213).
50 As Allison (1990: 129) observes, Kant's own language is confusing insofar as he uses *Wille* for both.
51 Guyer (2018: 125ff) shows how Kant adhered to such a distinction throughout his career even if the vocabulary changes, and why this is key to addressing the Moral Leeway question.
52 I use 'act' here insofar as it involves two components: the pursuit of a purpose and the implementation of a type of action.
53 This categorical imperative results from the application of *the* Categorical Imperative (CI): it is one of the 'imperatives of duty (. . .) derived from this single imperative', the CI (GMM AA04: 421; see Onof 1998).
54 This purpose is here defined in general terms by our predisposition to animality and humanity (see above).
55 Partial or complete compliance will correspond to different types of evil (see further).
56 This involves more than just complying with the universal principle of right (MM AA06: 230–1), namely complying with broad duties to others, if only out of self-love.
57 What about mere permissibility? This is action that is constrained by maxims of duty so all that is relevant at the intelligible level is the adoption of these maxims.
58 See Dirk Setton (2013) for an insightful interpretation of this respect in terms of auto-affection.
59 The predisposition to animality, which defines '*mechanical* self-love', accounts for the quest for sexual satisfaction; the predisposition to humanity, which defines '*comparing* self-love' (REL AA06: 26–7), accounts for the desire to win a Rhinemaiden for himself.
60 The leitmotiv will of course also have other dramatic functions in its reappearance (see Scruton 2016: 98).
61 One might wonder whether there is a secondary incentive of duty in Alberich's choice of action: because of his archetypal function in the Ring story's source of evil, it is arguably not the case.

62 Hence, *pace* Kosch (2006: 55n26), Kant's distinction *Wille-Willkür* is useful here (see further).
63 Kant *should* be committed to this rational self-sufficiency of purposiveness as consequence of his understanding of the difference purposive/mechanical causality (see Chapter 4), but I am not claiming there is evidence that he is. Hence, in this brief discussion of the *Gesinnung*, I put the emphasis upon what is needed to address the Problem.
64 Peters (2018: 505–6) argues that such a causal interpretation would eliminate leeway in individual choices. This is partly a consequence of overlooking the atemporal nature of the choice of *Gesinnung* which will, as I shall show in Chapter 6, itself be reflected as leeway in time. But it is also true that Kant's text in the REL suggests no *further* atemporal leeway than this fundamental choice (see further): any such leeway would amount to freedom of indifference which Kant rejects.
65 *Pace* Pasternack (2014: 116), like the acts of *Willkür*, the *Gesinnung*-adoption is not to be thought of as temporally located. I thereby concur with Stephen Palmquist (2015b: 112) although he argues for temporally located acts of *Willkür* while I also view them as non-temporal but with a temporal manifestation (see Chapter 6). Kant's remarks about the manifestation of a *Gesinnung* 'from youth on' (REL AA06: 25) can most charitably be interpreted as indicating that it is manifested at any point during the life of a fully fledged rational agent. It is implausible to make the inception of moral life of supreme importance through a decision (*Gesinnung*-adoption) affecting the whole of it, moral conversions perhaps excepted.
66 Allison (2020: 502) usefully refers to the *Gesinnung* as a higher-order maxim.
67 As Palmquist (2015a: 236) shows, psychological and metaphysical interpretations of *Gesinnung* are problematic: this is why it belongs to a volitional account of freedom.
68 For instance, that Björn Borg should have excelled at his discipline involves a strife for self-improvement, i.e. a moral characteristic ascribable to a good *Gesinnung*, but the fact that this discipline was tennis was determined by various contingent circumstances (see Borg 1980).
69 Above, I indicated that a subjective basis of maxim-adoption is necessary for this coherence.
70 There are thus arguably morally relevant choices to be made beyond the choice of acting morally, e.g. if competing duties need to be ranked (Onof 1998).
71 I use 'real' here to indicate that the metaphysical account makes metaphysical claims about what is required of the noumenal causality of freedom. The volitional account uses a *causal model* to describe much of what is involved in choice; it makes no metaphysical claims.
72 I agree with Insole's (2013: 127–34) penetrating analysis of Kant's inexplicability of evil claim, especially in relation to the Augustinian understanding of evil as nothingness. I would add that this nothingness is essentially the unknown for the agent, i.e. it amounts to the agent embracing randomness, which accounts for the incorporation of the incentive of self-love through which the agent lets the unknown Ground steer his agency.
73 A change of heart is also a possibility (REL AA06: 44ff; see below). Note that, while Allison (1990) identified propensity to evil and evil *Gesinnung*, Pasternack (2014: 116–17) and Allison (2020: 503) distinguish the first as feature of the human species logically preceding the second as feature of the individual agent. This is a more plausible interpretation although Kant's text (REL AA06: 25) is not clear on this issue.

74 The use of a causal interpretation of Kant's Theory of Choice circumvents problems of compatibility between GMM, CPrR and REL, as identified by some commentators (e.g. Guyer 2009).
75 Fugate (2012: 362–3) argues that we should interpret Kant's claim that immoral action is an incapacity (*Unvermögen*, REL AA06: 29) as amounting to the negation of a capacity. But the evidence of immoral acts would then lead us to claim that human agents both have and do not have a capacity, which is contradictory. It can therefore only mean that we are not exercising a capacity in immoral actions. While this is problematic on traditional understandings of the problem as Fugate points out (see Chapter 4), it is not on my interpretation. Indeed, it is precisely the non-exercise of my rational capacity (at least not in its fullness, i.e. as determining the law of my action). This does not mean that 'lawlessness' (2012: 354) ensues, but the law is no longer one I give myself, but one that I let the Ground determine.
76 See Palmquist (2015b: 144) for an enlightening mapping of this tripartite division upon our three predispositions.
77 Pasternack (2014: 119) offers an interesting analysis of this as a case of self-deception.
78 This differs from Allison's (1990: 94) hierarchy of maxims which is based upon degrees of generality.
79 A maxim towards which the agent displays frailty would arguably play a role similar to that of Hume's (T 2.2.9.15, 1978: 387) sympathy.
80 This requires assuming a hypothetical endless life, as per the Postulate of Immortality (CPrR AA05: 122).
81 I take it to be in the spirit of Kant's notion of *Gesinnung* as Palmquist (2015a; see above) interprets it.
82 There is arguably scope to view this as a broadly Kantian proposal that could be grounded in Kant's regulative principle of pure reason (A 652/B 680), following Adrian Piper's (2012) insightful interpretation of the Categorical Imperative.
83 There is also a temporal dimension to Kant's understanding of the formation of character (Refl. 5611 AA18: 252).
84 This might also seem close to Williams's (1981: 5) understanding of moral character as defined by certain fundamental desires which he also calls 'projects'. However, the agent's pursuit of her purpose cannot be dependent upon the manifestation of certain inclinations, however fundamental they may be.
85 See Sartre's (1958: 564; see Onof 2011a: 53–4) 'projet fondamental'.

Chapter 6

1 That is: the maxims characterise the intelligible character (Chapter 5), which appears as the empirical character specified in terms of subjective principles (Chapter 4).
2 In the 'Typic of the pure practical faculty of judgment' (CPrR AA05: 67–8), Kant restricts the role of practical judgement to determining how the moral law is to be applied. The MM deals with this issue, taking into account what is specific about 'the particular *nature* of man' (MM AA06: 217), to derive the duties specific to human agents. Kant is confident that this power is shared by all human agents (see GMM AA04: 403–4: this covers both our ability to know which maxims are moral and our ability to employ them appropriately).

3 Clarifying this issue arguably has consequences for the controversial question of whether one ought to φ out of duty when an inclination to φ is also present. Timmermann (2009: 53) argues that one ought to, which I think is correct. But it would also seem that overriding inclinations directed to the good is at least strange, and in fact unnecessary, as Kerstein (2002: 118–19) argues. On my proposal, if the inclination is directed to the good, then acting out of duty involves a causal role for this inclination in the psychological account of the action, i.e. the action will satisfy this inclination-to-the-good. This does not amount to acting *from* self-love, i.e. taking the satisfaction of this inclination as *ground* of my action (see also Onof 2011b: 125–6) because my free will controls my intention/action by either grounding/further developing an inclination or *endorsing* an existing such inclination, both out of duty (see further).
4 Although there is no space to discuss this, I would argue, *pace* Saunders (2018), that Kant's recognition of the temperament's contribution to the empirical character, which is well defined *because* of the framework of transcendental idealism, creates the space for *degrees* of responsibility, as required by our moral/legal practice. While, in any infringement of duty, the agent ought to have done otherwise (A555/B583), the greater burden upon certain agents to tame their temperament is recognised in apportioning responsibility.
5 The differences between Kant's solution to the Problem at that time and their final form in the CPR (see Chapter 2) do not concern the predetermination/determinism issue.
6 That is typically described with partial differential equations.
7 On the issue of the parity/disparity between inner and outer sense, see Kraus (2019) and Lian (2020).
8 The absence of such a structure accounts for Kant's repeated claim that the act of thinking requires a spatial representation (e.g. B154).
9 This problem of lack of criteria for contents of consciousness was famously discussed by Wittgenstein (1992:§258) in relation to the possibility of ostensive definitions of sensations .
10 This is why time itself cannot be perceived (B225).
11 Note that the manifold itself is altered if it is only reproduced (e.g. by the memory) once the mental event at stake is in the past. This alteration need not concern us here.
12 There is no possibility of circumventing the distorting effect of introspection by accessing the contents of inner sense through some 'inner perception', as Brentano (1973: 29–30) proposes.
13 I refer to *the whole of* ℂ because, as indicated earlier, while perceptual circumstances are reliably identifiable, since other circumstances are not, when considering the circumstances as a whole, an interpretation is required (see later).
14 Epistemic determination is, unlike in outer sense, also metaphysical determination. Here it is determination of the state of inner sense as circumstances of application of some maxim. For all actions (i.e. not our unconscious behaviour), some involvement of the subject's will is thus required. More generally, *the possibility of objectivity in inner sense depends upon our will*. This does not entail that freedom is thus shown to be real *qua* transcendental condition though, because there is no guarantee that what provides the determination is not determined by some more remote cause.
15 It is useful to look to Heidegger (1962: 191) to understand this. He claims that every interpretation requires some prior *decision* defining a 'fore-structure'. This involves a 'fore-having', i.e. the determinate perceptual circumstances and indeterminate

other contents of inner sense; a 'fore-conception', insofar as 'the interpretation has already *decided* for a definite way of conceiving' (1962: my emphasis) what is to be interpreted, here, the choice of maxim (M); and a 'fore-sight' (1962), which is arguably my grasp of the incentive to act upon. This use of Heidegger's fore-structure is plausible independently of his problematic critique of objectivity (see Onof 2006).

16 The manifestation of the act of *Willkür* in time is therefore made possible by the absence of knowledge about the full circumstances which are always novel in some respects. Our ignorance here is addressed by our freedom. Because in artificial intelligence, the machine exhibits no such ignorance, it could never claim to be free. It always has an answer based upon prior machine learning using algorithms, whose parameters are freely chosen by the user of the technology.
17 The attitude may, additionally, comprise feelings of resentment, pity, etc.
18 Is there a manifestation of the adoption of a *Gesinnung*? Dirk Setton (2013: 98–9) plausibly proposes that this act has a transcendental pre-timeliness. Alternatively, it is manifested with the first manifestation of an agent's maxim.
19 This is therefore also the temporal locus of our responsibility: it is because the agent endorses a maxim as to-be-acted-upon at t, that she is responsible for reasons B and D causing her intention and action.
20 In outer sense, circumstances are identical to past ones as long their spatial determinations are identical.
21 All actions are therefore, in a sense, what Kane (2014b: 26) would call 'self-forming actions', although differences of degree will arise: in most cases, I only endorse an extension of the range of application of a maxim to circumstances similar to past ones.
22 Indregard (2018) also introduces a distinction between the unchanging causal law(s) of the empirical character and something about it that changes. But the suggestion it is causal powers which change conflicts with their necessary function as timeless grounds of temporal determination (Chapter 2).
23 The empirical character was not part of Kant's account when he wrote this (before 1780).
24 This is, for instance. the case of Pereboom's (2006: 552ff) interpretation.
25 By not analysing the reasons for psychology's non-mathematisability, Bojanowski (2006: 175) overlooks the importance of the nature of inner sense for this impossibility.
26 I underscored the function of such an endorsement in arguing against Frankfurt-style counter-examples (Chapter 3).
27 It might seem that Kant claims that only the incentive is uncertain. But the incentive is, through incorporation, the matter of the maxim (REL AA06: 36), so this amounts to uncertainty about the maxim's content, specifically, its purpose Φ.
28 Knowing the maxims I adopt does not amount to noumenal knowledge since it provides no knowledge of the intelligible character, only a way of understanding it in voluntaristic terms. But knowing, for instance, that I acted on a moral maxim would imply knowledge that the incentive of duty grounds this action.
29 Both the willing and its manifestation in an intention *qua* event can be subsumed under what the scholastics referred to as 'elicited actions' (e.g. Aquinas 2012: Second Book, Part 1, Question 18, Article 6).
30 For the scholastics, this would be an 'imperated action', caused by an 'elicited action' (e.g. Aquinas 2012: Second Book, Part 1, Question 18, Article 6).
31 Mind-→body interaction is a unique case where final causality is realised through efficient causality (of a representation). Note also that, since the representation is

produced by the agent's free will, the action thereby qualifies as what Kant calls a product of 'art' in the CJ, i.e. of a 'production through freedom' (CJ AA05: 303). This contrasts with the purposiveness of organisms where we have no understanding of how it might emerge (Ginsborg 2006: 459) from natural 'mechanical' causality (CJ AA05: 370).

32 This account is also faithful to the scholastics' understanding of the physical $\varphi(\mathbb{C})$ action as efficiently caused by the will's intention to $\varphi(\mathbb{C})$ (see Stump 2003: 279).

33 This principle applies also to hypothetical imperatives, but the impossibility of acting on a hypothetical imperative is not a problem because such action is only conditionally required.

34 Scholten (2021a: 38) introduces a distinction between such real possibility independently of the nature of the agent, and this possibility *for* the agent. But this does not seem relevant: what is at stake is the real possibility of the agent $\varphi(\mathbb{C})$-ing.

35 The textual evidence (e.g. CPrR AA05: 30) cannot be examined here, but it is not decisively for or against an epistemic interpretation (see Kohl 2015b). For instance, *pace* Scholten (2021a: 35), when Kant says that the agent 'rightly concludes that he must also be able to' (REL AA06: 49n) do something, the fact that the agent can do it is clearly implied. This favours Vilhauer's (2023) interpretation which is epistemic but has factual implications.

36 Vihauer argues that this leeway requires transcendental idealism, in line with Kant's claim in the Resolution (Chapter 4). Scholten (2021a: 34–5) proposes a Frankfurt-style argument against this claim. Briefly, the idea is that Jones will give false testimony against White although if 'Jones were about to refrain from giving false testimony' a device implanted in his brain by Black would ensure that he does. And Scholten uses this to claim that Jones can freely give false testimony without alternative possibilities. This, however, begs the question against a libertarian understanding of deliberation since, as with the initial Frankfurt-style examples I examined in Chapter 2, this makes the assumption that there is a point in time before Jones has produced his intention at which it would be determined that he would produce it. The existence of such a time is, however, denied by the libertarian. Moreover, any improvement of the example along the lines proposed by Pereboom (2014b) and examined in Chapter 3 would have to involve identifying a time for the intervention after which the agent would certainly refrain from giving false testimony: as I argued there, any such time would only point to some prior deliberation with alternative possibilities available.

37 At this time, Kant claimed that, only in acting otherwise than following (the prevailing) inclination, is rationality involved. Action on inclinations therefore involved no free 'intervention' of *Willkür*, unlike the later Incorporation Thesis (Chapter 5), which raises the question of the agent's responsibility on this picture.

38 In Zeno's paradox, these times occur with delays from *t* which are halved at every step. Note also that I should be spelling out that what causes an event is the causality of a cause, but I am simplifying here in line with my remark (Chapter 2) about the fact that the manifestation of the causality of a cause defines an event.

39 These are circumstances of inner sense, but the interaction will involve these becoming relevant to outer sense causality as I explain further.

40 I agree with Allais (2018) that the domain of appearances is not closed. She, however, uses the always-incomplete determinateness of objects to argue for the existence of open futures. But in fact there is no limit to the determinacy of an occurrence for Kant: it is just set as a task according to the Second Analogy (see also the causal task

principle, Chapter 3). So when no action is involved, the task is to seek among causes active before or at t', causal determinants for an event after t'. If we now add an action to this picture, we still have the problem of how it fits in with the event that is already determinable to any required level of determinacy.

41 The attempt to explain mind-body interaction through a causal role of 'circumstances' also underpins Peter Tse's 'criterial causation' account of neural firing. On Tse's (2013: 25–6; 115–19; 136) proposal, the mind brings about an alteration of informational criteria for a post-synaptic neuron to fire, through its realisation (token-identity of mental and physical events is assumed) in a neuron. Interestingly, this enables Tse to account for both general and specific intentions. The proposal fails in my view, however, because the mental event is only causally effective through its neuronal realisation and therefore its nature is constrained by a prior distribution of possible neuronal states (in an assumed quantum physical setting): such constraints do not leave us with the required leeway.

42 The Kantian worry that this would be incompatible with the CJ's formal purposiveness of nature (CJ AA05: 181) can be addressed by appealing to the CJ's unification of nature and freedom (CJ AA05: 434ff).

43 It could be that the contribution of consciousness (inner sense) is *required* for further determination of a physical effect. More likely, this is only one way in which quantum level indeterminacy might be resolved ('collapsed') into a deterministic process at coarser scales (Wigner 1983; see further).

44 Excluding my contribution to natural causality, i.e. what I called 'Ground' in Chapter 5.

45 This infinity may not be realisable because of the quantum nature of matter which might make the divisibility of space physically irrelevant below a threshold defined by Planck's constant. But that is not a problem as we shall see further.

46 This causal role of intentions would be a case of 'intelligent top-down causation' (see Ellis 2011). This would only be permissible if the physical process exhibited some essential lack of determinacy, which we know to be the case at the quantum scale. Hence, on Pringe's (2007) interpretation, this would be regulative, not constitutive, of objective experience (see endnote 48).

While this concurs with Steward's (2012: 230–1) claim that 'non-physical influences' (here, mental) are relevant to physical processes, I do not understand laws as merely constraining these processes (see Chapter 3, endnote 9): rather, a law requires that circumstances be specified, and at the quantum level these may include non-physical factors. If this seems odd, note that at this level, we are arguably not dealing with fully fledged objects (see endnote 48).

47 There are two differences with Kant's series. First, the quantum events result from an external forcing upon the system, in the form of high-frequency perturbations. However, there is a causal role played by each occurrence since their accumulation brings about the physical action in circumstances defined by the perturbations. So this can be viewed as an instantiation of Kant's Zeno series. Second, in the quantum series, there is no last event when $n \to +\infty$ (there is a second discontinuity as the perturbations stop). Although Kant's series have a last event, that is not necessary for my proposal.

48 Hernàn Pringe's interpretation of quantum causality as having a regulative role is particularly attractive. He accounts for the compatibility of quantum and classical causality by referring to the analogy between this problem and that of the Third Antinomy (Pringe 2007: 156–9): the indeterminacy at the quantum level does not concern fully fledged objects, hence the Second Analogy holds.

49 Note that endorsing Stapp's theory about willings as causes of wave function collapses does not commit one to endorsing consciousness generally as the only cause of such collapses, as in Wigner (1983) - see endnote 43.

Chapter 7

1. Specifically, (a) it is necessary that freedom of the will be located outside the temporal order, so as to define a non-natural ground of psychological causality; (b) the metaphysical framework of transcendental idealism is apparently the only one in which the requirements in (a) can plausibly be met.
2. Morality could be centred around a value (e.g. love) or purpose (e.g. quest for meaning) that is taken as fundamental feature to our humanity (a role Kant assigns to rationality). It would thereby count as autonomy but define an alternative to Kant's moral law. The causality of reason would still define the driving cause of free agency, but in the case of moral action, it would be subservient to this value or purpose. Although all imperatives would thereby be hypothetical, moral imperatives would be conditional by this value or purpose taken as absolute.
3. One might well point out that this conception of choice does not include a concept of the 'I' who chooses. This issue requires going beyond materials available in Kant's theory and cannot be examined here.
4. This is Kant's mere 'empirical consciousness' (A122; B153).
5. Additionally, transcendental idealism requires that cognitive self-consciousness (apperception) be distinguished from inner sense as spontaneity. Today, what Block (1995) calls 'access consciousness' which is approximately 'awareness' but with a focus upon cognition is typically accounted for in functionalist terms, thereby leaving out the role of epistemic spontaneity that is crucial for Kant. But such functionalist reduction is questionable as Allison (1996: 53ff) showed in his critique, both exegetical and systematic, of Patricia Kitcher's (1990: 74–5; 111–12) functionalist interpretation of representational content in Kant.
6. That does not prevent it from also being viewed as 'highly plausible' (Pereboom 2006: 567).
7. Strawson argued that our reactive attitudes would not be impacted by the truth of determinism. Aside from the problems with this proposal (Chapter 1), Strawson's understanding of morality implies that 'there is no (...) independent notion of responsibility that explains the propriety of the reactive attitudes' (Watson 2004: 222). Such a claim is incompatible with my understanding of freedom in terms of moral responsibility.
8. This is no Berkeleyan idealistic claim but a short form for a more complex claim clarified below.
9. See endnote 11.
10. This is because the types of non-causal explanation that some authors appeal to in rejecting Salmon's claim are not relevant here (e.g. Nerlich 1979; Sober 1983).
11. In an argument directed at a more general form of transcendental realism, some role for perception would presumably remain since it is required to verify the fulfilment of the criteria of ontological commitment; and so would a role for causality insofar as this need not be a direct perception of the objects/events of the theory.

12 Two comments: first, it could be argued that I am just referring to the laws of physics and should rather refer to the laws of nature, but I prefer to avoid a reference to nature here. Second, the naturalist may object to an apparent conflation of epistemology and ontology here. However, observability, as criterion of ontological commitment, must be verifiable in principle, else it would be meaningless.
13 I use 'thing' very generally here as something that exists.
14 If this premise is rejected, then there are possible circumstances in which some natural objects/events are not natural. These objects/events cannot then have natural intrinsic properties, because if they did, the property of being natural would also be intrinsic to them. So these objects/events would define parts of nature that are not real in-themselves. This leads to (11) and (12), i.e. conclusion B below, by noting that if the domain of nature were real in-itself, all its parts would inherit natural intrinsic properties from those of the whole and hence would be real in-themselves.
15 While this separation of space and time is unproblematic in a Newtonian universe, in special relativity (see Section D), this is not the case. It will therefore be more useful to think of a totality relative to an initial observer. So W_s is a world of objects observable for a given observer, and the objects there in do not belong to a single time. In terms of events, the light cones will define W_t as those events that are accessible to the observer.
16 One might conceive of using a radar signal travelling beyond the totality to check if anything lies beyond, but this signal's presence outside it would mean that W_s is no longer the totality.
17 Note that the observability of parts of W_s/W_t is not sufficient for objectivity: all the parts of a unicorn are observable.
18 I avoid using 'possible world' so as not to create confusion around the meaning of 'world'.
19 The definitions of W_s/W_t are rigid designators, just as any natural kinds are. They identify different objects/events in different possible scenarios considered as actual. This is what Chalmers (1996: 60–2) calls the 'primary intension' of these definitions. The object/event thus picked out in the actual scenario can now be considered in different possible counterfactual scenarios. Because of the rigid designation it is always the same object/event that is picked out in these counterfactual scenarios: this is the 'secondary intension' (1996: 60–2).
20 The observation carried out by this new observer should be understood as an observation of the previous observer and her observations which, by transitivity is an observation of W_s/W_t. This is necessary to take the limitations imposed by special relativity into account (see endnote 15 and Section D).
21 While the argument in this remark relies upon the questionable assumption that such a subworld could be isolated, it is worth noting that our best theories suggest that the world is not infinite.
22 This differentiates the required metaphysics from scientific realism.
23 I argue directly for this impossibility in Onof (2024).
24 'Object' here refers to both the naturalist's objects and events.
25 I have not included a proof of this claim, but essentially, it follows from our cognitive capacities' being designed for knowledge of what is spatio-temporal.
26 Perception is here understood broadly to cover all possible sensations as indicative of some causal impact upon the senses.
27 It is simultaneously an epistemological claim of course.

28 It is therefore what Kant would call a *regulative* claim of reason (see Chapter 2, Onof 2020 and 2021a).
29 More generally, it is essentially the spatio-temporality of objective reality that accounts for its not being real-in-itself, whether it be in its intuitive manifestation as in my argument, or its conceptual manifestation as in the First Antinomy. As Ameriks (2003: 99ff) shows, there is therefore no 'short argument' to transcendental idealism.
30 See Buroker (1981), van Cleve (1991) and Onof (2024) for arguments for transcendental idealism using incongruent counterparts.
31 Note that the property of being incongruent counterparts depends upon the space in which these parts are embedded: it is a feature of the topological mereology of space. This can be seen by constructing in a plane two identical non-isosceles right-angle triangles that share their hypotenuses. They are incongruent in 2-d but not in 3-d.
32 In time, this outsideness means that the observation begins before the event begins.
33 Note: (i) I did not show the latter as an impossibility, but claim (11) is derived analytically so that modal claims could be made in that proof; (ii) I am not saying, of course, that this dependence of parts upon what is external proves transcendental idealism, but it is at the heart of the proof.
34 In Onof (2023), I propose alternative arguments for unicity and infinity based upon the possibility of geometric representations.
35 That it should in fact have been a key motivating factor is not only a consequence of the role freedom plays for morality (Bxxv), but is also explained by the fact that the freedom of engaging in such a critique (see also Chapter 5 is a condition for the very existence of the faculty of reason for Kant (A738/B766; see Pinkard 2002: 20–1).
36 I leave aside questions relating to quantum theory to which I alluded in Chapter 6 (see endnote 48) and for which Kant's idealism provides a fertile framework today (Bitbol, Kerszberg and Petitot 2009). Quantum indeterminacy concerns quantum scales and does not invalidate the applicability of the Second Analogy (Chapter 4) at coarser scales. This requires viewing 'quantum objects' as not fully fledged objects in the Kantian sense (Pringe 2007: 118–19).
37 Kant's space is three-dimensional (B40/41) and Euclidean (see AA10: 466; A716–17/B744–5). Does that mean that he cannot accommodate non-Euclidean spaces? Michael Friedman (1992b: 82) demonstrated that, insofar as Kant understands constructions in pure intuition as the source of geometric knowledge, non-Euclidean geometry is impossible. But non-Euclidean geometries could find a place in a Kantian framework as formal mathematical theories (we might need to enrich Kant's logico-mathematical toolkit to include polyadic logic and Cauchy-Weierstrass's conception of continuity – see Friedman 1992a: 71-80) which would be sufficient for their use in physics.
38 An early interpreter of GR, Sellien, thus argued (see his *Habilitationsschrift*) that Kant's understanding of space in transcendental idealism is as *intuitive* space (Howard 1984: 625).
39 These events are just the content of manifolds in intuition for a possible observer, structured by the forms of space and time. As such they are indeterminate. This is an advantage, however, since that enables the problem of the hole argument (Earman and Norton 1987) to be addressed (see Brighouse 1994).
40 Objective determinations in this tangent space will involve 'normal coordinates'.
41 Much more could be said about the relevance of Kant's idealism to, and compatibility with, SR and GR. Palmquist (2010: 50) reports how Ilse Schneider, a student close to Einstein, argued that Einstein's SR could not be said to refute Kant's views on space/

time. Further, Palmquist (2011: 101–2) shows how Einstein's conception of space/time as a kind of mental construct is profoundly indebted to Kant's anti-Newtonian conception thereof. Von Weizsäcker (1979: 16; see Palmquist 2011: 100) shows how Kant's thinking about simultaneity (B256-263/A211-5) sets the framework for Einstein's own theorising in SR. Finally, note that the role of possible observation/experience is arguably essential to GR: Hermann Weyl (1918: 3; 181–2; see Ryckman 2005: 133–4) identifies the ineliminability of coordinate systems in GR as attesting to the constitutive role of transcendental subjectivity, i.e. the forms of space/time, in his transcendental-phenomenological idealist account.

42 By introducing a ground of nature, the reality of nature is not demoted to a status comparable to that of a *virtual* (i.e. simulated as in the 'Matrix' films – see Chalmers 2015) as opposed to a non-virtual (non-simulated) reality (Chalmers 2022). While Chalmers argues that virtual realities are real, I would reply that this is not the case for the virtual realities we could create because they could never be real in the way our objective reality is. This follows from the fact that only the latter's causality is grounded in reality in-itself. This ground of nature, however, although more fundamental *qua* ground, is not a 'higher-level' reality *for us*: for our discursive cognition of spatio-temporal objects, there is only one objective reality, that of nature.

43 To see why property dualism calls for a transcendental turn, see Onof (2008).

44 Note that this is broadly how Langton (1998) interprets Kant's idealism using a questionable reading of the Amphiboly chapter of the CPR.

45 Although criticising physicalism, Strawson claims to be a materialist.

46 The intrinsic nature of reality must be able to give rise to experience. Whether that makes it pan-psychist or pan-proto-psychist is an open question (see Chalmers 2015).

47 Some argue that there is scope for a scientific understanding of the phenomenal character of our consciousness, a science which would be of a radically different type from what we now understand as science since it would rely upon subjective reports and would not involve analysing functional relations (Chalmers 2010). But even such a science would not claim to explain how phenomenal properties ground physical properties.

48 Arguably, qualia define an epistemic condition (additionally to Kant's transcendental conditions): they are required for consciousness of a manifold of sensations, but this cannot be discussed here.

49 As I indicated in Chapter 5, it does, however, enable Kant to argue for an enrichment of the concept of transcendental freedom as capacity for autonomy.

50 I thereby reject Prichard's (1912: 36) claim that grounding practical normativity is wrongheaded. Bittner (1989: 1–22) identifies the need for a normative starting point in his analysis of the lack of satisfactory answers to 'why be moral?'. He shows there are vicious circles involved, insofar as these answers make covert moral assumptions. While Bittner is right in his diagnosis that we cannot derive moral requirements without presupposing an 'ought', this 'ought' arguably need not be a moral one. One of the most impressive contemporary attempts to provide a foundation for morality (Korsgaard 1996a) derives the requirement to value humanity as an end-in-itself from the minimal assumption that one has values (Korsgaard 1996a: 100–26).

51 This is even true when the agent seeks to 'lose control': the agent, e.g., wants to use drugs in a controlled way and suffers when this control evades her.

52 Moral norms would arise from the recognition of the limits of this control and specifically the need to identify a value grounding the unity of my agency: a universalisability requirement will arguably follow from this.

53 What I propose to fill in the argument is close in spirit to Carnois's (1987: 101–3) view that heteronomy undermines what makes freedom effective: '[i]n a way, it annihilates itself'.

54 I specify 'random' to distinguish these inclinations from certain values which might define inclinations but be essential features of our agency on an non-Kantian understanding of it (just as rationality is essential for Kant). This could be the case for love, for instance. This is distinct from Bernard Williams's (1984: 5) contention that certain desires are endorsed as what defines an agent essentially because if it is *qua* inclinations (as opposed to essential features of what it is to be a human agent) that they do so, then the randomness of this adoption will, as I argue, lead to other inclinations being allowed to govern us.

55 There is no space to address this here, but some light can be shed upon why we choose evil: this is an attempt to extend our control beyond its proper domain. That is, I seek to bring the ground of natural causality under my control to serve my self-love: as shown in Chapter 5, in immoral decisions, I channel the driving force of this Ground through my practical rationality (thereby conditioning the latter) towards a purpose defined by my self-love. The slippery slope described earlier is just the manifestation of the failure of such extended control.

56 In Kantian moral scholarship, the view that moral normativity requires Kant's metaphysics is not popular. This often suggests an implicit assumption that the Problem is a separate one that could be given a compatibilist treatment (see Vilhauer 2004: 720). This is, however, anathema to Kant (Chapter 5) and relying upon compatibilism is problematic (Chapter 1).

References

Translations of Kant's works (with abbreviations)

CPR *Critique of Pure Reason* (1998), Paul Guyer and Allen W. Wood (trans.). Cambridge: Cambridge University Press(when not otherwise mentioned, this translation is used).
CPrR*Critique of Practical Reason* (1993), Lewis White Beck (ed. and trans.). New York: Macmillan.
(1996), Werner S. Pluhar (trans.). Indianapolis and Cambridge: Hackett.
CJ *Critique of Judgement* (1987), Werner Pluhar (trans.). Indianapolis: Hackett.
GMM *Groundwork of the Metaphysics of Morals* (1976), Lewis White Beck (trans.). Indianapolis: Bobbs-Merrill.
MM *Metaphysics of Morals* (1995), Mary Gregor (trans.). Cambridge: Cambridge University Press.
Prol *Prolegomena to any Future Metaphysics* (2004), Gary Hatfield (trans.). Cambridge: Cambridge University Press.
REL *Religion within the Bounds of Bare Reason* (2009), Werner S. Pluhar (trans.). Indianapolis: Hackett.
MFNS *Metaphysical Foundations of Natural Science* (1970), James Ellington (trans.). Indianapolis: Bobbs-Merrill.
Refl *Notes and Fragments* (2010), Paul Guyer (ed.), Curtis Bowman, Paul Guyer and Frederick Rauscher (trans.). Cambridge: Cambridge University Press.

Other sources

Adickes, E. (1889), *Immanuel Kants Kritik der reinen Vernunft*. Berlin: Mayer & Müller.
Adickes, E. (1924), *Kant's Analogies of Experience*. Berlin: Pan Verlag Rolf Heise.
Allais, L. (2015), *Manifest Reality: Kant's Idealism and His Realism*. Oxford: Oxford University Press.
Allais, L. (2018), 'The Compatibility of Kantian Determinism with an Open Future', in Violetta L. Waibel, Margit Ruffing and David Wagner (eds), *Natur und Freiheit. Akten des XII. Internationalen Kant Kongresses*, 713–28. Berlin: de Gruyter.
Allison, H. E. (1983), *Kant's Transcendental Idealism. An Interpretation and Defense*. New Haven and London: Yale University Press
Allison, H. E. (1990), *Kant's Theory of Freedom*. Cambridge: Cambridge University Press.
Allison, H. E. (1996), *Idealism and Freedom*. Cambridge: Cambridge University Press.
Allison, H. E. (2020), *Kant's Conception of Freedom*. Cambridge: Cambridge University Press.
Allison, H. E. (2004), *Kant's Transcendental Idealism. An Interpretation and Defense*. New Haven & London: Yale University Press.
Ameriks, K. (1982), *Kant's Theory of Mind*. Oxford: Clarendon Press.

Ameriks, K. (2000), *Kant and the Fate of Autonomy. Problems in the Appropriation of the Critical Philosophy*. Cambridge: Cambridge University Press.
Ameriks, K. (2003), *Interpreting Kant's Critiques*. Oxford: Oxford University Press.
Anscombe, G. E., ed. (1981), 'Causality and Determination', in *Metaphysics and the Philosophy of Mind: The Collected Philosophical Papers of GEM Anscombe. Volume Two*, 133–47. Minneapolis: University of Minnesota Press.
Aquila, R. E. (1981), 'Intentional Objects and Kantian Appearances', *Philosophical Topics*, 12(2): 9–37.
Aristotle (1986), *De Anima*, trans. Hugh Lawson-Tancred. Harmondsworth: Penguin.
Aristotle (1995), *Physics*. Books I-VIII, trans. P. H. Wicksteed and F. M. Cornford. Cambridge, MA: Harvard University Press.
Aristotle (2006), *Nicomachean Ethics*, trans. C. C. W. Taylor. Oxford: Oxford University Press.
Armstrong, D. (1997), *A World of States of Affairs*. Cambridge: Cambridge University Press.
Augustine (1993), *De Libero Arbitrio. On the Free Choice of the Will*. Thomas Williams, [trans.], Cambridge and Indianapolis: Hackett Publishing Company.
Ayer, A. J. (1954), 'Freedom and Necessity', in his *Philosophical Essays*, 3–20. New York: St Martin's Press.
Baiasu, S. (2020), 'Free Will and Determinism: A Solution to the Kantian Paradox', in M. Kisner and J. Noller (eds), *The Concept of Will in Classical German Philosophy: Between Ethics, Politics, and Metaphysics*, 7–27. Berlin: De Gruyter.
Bayne, S. (2004), *Kant on Causation: On the Fivefold Routes to the Principle of Causation*. Albany: State University of New York Press.
Beck, L. W. (1960), *A Commentary on Kant's Critique of Practical Reason*. Chicago: University of Chicago Press.
Beck, L. W. (1987), 'Five Concepts of Freedom in Kant', in Stephan Körner and J. T. J. Srzednick (eds), *Philosophical Analysis and Reconstruction*, 35–51. Dordrecht: Springer.
Bennett, J. (1984), 'Kant's Theory of Freedom', in A. Wood (ed.), *Self and Nature in Kant's Philosophy*, 102–12. Ithaca: Cornell University Press.
Berkeley, G. (1848–1957), *The Works of George Berkeley, Bishop of Cloyne*, ed. A. A. Luce and T. E. Jessop. London: Thomas Nelson and Sons.
Bird, G. (2006), *The Revolutionary Kant*. Peru: Open Court.
Bitbol, M., P. Kerszberg and J. Petitot, eds (2009), *Constituting Objectivity: Transcendental Perspectives on Modern Physics*, vol. 74. Berlin: Springer Science & Business Media.
Bittner, R. (1974), 'Maximen', in G. Funke and J. Kopper (eds), *Akten des 4. Internationalen Kant-Kongresses (Mainz)*, 485–98. Berlin: de Gruyter.
Bittner, R. (1983), *Moralisches Gebot oder Autonomie*. Freiburg/Munich: Karl Alber.
Bittner, R. (1989), *What Reason Demands*. Cambridge: Cambridge University Press.
Block, N. (1995), 'On a Confusion about a Function of Consciousness', *Behavioral and Brain Sciences*, 18: 227–47.
Blöser, C. (2021), 'Kant's Justification of Freedom as a Condition for Moral Imputation', in M. Hausmann and J. Noller (eds), *Free Will. Historical and Analytical Perspectives*, 283–312. London: Palgrave.
Bohm, D. and B. J. Hiley (2003), *The Undivided Universe: An Ontological Interpretation of Quantum Theory*. London: Routledge.
Bojanowski, J. (2006), *Kants Theorie der Freiheit*. Berlin: De Gruyter.
Borg, B. (1980), *My Life and Game*. London: Sidgwick and Jackson.

Bourget, D. and D. J. Chalmers (2014), 'What Do Philosophers Believe', *Philosophical Studies*, 170(3): 465–500.
Boutroux, E. (1926), *La Philosophie de Kant*. Paris: Vrin.
Bratman, M. (2003), 'A Desire of One's Own', *Journal of Philosophy*, 100(5): 221–42.
Breitenbach, A. (2006), 'Mechanical Explanation of Nature and Its Limits in Kant's Critique of Judgment', *Studies in History and Philosophy of Biological and Biomedical Sciences*, 37(4): 694–711.
Brentano, F. C. (1973), *Psychology from an Empirical Standpoint*, trans. A. C. Rancurello, D. B. Terrell and L. L. McAlister. Abingdon: Routledge.
Brewer, K. and E. Watkins (2019), 'A Difficulty Still Awaits: Kant, Spinoza, and the Threat of Theological Determinism', *Kant Studien*, 103: 163–87.
Brewer, T. (2002), 'Maxims and Virtues', *The Philosophical Review*, 111: 525–72.
Brighouse, C. (1994), 'Spacetime and Holes', in D. Hull, M. Forbes and R. M. Burian (eds), *PSA 1994*, vol. 1, 117–25.
Broad, C. D. (1952), *Ethics and the History of Philosophy: Selected Essays*. New York: Humanities Press.
Buchdahl, G. (1992), *Kant and the Dynamics of Reason: Essay on the Structure of Kant's Philosophy*. Oxford: Basil Blackwell.
Buroker, J. V. (1981), *Space and Incongruence: The Origin of Kant's Idealism*. Dordrecht: D. Reidel.
Buroker, J. V. (2006), *Kant's Critique of Pure Reason. An Introduction*. Cambridge: Cambridge University Press.
Byrd, J. (2008), 'A Remark on Kant's Argument from Incongruent Counterparts', *British Journal for the History of Philosophy*, 16(4): 789–800.
Carnois, B. (1987), *The Coherence of Kant's Doctrine of Freedom*, trans. D. Booth. Chicago: University of Chicago Press.
Carroll, L. (2015), *Through the Looking-Glass*. London: Macmillan.
Chalmers, D. J. (1996), *The Conscious Mind*. Oxford: Oxford University Press.
Chalmers, D. J. (2005), 'The Matrix as Metaphysics', in Christopher Grau (ed.), *Philosophers Explore the Matrix*, 132–76. Oxford: Oxford University Press.
Chalmers, D. J. (2010), *The Character of Consciousness*. Oxford: Oxford University Press.
Chalmers, D. J. (2015), 'Panpsychism and Panprotopsychism', in T. Alter and Y. Nagasawa (eds), *Consciousness in the Physical World: Perspectives on Russellian Monism*, 246–76. Oxford: Oxford University Press.
Chalmers, D. J. (2022), *Reality+: Virtual Worlds and the Problems of Philosophy*. London: Penguin Books.
Chiba, K. (2012), *Kants Ontologie der raumzeitlichen Wirklichkeit*. Berlin: De Gruyter.
Chignell, A. (2017), 'Kant on Cognition, Givenness, and Ignorance', *Journal of the History of Philosophy*, 55(1): 131–42.
Chisholm, R. (1971), 'Reflections on Human Agency', *Idealistic Studies*, 1: 33–46.
Chisholm, R. (1976), *Person and Object: A Metaphysical Study*. La Salle: Open Court.
Churchland, P. M. (1985), 'Reduction, Qualia and the Direct Introspection of Brain States', *Journal of Philosophy*, 82: 8–28.
Clarke, R. (1993), 'Toward a Credible Agent-Causal Account of Free Will', *Noûs*, 27: 191–203.
Clarke, R. (2003), *Libertarian Accounts of Free Will*. Oxford: Oxford University Press.
Danto, A. C. (1967), 'Naturalism', in Paul Edwords (ed.), *The Encyclopaedia of Philosophy*, 448–50. New York: The Macmillan Co. and The Free Press.
Davidson, D. (1963), 'Actions, Reasons, and Causes', *The Journal of Philosophy*, 60(23): 685–700.

Davidson, D. (1980), *Essays on Actions and Events* Oxford: Oxford University Press.
Dennett, D. C. (1978), *Brainstorms: Philosophical Essays in Mond and Psychology*. Montgomery: Bradford.
Dennett, D. C. (1991), *Consciousness Explained*. Boston: Little, Brown.
Dupré, J. (1984), 'Probabilistic Causality Emancipated', in P. French, T. Uehling, Jr and H. Wettstein (eds), *Midwest Studies in Philosophy IX*, 169–75. Minneapolis: University of Minnesota Press. doi: 10.1111/j.1475-4975.1984.tb00058.x
Dupré, J. (1993), *The Disorder of Things. Metaphysical Foundations of the Disunity of Science*. Cambridge, MA: Harvard University Press.
Earman, J. and J. D. Norton (1987), 'What Price Spacetime Substantivalism', *British Journal for the Philosophy of Science*, 38: 515–25.
Ekstrom, L. W. (2000), *Free Will: A Philosophical Study*. Boulder, CO: Westview Press.
Ekstrom, L. W. (2003), 'Free Will, Chance, and Mystery', *Philosophical Studies*, 113(2): 153–80.
Ellis, G. F. R. (2011), 'Top-Down Causation and Emergence: Some Comments on Mechanisms', *Royal Society: Interface Focus*, 2(1): 126–40.
Erdmann, B. (1878), *Kants Criticismus in der ersten und zweiten Auflage der Kritik der reinen Vernunft. Eine historische Untersuchung*. Leipzig: Leopold Voss.
Ertl, W. (1998), *Kants Auflösung der 'dritten Aintinomie'*. München: Verlag Karl Alber.
Ertl, W. (2014), '"Ludewig" Molina and Kant's Libertarian Compatibilism', in A. Aichele and M. Kaufmann (eds), *A Companion to Luis De Molina*, 405–45. Boston: Brill.
Ertl, W. (2020), *The Guarantee of Perpetual Peace*. Cambridge: Cambridge University Press.
Ertl, W. (2024), 'Free Will and Determinism in Kant: The Pitfalls of Domestication', under review.
Ferrari, J. (2018), 'Finalité, Nature et Liberté', in V. L. Waibel, M. Ruffing and D. Wagner (eds), *Natur und Freiheit. Akten des XII. Internationalen Kant Kongresses*, 1615–23. Berlin: de Gruyter.
Fischer, J. M. (1986), 'Introduction: Responsibility and Freedom', in J. M. Fischer (ed.), *Moral Responsibility*, 9–61. Ithaca: Cornell University Press.
Fischer, J. M. (1994), *Kant's Analogies of Experience*.
Fischer, J. M. (2006), *My Way: Essays on Moral Responsibility*. Oxford: Oxford University Press.
Fischer, J. M., R. Kane, D. Pereboom and M. Vargas (2014), *Four Views on Free Will*. Oxford: Blackwell.
Fischer, J. M. and M. Ravizza (1998), *Responsibility and Control: A Theory of Moral Responsibility*. Cambridge: Cambridge University Press.
Frankfurt, H. (1969), 'Alternate Possibilities and Moral Responsibility', *Journal of Philosophy*, 66: 829–39.
Frankfurt, H. (1971), 'Freedom of the Will and the Concept of a Person', *Journal of Philosophy*, 68: 5–20.
Franks, W. F. (2005), *All or Nothing: Systematicity, Transcendental Arguments and Skepticism in German Idealism*. Cambridge, MA: Harvard University Press.
Friedman, M. (1992a), *Kant and the Exact Sciences*. Cambridge, MA: Harvard University Press.
Friedman, M. (1992b), 'Kant on Causal Laws and the Foundations of Natural Science', in Paul Guyer (ed.), *The Cambridge Companion to Kant*, 161–97. Cambridge: Cambridge University Press.

Friedman, M. (2008), 'Einstein, Kant and the A Priori', in M. Massimi (ed.), *Kant and Philosophy of Science Today*, vol. 63. *Royal Institute of Philosophy Supplement*, 95–112. Cambridge: Cambridge University Press.

Fugate, C. D. (2012), 'On a supposed solution to the Reinhold/Sidgwick problem in Kant's Metaphysics of Morals', *European Journal of Philosophy*, 23(3): 349–73.

Gardner, S. (1999), *Kant and the Critique of Pure Reason*. Abingdon: Routledge.

Gerhardt, V. (2018), *Selbstbestimmung. Das Prinzip der Individualität*, 2nd edn. Stuttgart: Reklam.

Ginet, C. (1990), *On Action*. Cambridge: Cambridge University Press.

Ginet, C. (1997), 'Freedom, Responsibility and Agency', *The Journal of Ethics*, 1: 85–98.

Ginet, C. (2000), 'Review of *The Works of Agency: On Human Action, Will, and Freedom* by Hugh J. McCann', *Philosophical Review*, 109(4): 632–5.

Ginet, C. (2002), 'Reasons Explanations of Action: Causalist versus Noncausalist Accounts', in R. Kane (ed.), *The Oxford Handbook of Free Will*, 386–405. Oxford: Oxford University Press.

Ginsborg, H. (2006), 'Kant's Biological Teleology and Its Philosophical Significance', in G. Bird (ed.), *The Blackwell Companion to Kant*, 455–70. Oxford: Blackwell.

Goff, P. (2017), *Consciousness and Fundamental Reality*. Oxford: Oxford University Press.

Griffith, M. (2017), 'Major Positions in the Free Will Debate', in K. Timpe, M. Griffith and N. Levy (eds), *The Routledge Companion to Free Will*, 1–4. Abingdon: Routledge.

Guyer, P. (1987), *Kant and the Claims of Knowledge*. Cambridge: Cambridge University Press.

Guyer, P. (1998), 'The Value of Reason and the Value of Freedom', *Ethics*, 109(1): 22–35.

Guyer, P. (2006), *Kant*. Abingdon: Routledge.

Guyer, P. (2009), 'Problems with Freedom: Kant's Argument in Groundwork III and Its Sunsequent Emendations', in J. Timmermann (ed.), *Kant's Groundwork of the Metaphysics of Morals. A Critical Guide*, 176–202. Cambridge: Cambridge University Press.

Guyer, P. (2018), 'The Struggle for Freedom: Freedom of Will in Kant and Reinhold', in Eric Watkins (ed.), *Kant on Persons and Agency*, 120–37. Cambridge: Cambridge University Press.

Guyer, P. (2022), 'Review of 'Henry Allison: Kant's Conception of Freedom: A Developmental and Critical Analysis', *Kant Studien*, 113(2): 375–9.

Haji, I. (2000), 'Libertarianism and the Luck Objection', *Journal of Ethics*, 4: 329–37.

Haji, I. (2004), 'Active control, agent causation, and free action', *Philosophical Explorations*, 7: 131–48.

Heidegger, M. (1962), *Being and Time*. Oxford: Blackwell.

Heimsoeth, H. (1973), 'Freiheit und Charakter', in G. Prauss (ed.), *Kant. Zur Deutung seiner Theorie von Erkennen und Handeln*, 292–309. Köln: Kiepenheimer und Witsch.

Hempel, C. and P. Oppenheim (1948), 'Studies in the Logic of Explanation', *Philosophy of Science*, 15: 135–75.

Henrich, D. (1960), 'Der Begriff der Sittlichen Einsicht und Kants Lehre vom Faktum der Vernunft', in Dieter Henrich, W. Schulz and K.-H. Volkmann-Schluck (eds), *Die Gegenwart der Griechen im neueren Denken*, 77–195. Tübingen: Mohr.

Henrich, D. (1975), 'Die Deduktion des Sittengesetzes', in A. Schwan (ed.), *Denken im Schatten des Nihilismus*, 55–112. Darmstadt: Wissenschaftliche Buchgesellschaft.

Herman, B. (1985), 'The Practice of Moral Judgment', *Journal of Philosophy*, 82(8): 414–36.

Herman, B. (1996), 'Making Room for Character', in S. Engstrom and J. Whiting (eds), *Aristotle, Kant, and the Stoics: Rethinking Happiness and Duty*, 36–60. Cambridge: Cambridge University Press.

Herrera, L. (2000), 'Kant on the Moral *Triebfeder*', *Kant Studien*, 91: 395–410.

Herring, H. (1953), 'Das Problem der Affektion bei Kant', *Kant Studien Ergänzungshefte*, 67. Berlin: De Gruyter.

Hitchcock, C. (2004), 'Do All and Only Causes Raise the Probabilities of Effects?' in J. Collins, N. Hall and L. A. Paul (eds), *Causation and Counterfactuals*, 403–17. Cambridge, MA: MIT Press.

Hobbes, T. (1651/1997), *Leviathan*, ed. R. E. Flatman and D. Johnston. New York: W.W. Norton & Co.

Hobbes, T. (1654/1999), *Of Liberty and Necessity*, in V. Chappell (ed.), *Hobbes and Bramhall on Liberty and Necessity*, 15–42. Cambridge: Cambridge University Press.

Hobbes, T. (1656/1999), *The Questions Concerning Liberty, Necessity, and Chance*, in V. Chappell (ed.), *Hobbes and Bramhall on Liberty and* Necessity, 15–42, Cambridge: Cambridge University Press.

Hogan, D. (2009), 'Noumenal Affection', *Philosophical Review*, 118(4): 501–32.

Hogan, D. (2021), 'Handedness, Idealism, and Freedom', *Philosophical Review*, 130(3): 385–449.

Holton, R. (2009), *Willing, Wanting, Waiting*. Oxford: Oxford University Press.

Honderich, T. (1988), *A Theory of Determinism: The Mind, Neuroscience, and Life-Hopes*. Oxford: Clarendon Press.

Honderich, T. (2011), 'Effects, Determinism, Neither Compatibilism Nor Incompatibilism, Consciousness', in R. Kane (ed.), *The Oxford Handbook of Free Will*, 442–56. Oxford: Oxford University Press.

Honderich, T. (n.d.), 'Immanuel Kant: For Determinism in a Way and also Indeterminism, and for Freedom of Origination Being Consistent with the Determinism', *The Determinism and Freedom Philosophy* Website. https://www.ucl.ac.uk/~uctytho/dfwVariousKant.htm (accessed 21 February 2021).

Howard, Don A. (1984), 'Realism and Conventionalism in Einstein's Philosophy of Science: The Einstein-Schlick Correspondence', *Philosophia Naturalis*, 21(2–4): 616–29.

Hume, D. (1748/1975), *Enquiries Concerning Human Understanding and Concerning the Principles of Morals*, ed. Peter H. Nidditch. Oxford: Oxford University Press.

Hume, D. (1978), *A Treatise of Human Nature*, ed. L. A. Selby-Bigge and P. H. Nidditch. Oxford: Clarendon Press.

Humphreys, P. (1989), *The Chances of Explanation: Causal Explanations in the Social, Medical, and Physical Sciences*. Princeton: Princeton University Press.

Hunt, D. (2005), 'Moral Responsibility and Buffered Alternatives', *Midwest Studies in Philosophy*, 29: 126–45.

Illies, C. (2007), 'Orientierung durch Universalisierung: Der Kategorische Imperativ als Test für die Moralität von Maximen', *Kant Studien*, 98(3): 306–28.

Indregard, J. J. (2018), 'A Gradual Reformation: Empirical Character and Causal Powers in Kant', *Canadian Journal of Philosophy*, 48(5): 662–83.

Insole, C. J. (2013), *Kant and the Creation of Freedom. A Theological Problem*. Oxford: Oxford University Press.

Irwin, T. (1984), 'Morality and Personality: Kant and Green', in Allen W. Wood (ed.), *Self and Nature in Kant's Philosophy*, 31–56. Ithaca: Cornell University Press.

Isham, C. J. (1995), *Lectures on Quantum Theory*. London: Imperial College Press.

Itano, W. M. (2009), 'Perspectives on the Quantum Zeno Paradox', *Journal of Physics: Conference Series*, 196: 012018. doi: 10.1088/1742-6596/196/1/012018

Itano, W. M., D. J. Heinzen, J. J. Bollinger and D. J. Wineland (1990), 'Quantum Zeno Effect', *Physical Review A*, 41(5): 2295.

James, W. (1997), *The Meaning of Truth*. Amherst: Prometheus Books.

Jauernig, A. (2021), *The World According to Kant. Appearances and Things in Themselves in Critical Idealism*. Oxford: Oxford University Press.

Jorati, J. (2017), 'Gottfried Leibniz', in K. Timpe, M. Griffith and N. Levy (eds), *The Routledge Companion to Free Will*, 293–302. Abingdon: Routledge.

Kane, R. (1985), *Free Will and Values*. Albany: SUNY Press.

Kane, R. (1996), *The Significance of Free Will*. Oxford: Oxford University Press.

Kane, R. (2011), 'Rethinking Free Will: New Perspectives on an Ancient Problem', in R. Kane (ed.), *The Oxford Handbook of Free Will*, 381–404. Oxford: Oxford University Press.

Kane, R. (2014a), 'New Arguments in Debates on Libertarian Free Will: Responses to Contributors', in D. Palmer (ed.), *Libertarian Free Will*, 179–214. Oxford: Oxford University Press.

Kane, R. (2014b), 'Libertarianism', in J. M. Fischer, R. S. Kane, D. Pereboom and M. Vargas (eds), *Four Views on Free Will*, 5–43. Oxford: Blackwell.

Keil, G. (2018), *Willensfreiheit und Determinismus*. Ditzingen: Reclam.

Kemp Smith, N. (1962), *A Commentary to Kant's Critique of Pure Reason*. New York: Humanities.

Kemp Smith, N. (1979), *A Commentary to Kant's Critique of Pure Reason*, 2nd edn. London and Basingstoke: McMillan.

Kerstein, S. J. (2002), *Kant's Search for the Supreme Principle of Morality*. Cambridge: Cambridge University Press.

Kitcher, P. (1990), *Kant's Transcendental Psychology*. Oxford: Oxford University Press.

Köhl, H. (1990), *Kants Gesinnungs Ethik*. Berlin: de Gruyter.

Kohl, M. (2014), 'Transcendental and Practical Freedom in the *Critique of Pure Reason*', *Kant Studien*, 105(3): 313–35.

Kohl, M. (2015a), 'Kant on Freedom of Empirical Thought', *Journal of the History of Philosophy*, 53(2): 301–26.

Kohl, M. (2015b), 'Kant and "Ought Implies Can"', *The Philosophical Quarterly*, 65(261): 690–710.

Korsgaard, C. M. (1996a), *The Sources of Normativity*. Cambridge: Cambridge University Press.

Korsgaard, C. M. (1996b), *Creating the Kingdom of Ends*. Cambridge: Cambridge University Press.

Kosch, M. (2006), *Freedom and Reason in Kant, Schelling and Kierkegaard*. Oxford: Clarendon Press.

Koutsoyannis, D., C. Onof, A. Christofides and Z. Kundzewicz (2022), 'Revisiting Causality using Stochastics: 1. Theory', *Proceedings of the Royal Society A*, 1–21. https://doi.org/10.1098/rspa.2021.0835

Kraus, K. (2019), 'The Parity and Disparity between Inner and Outer Experience in Kant', *Kantian Review*, 24(2): 171–95.

Langton, R. (1998), *Kantian Humility*. Oxford: Clarendon.

Langton, R. (2006), 'Kant's Phenomena: Extrinsic or Relational Properties? A Reply to Allais', *Philosophy and Phenomenological Research*, 73(1): 170–85.

Laplace, P. S. de (1902), *A Philosophical Essay on Probabilities*, trans. F. W. Truscott and F. L. Emory. New York: Wiley.
Lehrer, K. (1968), 'Cans without Ifs', *Analysis*, 29(1): 29–32.
Lehrer, K. (2004), 'Freedom and the Power of Preference', in M. O.'Rourke and J. K. Campbell (eds), *Freedom and Determinism*, 47–69. Cambridge, MA: MIT Press.
Leibniz, G. W. (1710/1983), *Theodicy*. La Salle: Open Court.
Lewis, D. (1983), 'Extrinsic Properties', *Philosophical Studies*, 44: 197–20.
Liang, Y. (2020), 'Kant on Inner Sensations and the Parity between Inner and Outer Sense', *Ergo*, 7(10): 307–38.
Libet, B. (1985), 'Unconscious cerebral initiative and the role of conscious will in voluntary action', *Behavioral and Brain Sciences*, 8: 529–66.
Locke, J. (1690/1975), *An Essay Concerning Human Understanding*, ed. Peter H. Nidditch. Oxford: Oxford University Press.
Ludwig, B. (2015), 'Die *Kritik der reinen Vernunft* hat die Wirklichkeit der Freiheit nicht bewiesen, ja nicht einmal deren Möglichkeit. Über die folgenreiche Fehlinterpretation eines Absatzes in der Kritik der reinen Vernunft', *Kant Studien*, 106(3): 398–417.
McCann, H. J. (1998), *The Works of Agency: On Human Action, Will and Freedom*. Ithaca: Cornell University Press.
McDowell, J. (1996), *Mind and World*. Cambridge, MA: Harvard University Press.
McKenna, M. and D. Pereboom (2016), *Free Will: A Contemporary Introduction*. London: Routledge.
McLear, C. (2020), 'On the Transcendental Freedom of the Intellect', *Ergo: An Open Access Journal of Philosophy*, 7(2): 35–104.
Meerbote, R. (1984), 'Kant on Freedom and the Rational and Morally Good Will', in Allen Wood (ed.), *Self and Nature in Kant's Philosophy*, 57–72. Ithaca: Cornell University Press.
Mele, A. R. (1995), *Autonomous Agents: From Self-Control to Autonomy*. Oxford: Oxford University Press.
Mele, A. R. (1999), 'Ultimate Responsibility and Dumb Luck', *Social Philosophy and Policy*, 16: 274–93.
Mele, A. R. (2006), *Free Will and Luck*. Oxford: Oxford University Press.
Mellor, D. H. (1995), *The Facts of Causation*. Abingdon: Routledge.
Melnick, A. (1973), *Kant's Analogies of Experience*. Chicago: University of Chicago Press.
Mill, J. S. (1963–91), *The Collected Works of John Stuart Mill*, ed. John M. Robson. Toronto: University of Toronto Press. London: Routledge and Kegan Paul.
Mumford, S. (2015), 'Freedom and Control: On the Modality of Free Will', *American Philosophical Quarterly*, 52(1): 1–11.
Nagel, T. (1986), *The View from Nowhere*. Oxford: Oxford University Press.
Natorp, P. (1981), 'On the Objective and Subjective Grounding of Knowledge', L. Phillips and D. Kolb (trans.), *Journal of the British Society for Phenomenology*, 12: 245–66.
Nell (O'Neill), O. (1975), *Acting on Principle*. New York: Columbia University Press.
Nerlich, G. (1979), 'What Can Geometry Explain?' *British Journal for the Philosophy of Science*, 30: 69–83.
Noller, J. (2021), 'Ambivalent Freedom: Kant and the Problem of *Willkür*', in M. Hausmann and J. Noller (eds), *Free Will. Historical and Analytical Perspectives*, 251–66. London: Palgrave.
O'Connor, T. (2000), *Persons and Causes: The Metaphysics of Free Will*. Oxford: Oxford University Press.

O'Connor, T. (2005), 'Freedom with a Human Face', *Midwest Studies in Philosophy*, 29: 207–27.
O'Connor, T. (2011), 'Agent-Causal Theories of Freedom', in R. Kane (ed.), *The Oxford Handbook of Free Will*, 309–28. Oxford: Oxford University Press.
O'Connor, T. and C. Franklin (2019), 'Free Will', *Stanford Encyclopaedia of Philosophy*, 1–77. https://plato.stanford.edu/entries/freewill/
O'Neill, O. (1983), 'Kant after Virtue', *Inquiry*, 26: 387–405.
O'Neill, O. (1989), *Constructions of Reason*. Cambridge: Cambridge University Press.
Onof, C. (1998), 'A Framework for the Derivation and Reconstruction of the Categorical Imperative', *Kant Studien*, 89: 410–27.
Onof, C. (2006), 'Hermeneutic Conditions and the Possibility of Objective Knowledge', in K. Boudouris and K. Kalimtzis (eds), *Philosophy, Competition and the Good Life*, 225–30. Athens: Ionia Publications.
Onof, C. (2008), 'Property Dualism, Epistemic Normativity and the Limits of Naturalism', *Philosophy and Phenomenological Research*, 76(1): 60–85.
Onof, C. (2009a), 'Critical Notice of "Consciousness and Its Place in Nature: Does Physicalism Entail Panpsychism?" by Galen Strawson et al.', A. Freeman (ed.), *Journal of Mind and Behavior*, 30(1–2): 79–92.
Onof, C. (2009b), 'Reconstructing the Grounding of Kant's Ethics: A Critical Assessment', *Kant Studien*, 100(4): 496–517.
Onof, C. (2011a), 'Existentialism, Metaphysics and Ontology', in F. Joseph, J. Reynolds and A. Woodward (eds), *The Continuum Companion to Existentialism*, 39–61. London/New York: Continuum.
Onof, C. (2011b), 'Moral Worth and Inclinations in Kantian Ethics', *Kant Studies*, 116–61. Online. https://kantstudiesonline.net/articles
Onof, C. (2019a), 'Review of Eric Watkins's [ed.] "Kant on Persons and Agency"', *Critique*. https://virtualcritique.wordpress.com/2019/02/24/new-work-on-kant-iv-kant-on-persons-and-agency/
Onof, C. (2019b), 'Reality in-itself and the Ground of Causality', *Kantian Review*, 24(2): 197–222.
Onof, C. (2020), 'The Role of Regulative Principles and Their Relation to Reflective Judgement', in S. Baiasu and A. Vanza (eds), *Kant and the Continental Tradition. Sensibility, Nature and Religion*, 101–30, Abingdon: Routledge.
Onof, C. (2021a), 'The Third Antinomy's Cosmological Problem and Transcendental Idealism', in B. Himmelmann and C. Serck-Hanssen (eds), *The Court of Reason. Proceedings of the 13th International Kant Congress*, 597–606. Berlin: de Gruyter.
Onof, C. (2021b), 'Review of Henry Allison: Kant's Conception of Freedom', *Studi Kantiani*, 34: 231–6.
Onof, C. (2021c), 'Kant and the Possibility of Transcendental Freedom', *Kant Studien*, 112(3): 343-31.
Onof, C. (2023), 'The Unicity, Infinity and Unity of Space', *Kantian Review*, 28(2): 1–23.
Onof, C. (2024), 'Incongruent Counterparts, Transcendental Idealism and Consciousness', forthcoming.
Onof, C. and D. Schulting (2015), 'Space as Form of Intuition and as Formal Intuition: On the Note to B160 in Kant's Critique of Pure Reason', *Philosophical Review*, 124(1): 1–58.
Onof, C. and D. Schulting (2023), 'Chapter 21: Analytic of Teleological Judgement', in S. Baiasu and M. Timmons (eds), *The Kantian Mind*, 247–59. London: Routledge.
Otsuka, M. (1998), 'Incompatibilism and the Avoidability of Blame', *Ethics*, 108: 685–701.

Palmquist, S. R. (2010), 'The Kantian Grounding of Einstein's Worldview: (I) The Early Influence of Kant's System of Perspectives', *Polish Journal of Philosophy*, 4(1): 45–64.

Palmquist, S. R. (2011), 'The Kantian Grounding of Einstein's Worldview: (II) Simultaneity, Synthetic Apriority and the Mystical', *Polish Journal of Philosophy*, 5(1): 97–116.

Palmquist, S. R. (2015a), 'What Is Kantian Gesinnung? On the Priority of Volition over Metaphysics and Psychology in Religion within the Bounds of Bare Reason', *Kantian Review*, 20(2): 235–64.

Palmquist, S. R. (2015b), *Comprehensive Commentary on Kant's Religion within the Bounds of Bare Reason*. Hoboken: Wiley-Blackwell.

Pasternack, L. R. (2014), *Kant on Religion within the Boundaries of Mere Reason*. London: Routledge.

Pereboom, D. (2004), *Living Without Free Will*. Cambridge: Cambridge University Press.

Pereboom, D. (2006), 'Kant on Transcendental Freedom', *Philosophy and Phenomenological Research*, 73(3): 537–64.

Pereboom, D. (2014a), *Free Will, Agency, and Meaning in Life*. Oxford: Oxford University Press.

Pereboom, D. (2014b), 'Hard Incompatibilism', in J. M. Fischer, R. S. Kane, D. Pereboom and M. Vargas (eds), *Four Views on Free Will*, 85–125, Oxford: Blackwell.

Pereboom, D. (2022), *Free Will*. Cambridge: Cambridge University Press.

Peters, J. (2018), 'Kant's Gesinnung', *Journal of the History of Philosophy*, 56(3): 497–518.

Pink, T. (2011), 'Freedom and Action without Causation: Noncausal Theories of Freedom and Purposive Agency', in R. Kane (ed.), *The Oxford Handbook of Free Will*, 349–65. Oxford: Oxford University Press.

Pinkard, T. (2002), *German Philosophy 1760–1860. The Legacy of Idealism*. Cambridge: Cambridge University Press.

Piper, A. (2012), 'Kant's Self-Legislation Procedure Reconsidered', *Kant Studies Online*, 203–77. https://kantstudiesonline.net/articles

Prauss, G. (1974), *Kant und das Problem der Dinge an sich*. Bonn: Bouvier.

Prichard, H. A. (1909), *Kant's Theory of Knowledge*. Oxford: Clarendon Press.

Prichard, H. A. (1912), 'Does Moral Philosophy Rest on a Mistake?' *Mind*, 21(81): 21–37.

Pringe, H. (2007), *Critique of the Quantum Power of Judgment*. Berlin: de Gruyter.

Puls, H. (2016), *Sittliches Bewusstsein Und Kategorischer Imperativ in Kants Grundlegung: Ein Kommentar Zum Dritten Abschnitt*. Berlin: De Gruyter.

Quarfood, M. (2006), 'The Circle and the Two Standpoints (GMS III, 3)', in C. Horn and D. Schönecker (eds), *Groundwork for the Metaphysics of Morals*, 285–300. Berlin: De Gruyter.

Quine, W. v. O. (1948), 'On What There Is', *The Review of Metaphysics*, 2(1): 21–38.

Quine, W. v. O. (1996), 'Progress on Two Fronts', *Journal of Philosophy*, 93: 159–63.

Reath, A. (2013), *Kant's 'Critique of Practical Reason': A Critical Guide*. Cambridge: Cambridge University Press.

Reichenbach, H. (1956), *The Direction of Time*. Berkeley and Los Angeles: University of California Press.

Reid, T. (1788/1969), *Essays on the Active Powers of the Human Mind*, ed. B. Brody. Cambridge, MA: MIT Press.

Reinhold, K. L. (1975), 'Einige Bemerkungen über die in der Einleitung zu den "Metaphysischen Anfangsgründen der Rechtslehre" von I. Kant aufgestellten Begriffe von der Freiheit des Willens', in R. Bittner and K. Kramer (eds), *Materialen zu Kants Kritik der praktischen Vernunft*, 252–274. Frankfurt am Main: Suhrkamp Verlag.

Robinson, W. S. (2004), *Understanding Phenomenal Consciousness*. Cambridge: Cambridge University Press.

Rosefeldt, T. (2007), 'Dinge an sich und sekundäre Qualitäten', in J. Stolzenberg (ed.), *Kant in der Gegenwart*, 167–209. Berlin: de Gruyter.

Rosefeldt, T. (2012), *Kant's Analogies of Experience*. 99–109.

Russell, B. (1927), *The Analysis of Matter*. London: Routledge.

Ryckman, T. (2005), *The Reign of Relativity*. Oxford: Oxford University Press.

Salmon, W. (1984), *Scientific Explanation and the Causal Structure of the World*. Princeton: Princeton University Press.

Sartre, J.-P. (1958), *Being and Nothingness*. London: Methuen.

Saunders, J. (2018), 'Kant and Degrees of Responsibility', *Journal of Applied Philosophy*, 36(1): 137–54.

Saunders, J. (2021), 'Recent Work on Freedom in Kant', *British Journal for the History of Philosophy*, 29(6): 1177–89.

Schaffer, J. (2000), 'Overlappings: Probability-Raising without Causation', *Australasian Journal of Philosophy*, 78: 40–6.

Schlick, M. (1939), 'When Is a Man Responsible?' in D. Rynin (trans.), *Problems of Ethics*, Eaglewood Cliffs: Prentice-Hall Publishing.

Scholten, M. (2021a), 'Ought Implies Can, Asymmetrical Freedom, and the Practical Irrelevance of Transcendental Freedom', *European Journal of Philosophy*, 29(1): 25–42.

Scholten, M. (2021b), 'Kant's Reply to the Consequence Argument', *International Journal of Philosophical Studies*, 29(2): 135–58.

Scholten, M. (2022), 'Kant Is a Soft Determinist', *European Journal of Philosophy*, 30: 79–95.

Schönecker, D. (1999), *Kant: Grundlegung III. Die Deduktion des kategorischen Imperativs*. Freiburg und München: Alber.

Schönecker, D. (2005), *Kants Begriff transzendentaler und praktischer Freiheit: Eine entwicklungsgeschichtliche Studie*. Kantstudien-Ergänzungshefte 149. Berlin: de Gruyter.

Schopenhauer, A. (1960), *Essay on the Freedom of the Will*, trans. K. Kolenda. Indianapolis: Bobbs-Merrill.

Schulting, D. (2017), *Kant's Radical Subjectivism*. London: Palgrave.

Scruton, R. (2016), *The Ring of Truth*. London: Penguin eBook.

Sellars, W. (1974), *Essays in Philosophy and Its History*. Dordrecht and Boston: D. Reidel.

Setton, D. (2013), 'Absolute Spontaneity of Choice: The Other Side of Kant's Theory of Freedom', *Symposium*, 17(1): 75–99.

Sidgwick, H. (2005), *The Methods of Ethics*. Indianapolis: Hackett.

Skyrms, B. (1980), *Causal Necessity*. New Haven and London: Yale University Press.

Sober, E. (1983), 'Equilibrium Explanation', *Philosophical Studies*, 43: 201–10.

Sotnak, E. (1999), 'The Range of Leibnizian Compatibilism', in Rocco J. Gennaro and C. Huenemann (eds), *New Essays on the Rationalists*, 200–23. Oxford Scholarship Online.

Speak, D. (2011), 'The Consequence Argument Revisited', in R. Kane (ed.), *The Oxford Handbook of Free Will*, 115–30. Oxford: Oxford University Press.

Spinoza, B. (1992), *The Ethics and Selected Letters*, ed. S. Feldman, trans. S. Shirley. Indianapolis: Hackett Publishing.

Stang, N. F. (2014), 'The Non-identity of Appearances and Things in Themselves', *Noûs*, 48(1): 106–36.
Stang, N. F. (2015), 'Who's Afraid of Double Affection?' *Philosophers' Imprint*, 15(18): 1–28.
Stapp, H. P. (2011), *Mindful Universe. Quantum Mechanics and the Participating Observer*. Berlin and Heidelberg: Springer.
Steward, H. (2012), *A Metaphysics for Freedom*. Oxford: Oxford University Press.
Strawson, G. (1986), *Freedom and Belief*. Oxford: Clarendon.
Strawson, G. (1994), 'The Impossibility of Moral Responsibility', *Philosophical Studies*, 75: 5–24.
Strawson, G. (2002), 'The Bounds of Freedom', in Robert H. Kane (ed.), *The Oxford Handbook of Free Will*, 441–60. Oxford: Oxford University Press.
Strawson, G. (2006), 'Realistic Materialism: Why Physicalism Entails Panpsychism', *Journal of Consciousness Studies*, 13(10–11): 3–31.
Strawson, P. F. (1966), *The Bounds of Sense*. London: Methuen.
Strawson, P. F. (1974), *Freedom and Resentment, and Other Essays*. London: Methuen & Co.
Strohmeyer, I. (1995), *Transzendentalphilosophie und Quantenphysik*. Heidelberg: Spektrum.
Strohmeyer, I. (2013), 'Kausalität und Freiheit', *Kant Studien*, 104(1): 63–99.
Stump, E. (2003), *Aquinas*. Abingdon: Routledge.
Taylor, C. and D. Dennett (2011), 'Who's Still Afraid of Determinism', in R. Kane (ed.), *The Oxford Handbook of Free Will*, 221–40. Oxford: Oxford University Press.
Sturma, D. (2018) 'The Practice of Self-Consciousness: Kant on Nature, Freedom, and Morality', in Eric Watkins (ed.), *Kant on Persons and Agency*, 138–152. Cambridge: Cambridge University Press.
Tetens, J. N. (1777), *Philosophische Versuche über die menschliche Natur und ihre Entwicklung*, 2 vols. Leipzig: Weidmann.
Thorp, J. (1980), *Free Will: A Defence against Neurophysiological Determinism*. London: Routledge and Kegan Paul.
Timmermann, J. (2000), 'Kant's Puzzling Ethics of Maxims', *Harvard Review*, VIII: 39–52.
Timmermann, J. (2003), *Sittengesetz und Freiheit. Untersuchungen zu Immanuel Kants Theorie des freien Willens*. Berlin: de Gruyter.
Timmermann, J. (2009), *Acting from Duty*, in J. Timmermann (ed.), *Groundwork of the Metaphysics of Morals. A Critical Guide*, 45–62. Cambridge: Cambridge University Press.
Timmermann, J. (2022), *Kant's Will at the Crossroads. An Essay on the Failings of Practical Rationality*. Oxford: Oxford University Press.
Trendelenburg, A. (1862), *Logische Untersuchungen*. Leipzig: Hinzel.
Tse, P. U. (2013), *The Neural Basis of Free Will*. Cambridge, MA: MIT Press.
Vaihinger, H. (1881–92), *Commentar zu Kants Kritik der reinen Vernunft*, 2 vols. Stuttgart: W. Spermann.
van Cleve, J. (1991), 'Incongruent Counterparts and Things in Themselves', in J. van Cleve and R. R. Frederick (eds), *The Philosophy of Right and Left*, 341–52. Dordrecht: Kluwer Academic.
van Cleve, J. (1999), *Problems from Kant*. Oxford: Oxford University Press.
van Inwagen, P. (1983), *An Essay on Free Will*. Oxford: Clarendon Press.
van Inwagen, P. (1989), 'When is the Will Free?', *Philosophical Perspectives*, 3: 399–422.
van Inwagen, P. (1993), *Metaphysics*. Boulder: Westview.

van Inwagen, P. (2000), 'Free will Remains a Mystery', J. E. Tomberlin (ed.), Philosophical Perspectives. *Noûs*, 34: 1-19.
Vihvelin, K. (2000), 'Libertarian Compatibilism', *Philosophical Perspectives*, 14: 139-66.
Vihvelin, K. (2004), 'Free Will Demystified: A Dispositional Account', *Philosophical Topics*, 32: 427-50.
Vihvelin, K. (2013), *Causes, Laws, and Free Will: Why Determinism Doesn't Matter*. Oxford: Oxford University Press.
Vilhauer, B. (2004), 'Can We Interpret Kant as a Compatibilist about Determinism and Moral Responsibility?' *British Journal for the History of Philosophy*, 12: 719-30.
Vilhauer, B. (2010), 'The Scope of Responsibility in Kant's Theory of Free Will', *British Journal for the History of Philosophy*, 18: 45-71.
Vilhauer, B. (2023), 'An Asymmetrical Approach to Kant's Theory of Freedom', in D. Heide and E. Tiffany (eds), *The Idea of Freedom: New Essays on the Kantian Theory of Freedom*. Oxford: Oxford University Press, forthcoming.
von Weizsäcker, C. F. (1979), 'Einstein's Importance to Physics, Philosophy and Politics', in M. Skopec and M. Skopec (trans.), P. Aichelburg and R. U. Sexl (eds), *Albert Einstein: His Influence on Physics, Philosophy and Politics*, 159-68. Braunschweig: Friedr. Vieweg & Sohn.
von Wright, G. H. (1980), 'Freedom and Determination', *Acta Philosophica Fennica*, 31: 5-88.
Vuillemin, J. (2017), 'Sommes-nous libres?' *Philosophia Scientiae*, 21(2): 163-74.
Wagner, R. (1900), *Das Rheingold*. Leipzig: Reclam.
Wagner, R. (1918), *The Rhinegold and the Valkyrie*, trans. M. Armour, illus. Arthur Rackham. London: William Heinemann Ltd.
Wagner, R. (1980), *Der Ring des Nibelungen*. Mainz: Goldmann Schott.
Walker, R. C. S. (1978), *Kant*. London: Routledge and Kegan Paul.
Ware, O. (2023), *Kant on Freedom*. Cambridge: Cambridge University Press.
Watkins, E. (2005), *Kant and the Metaphysics of Causality*. Cambridge: Cambridge University Press.
Watson, G. (1975), 'Free Agency', *Journal of Philosophy*, 72: 205-20.
Watson, G. (2004), *Agency and Answerability: Selected Essays*. Oxford: Clarendon Press.
Weyl, H. (1918), *Raum-Zeit-Materie*. Berlin: Springer.
Widerker, D. (1995), 'Libertarianism and Frankfurt's Attack on the Principle of Alternative Possibilities', *The Philosophical Review*, 104: 247-61.
Widerker, D. (2000), 'Frankfurt's Attack on Alternative Possibilities', *Philosophical Perspectives*, 14: 181-201.
Wigner, E. (1983), 'Remarks on the Mind-Body Problem', in J. A. Wheeler and W. H. Zurek (eds), *Quantum Theory and Measurement*, 168-81. Princeton: Princeton University Press.
Willaschek, M. (1992), *Handlungstheorie und Moralnbegründing bei Kant*. Suttgat: J.B. Metzerg.
Willaschek, M. (2018), 'Freedom as a Postulate', in E. Watkins (ed.), *Kant on Persons and Agency*, 102-19. Cambridge: Cambridge University Press.
Willaschek, M. and E. Watkins (2020), 'Kant on Cognition and Knowledge', *Synthese*, 197(8): 3195-213.
Williams, B. (1981), 'Persons, Character and Morality', in J. Rachels (ed.), *Moral Luck*, 1-19. Cambridge: Cambridge University Press.
Wittgenstein, L. (1992), *Philosophical Investigations*. Oxford: Wiley/Blackwell.
Wolf, S. (1990), *Freedom within Reason*. Oxford: Oxford University Press.

Wood, A. W. (1984), 'Kant's Compatibilism', in Allen W. Wood (ed.), *Self and Nature in Kant's Philosophy*, 73–101. Ithaca and London: Cornell University Press.
Wood, A. W. (1999), *Kant's Ethical Thought*. Cambridge: Cambridge University Press.
Wood, A. W. (2008), *Kantian Ethics*. Cambridge: Cambridge University Press.
Wuerth, J. (2014), *Kant on Mind, Action, and Ethics*. Oxford: Oxford University Press.
Xie, S. S. (2009), 'What Is Kant: A Compatibilist or an Incompatibilist?' *Kant Studien*, 100: 53–76.

Index

account
   metaphysical 3, 4, 7, 27, 29, 44, 47, 48, 63–70, 75–83, 91–3, 101, 102, 107–12, 119–23, 128, 130, 133–8, 149, 168–71, 186, 193, 207, 213–16
   physical 6, 7, 96, 143, 144, 157–61, 164, 193, 194
   psychological 3–5, 7, 9, 13, 24, 26, 27, 46, 49, 51, 54, 58, 63–79, 82, 83, 91, 96, 107, 108, 143–9, 156, 159, 164, 167–71, 192, 193, 209, 218
   volitional 3–5, 13–16, 24–7, 31, 46–9, 54, 60–83, 93, 94, 103–11, 119–23, 126–37, 140, 143–6, 149, 154, 157, 164, 168–71, 193, 194, 207, 214, 216
action
   -token 131, 144–7, 156
   -type 145–7, 156
addiction 16
affection
   auto- 215
   double 32–3
   empirical 32–5, 182, 183
   noumenal 200
   self- 114
   transcendental 32–5, 182, 183
Allais, Lucy 9, 29, 33
Allison, Henry 5, 9, 20, 27–9, 34–45, 54, 59, 93–6, 100–8, 112–23, 128, 129, 133, 134, 138, 150, 184, 190, 191, 202, 208–17
altered
   -law interpretation 3, 4, 8, 44, 48, 52–4, 79–83, 92, 106, 151, 168, 193, 204
   -past interpretation 3, 44, 48–53, 151, 161, 193
Ameriks, Karl 9, 31, 32, 102, 112, 113, 158, 201
Anscombe, Elizabeth 61
apperception 36, 84, 93
Aquila, Richard 32

Aquinas, Thomas 219
Argument
   Consequence 2, 8, 11, 14–16, 43–4, 48, 53, 55, 58, 79–80, 83, 85, 94, 106, 117, 169–71, 193, 195, 198, 203–4
   Infinite Regress 4, 6, 8, 55, 70–82, 106, 110, 117, 134–6, 141, 148, 167, 169, 185, 190, 193
   Luck 4–5, 8, 62, 68, 117, 132–3, 164, 194, 207
   from Manipulation 3, 8, 16–25, 49, 57, 79, 100, 145, 167, 193, 204, 210
Aristotle 12, 26, 161, 206
asymmetry of leeway 5, 111, 123, 203
Augustine 137
autonomy (autonomous-ly) 5, 6, 73, 94, 102, 114, 115, 121–6, 130, 132, 136–8, 168–71, 190–2, 212, 213, 222, 225

Baiasu, Sorin 202
Bayne, Stephen 38
Beck, Lewis White 100–3, 108, 128, 207, 212, 215
Beebee, Helen 198
belief-desire model 5, 11, 74, 77, 79, 96, 147, 149, 171, 194, 205
Bennett, Jonathan 49–51, 198, 204
Bitbol, Michel 2, 24
Bittner, Rudiger 113, 209, 213
blameworthy, blameworthiness 9, 20–3, 26, 56, 106, 171–2, 205, 211
Bojanowski, Jochen 45, 101–2, 105, 211–14, 219
brain 1, 11, 47, 56–7, 60, 67, 79–80, 162–4, 172, 220
Bratman, Michael 19–20, 102, 145
Breitenbach, Angela 211
Brewer, Talbot 125, 146
Buroker, Jill Vance 28, 201, 224

Carroll, Lewis   21
category   32, 36, 38, 116, 187, 201–2, 209
causality
  law of   96, 120–5, 129–30, 137–8, 208
  psychological   4–7, 78–83, 105–6, 109–11, 134, 143, 151–4, 167–71, 186, 193, 214, 222
causal task principle   62, 69, 220
cause
  noumenal   46, 84, 202
  transcendental   91, 147, 171, 183, 208
Chalmers, David   98, 170, 189, 200, 223, 225
character
  empirical   3–5, 51, 53, 82, 88–92, 95–9, 107–9, 118, 125, 127, 133–4, 143–58, 164, 168–71, 194, 204, 208–9, 217–19
  intelligible   45, 50–3, 88–9, 92, 94, 97–9, 107, 109, 118–26, 130–1, 134, 137–8, 143–4, 147, 150, 152, 156, 158, 161–2, 168–71, 204, 208–9, 213, 217, 219
Chignell, Andrew   201
choice, theory of   5, 8, 111–12, 132–3, 136–40, 143, 154, 194, 217
Clarke, Randolph   59–68, 71–2, 78, 131, 163, 199, 206
compatibilism
  semi-   1, 199
  -source (compatibilist, -source)   3, 8, 15, 18, 20, 23–5, 29, 31, 45–6, 55–7, 74, 143, 145, 167–8, 193, 210
complement of sufficiency (of determinacy)   45, 48, 53, 73, 82, 93, 153, 155, 170
compulsion, compulsive   17, 20
consciousness
  empirical   5, 109
  self-   36, 222
constitutive   12, 33, 36, 75, 86–7, 174, 202, 221, 225
control
  guidance   21, 24, 27, 199
  regulative   21, 49, 55, 124, 191, 199
cosmological   3, 40, 46, 82–5, 88–90, 93, 208
counterfactual   50–1, 178–9, 198–9, 203–4, 223

creator   5, 28, 49, 80, 125
critical philosophy   8, 83, 186–7
Crusius, Christian August   133–4

Davidson, Donald   5, 65, 74, 78, 199–200, 207
Dennett, Daniel   23, 59, 189
disability   16
disappearing agent   59, 62, 172
dispositionalism, new   199
dual-aspect theory   33, 54, 87, 89, 181, 201

Ekstrom, Laura Waddell   15, 59
empirical law   33, 38–9, 187–8
empiricism, empiricist   117, 183, 199
Ertl, Wolfgang   42, 83, 90, 95–8, 106, 108, 138, 150, 200, 203–4, 209
ethics   47, 84, 102, 135, 138, 145, 191, 193, 214–15
explanatory self-sufficiency of willings   4, 73, 109, 110, 142, 170

fact of reason   115–20, 168–70, 194, 208, 212
Fischer, John Martin   17, 20–2, 45, 56–7, 93–4, 102, 198–9
forgiveness   172
Frankfurt, Harry   19–20, 25, 56, 101–2, 199, 205, 214
Frankfurt-style example   4, 8, 55–8, 81, 193, 202, 205, 219–20
freedom
  causality of   4–5, 82, 89, 109–10, 121–2, 128–9, 132, 136–8, 141, 144–6, 154, 158, 162, 168, 169, 194–5, 209, 214, 216
  practical (P-freedom)   4, 8, 82–4, 93, 98–106, 109, 111, 116, 130, 168, 193, 209–12
  transcendental (T-freedom)   4–5, 8, 40–8, 54, 82–95, 98–118, 121–3, 168–9, 203, 207–13, 225
Friedman, Michael   38, 45, 96, 186–7, 208, 224
Fugate, Courtney   108, 138, 217

Gardner, Sebastian   29, 35, 46, 112, 181, 200–1

Gerhardt, Volker   40
Gesinnung   5–6, 8, 118–19, 133–43, 146, 148, 164, 167–71, 190, 194, 213, 216–19
Ginet, Carl   65–6, 69, 207
Ginsborg, Hannah   220
God   5, 27, 36, 49, 64, 98, 102, 125–6, 139–40, 175, 185, 200, 204, 210, 214
Goff, Philip   189–90
gratitude   172
ground   129, 132, 136–7, 215–17, 221, 226
guilt   3, 195
Guyer, Paul   8, 33–4, 38–41, 46, 93, 113, 120, 191, 202–3, 208, 215, 217

Haji, Ishtiyaque   59, 63, 65, 207
happiness   102, 129–30, 210
hard incompatibilism   2, 6, 14–15, 43–4, 167, 171, 173, 195, 211
Heidegger, Martin   153, 218–19
Heimsoeth, Heinz   150, 204
Henrich, Dieter   113, 211
Herman, Barbara   214
Historical Agency problem   3, 49–52, 81–2
Hobbes, Thomas (Hobbesian)   3, 16, 18, 74
Hogan, Desmond   9, 32, 116, 200
Homeless Agent problem   3, 11, 25–6, 44, 47, 49, 55, 58, 81–2, 107
Honderich, Ted   2, 61, 173
Hume, David (Humean)   16, 18, 23, 25, 37, 59, 117, 197, 199, 217

idealism, transcendental   3–9, 28–36, 41–6, 53–5, 62, 67, 73, 80–6, 89, 106, 110, 115–18, 152, 158, 164–71, 174–5, 180–6, 189–90, 193–7, 200, 202, 206–12, 218–24
imperative
  categorical (CI)   104–7, 112, 119, 121, 123, 130–2, 136, 210–15, 217
  hypothetical   104, 113, 117, 119, 131–2, 220, 222
  of prudence   119, 124, 131–2
  of skill   119, 124, 131–2
incentive
  primary   128–33, 155, 214

  secondary   128, 132, 137, 155, 214–15
inclination   27, 43–4, 52, 56, 58, 101, 103, 124, 128–9, 136, 138, 140, 146–9, 157, 173, 191–2, 194, 215–20, 226
incompatibilism   1–2, 6, 14–17, 23, 42–4, 49, 55, 58, 94, 101, 167, 171, 173, 195, 200–3, 209, 211
incorporation thesis   5, 93, 127–9, 132, 138, 147, 155, 168, 170, 216, 219–20
indeterminism (indeterministic)   4, 55, 59–63, 71, 163, 206
Indregard, Jonas Jervell   108, 147, 219
inner sense   5, 8, 95–7, 109, 114, 144, 151–8, 161–4, 169–71, 194, 208–9, 212, 218–22
Insole, Christopher   125, 137, 147, 214, 216
intention   6–8, 13, 44–9, 52–3, 56, 66–70, 73–82, 96–7, 138–9, 144, 149, 154–5, 158, 162–4, 173, 195, 203–7, 214, 218–20
interpretation of transcendental idealism
  metaphysical   3, 8, 33, 35, 54, 115, 139
  methodological   34–5, 93, 103, 115, 201, 212
Irwin, Terence   150, 202

Kane, Robert   12, 57, 60, 63, 94, 191, 214, 219
Keil, Geert   12, 104, 133
Kohl, Markus   96, 100–3, 106, 124, 147, 159–60, 210–14, 220
Korsgaard, Christine   108, 127, 201, 215, 225
Kosch, Michelle   108, 114, 120–3, 138, 216

Langton, Rae   176, 225
law
  empirical   33, 38–9, 187–8
  limited-instantiation-scope   151
  moral   4–5, 106–7, 111–16, 119–39, 147, 159, 168–71, 191, 210–13, 217, 222
leeway   1, 3–5, 12, 15–20, 23, 25, 43, 46, 49, 54–9, 62, 65, 75, 81, 94, 99, 107–8, 111, 123–4, 133, 140, 143, 149–50, 170, 200, 202–5, 211, 213, 216, 220–1

Leeway
  Moral   4–5, 107–8, 111–12, 119–20, 125, 137–8, 140, 143, 194, 215
  Temporal   4–5, 54, 107–8, 143–9, 152–7, 164–5, 170, 194, 204, 216
Leibniz, Gottfried Wilhelm (Leibnizian)   20, 27, 34, 37, 43, 46, 47, 117, 133, 199–200
Lewis, David   176, 180, 198–200, 203
libertarianism (libertarian)   1–8, 12–15, 40–3, 46, 49, 54–82, 93–5, 100–7, 111, 113, 117, 124, 133, 141, 163–4, 167–72, 191–8, 202–3, 206–10, 220
  agent-causal   4, 6, 40, 55, 63–79, 193, 203, 206, 207
  event-causal   4, 27, 55, 59–68, 72, 77–8, 172, 193, 206–7
  non-causal   4, 55, 63–8, 74, 77, 207
Libet, Benjamin   211

McCann, Hugh   66–7, 74, 77, 93, 207
McDowell, John   214
McKenna, Michael   18–23, 42, 200
maxim   5, 8, 122–50, 154–60, 164, 168–70, 194, 209, 213–19
Mele, Alfred   21, 59–60, 65, 199, 207
Melnick, Arthur   38
mereology, topological   184–5, 224
mesh theory (real-self view)   18–28, 117, 199
mind-body   6, 8, 77, 80, 169, 171, 194
morality   5–6, 16, 47, 49, 98, 107, 112, 115, 117, 121, 123, 128, 131–2, 148, 160, 169, 190, 194, 197, 210–13, 222–5
mysterianism   2, 11, 14–15, 110, 171

Natorp, Paul   187
naturalism   2, 6–9, 40, 49, 55, 75, 167, 171, 174–8, 183–9, 193, 195, 198
neural   12, 60, 162–3, 169, 221
neuroscience, neuroscientist   17, 19, 22, 57
normativity (normative)   6, 15, 106–7, 111–12, 115, 123–6, 140–1, 148, 158, 164–9, 190–4, 197, 225–6
noumenon (noumenal)   9, 42–7, 51–4, 80, 84, 88, 93, 109, 118, 125–6, 136–9, 157, 168, 200–4, 208, 212–16, 219

object, transcendental   32–6, 89–90, 201
object-duality   32–3
observational truth   175
O'Connor, Timothy   58–62, 65–79, 141, 198, 205–7
O'Neill, Onora   127, 209
open futures   156
ought implies can   6, 8, 94, 99, 112, 124, 144, 158, 169, 194, 210–11, 214

Palmquist, Stephen   129, 134, 140, 216–17, 224–5
Paradox
  of Observed Totalities   177–80, 185–6, 193
  of Self-Determination   4, 6, 72–3, 184–6, 193
  Zeno's   161, 163, 220
Pasternack, Lawrence   134, 137–9, 216–17
Pereboom, Dirk   16–23, 42, 48, 56–60, 63–6, 72, 94, 100, 108, 163, 172–3, 199–200, 203, 205, 207, 212–12, 219–22
permissibility (permissible)   47–8, 82–3, 86, 100, 106, 110–11, 132, 137, 211, 214–15, 221
phobia, phobic   20, 199
physics   6, 60, 163, 178, 186–9, 223–4
Pink, Thomas   4, 69, 73–7
Pinkard, Terry   224
Piper, Adrian   217
Plato (Platonic)   212
possibility
  logical (possible, logical)   3–4, 13, 31, 34, 42–8, 73, 76, 82–3, 87–8, 203
  real (possible, real)   46–7, 54, 73, 76–7, 82–4, 87–92, 105–6, 111, 117, 137–8, 159, 168, 193–5, 201, 203, 208, 210, 220
possible world   21, 50, 98, 113, 195, 198–203, 223
postulates of practical reason   116, 210, 212, 217
praiseworthy-praiseworthiness   172
predetermination (predetermined)   7–8, 24, 117, 133, 144, 147–53, 156–7, 218
Prichard, Harold Arthur   34, 201, 225

Pringe, Hernan   164, 221, 224
probability
  -fork model   60, 63–4
  -pool model   60
punishment   139, 171, 195, 207

quantum
  physics/mechanics/theory   60, 69, 163–4, 198, 205, 221, 224
  Zeno effect   163
quantum indeterminacy   11, 60, 61, 221, 224
Quarfood, Marcel   112
Quine, William van Orman   174–5

rationalism   199
rationality account, *see* reasons-responsive theory
Ravizza, Mark   20–2, 45, 93, 102, 199
reactive attitudes   14, 16, 172, 197, 222
realism, transcendental   40, 43, 49, 85, 94, 105, 117, 174–6, 179, 186, 202
real-self view, *see* mesh theory
reason, causality of   4–5, 8, 93–4, 98, 105, 120–6, 129–32, 135–8, 168–9, 194, 209, 222
reasons-responsive theory (rationality account)   20–31, 54–6, 93, 99, 102, 118, 200, 205
Reciprocity Thesis   5, 112–15, 121–2, 169, 190
regulative (claim, principle, role)   33, 36, 86, 98, 104, 112, 115, 202, 204, 207–8, 217, 221, 224
Reinhold, Karl Leonhard   108, 138, 213
relativity
  general (GR)   186
  special (SR)   37, 186, 223
resentment   16, 172, 219
respect (for the moral law)   128–32, 147
responsibility   1, 6, 12–13, 17–24, 51, 55–8, 63, 91, 107, 124–5, 139, 171, 186, 191, 195, 197, 199, 204–5, 211, 218–22
Rosefeldt, Tobias   9, 33, 49–51, 99, 204, 209

Sartre, Jean-Paul (Sartrean)   142, 217
Saunders, Joe   2, 218

Schoenecker, Dieter   100–2, 106, 211, 213
Scholten, Matthe   42–3, 48, 51, 94, 106, 202–3, 209–13, 220
Schopenhauer, Arthur   108
Schulting, Dennis   32, 35, 110, 158, 181, 185, 197
Second Analogy   3, 37–9, 43, 45, 52, 62, 92, 96–7, 161, 202–3, 208, 220–1, 224
second problem of free will   125
self-determination   4–7, 24, 27, 67, 72–3, 128, 184–6, 193
self-love   128–32, 138, 155, 215–16, 218, 226
Sellars, Wilfrid   101, 115, 214
Setton, Dirk   215, 219
Sidgwick, Henry   108
single-instantiation clauses   169
Skyrms, Brian   50, 61
solution, Kantian   2, 6–8, 81, 161, 165, 167–70
solution-thing (in Third Antinomy)   45, 47, 52–3, 82–4, 87–90, 117, 203
sourcehood   4, 12, 15–17, 21–5, 43, 46, 49, 56–8, 62, 64, 70, 72, 94, 101, 107, 111, 143, 171, 173, 193, 202
space   8, 35, 42, 109, 125, 152, 162, 177–88, 195, 203, 221, 223–5
spontaneity   36, 67, 93, 101, 112–14, 120, 132, 155, 194, 211–12, 215, 222
Stang, Nick   9, 32–3
Stapp, Henry   163–4, 222
Steward, Helen   197, 205, 221
Strawson, Galen   4, 70–8, 141, 185, 189, 207, 225
Strawson, Peter   8, 14, 16, 23, 34, 38, 101, 105, 172, 199, 211, 222
Strohmeyer, Ingeborg   46, 164
Stump, Eleanor   220
substance   3, 27, 37–40, 44, 47, 54, 109, 158, 162, 187, 202–3, 209

teleology (teleological)   4, 26, 67, 75, 80, 109–10, 197
temperament   51, 99, 119, 148, 151, 218
Theory of Choice   5, 8, 111–12, 132–3, 136, 138, 140, 143, 154, 194, 217

Third Antinomy 31, 39–41, 44, 46, 52, 158, 221
   Resolution of 3, 4, 8, 41, 44, 46, 53, 81–107, 111, 145, 169, 193, 207, 214
Timeless Agency problem 3, 48–9, 53, 81–2, 108–12, 127, 135, 140, 143–6, 164–5, 194, 204
Timmermann, Jens 46, 124, 127–30, 147, 215, 218
Tse, Peter 221

van Cleve, James 200, 224
van Inwagen, Peter 2, 14–15, 43–4, 64, 69, 83, 85, 94, 110, 117, 198, 205–6
Vihvelin, Kadri 198–200
Vilhauer, Benjamin 9, 39, 53, 106, 151, 160, 209, 213, 220, 226
volition, *see* willing
Vuillemin, Jules 212

Wagner, Richard 132
Walker, Ralph 48–52, 151
Watkins, Eric 9, 37–41, 45, 53, 92, 98, 109, 116, 125, 200, 206–7

Watson, Gary 19–20, 102, 199, 222
Widerker, David 56–7, 198
Wigner, Eugene 60, 163, 221–2
Willaschek, Markus 104, 115–17, 212–13
Wille 5, 16, 108, 129–32, 168, 215–16
Williams, Bernard 214, 217, 226
willing (or volition) 3–4, 18, 29, 56, 66–7, 73–9, 94, 109–12, 123, 126–7, 134–5, 141, 147, 170–1, 191, 193, 207, 214, 219, 222
Willkür 5, 97, 108, 126–35, 140, 148, 154–5, 168, 171, 214, 216, 219–20
Wittgenstein, Ludwig 218
Wolf, Susan 55, 99, 123, 204
Wolff, Christian (Wolffian) 20, 27, 37, 133
Wood, Allen 9, 42, 48–54, 93–4, 108, 115, 118, 137, 204, 208
Wuerth, Julian 209–15

Zeno 161–4, 220–1

www.ingramcontent.com/pod-product-compliance
Lightning Source LLC
Chambersburg PA
CBHW071824300426
44116CB00009B/1422